Sámi Educational History in a Comparative International Perspective

"This very important volume on indigenous educational history presents a critical investigation on the impact of educational ideologies, policies and practices on indigenous peoples' lives. The historical role of school as a tool for assimilation and suppression shows similarities across the globe. At the same time, there are interesting differences even between Sámi experiences in different countries of the North. Colonisation through education is no simple, unified story. This is the first comprehensive volume on Sámi educational history. The comparison with other indigenous peoples situates the Arctic experiences within a globally comprehensible context."

—Reetta Toivanen, *Professor of Sustainability Science (Indigenous Sustainabilities), Helsinki Institute of Sustainability Science, University of Helsinki, Finland*

"This is an important work for scholars, students and policymakers wanting to understand the history of and current context for Sámi education across the North. However, it goes beyond the borders of Sámi lands to address issues of Indigenous education in multiple nations. This work adds a much needed critical perspective not only to Circumpolar education research but also to North-South and East-West comparative discussions of Indigenous education, identities, and rights."

—Diane Hirshberg, *Professor of Education Policy, University of Alaska Anchorage, USA*

"A welcome and much needed anthology that takes a critical perspective on the history and future of Indigenous education. The juxtaposition of chapters from the traditionally separate disciplines of educational history and educational science provides a novel and richly rewarding perspective. Whilst the book takes its starting point from an examination of Indigenous education within Scandinavia, the opportunity to explore Indigenous education in diverse international contexts across the globe is unique."

—Mhairi C. Beaton, *Senior Lecturer in Special Educational Needs, Carnegie School of Education, Leeds Beckett University, UK*

Otso Kortekangas · Pigga Keskitalo ·
Jukka Nyyssönen · Andrej Kotljarchuk ·
Merja Paksuniemi · David Sjögren
Editors

Sámi Educational History in a Comparative International Perspective

palgrave
macmillan

Editors
Otso Kortekangas
Division of History of Science, Technology
and Environment
KTH Royal Institute of Technology
Stockholm, Sweden

Department of History
Stockholm University
Stockholm, Sweden

Jukka Nyyssönen
The Arctic University Museum of Norway
UiT—The Arctic University of Norway
Tromsø, Norway

Merja Paksuniemi
Department of Education
University of Lapland
Rovaniemi, Finland

Pigga Keskitalo
Department of Education
University of Lapland
Rovaniemi, Finland

Andrej Kotljarchuk
Department of History
Södertörn University
Huddinge, Stockholms Län, Sweden

David Sjögren
Department of Education
Uppsala University
Uppsala, Sweden

ISBN 978-3-030-24111-7 ISBN 978-3-030-24112-4 (eBook)
https://doi.org/10.1007/978-3-030-24112-4

© The Editor(s) (if applicable) and The Author(s), under exclusive license to Springer Nature
Switzerland AG, part of Springer Nature 2019
This work is subject to copyright. All rights are solely and exclusively licensed by the Publisher, whether
the whole or part of the material is concerned, specifically the rights of translation, reprinting, reuse
of illustrations, recitation, broadcasting, reproduction on microfilms or in any other physical way, and
transmission or information storage and retrieval, electronic adaptation, computer software, or by
similar or dissimilar methodology now known or hereafter developed.
The use of general descriptive names, registered names, trademarks, service marks, etc. in this
publication does not imply, even in the absence of a specific statement, that such names are exempt
from the relevant protective laws and regulations and therefore free for general use.
The publisher, the authors and the editors are safe to assume that the advice and information in this
book are believed to be true and accurate at the date of publication. Neither the publisher nor the
authors or the editors give a warranty, expressed or implied, with respect to the material contained
herein or for any errors or omissions that may have been made. The publisher remains neutral with
regard to jurisdictional claims in published maps and institutional affiliations.

This Palgrave Macmillan imprint is published by the registered company Springer Nature Switzerland AG
The registered company address is: Gewerbestrasse 11, 6330 Cham, Switzerland

Contents

1 Introduction   1
Otso Kortekangas, Pigga Keskitalo, Jukka Nyyssönen,
Andrej Kotljarchuk, David Sjögren and Merja Paksuniemi

**2 Sámi Schools, Female Enrolment, and the Teaching
Trade: Sámi Women's Involvement in Education
in Early Modern Sweden**   13
Daniel Lindmark

**3 Out of the "Pagan Darkness": Christian Education
in Finnish Lapland**   27
Ritva Kylli

**4 Narratives of Sámi School History in Finland:
Assimilation and Empowerment**   47
Jukka Nyyssönen

vi   Contents

5   Indigenous People, Vulnerability and the Security
     Dilemma: Sámi School Education on the Kola
     Peninsula, 1917–1991   63
     Andrej Kotljarchuk

6   The Perspective of Former Pupils: Indigenous Children
     and Boarding Schools on the Kola Peninsula, 1960s
     to 1980s   83
     Lukas Allemann

7   The Development of Sámi Children's Right
     to Learn Sámi in the Russian School Context   105
     Ekaterina Zmyvalova and Hanna Outakoski

8   Sámi Issues in Norwegian Curricula:
     A Historical Overview   125
     Torjer A. Olsen

9   The History of the Sámi Upper Secondary School
     in Guovdageaidnu: Language Policy Development   143
     Inker-Anni Linkola-Aikio

10   Christian Morality and Enlightenment to the Natural
     Child: Third-Sector Education in a Children's Home
     in Northern Finland (1907–1947)   161
     Merja Paksuniemi and Pigga Keskitalo

11   History of Early Childhood Education
     in the Sámi Language in Finland   187
     Marikaisa Laiti

12   A Historical Perspective of Indigenous Education
     Policy in Japan: The Case of Ainu Schools   207
     Yoko Tanabe

Contents   vii

13   Indigenous in Japan? The Reluctance of the Japanese
     State to Acknowledge Indigenous Peoples and Their
     Need for Education   225
     Madoka Hammine

14   School Histories in Amazonia: Education
     and Schooling in Apuriná Lands   247
     Pirjo Kristiina Virtanen and Francisco Apuriná

15   Revitalization of Oral History in Wixárika
     Community-Based Schools and Museums: Working
     Towards Decolonisation of Art Education Among
     the Indigenous Peoples of Mexico   265
     Lea Kantonen

16   A Community of Ako, 1987–1995: Teaching
     and Learning in the ELTU and Po Ako, Auckland,
     Aotearoa NZ   283
     Mere Kepa

17   Education for Assimilation: A Brief History
     of Aboriginal Education in Western Australia   299
     Elizabeth Jackson-Barrett and Libby Lee-Hammond

18   Conclusion: Promising Prospects—Reflections
     on Research on Sámi Education Yesterday,
     Today and Tomorrow   317
     Otso Kortekangas

Index   327

Notes on Contributors

Lukas Allemann is an anthropologist and historian at the Arctic Centre at the University of Lapland (Finland). He is currently completing his Ph.D. thesis on the history and consequences of social engineering among Northern indigenous minorities in the Soviet Union, based on the example of the relocation of the Sámi people, and using mainly oral history methods. He holds a master's degree from the University of Basel (Switzerland) in Eastern European history and Russian language and literature.

Francisco Apuriná is a doctoral researcher in anthropology at the University of Brasília. His dissertation looks at the impacts of the highway construction to the Apuriná material and immaterial cultural tradition. He lives in SouthWestern Amazonia, Brazil. His research topics include, among others, sustainability of Indigenous peoples, shamanism, and Indigenous postgraduate education. He has also worked as a public servant in Indigenous state agencies as well as a consult in projects dealing with Indigenous communities in Brazil.

Madoka Hammine is a Ph.D. Candidate at Faculty of Education, University of Lapland in Finland. Her thesis focuses on two case studies of Sámi languages in Finland and Ryukyuan languages in Japan. Her research interests include heritage language teaching and learning, indigenous language education, teacher education, and language policy for maintaining language diversity. She is currently participating in a research traineeship at Ca' Foscari University in Italy.

Elizabeth Jackson-Barrett is a lecturer and senior indigenous researcher within the School of Education at Murdoch University. Elizabeth is passionate about improving educational outcomes for Aboriginal students regardless of education context.

Elizabeth works alongside colleague Associate Professor Libby Lee-Hammond in the following projects; On Country Learning: Promoting Remote Australian Aboriginal Children's Wellbeing and Creativity. *Djarlgarra Koolunger: Kids of the Canning* an OCL Program aimed at Connecting Culture Curriculum and Communities in Early Years Aboriginal Education; and *Walliabup Connections* for Burdiya Aboriginal Corporation. In 2018, the On Country Learning project was a finalist in the UNAAWA Human Rights Award in Western Australia.

Lea Kantonen Doctor of Arts, is a professor of artistic research at the University of the Arts Helsinki's Academy of Fine Arts and a researcher with the University of the Arts Helsinki's ArtsEqual initiative. She is interested in artistic dialogue with people from different cultures, language domains, generations, and professions. Her other interests include translation as part of the artistic process. She is involved in the Indigenous Research Methods in Academia project of the universities of Helsinki, Finland, the Arctic University of Norway, and the Sámi University of Applied Sciences. Lea Kantonen and her partner, Pekka Kantonen, have carried out multilingual performances and workshops on different interpretations of knowledge with Wixárika artists and teachers in Mexico.

Dr. Mere Kepa is a consultant/community researcher, a Maori cultural critic, a published writer, and a social innovator who works to inspire a new vision of Indigenous Maori, Pasifika Peoples, and Migrant Peoples life. She is the consultant researcher to the *Waimaori tatou taonga: Healthy water our treasure* pilot study and the *Nga Kaumatua, o Matou Taonga: Supporting kaumatua health in a changing world: A feasibility* *study in Te Tai Tokerau* based at the James Henare Maori Research Centre, the University of Auckland, New Zealand.

Mere is convener of *Friends of the Berm@Takahiwai*, a community environmental project funded by the local district council and Creative Northland.

Pigga Keskitalo, Ph.D., a Title of Docent at the University of Helsinki, is a University Researcher at the Faculty of Education, University of Lapland and she also works part-time as a researcher at Sámi University of Applied Sciences in Norway.

Otso Kortekangas, Ph.D. teaches Sámi history at the Department of History, Stockholm University, Sweden. He is also a postdoctoral researcher at the Division of History of Science, Technology and Environment at the KTH Royal Institute of Technology in Stockholm. Kortekangas has published a substantial number of scholarly articles, mainly on Sámi history and educational history.

Andrej Kotljarchuk is senior researcher at the Institute of Contemporary History, Södertörn University, Sweden. Recent publications include the edited volume *Minorities in Stalin's Soviet Union. New Dimensions of Research* (Södertörn University, 2017); the monograph *In Forge of Stalin. Swedish colonists of Ukraine in the totalitarian experiments of the 20th century* (Stockholm, 2014), the book chapters "Propaganda of Hatred and the Great Terror. A Nordic Approach", in *Minorities in Stalin's Soviet Union*; "Nordic fishermen in the Soviet Union: Ethnic Purges and the Cleansing of Cultural Landscape" in *The Barents and the Baltic Sea Region: Contacts, Influences and Social Change* (Rovaniemi, 2017).

Ritva Kylli is a University lecturer of Arctic and Northern History, and Adjunct professor of Finnish and North European History at the University of Oulu, Finland. She specialises in the study of Sámi history and has conducted research on cultural encounters (e.g. relations between the church and the Sámi in Finnish Lapland). She has most recently concentrated on food, health, and environmental history of the Arctic.

Marikaisa Laiti works as the leader of an early childhood education centre in Inari, Finland. Earlier, she has worked as a research assistant at the University of Oulu. She has also managed her own kindergarten and worked as an early education teacher in Kittilä municipality. She graduated from the University of Lapland with a Ph.D. degree in education in 2018. She has a Masters' degree in education 1996 and has finished her bachelors' degree with an early education teacher qualification 2009 at Oulu University. Her main research focuses have been Sámi everyday life and Sámi early childhood education.

Libby Lee-Hammond is Associate Professor of Early Childhood Education at Murdoch University, Australia, where she teaches early childhood education and critical pedagogies. Libby has Skolt Sámi maternal ancestry. Her research has focussed on working alongside Australian Aboriginal communities, particularly with parents and young children in early years' programmes both within schools and in prior to school settings. Libby is committed to addressing social inequalities through her research in education. Her work in On Country Learning with Elizabeth Jackson-Barrett has been recognised by ARNEC as an Innovative Pedagogical Approach in the Early Years in the Asia Pacific Region.

Daniel Lindmark born in 1960, is a professor of church history at the Faculty of Arts and a professor of history and education at Umeå School of Education, Umeå University. His research fields include educational history, print culture, popular religion, and religious use of history. Large parts of his research concern the religious history of the North, including Sámi missionary and educational history. He was in charge of the white paper project on the historical relations between the Church of Sweden and the Sámi (2012–2017) and edited its publications together with Olle Sundström, including the English conclusion, *The Sámi and the Church of Sweden: Results from a White Paper Project* (2018).

Inker-Anni Linkola-Aikio, Ph.D. is Associate professor at Sámi allaskuvla (Sámi University of Applied Sciences), Norway.

Dr. artium Jukka Nyyssönen works as a researcher in the Department of Cultural Sciences at Arctic University Museum of Norway, at the UiT—the Arctic University of Norway. He defended a doctoral thesis in 2007 on Sámi identity politics in Finland, in addition to which, he has published on Sámi politics in Finland, Sámi research, historiography, environmental history, and history of education. Currently he leads the research project "Societal Dimensions of Sámi research".

Torjer A. Olsen (Ph.D. in religious studies 2008) is a professor in Indigenous studies at the Centre for Sámi Studies, UiT The Arctic University of Norway. Olsen is the leader of the international research project "Indigenous Citizenship & Education". His research interests include indigenous issues in education, gender and privilege in indigenous research, and Christianity in Sámi settings.

Hanna Outakoski is senior lecturer in North Sámi at the Department of Language Studies at Umeå University, Sweden. She is currently doing research on literacy instruction at Sámi schools and in Sámi teacher education. Apart from literacy studies, her research interests lie on North Sámi grammar and syntax, as well as on the possibilities and potential of using virtual worlds and virtual classrooms for language revitalization.

Merja Paksuniemi, Ph.D. is a senior lecturer at the Faculty of Education, University of Lapland.

David Sjögren is Associate Professor (docent) in History, Senior Lecturer in Education and Director of Studies at the Department of Education, Uppsala University, Sweden. Sjögren has since 2005 done research in the field of educational history and Sámi and Roma history.

Yoko Tanabe is a doctoral candidate at the Institute of Education, University College London (UK). She currently teaches at Tokai University, Japan, as a part-time lecturer. Her research interests lie in the intersection of indigenous education, language, and school history, particularly in the context of Japan and Norway. Her major works include: St. Louis Correspondence—the Ainu Experience at the 1904 St. Louis World's Fair (Kamakura shunjūsya publishing, 2016), The Church Missionary Society's Japan Mission and the Hakodate Ainu School (Shumpūsya publishing, 2018).

xiv **Notes on Contributors**

Pirjo Kristiina Virtanen is a faculty member of Indigenous studies at the University of Helsinki, Finland. For the past 15 years, she has carried out fieldwork with the Apurinã and Manchineri, in particular in Brazil. Her research interests include Indigenous leaderships, Indigenous politics, Amazonian Indigenous adolescence, Amazonian iconography and art, ethnohistory, and epistemological plurality. Her work has been published in numerous journal articles, monographs, and edited volumes. She has also co-authored various indigenous school materials.

Ekaterina Zmyvalova is a Ph.D. candidate in Sámi studies at Umeå University (Sweden). Zmyvalova graduated from the Faculty of Law of NArFU (the Northern Arctic Federal University (Arkhangelsk, Russia) in 2013 with a diploma with honors. In 2015, she completed the Indigenous Studies master programme in UiT—the Arctic University of Norway (Tromsø, Norway). Zmyvalova's primary research interests are the rights of indigenous peoples of Russia and Scandinavia. Her latest articles are published in journals such as *Arctic Review on Law and Politics* and *International Journal on Group and Minority Rights*.

List of Figures

Fig. 12.1   Elementary school enrolment rate in Japan
(1890–1930). *Source* Ministry of Education
(1972, p. 497), Ogawa (1997, p. 10)   219

Image 3.1   Sámi woman reading (No date. Photo by Juhani Ahola)   36
Image 12.1   Ainu School. (n.d.). Hakodate City Central Library   217

Map 7.1   The dark grey area in this map illustrates
the traditional Sámi territory, Sápmi, which
extends from Scandinavia over to the Kola Peninsula
in the east. The dotted line in the Kola Peninsula
marks the borders of the territory of the Lovozero
district. The MO shares a national border with
Norway in the north and with Finland further south.
(Copyright granted by Aleksei Larionov)   108

List of Tables

Table 2.1	Distribution of students according to sex at respective Sámi School, 1732–1850	18
Table 2.2	Distribution of students according to sex and enrolment decade at the Sámi Schools of Jokkmokk, Jukkasjärvi and Gellivare, 1732–1819	19
Table 7.1	Provision of the Sámi language and culture teaching in the Lovozero School from 2009 to 2017 showing the change in the content of the extra-curricular subject and in the school form that changed from a boarding school to a municipal school	116
Table 7.2	Pupils learning the Sámi language in the Lovozero School (2009–2017)	117
Table 9.1	Names of the school in different periods	148
Table 12.1	The 1901 school curriculum for government Ainu schools	210
Table 12.2	Analysis of Hakodate Ainu training school timetable 1895 (Nettleship 1895c)	216

1

Introduction

Otso Kortekangas, Pigga Keskitalo,
Jukka Nyyssönen, Andrej Kotljarchuk,
David Sjögren and Merja Paksuniemi

This book pursues two aims. The first aim is to critically examine the history of education of various indigenous groups, and the second aim is to build on the gained critical insights to examine the need for and possibility of future educational initiatives within indigenous education. While the focus is on the Sámi education, the scope of this volume is global, stretching from Asia and Oceania to Sápmi (the

---

O. Kortekangas (✉)
Division of History of Science, Technology and Environment, KTH Royal Institute of Technology, Stockholm, Sweden
e-mail: otso.kortekangas@historia.su.se

Department of History, Stockholm University, Stockholm, Sweden

P. Keskitalo
Department of Education, University of Lapland, Rovaniemi, Finland
e-mail: pigga.keskitalo@ulapland.fi

© The Author(s) 2019
O. Kortekangas et al. (eds.), *Sámi Educational History in a Comparative International Perspective*,
https://doi.org/10.1007/978-3-030-24112-4_1

Sámi areas in Russia and the Nordic countries of Finland, Sweden and Norway) and the Americas, which in a way resonates with the recent trends in indigenous studies. Many researchers have called for a paradigm shift in indigenous research (e.g. Kuokkanen 2007; Wilson 2001). Shawn Wilson (2001) offers an alternative to the Eurocentric way of doing research using the major classic paradigms (e.g. positivism, post-positivism, critical theory, constructivism). According to Wilson (2001), an indigenous paradigm is to be found in the fundamental belief that knowledge is relational to and shared in connection with all of creation, including the cosmos, animals, plants and the Earth. Wilson (2001) continues and elaborates the decolonising tradition that Linda Tuhiwai Smith (2001) famously championed. In a Sámi context, the decolonising methodologies have recently been promoted and applied by many researchers, including Evjen and Beck (2015). In short, decolonising simply implies a shift in the researcher's perspective. Whereas scholars of indigenous cultures have conventionally looked at culture from the outside, within the framework of certain methodologies, the

---

J. Nyyssönen
The Arctic University Museum of Norway, UiT—The Arctic University of Norway, Tromsø, Norway
e-mail: jukka.kalervo@uit.no

A. Kotljarchuk
The School of Historical and Contemporary Studies, Södertörn University, Huddinge, Sweden
e-mail: andrej.kotljarchuk@sh.se

D. Sjögren
Department of Education, Uppsala University, Uppsala, Sweden
e-mail: david.sjogren@edu.uu.se

M. Paksuniemi
Department of Education, University of Lapland, Rovaniemi, Finland
e-mail: merja.paksuniemi@ulapland.fi

decolonising of research aims at an insider perspective, taking the epistemology of the studied cultures as a starting point of research. Many of the chapters in this anthology stress the importance of decolonisation in the studies of indigenous education.

While Wilson's (2001) notion of the new indigenous paradigm is tempting and promising, engaging in history has always differed from thinking about it in theoretical terms. Bruno Latour (2016) reminds us that a global view (not to be confused with Wilson's cosmic view) is always blurred by our own limitations as scholars and individuals. As researchers, we are always affected by the places in which we live and work (i.e. by the epistemological contexts of these places) (Latour 2016). Hence, the articles of this collection are deeply embedded in their researchers' political-institutional and temporal contexts. Thematically, methodologically and contextually, most of the researches in the articles 'took place' during the process of introducing the mass education systems of the twentieth century, with the inbuilt aims of nation-building and citizenship education. What is shared by most of the articles, however, is the goal of deconstructing these projects and their state-internal trajectories (also see Tröhler 2016). Our aim is international and comparative and includes a variety of perspectives from the more conventional history of education to the educational science articles which apply decolonising methodologies.

The chapters of this anthology provide critical constructivist reviews of the histories of education in various national settings and from a variety of interdisciplinary perspectives. Many of the chapters share the relational knowledge interest in the ideals produced by the institutions (i.e. the church and the state) which organise tuition, the institution of the school itself and those produced in researches into these institutions. The authors of this edition scrutinise the production of the competing state narratives and the empowering counter-narratives, which is one overarching aim of this book: enhancing the school experiences of the students who belong to indigenous minorities in their multiplicity of backgrounds and better addressing their needs by responding to some of the issues and challenges of the current education.

4   O. Kortekangas et al.

The main focus of this book is the history of education and the school experiences of the Sámi. However, a large number of chapters concentrate on the educational histories of other indigenous peoples. The comparative approach in this book pursues two goals. First, we intend to deepen our understanding of the similarities and differences of our international cases. Second, considering the design of the book, we hope that the Sámi cases will benefit most from these comparisons.

Histories of the Sámi Education

Internationally, the *civilising* dimension of education has been a central, albeit contentious, issue in research on the education of indigenous and colonised populations. The educational ideologies and practices targeting indigenous peoples have produced and reproduced biological, cultural and economic hierarchies. Nonetheless, the education of natives has in many cases been considered to be of paramount importance, especially in the colonised societies which often advocated the introduction of educational institutions. The cultural cost has been high and the coverage has been limited, leading to inequalities affecting educational access and benefits. Many studies have already established the duality of education: while education has in many ways been exclusive and assimilative, it has also distributed skills and know-how which can actively be used by the resistant subject populations or movements advocating cultural revival. Research has been a leading field in helping the development of decolonising and deconstructing criticism (e.g. Whitehead 2005). In the historiography of the Sámi education, studies on the state-Sámi relationships and education have in the past two decades been followed by more critical studies, inspired by the tradition of post-colonial and indigenous studies.

The critical turn in the Norwegian studies on school history occurred earlier than that in Finland or Sweden, with the publication of Knut Einar Eriksen and Einar Niemi's seminal *Den finske fare* (The Finnish menace) (1981). While the book was chiefly concerned with the security policies affecting national minorities, the passages on both school institution and policies on assimilation dominate references to the

1 Introduction 5

book, which, despite some criticisms, has remained exceptionally influential in numerous readings and national debate.[1] Arguably, the Norwegian research on schools and the Sámi has been largely influenced by the readings and interpretations of this pioneering book.

The history of the Sámi education in Norway features prominently in a Nordic comparison for the extremity and longevity of the explicated and established state-funded assimilative policies. These language assimilation policies targeted the Kven (a Finnish-speaking minority in Northern Norway) and the Sámi pupils in certain districts, mainly because of national security concerns, and since the Sámi were seen as dying people who had to be brought out of their misery by improving their means of subsistence. This history of assimilation has become a structuring component of the Sámi history in Norway. It is still a sensitive issue that can spark off debates, the consequences of which will be the concern of the Conciliation Committee in the near future.

In Sweden, the Sámi educational history can be divided into two broad historiographical traditions. The first is an old tradition with a starting point in the 1950s and 1960s, mostly interested in the early modern period and especially the 'Lapp schools' of the eighteenth and nineteenth centuries. Questions about student composition, recruitment patterns and education goals and purposes dominated the research interests of this tradition (e.g. Norberg 1955; Johansson and Flodin 1991; Andersén 1990). This tradition soon manifested itself in Egil Johansson's (1977, 1993) pioneering work on literacy, and within the framework of Johansson's work, the ecclesiastical (folk) education in Sápmi became eventually central to this orientation of the Sámi education history. For the early modern period, the scholarship of Daniel Lindmark was key to pioneering research and generating new research questions (e.g. Lindmark 2006).

The second tradition has been dominant since the 1990s. It chiefly focused on the significance of establishing the nomad school system in

---

[1] Compared to Finland, where the study of Esko J. Kähkönen remained a marginal book in the national debate—a book considered marginal for its theme by the itinerant church teachers called catechists. Esko I. Kähkönen, *Katekeetat Suomen Lapissa 200 vuotta* (Rovaniemi: Lapin korkeakoulun kasvatustieteellisiä julkaisuja A 4, 1988), passim.

the early 1900s. Interest in this tradition stemmed from the possibility of investigating the consequences of Sweden's policies on the Sámi at the turn of the twentieth century. Interpreting the motives of historical actors and the design of the nomad school system dominated the research area for a long time. Sten Henrysson and Johnny Flodin's (1992) reviews of the Sámi education and Lars Elenius' book (2006) about policies on the minorities (the Sámi and Finnish-speaking minorities of Northern Sweden) are early examples of scholarly interest in the Sámi education in the twentieth century. In recent years, many academic articles and books have been written on the topic of the Sámi education. In the modern time, the main attention has been on the education of the nomadic reindeer-herding fell Sámi and the nomad school system. A persistent limitation in the Swedish research has been the failure to include the education of the Sámi children who did not attend the nomad schools. Although the Swedish educational authorities created the nomad schools—since they prioritised the livelihood of reindeer-herding for national economic purposes—the Sámi who had livelihoods other than large-scale reindeer-herding were sent to regular Swedish primary schools, leading to linguistic and cultural assimilation in many cases.

Since the publication of Elenius' book (2006), comparative perspectives have characterised the works on the Sámi education in Sweden, whether internationally (e.g. Nordblad 2013; Kortekangas 2017) or in the context of national minority policies (e.g. Sjögren 2010). As a result of these comparative approaches, the Swedish research has highly deepened our understanding of the nomad school system, which includes the underlying patterns of thoughts and ideas that constituted the fundamental elements of the nomadic school reform in 1913, knowledge about the role of different actors at the central, regional and local levels, knowledge about the difficulties involved in implementing the reform processes and, in recent years, insights into the former pupils' experiences. In contrast to this relatively well-known history of education, there is a lack of research on the Sámi educational history from the 1960s onwards.

In Finland, debates among the historians about the education of the Sámi were non-existent for a long time. The educational issues were

1 Introduction 7

discussed in the context of local histories, including the history of the building and subsequently the dismantling of the school institution. Criticisms were sometimes voiced about the lack of cultural sensitivity in this project, while the dominant narrative was concerned with progress and national integration at the municipality level. Researchers with ties to the Sámi movement of the 1970s carried out foundational studies, working on issues related to language and education. One outcome of this connection was the coupling of educational questions with those of language and language loss—an issue that had engaged the Sámi movement all through its existence (and still does) but which also began to dominate the scholars' research interest in Finland (see Saamelaiskomitea 1973; Aikio 1988), perhaps at the cost of other cultural norms that were violated and lost.

Historians were late to debate the key issues relevant to the Sámi education; however, once they did, a new research field was immediately established. The field is distinct in the way the politics of research has been successful in penetrating the (mainstream) political discourses. The histories of assimilation and those of the darker sides of school dormitories have managed to change the way that the Sámi policies and perhaps also the state of Finland are seen. Another substantial change, catering for the above-mentioned political interest, has been the change of focus from institutional history towards the histories of school and dormitory experiences among individual pupils (e.g. Keskitalo et al. 2014). These responses are being voiced against the triumphant discourses of the Finnish success in the PISA studies and the centenary celebrations of the Finnish independence when the Sámi educational history was barely criticised[2] and at the time when the educational system was a major source of national pride.

The Sámi school experience in Russia and in the Soviet Union is exceptional, mainly because of the early introduction of the minority-friendly institutions, including those that were already engaged in educating teachers of the native languages in the 1880s. This was the

---

[2]The issue was raised in a 'Suomi 100 seminar', organised to discuss Finland's 100 years of independence 'Saamelaisten historia itsenäisessä Suomessa: politiikka ja kokemukset' in Inari, Finland, 21 September 2017.

time when the first Sámi language schools were established on the Kola peninsula and sponsored by the state, the Russian Orthodox church and the local communities. The Russian Revolution of 1917 reinforced the position of these institutions. Another aspect concerns the harsh disruptions of the policies during the Great Terror and the long period of assimilation, which, as shown by Andrej Kotljarchuk, were motivated by political and security concerns. This break dealt a severe blow to the Sámi society and impacted the Sámi intelligentsia. In 1938, the Soviet government abolished all the Sámi schools as well as those of the other indigenous groups. The resumption of the Sámi classes in Russia was allowed only during the *perestroika*.

The number of studies on the Sámi education is limited, mainly because many leading scholars were arrested during Stalin's era. The first reviews of the Sámi education in the Soviet Union were published by David Zolotarev (1927) and Zakharii Cherniakov (1934). However, in the 1930s, both scholars were arrested by the NKVD for leading the 'Sámi counter-revolutionary nationalistic movement' and sent to the Gulag. Zolotarev (Russian by origin) died in prison in 1935. Cherniakov (a Jew from Belarus) survived the Gulag; however, his opus magnum *Essays on Sámi Ethnography* was published posthumously by the University of Lapland (Cherniakov 1998). In a chapter of the book entitled 'Sámi literacy and education in past and present', Cherniakov discusses the role of the Sámi school education for the development and the preservation of the Kola Sámi identity. He described the attempt of the early Soviet politicians at establishing the native language schools and argued that the Latin alphabet should be used for the Russian Sámi students, mainly because the Kola Sámi people perceived this alphabet as non-Russian and thus native. The author describes the decline of the Sámi school education, which forced the small number of Kola Sámi people to share their school and out-of-school environments with the local Russian and Komi children. Cherniakov was critical of the bilingual Sámi-Russian schools and of Sámi-Russian bilingualism in general; he believed that with the help of the native monolingual schools he could revive the native language. Finally, in 2002, Nikolay Bogdanov, an official of the Murmansk Regional Committee of the Affairs of Indigenous Peoples, published online a report on the history of the school education for Kola Sámi, in which he reviewed the Sámi school education from the tsarist era until the present-day. In his article, Bogdanov emphasises that the long-term crisis in the Sámi school education system was caused by political repression and forced relocation of the Sámi people on the Kola Peninsula (Bogdanov 2002).

Towards an International Research Frame

The selection of the chapters in this book reflect the recent historiographical developments within the Sámi studies in the Nordic countries. Whereas some of the chapters offer a conventional history of the educational tradition, others are written according to recent developments, aiding the framing of the Sámi history in a globally indigenous context.

Daniel Lindmark and Ritva Kylli's chapters discuss the early modern Sámi education in Sweden (including modern-day Finland). Jukka Nyyssönen's historiographical overview of the Sámi education in Finland is followed by the chapters written by Andrej Kotljarchuk, Lukas Allemann and Ekaterina Zmyvalova and Hanna Outakoski on the variety of roles that the Sámi language has played (or not played) in the Russian/Soviet educational context. Torjer A. Olsen discusses some key moments of the Sámi education in Norway, followed by Inker-Anni Linkola-Aikio's study on the position of Sámi language in the upper secondary education and vocational education systems of Norway. The chapters written by Merja Paksuniemi and Pigga Keskitalo and Marikaisa Laiti treat the Sámi language education in Finland.

After these chapters on the Sámi education, the focus turns to other indigenous groups. The chapters by Yoko Tanabe and Madoka Hammine discuss the education history of Japan's indigenous populations (the Ainu and the Ryukyu). The chapters written by Pirjo Kristiina Virtanen and Francisco Apurinã de Moura Cândido and Lea Kantonen focus on Latin American education by reviewing the indigenous education histories of Brazil and Mexico. Finally, Mere Kepa and Elizabeth Jackson-Barrett and Libby Lee-Hammond provide useful

10 O. Kortekangas et al.

scholarly insights from two strong geographical areas for studies of indigenous education, Australia and New Zealand. The book ends with a comparative summary of the chapters, written by Otso Kortekangas.

References

Aikio, M. (1988). *Saamelaiset kielenvaihdon kierteessä, Kielisosiologinen tutkimus viiden saamelaiskylän kielenvaihdosta 1910–1980.* Helsinki: SKS.

Andresén, S. (1990). *Eleverna vid Jukkasjärvi lappskola 1743–1820.* Umeå: Umeå universitet Forskningsarkivet.

Bogdanov, N. B. (2002). Богданов, Н. Б. История становления системы образования Кольских саамов или этапы становления саамской педагогики [History of the Educational System of Kola Sámi and the Formation of Sámi Pedagogic]. Available 28 August 2017 on www.sami.ru.

Cherniakov, Z. E. (1934). Черняков, З. Е. *Отчёт о командировке в Полярный район Мурманского округа 1933 г* [Report on the Field Studies in Polarnyi Rayon of the Murmansk District in 1933] (pp. 13–19). Murmansk: Komitet Novogo Alfavita.

Cherniakov, Z. E. (1998). Черняков, З. Е. *Очерки саамской этнографии* [Essays on Sámi Ethnography] (L. Rantala, Ed.). Rovaniemi: University of Lapland.

Elenius, L. (2006). *Nationalstat och minoritetspolitik: Samer och finskspråkiga minoriteter i ett jämförande nordiskt perspektiv.* Lund: Studentlitteratur.

Eriksen, K. E., & Niemi, Einar. (1981). *Den finske fare: sikkerhetsproblemer og minoritetspolitikk i nord 1860–1940.* Oslo: Universitetsforlaget.

Evjen, B., & Beck, D. R. (2015). Growing Indigenous Influence on Research, Extended Perspectives, and a New Mehtodology: A Historical Approach. In K. W. Shanley & B. Evjen (Eds.), *Mapping Indigenous Presence: North Scandinavian and North American Perspectives.* Tucson: The University of Arizona Press.

Henrysson, S., & Flodin, J. (1992). *Samernas skolgång till 1956.* Umeå: Umeå University.

Johansson, C.-H., & Flodin, J. (1991). *Åsele lappskola 1732–1820.* Umeå: Umeå universitet Forskningsarkivet.

Johansson, Egil. (1977). *The History of Literacy in Sweden: In Comparison with Some Other Countries.* Umeå: Umeå University.

Johansson, E. (1993). *Kan själva orden.* Umeå: Umeå University.

Keskitalo, P., Lehtola, V.-P., Paksuniemi, M. (Eds.). (2014). *Saamelaisten kansanopetuksen ja koulunkäynnin historia Suomessa*. Turku: Siirtolaisuusinstituutti.
Kortekangas, O. (2017). *Tools of Teaching and Means of Managing: Educational and Sociopolitical Functions of Languages of Instruction in Elementary Schools with Sámi Pupils in Sweden, Finland and Norway 1900–1940 in a Cross-National Perspective*. Turku: Iloinen tiede.
Kuokkanen, R. (2007). *Reshaping the University: Responsibility, Indigenous Epistemes, and the Logic of the Gift*. Vancouver and Toronto: UBC Press.
Kähkönen, E. I. (1988). *Katekeetat Suomen Lapissa 200 vuotta*. Rovaniemi: Lapin korkeakoulun kasvatustieteellisiä julkaisuja A 4.
Latour, B. (Ed). (2016). *Reset Modernity!* Karlsruhe: ZKM Center for Art and Media.
Lindmark, D. (2006). Pietism and Colonialism. Swedish Schooling in Eighteenth-century Sápmi. *Acta Borealia, 23*(2), 116–129.
Norberg, E. (1955). *Arjepolgs lappskola. Anteckningar*. Stockholm: Föreningen för svensk undervisningshistoria.
Nordblad, J. (2013). *Jämlikhetens villkor: Demos, imperium och pedagogik i Bretagne, Tunisien, Tornedalen och Lappmarken 1880–1925*. Göteborg: University of Gothenburg.
Saamelaiskomitean mietintö. (1973). Liite: Tutkimusraportit.
Sjögren, D. (2010). *Den säkra zonen: Motiv, åtgärdsförslag och verksamhet i den särskiljande utbildningspolitiken för inhemska minoriteter 1913–1962*. Umeå: Umeå University.
Smith, L. T. (2001). *Decolonizing Methodologies*. London: Zed Books.
Tröhler, Daniel. (2016). Curriculum History in Europe: A Historiographic Added Value. *Nordic Journal of Educational History, 3*(1), 10–11.
Whitehead, C. (2005). The Historiography of British Imperial Education Policy, Part I: India. *History of Education, 34*(3), 315–318.
Wilson, S. (2001). What Is an Indigenous Research Methodology? *Canadian Journal of Native Education, 25*(2), 175–179.
Zolotarev, D. A. (1927). Золотарев, Д. А. *Лопарская экспедиция 1927 года* [The 1927 Lappish Expedition]. Leningrad: State Russian Geographical Society Press.

2

Sámi Schools, Female Enrolment, and the Teaching Trade: Sámi Women's Involvement in Education in Early Modern Sweden

Daniel Lindmark

The encounter between Swedish and Sámi culture in the early modern period was very complex (Fur 2016). It involved both reciprocal contacts and a certain degree of coercion and resistance. In the seventeenth century, the State of Sweden made itself visible in Sápmi in the institution of fiscal, judicial, and mercantile systems, and the Sámi people were affected by the mining industry, tax collection, and missionary efforts. The established Lutheran church tried to impose Christian beliefs, rituals and customs, and education became a key missionary activity.

The first school for Sámi opened in Lycksele in 1632. In 1723, the Swedish Diet decided to establish a school system with one residential school in each Sámi parish. Around the year of 1740, the Sámi schools started to change their recruitment policy. They were no longer supposed to prepare Sámi boys for future clerical careers. Instead, the most proficient students were trained to serve as itinerant catechists. At the

D. Lindmark (✉)
Umeå School of Education and Faculty of Arts,
Umeå University, Umeå, Sweden
e-mail: daniel.lindmark@umu.se

© The Author(s) 2019
O. Kortekangas et al. (eds.), *Sámi Educational History in a Comparative International Perspective*,
https://doi.org/10.1007/978-3-030-24112-4_2

same time, the schools started to accept female students. This article will discuss how these changes were interconnected and especially how female enrolment should be interpreted, primarily in relation to the gender pattern of the various positions within the educational field, the "teaching trade."

Previous Research and Sources Used

Over the years, Sámi education in Early Modern Sweden has attracted quite an interest among scholars. Elof Haller (1896) and Bill Widén (1964) have written very useful overviews of the educational efforts made by the ecclesiastical authorities in the eighteenth century. There are also studies focusing on certain areas, for instance Gellivare Parish (Öberg 1979) and Jukkasjärvi Parish (Anderzén 1992). The Sámi school system of 1723 has been in focus of many studies, starting with Erik Nordberg's (1955) comprehensive book on Arjeplog Sámi School. The first quantitative analyses of student recruitment to the Sámi schools were undertaken in a large research project at Umeå University starting in 1986. This project, which also involved studies of educational media in Sápmi (Forsgren 1988, 1990), resulted in a number of reports on individual schools and a concluding book (Henrysson et al. 1993). Starting my academic career in this project (Lindmark 1988, 1990), I have written about the ideological background and educational practice of the Sámi school system of 1723 (Lindmark 2006a, b). The gender pattern of the Sámi school has been touched upon in previous research (Henrysson et al. 1993; Lindmark 2016) but never made subject to a more systematic analysis in relation to female teaching opportunities.

The analysis of student recruitment is based upon school enrolment registers from six of the Sámi schools founded in the eighteenth century (*Catalogus Discentium, Scholæ Matrickel*, etc.). The information in these registers has been processed in previous research (Anderzén 1992; Henrysson et al. 1993), and most of the records have also been published (e.g. Alm and Henrysson 1991). This article makes use of both the published and processed enrolment registers.

The Sámi School of the Eighteenth Century

After repeated reports on extant Sámi religious practice and several proposals for improved religious instruction, the Diet of 1723 decided to set up a school system for the Sámi population. The School Ordinance of 1723 was supplemented with financial regulations in 1729 and the School Instruction of 1735. The new school system meant one residential school in each of the following seven Sámi parishes, in addition to the existing Skyttean School in Lycksele (1632): Åsele (1732), Jokkmokk (1732), Arjeplog (1743), Utsjoki (1743; discontinued in 1750), Jukkasjärvi (1744), Föllinge (1748), and Gellivare (1756). Consequently, by the middle of the century, all schools were in operation.

In 1739, a special organisation for ecclesiastical and educational matters was instituted, the Board of Ecclesiastical Affairs in the Laplands (Sw. *Direktionen över lappmarkens ecklesisastikverk*). This national board of clergy and laymen was superior to the consistories of Härnösand and Åbo in matters concerning the Laplands, including the Sámi schools.

The schoolmaster of the Sámi School was an ordained minister, and he was required to master the Sámi language, which was the primary language of instruction (School Instruction in Haller 1896, 148–155; Lindmark 1988, 8–14). In order to improve his language skills, the schoolmaster was recommended to initially accept bilingual children— also among colonists—but after the first year, Sámi children from remote areas were to be prioritised. The explicit idea was to teach the students so thoroughly that they could serve as catechists among their own people. According to the School Instruction, it was the duty of vicars and deans to make sure that Sámi parents took advantage of the services offered by these itinerant catechising teachers.

The School Instruction restricted the schoolmaster's teaching duty to six students at a time. If the schoolmaster could manage more students, he was free to take on a heavier burden, but such students attended school at their own expense. The students were supposed to leave school after two years of study, when they had been "informed in the most necessary parts of Christianity" (Lindmark 1988, 12). If they needed more time to meet the learning goals, the schoolmaster could keep them longer.

The teaching in the Sámi School was restricted to reading and religion. The School Instruction refers to the basic books of Christian teaching: the ABC book, the Small Catechism, the Exposition, and the Hymnbook. While the Small Catechism was to be mastered by heart, the Hymnbook was to be used for reading exercises. The Schoolmaster was requested to diligently explain the Exposition to enable the students to develop firm concepts, especially regarding God and his demands. The Instruction specifically pointed out the need for clear teaching of the first three Commandments concerning the duties towards God Almighty.

The Sámi School was a residential school, where the state provided teaching, clothing, boarding, and lodging at no expense for the students. The School Instruction made clear that no abuse of the students would be tolerated. They were entitled to three meals a day, and the school inspector, usually the dean, was urged to make sure that the students were fed and clad in accordance with the regulations. Also in other respects, the Instruction tried to prevent abuse. Among other things, the schoolmaster was not allowed to take any enrolment fees, nor have the students work for him.

During their schooldays, the students were requested to spend all their time at the residential school, including the holidays. The schoolmaster was to keep them under constant surveillance, and it was totally forbidden for the students to visit their parents before they were firmly grounded in their Christian faith.

The isolation of the individual student was to be maintained until the teaching had reached its goal: the student would so completely internalise the new norms "that he would be able to control and guide himself." In order to reach that goal, the schoolmaster was not allowed to use penalties or corporal punishment; instead, "with each and every motive and idea at hand encourage them, until they themselves can find the necessity in doing this Divine work" (Lindmark 1988, 12).

Student Enrolment in the Sámi School

All in all, there were 1894 students enrolled in the six Sámi Schools during the period 1732–1850 (Henrysson et al. 1993; Lycksele and Utsjoki schools not included). In the beginning the schools recruited boys only, but in the 1740s a change took place. In 1741, Dean Carl Solander argued in favour of accepting girls as students by referring to their better opportunities to teach others as they spent more time at home. In 1747, a formal decision was made, according to which the Board of Ecclesiastical Affairs recommended the schools to replace the boys who left school in the coming year with girls (Nordberg 1955, 95). Most schools went for coeducation right away, but in 1747 Vicar Pehr Fjellström in Lycksele put forward the idea that boys and girls should be accepted every second year, which would create preconditions for keeping the two sexes separated from each other. In 1749, the Skyttean School accepted girls only, but from the next year on coeducation became the prevailing model there, too (Haller 1896, 117).

As can be seen from Table 2.1, the overall rate of female students was 36% (687 girls out of a total student body of 1894). Female enrolment ranged from 27% in Åsele to 44% in Gellivare. Table 2.2 displays how female enrolment developed over time in the Sámi Schools of Jokkmokk, Jukkasjärvi, and Gellivare.

During the 90 years that Table 2.2 covers, the female students represented on average one-third of the student body in the three schools taken together. Table 2.2 shows that male students dominated in the beginning, but already in the 1750s, every fourth student was a girl. In the two decades after the turn of the century, the schools achieved gender balance (48% girls, and 52% boys). Gellivare Sámi School was the only one where the female students outnumbered their male counterparts. Jokkmokk Sámi School did not accept any female students during its first two decades of operation. The first girls accepted in each of the three schools were enrolled in 1749 (Jukkasjärvi), 1753 (Jokkmokk) and 1756 (Gellivare), respectively. In the schools of Arjeplog and Åsele, the first female students appeared in 1747 and 1748, respectively.

Table 2.1 Distribution of students according to sex at respective Sámi School, 1732–1850

Sex	Jokkmokk	Åsele	Arjeplog	Jukkasjärvi	Föllinge	Gellivare	Total
Female	144 (36%)	88 (27%)	120 (43%)	80 (29%)	86 (39%)	169 (44%)	687 (36%)
Male	256 (64%)	241 (73%)	161 (57%)	195 (71%)	137 (61%)	217 (56%)	1207 (64%)
Sum	400 (100%)	329 (100%)	281 (100%)	275 (100%)	223 (100%)	386 (100%)	1894 (100%)

Source Henrysson et al. (1993, 63)

2 Sámi Schools, Female Enrolment, and the Teaching Trade ...   19

Table 2.2 Distribution of students according to sex and enrolment decade at the Sámi Schools of Jokkmokk, Jukkasjärvi and Gellivare, 1732–1819

Decade	Jokkmokk		Jukkasjärvi		Gellivare		All three schools	
	F	M	F	M	F	M	F	M
1730–1739	–	23	–	–	–	–		23 (100%)
1740–1749	–	19	2	24	–	–	2 (4%)	43 (96%)
1750–1759	7	23	8	24	4	11	19 (25%)	58 (75%)
1760–1769	8	20	3	39	10	19	21 (21%)	78 (79%)
1770–1779	12	17	14	28	8	20	34 (34%)	65 (66%)
1780–1789	12	16	18	25	12	15	42 (43%)	56 (57%)
1790–1799	10	22	9	23	10	20	29 (31%)	65 (69%)
1800–1809	15	19	17	20	15	12	47 (48%)	51 (52%)
1810–1819	16	16	8	13	16	15	40 (48%)	44 (52%)
Total	80	175	79	196	75	112	234 (33%)	483 (67%)

Note The Jokkmokk Sámi School started in 1732, Jukkasjärvi Sámi School in 1744, and Gellivare Sámi School in 1756
Sources Henrysson et al. (1993, 73) (Jokkmokk); Anderzén (1992, 129) (Jukkasjärvi); and Alm and Henrysson (1991, 34) (Gellivare)

According to available records, male and female students seem to have been treated the same way in the Sámi schools. The gender-specific differences were very small in terms of enrolment age, time spent in school and study results (Henrysson et al. 1993, 72–74; Anderzén 1992, 128–130).

Schooling for Prospective Ministers and Catechists

When the Sámi school system of 1723 was established, there was no mention of female enrolment. Why was that? One explanation takes into account the intentions behind previous schooling efforts. The Skyttean School that was founded in Lycksele in 1632 aimed at preparing Sámi boys for further studies. The idea was to create a corps of native Sámi ministers to secure proficiency in the Sámi language (Rasmussen 2016). The actual curriculum of the Skyttean School bears witness to this ambition. Still at the beginning of the eighteenth century Latin was taught. It is also known that some of the students

20   D. Lindmark

continued their studies at schools in Umeå and Härnösand, for instance Olof Sjulsson, who gave up his studies and became a county sheriff (Lindmark 2006a, 73).

Not many ministers were recruited among the Sámi. During almost three centuries, from 1584 to 1876, only ten of the ministers in the Church of Sweden had two Sámi parents. Seven of the ten Sámi ministers were ordained before 1710, and all but one served in Sámi parishes. No more than one of them was a possible student of the Skyttean School in Lycksele (Rasmussen 2016).

The idea of recruiting clergymen from the Sámi population was not abandoned entirely until the middle of the eighteenth century. The Diet of 1738/1739 wanted the schoolmasters of the Sámi schools to make sure that suitable candidates were encouraged to continue their studies in order to qualify for ministerial service among the Sámi people. In 1743 the Board of Ecclesiastical Affairs decided to keep a candidate for the ministry in the Skyttean School of Lycksele (Widén 1964, 55).

The ecclesiastical authorities changed the recruitment policy around 1740. Now sons of Swedish ministers in the Sámi parishes were encouraged to follow in their fathers' footsteps. These candidates were considered to be more prone to academic studies, and having grown up in Sápmi, they were familiar with the Sámi culture and mastered the Sámi language. Scholarships dedicated to students of Sámi background were offered to sons of the clergy, and the new recruitment policy soon created a corps of large bilingual clerical families that frequently intermarried. The Sámi school system had no role to play in the education of the new candidates, who usually were taught by their fathers or private tutors before being sent to the grammar schools of Härnösand, Piteå or Frösön and the upper secondary school of Härnösand (Haller 1896, 66–68; Lindmark 1990, 75–76).

The decision not to recruit ministers among the Sámi population seems to have coincided with the emergence of a new itinerant teacher category, the catechists. In 1743, the Board of Ecclesiastical Affairs started to demand each Sámi school to keep a couple of students for a prolonged period and train them for future service as catechists. Soon enough, ambulating catechists were hired in most Sámi parishes: Åsele 1744, Lycksele 1744, Arjeplog 1744, Jokkmokk 1745, Arvidsjaur 1749,

2 Sámi Schools, Female Enrolment, and the Teaching Trade ... 21

Jukkasjärvi 1750, Gellivare 1751. In the period 1744–1820, 158 catechists served in the Laplands of Sweden and Finland, receiving their salaries from the Board of Ecclesiastical Affairs (Widén 1965, 13–24, 134).

The catechists were educated in the Sámi Schools. This means that the schools at least occasionally could offer more academic teaching. There is evidence that some of the prospective catechists studied Latin and theology in Jokkmokk Sámi School in the 1740s. However, from 1750 focus was in general placed on the teaching of religion. First of all, the students had to master the lessons they were supposed to teach as catechists, not only to recite the wordings correctly, but also to reflect upon the contents by rephrasing it. Second, they received a practical education in teaching methods. Third, they were instructed how to conduct emergency baptisms and lead Sunday prayers. In contrast to the schoolmasters and missionaries, the catechists were not ordained, but they were encouraged to perform religious acts as laymen (Widén 1965, 54–62).

Extant records do not offer much information on the recruitment of catechists. However, the reports from the *visitatio classica* of 1749 provide an interesting example of selection and preparation of a candidate, even though the case is quite exceptional. When visiting the Sámi School of Jokkmokk in 1749, Superintendent Kiörning found out that student Anders Nilsson was "especially clever, virtuous and of good nature" (Anderzén 1999, 76). Among other things, he answered correctly the questions in the newly issued catechetical exposition, and he read fluently from the new Güttner Homily, even though its "orthography differed from what he previously had read." Consequently, he was appointed an itinerant teacher, starting with Nils Ericsson's children in Sjokksjokk. He was given a Güttner Homily and was admonished to "every Sunday read from it in cots for the people of the household and the neighbors" (Anderzén 1999, 77). Before leaving school, he would be trained in holding service in accordance with the order drawn up on the first page of the homily (Anderzén 1993, 1999, 76–77).

From Bill Widén's research it is known that 158 individuals were employed as catechists in the Swedish and Finnish Laplands in the period 1744–1820 (Widén 1965, 100–134). The vast majority of them were men. No more than 6 women worked as catechists (4%), and they can be found in two parishes only, Arjeplog (4) and Jokkmokk (2). The almost total exclusion of female students from the training for future service as itinerant catechists was the only major gender-specific difference of the eighteenth-century Sámi school system.

Female School Enrolment and the Gender Pattern of the Teaching Trade

Around the year of 1740, three important changes took place that might have affected the Sámi school and its way of operating. First, the policy for recruitment to clerical service shifted focus from Sámi youngsters to sons of ministers working in the Sámi parishes. The Sámi school would no longer serve as the first educational step for prospective ministers. Second, the Sámi school received a new educational task: to train proficient students for future service as catechists. Third, the Sámi schools started to accept female students.

The threefold reorientation of the Sámi schools did not in any essential way change the character of the teaching practice. The schools continued to offer basic education in reading and religion and occasionally teach more talented students at a higher level. This was the way the Skyttean School had functioned for more than one century, and the schools founded in the eighteenth century obviously operated in the same way.

Sámi schooling displayed a high degree of differentiation. Examination registers provide clear evidence of an individualised teaching practice. As soon as a vacancy occurred, a new student was accepted. The teaching began from the new student's level of knowledge, and all students developed knowledge and skills at their own pace. Depending on previous knowledge and aptitude for studies, the time in school could vary considerably.

Female enrolment in the Sámi schools does not seem to have been linked to any of the other changes. The explicit idea behind opening the schools for girls highlighted women as better teachers—from a practical point of view. It is also possible that female enrolment was promoted simply to broaden the recruitment basis. Some of the schools found it hard to recruit students, including Jokkmokk Sámi School. Certain scholars have also suggested that the girls were more dispensable in the reindeer herding economy (Henrysson et al. 1993, 72).

Although the Sámi schools were fairly inclusive by enrolling female students, a certain pattern of differentiation is clearly discernible when it comes to job opportunities within the teaching trade. There were four levels of teaching positions that were possible to reach for the Sámi population in the eighteenth century. The first level was the clergy, which included parish ministers and ordained schoolmasters in the Sámi schools. Only a restricted number of ministers were recruited from the Sámi population, but since the ministry was an entirely masculine affair, the exclusion was total for Sámi women regardless of their aptitude for studies.

The next level might have been the parish clerks, but since they seem not to have engaged in teaching in the Sámi parishes, they will be left out of this discussion. In the Sámi parishes, the catechists represented the next level of teaching staff. From an ethnic point of view, this was a group of educators among which Sámi individuals heavily dominated. Only a few catechists came from Swedish or Finnish settler families. Consequently, there was a general differentiation between ordained Swedish ministers and schoolmasters on the one hand, and Sámi catechists on the other hand. The salary and social status differed considerably between the two groups.

Among the catechists, a few women can be found. All in all, they did not represent more than 4% of the entire body, but in the parishes of Arjeplog and Jokkmokk their share was 12% (6 out of 51 catechists). Obviously, it was possible for women to become employed as catechists, but not everywhere and only as a marginal group. When women were hired, they usually were treated the same way as their male counterparts, receiving the same salary, and performing the same acts, etc. Consequently, female catechists conducted some of the acts that normally were reserved for men, including the leading of Sunday services. Catechist Ingri Månsdotter in Arjeplog Parish was even promoted to first catechist in 1779, only 23 years old. Then she served as head of the other catechists and fulfilled some of the clerical duties when the vicar was absent (Nordberg 1955, 137–139; Rydving 2016, 328). The third level of teaching in the Sámi parishes was a phenomenon referred to as "premium instruction," which meant that informal teachers (Anderzén [1992] uses the term "informants," Sw. *informatörer*) received a premium for having taught a named person to read or master the catechism. This model of teaching was often resorted to in cases when suitable candidates for the catechist positions were hard to find, and then the catechist salary was used for these premiums. Income from book sales could also be used for this purpose. This informal teaching model has not left many traces in the sources, but Sölve Anderzén has published a list of 91 informants having received premiums in Jukkasjärvi Parish between 1776 and 1786 (Anderzén 1992, 303–306). As big a share as 30% of the informants were women (27 out of 91). Obviously, this type of informal teaching of individuals at home allowed women to reach a high representation.

Consequently, the more informal the teaching duties were, the higher the representation of Sámi women. At the fourth and most informal level, the unpaid parent level, we can assume that Sámi women were overrepresented as teachers. The main argument for admitting female students to the Sámi schools was their better opportunities to teach, which indicates that mothers were more involved than fathers in parents' teaching of their children. In conclusion, even though female students were well integrated into the Sámi schools, the educational labour market in the Sámi parishes was highly differentiated along gender lines.

References

Alm, A., & Henrysson, S. (1991). *Gällivare lappskola 1756–1850: En elevmatrikel jämte analys.* Umeå: Research Archives.

Anderzén, S. (1992). *"Begrepp om salighetens grund, ordning och medel": Undervisningen i en Lappmarksförsamling: Jukkasjärvi församling 1744–1820.* Uppsala: Uppsala University.

Anderzén, S. (1993). "Förplichtat wara läsa för them": Byabön i Lappmarken vid 1700-talets mitt? In M. A. Sohlman, D. Lindmark, & K. Snellman

2 Sámi Schools, Female Enrolment, and the Teaching Trade ...   25

(Eds.), *Alphabeta varia: Läsebok för Egil* (pp. 9–22). Umeå: Research Archives.

Anderzén, S. (Ed.). (1999). *Jockmock 1749–1775: Ämbetsberättelser, visitationsprotokoll och andra berättelser med anknytning till skolmästaren och kyrkoherden Jonas Hollsten.* Umeå: Research Archives.

Forsgren, T. (1988). *Samisk kyrko- och undervisningslitteratur i Sverige 1619–1850.* Umeå: Research Archives.

Forsgren, T. (1990). *"…först at inhämta språket, och sedan deruppå lära sin Christendom…": Om finska böcker i sameundervisning i Torne och Kemi lappmarker före 1850.* Umeå: Research Archives.

Fur, G. (2016). Kolonisation och kulturmöten under 1600- och 1700-talen. In D. Lindmark & O. Sundström (Eds.), *De historiska relationerna mellan Svenska kyrkan och samerna: En vetenskaplig antologi* (pp. 241–282). Skellefteå: Artos.

Haller, E. (1896). *Svenska kyrkans mission i Lappmarken under frihetstiden.* Stockholm: Carlson.

Henrysson, S., et al. (1993). *Samer, präster och skolmästare: Ett kulturellt perspektiv på samernas och Övre Norrlands historia.* Umeå: Centre for Arctic Research.

Lindmark, D. (Ed.). (1988). *1812 års uppfostringskommittés enkät: Svaren från lappmarksförsamlingarna.* Umeå: Research Archives.

Lindmark, D. (1990). *En skola för staden, regionen och kyrkan: Elever, lärare och präster i Piteå skola före 1850.* Umeå: Research Archives.

Lindmark, D. (2006a). *En lappdrängs omvändelse: Svenskar i möte med samer och deras religion på 1600- och 1700-talen.* Umeå: Centre for Sami Research.

Lindmark, D. (2006b). Pietism and Colonialism: Swedish Schooling in Eighteenth-Century Sápmi. *Acta Borealia: A Nordic Journal of Circumpolar Societies, 23*(2), 116–129.

Lindmark, D. (2016). Svenska undervisningsinsatser och samiska reaktioner på 1600- och 1700-talen. In D. Lindmark & O. Sundström (Eds.), *De historiska relationerna mellan Svenska kyrkan och samerna: En vetenskaplig antologi* (pp. 341–369). Skellefteå: Artos.

Nordberg, E. (1955). *Arjeplogs lappskola.* Stockholm: Föreningen för svensk undervisningshistoria.

Öberg, I. (1979). *Mission och evangelisation i Gellivare-bygden ca 1740–1770.* Turku: Kyrkohistoriska arkivet vid Åbo Akademi.

Rasmussen, S. (2016). Samiske prester i den svenske kirka i tidlig nytid. In D. Lindmark & O. Sundström (Eds.), *De historiska relationerna*

26   D. Lindmark

mellan Svenska kyrkan och samerna: En vetenskaplig antologi (pp. 283–314). Skellefteå: Artos.

Rydving, H. (2016). Samisk kyrkohistoria: En kort översikt med fokus på kvinnor som aktörer. In D. Lindmark & O. Sundström (Eds.), *De historiska relationerna mellan Svenska kyrkan och samerna: En vetenskaplig antologi* (pp. 315–339). Skellefteå: Artos.

Widén, B. (1964). *Kristendomsundervisning och nomadliv: Studier i den kyrkliga verksamheten i lappmarkerna 1740–1809.* Turku: Åbo Akademi University.

Widén, B. (1965). *Kateketinstitutionen i Sveriges och Finlands lappmarker 1744–1820.* Turku: Åbo Akademi University.

3

Out of the "Pagan Darkness": Christian Education in Finnish Lapland

Ritva Kylli

In the early modern period in Europe, the formation of states and the building of empires inspired governments to take over remote and overseas areas. Fur and other natural resources in the Arctic region attracted Northern European states to expand their control to Greenland, Alaska and the northernmost parts of Fennoscandia (McCannon 2012, 77–78). In Sweden, the government and the church took it upon themselves to educate the Sámi people living in Finnish Lapland in the seventeenth century. The means to accomplish this mission, however, varied from century to century. Some forms of nationwide education were brought to the Sámi people, but the exceptional circumstances of northernmost Lapland were also taken into account in their education. Education was provided by priests sent from southern Finland, as well as Sámi educators trained for the job.

R. Kylli (✉)
University of Oulu, Oulu, Finland
e-mail: ritva.kylli@oulu.fi

© The Author(s) 2019
O. Kortekangas et al. (eds.), *Sámi Educational History
in a Comparative International Perspective*,
https://doi.org/10.1007/978-3-030-24112-4_3

Educating the Sámi was seen as a comprehensive process: The Sámi were taught how important it was to appreciate the family, as well as the church and the state—in other words, God in heaven and the king in Stockholm. This article examines what means were used to pull the Sámi out of their "pagan darkness" and how the "light of civilisation" was intended to be cast upon them, i.e. the various motives the Lutheran Church had for the Sámi education over the centuries. In the process of Christianising the Sámi, the church and the state produced a large body of documents, which also served as key source material for this article. My study focuses on the three parishes established during the seventeenth and eighteenth centuries in the Sámi area of what is now Finnish Lapland. These parishes were Utsjoki (*Ohcejohka*), Inari (*Aanaar*) and Enontekiö (*Eanodat*); of these, Enontekiö and Inari also included Finnish settlements established since the seventeenth century. My examination of these parishes extends to the beginning of the twentieth century. During that time, the Sámi adopted a new religion, in addition to becoming citizens of another realm at the beginning of the nineteenth century, when Finland became part of the Russian Empire. Before that, education for the Sámi people in Finnish Lapland had been in line with the Swedish school system for Lapland, as Finland was part of Sweden until the war in 1808–1809. Finland gained independence from Russia in 1917.

Education for "Savages"

In Sweden, the church—which had turned from Catholic to Lutheran faith after the Reformation in the sixteenth century—became interested in the Sámi people living in the remote areas of the nation at the beginning of the seventeenth century. The Sámi people who lived in the area that is now Finnish Lapland sustained themselves by hunting and fishing. In some Lappish villages, some of the Sámi had specialised in reindeer herding (Kylli et al. 2019). Representatives of the church and the state looked down on the residents of Lapland as primitive and pagan "savages"—as opposed to Christians—who needed to be brought into line with values of the majority culture. In the process, they would also become obedient citizens and good taxpayers. At the beginning of the seventeenth century, a decision was made to teach the Word of God to all of the Sámi people living in Swedish Lapland. The Sámi people who lived in what is now Enontekiö were told that Charles IX of Sweden wished them to start going to the church that had been built in their area and pay a tithe to the priest annually. At that point, the teaching of Christianity was relatively superficial, as the clergymen who arrived from the south once a year were often more interested in trading and collecting taxes than in systematically educating the people of Lapland (Kylli 2012b).

In the Great Northern War against Russia (1700–1721), Sweden lost its status as a Great Power. Among other areas, it had to cede the Livonia region, which was a nationally important area for grain cultivation. The nation's rulers turned their attention to Lapland and its natural resources, which they now wanted to use more broadly and effectively. They also wanted to tie the land of the Sámi more closely to the rest of the nation, which spurred the church to try to make the inhabitants of Lapland adopt the Christian faith more deeply than before. In 1723, Sweden issued a royal decree for teaching Christianity to the Sámi and establishing schools in Lapland. With the goal of making education more effective, a decision was made to build a special Lappish school in conjunction with each major church in Lapland (Kylli 2012b, 99–109). The Sámi parish of Utsjoki was part of the Kautokeino (*Guovdageaidnu*) parish region (in what is now Norway), and it was deemed best to locate the school, which had originally been planned for Kautokeino, in Utsjoki. In Kautokeino, the construction of the school had encountered a problem typical of subarctic Lapland: a lack of suitable logs. The nearest place where suitable trees grew was around 90 kilometres distant, whereas in Utsjoki the corresponding distance was around 20 kilometres. Sámi taxpayers in Utsjoki were ordered to fell the trees in the winter of 1726 and have their reindeer drag the logs to the intended location of the chapel (Kylli 2014, 31–32).

The plan was to hire a qualified priest as a schoolmaster who would also hold church services for the parish. In the church that had been built for the parish in 1700, the local Sámi church officer had been reading homilies on Sundays, but the church now wanted greater control of the Sámi people's education. However, the plan was not implemented because of insufficient funds, and the school building was left unused for more than ten years. In 1742, it was finally possible to send a schoolmaster to Utsjoki. He immediately noticed that the parents of the local Sámi children had put considerable effort into teaching the catechism. This was evident in the high level of rote learning, and many parishioners received high marks in the parish confirmation book for knowing the Apostles' Creed and the Lord's Prayer, for example (Kylli 2005, 115–122).

The Sámi people—a linguistic minority living in a remote northern area—can be seen as an "internal other" (Johnson and Coleman 2012), who became subject to a special education policy in Finland. In some respects, better care was taken with the Christian education of minorities in remote areas than with the education of Finns living inland. The books used in Christian education also found their way rather quickly to the northernmost parts of Lapland. This is evident in court records from Inari from 1760 (RA), when a married couple applied for financial assistance after their hut had been destroyed in a fire. One of the spouses had been net fishing and the other had been collecting reindeer lichen when their hut burned down, and the inventory of lost property specified six sheep, a copper pot, two hymnals and two catechisms. In other words, basic Christian books constituted a significant part of their property. In 1777, Sámi people in both Utsjoki and Inari complained about the lack of Christian textbooks and hoped that such books would be sold at the market to be held in Lapland, instead of many other, comparatively useless commodities. In the early nineteenth century, foreign Bible societies had the New Testament translated into the Sámi languages and made available to the Sámi (Kylli 2005, 162–164).

The schools that had been established in areas inhabited by the Sámi and other Arctic indigenous peoples since the seventeenth century also served as a means of assimilation (McCannon 2012, 95). The Lappish school that operated in Utsjoki in the eighteenth century could be considered the country's northernmost boarding school, with the state contributing to the students' cost of living and meals. For the pupils, living at and attending the Lappish school, even for a short period, marked a major life change. The children, aged ten and older, had to leave their families and move to a location near the church (Kylli 2005, 339). This must have been quite an ordeal, considering that, as the Sámi diet centres on meat and fish, the children were unfamiliar with a permanent living arrangement or a Finnish-type diet relying more on grain. Furthermore, some died in epidemics that spread through the school. In other words, a high price was paid by some in the effort to educate the children to become obedient citizens and church members (Anderzén 1992, 105).

For many inhabitants of Lapland, Christian knowledge and skills were not related in any way to their daily lives, so it was often difficult to translate Christian terms (which arose in the Mediterranean) into the Sámi language, which had many highly nuanced terms, such as for reindeer herding and other matters relevant to the life of the Sámi. The ethnic religion of the Sámi people was also seamlessly connected to essential aspects of their lives, such as successful livelihoods (Kylli 2012b, 12). Since the 1760s, the members of the fully Sámi parish of Utsjoki had been required to learn the Finnish language, as they were deemed to benefit from learning the language not only for their Christian education, but also for trading and other more secular activities. In 1804, a decision was made in Utsjoki to impose fines on parents who did not teach their children to read. In 1828, a similar decision was made concerning parents who did not teach their children to speak Finnish (Kylli 2005, 195).

The Worst Classroom in the World

Studies conducted in Swedish Lapland in the early eighteenth century found that the Sámi continued to rely on their old, indigenous religion and drums, particularly in an hour of need. However, Christian priests were prohibited from taking too strong a stand against the remnants of these old Sámi beliefs and practices. It was believed that with a Christian education, pagan customs would disappear over time (Kylli 2012b, 121). It took some time to find the best forms of teaching for the conditions prevailing in Lapland. The Lappish school in Utsjoki was discontinued in the early 1750s, as contemporaries found that having a catechist travel from hut to hut was, after all, the best way to teach

Christianity across a wide, sparsely populated region (Kylli 2014, 33). The first catechists in Utsjoki, who began their work in 1751, were former pupils of the Lappish school that had operated in Utsjoki in the 1740s; thus, the school can be regarded as having served as the first teacher training institution in Finnish Lapland (Kylli 2005, 346).

Education provided by catechists was a form of teaching particularly well suited for Sámi families: the parents did not need to send their children away to school, as a catechist visited their homes to teach reading and Christianity to their children once a year. From the very beginning, catechists provided education to girls and boys alike in Lapland (Kylli 2005, 348). However, this form of teaching was also problematic, as some people found a Sámi hut to be the worst possible classroom in the world (Læstadius 1977, 184). In 1857, a Sámi catechist who worked in Utsjoki described the chaos of teaching children in a hut as follows:

> As soon as the schoolman arrives in the reindeer village and steps inside a hut and sits down by the door, he is requested to step higher and food is prepared for him to eat. Then he is given bedclothes and shown his place. The schoolman's place is always in the middle of the hut. The children gather around him once he begins his work. If the children already know how to read, they are given hymnals to read or spell aloud together. But teaching, or having children read, is difficult in a Lappish hut, particularly when it is dark. Once the fireplace is lit, the hut fills with smoke and steam, and you can barely see anything. The dogs that herd the reindeer are so loud that you cannot hear anything. Many huts have as many as eight dogs – or even more. When they start to make a racket, fight, bark and howl, the schoolman must focus on protecting himself and the children from being bitten, and on preventing the dogs from taking the books from the children's hands and from pushing the children into the fire. (Hellander 1857)

The parents of Sámi children had been teaching Christianity diligently to their children in the early eighteenth century. However, in the latter half of the century it was discovered that some parents were eager to hand over this responsibility to the catechists. Before long, the learning outcomes began to decline, as the catechists could spend only a few days teaching individual Sámi children each year (Kylli 2005, 378). Sámi catechists could anyway convey special features of Sámi culture to the children better than priests from other parts of Finland—and, in the process, perhaps also strengthen the pupils' Sámi identity. The priests were not familiar enough with concepts of the Sámi lifestyle (or even the Sámi language), but the catechists were able to explain aspects of the indigenous religion of the Sámi, which also helped the children better understand Christianity. The catechists could teach that Christianity protected the children from Stallos, giant creatures that—according to Sámi mythology—lived in the forest and caught little children in their bags (Paulaharju 1965, 168–172, 228–229). In many schools in the Arctic region, teachers who had come from elsewhere were scornful of the ethnic religions and folklore of the indigenous peoples, which was very harmful for the collective memory of the local residents (McCannon 2012, 201).

The education of the Sámi needed to be adjusted to the exceptional circumstances of the north. In Lapland, the teaching provided by the catechists was customised to the Sámi lifestyle, but the ultimate goal of Christian education—in Lapland and elsewhere in the country—was confirmation: the completion of confirmation classes (Kylli 2005, 357). Even though the Lutheran church usually stressed the importance of the local language, the situation among the Sámi living in Finnish Lapland was not always that simple. The Sámi were forced to learn Finnish, the language of instruction, at least to some degree, before they were able to learn Christianity and, consequently, be confirmed and get married (Kielioloista Lapissa 1901). In practice, permission to get married was granted to Sámi people whose knowledge of Christianity left something to be desired, as long as they promised to improve their knowledge in the future. Not everyone did, and a priest working in Utsjoki in the early 1830s was left wondering why a Mountain Sámi woman he had examined could not even remember the name of Jesus (Paulaharju 1966, 203–211). The language barrier was too high for many Sámi people, and many parishioners missed the entire content of a Finnish church service (Kylli 2005, 238).

To address the Sámi's learning difficulties, in the nineteenth century basic literature for their Christian education began to be translated extensively into Sámi. Because Finns were a minority in the Russian Empire, representatives of the Finnish intelligentsia paid attention to minorities in Finland and spoke in favour of both the Sámi language and of providing education in the language. Linguists who had familiarised themselves with the issues were particularly concerned about the future of the Inari Sámi language, which was spoken only inside the borders of Finland. Their concern was not unfounded: by the beginning of the nineteenth century, with the large number of new Finnish settlements in the area, the Sámi spoken south of Inari had almost completely disappeared. As mentioned earlier, Finnish had been used extensively as the language of instruction in Utsjoki, for example, since the 1760s. However, the situation changed after the 1840s. Since 1849, priests and catechists with a knowledge of Sámi were paid better salaries, which inspired them to learn the native language of their parishioners. At the same time, the fines imposed on Sámi parents who did not teach Finnish to their children were discontinued. In the latter half of the nineteenth century, the parents of Sámi children attending church schools were allowed to choose between Sámi and Finnish as the language of education for their children (Kylli 2005, 198–206, 403).

During the days of the Lappish school in Utsjoki in the 1740s, the schoolmaster had been required to teach writing at noon on every school day to pupils who were adept at writing. In 1748, a Finnish provincial provost responsible for church administration visited Utsjoki. He advised the teacher of the Lappish school to stop teaching writing to the pupils and primarily focus on Christian doctrines, as it was feared that too much book learning would inspire rebellion among the people living in the remote areas (Kylli 2005, 340–341). Writing was not taught again in the Sámi region of Finnish Lapland until the latter half of the nineteenth century, but the interest in written expression had been so strong among some Sámi people that they had practiced writing on their own. A Sámi fisher explained that he had taken an interest in writing after seeing a priest make notes in the confirmation book at the church. At that time, the residents of Lapland had very little access to paper suitable for writing, let alone ink, so the Sámi had used bark as paper and reindeer blood as ink (Walle 1881).

The White Man's Burden

Even though the land of the Sámi was contiguous with Finland, it was often subject to colonialist policies (Anderzén 1996, 5–17). The priests often taught more than just Christianity: they also tried to make the Sámi adopt other virtues appreciated by the Finns, such as punctuality and modesty. Some priests even objected to the way the Sámi dressed, as the priests were not used to their parishioners wearing colourful clothes and Sámi hats (Andelin 1854; Utsjoen Lapinmaalta 1855). Colonialism often involved an attempt to control the hygienic practices of the colonised peoples (Collingham 2001). In 1860, a Sámi fisher reminisced about the eagerness of their former vicar to promote cleanliness among the parishioners. He defended the priest's "sternness and daily complaints about our filthiness, which caused many Utsjoki residents to stop living with animals and start going to church in clean clothes and with a clean face" (Matinpoika Lappalainen 1860).

In addition to the priests' personal preferences, global views—such as the classification of nations in the spirit of Darwinism—were incorporated into educating the Sámi. Finns felt superior to the Sámi people, even though the Sámi were considered a kindred people of the Finns. Many advocates of the majority culture predicted destruction and extinction for the "less developed, primitive Sámi people", because unlike "civilised nations", the Sámi had not developed a history, religion or artistic tradition of their own. However, not everyone thought the disappearance of primitive peoples was inevitable: the Sámi, they said, could still save their culture if they adopted the ideals of Finnish culture as part of their lives. Finns felt their national self-esteem increase when they could see themselves as a conquering people in relation to their minority and could teach the Sámi farming, Christianity and other aspects of their own majority culture (Isaksson 1995, 158–161; Kylli 2005, 444–480).

In the nineteenth century, people across Europe became interested in the idea of general popular education. After the Enlightenment, the American Revolution with its Declaration of Independence and the French Revolution in the late eighteenth century, people began to realise that education must be made equally accessible to all. This idea was reinforced by the nationalist movements of the nineteenth century, which wanted nations to thrive, even in terms of education.

Image 3.1 Sámi woman reading (No date. Photo by Juhani Ahola)

Primary schools began to be established in Finland during the latter half of the nineteenth century. The idea gained momentum in 1856, when Alexander II of Russia required popular education to be improved in Finland as part of a reform programme. After the Crimean War (1853–1856), plans were discussed to develop Finland into a major European industrial nation through education. In the 1850s, there were plans to develop broad-based education for children in Finland to provide them with teaching in theoretical subjects, such as the natural sciences and arithmetic, as well as music and physical education (Jalava 2011).

The ideals of the time were also reflected in education for the Sámi people: the clergymen's enthusiasm for promoting Finnish values in Lapland was also evident, as efforts to introduce educational reforms were often pursued among the Sámi at a very early stage. In the 1850s, a decision was made to improve the level of education in the Sámi parishes in one go by replacing the teaching provided by catechists with permanent schools located near churches. In 1857, it was declared that permanent schools would be established in conjunction with the churches in Utsjoki and Inari. It was thought that as young people were able to attend education in permanent schools for longer periods than before, educational goals would be more readily achieved. A diverse selection of subjects (such as choral singing, writing and arithmetic) was planned for the schools, with education provided by qualified teachers, even university graduates. In addition to knowledge of the subjects to be taught, the teacher was required to have knowledge of Sámi, the language spoken in the parish (NA, UKA, JI:1).

The plan was regarded as unrealistic from the very beginning, and when a primary school was finally established in the vicinity of the church in Utsjoki, soon it had to become a travelling school. Because of many problems, such as the lack of school buildings, in practice it was impossible to teach writing, arithmetic and singing, and teaching continued to focus on reading aloud (Kylli 2005, 380–383). In addition, at the beginning hiring qualified teachers was difficult, even impossible, as the first teacher training college in Finland was not established until 1863, with the foundation of Jyväskylä Teacher Seminary (Nurmi 1995).

Education continued to be provided by travelling catechists in the latter half of the nineteenth century and even into the twentieth century—which was evidence of how highly suitable this form of teaching was for sparsely populated Lapland (Lehtola 2014). In addition, many Sámi people continued to appreciate the education provided by the church because of its connection to Christianity (Nikunlassi and Nillukka 1985; Kylli 2012b). For these reasons, Christian education provided by catechists continued for decades despite the appearance of primary schools. Even though the plans for providing multifaceted popular education were realised more slowly than expected, it should be noted that clergymen did not question the ability of the Sámi people to adopt written culture and that Finland never complied with the *lapp skall vara lapp* ("the Sámi should remain Sámi") thinking that was applied in Sweden. This way of thinking was based on the idea that the reindeer-herding Mountain Sámi people would like to continue to herd reindeer even in the future. For this reason, special nomad schools were established in Sweden that did not burden the pupils with excessive book learning (Anderzén 1992, 148–149, 239–242; Norlin and Sjögren 2016, 414–420).

Nevertheless, the Romantic period (when Sámi people were sometimes seen, in the spirit of J. J. Rousseau, as "noble savages" who could teach new values to Finns) had made some Finnish priests think that the Sámi people would be happiest if they were able to ride their reindeer sleighs freely across the wild country, without the degenerative effect of book learning. The perception of the Sámi as primitive and wild people persisted among Finns even after the Sámi had proven themselves both willing to educate themselves and able to manage, for example, the administration of the municipalities independently (Kylli 2005, 384–385).

"Cultivating the Spirit in Tough Conditions"

Since the early modern period, there had been attempts to tie the Sámi people to the Swedish realm. In the eighteenth century, the Christian knowledge of the Sámi people in Finnish Lapland had flourished, but in the early nineteenth century, their knowledge began to deteriorate, partly because priests were no longer that interested in educating the Sámi. Enontekiö, in particular, was left to its own devices in the nineteenth century. According to a report issued in the 1860s, literacy was quite high among the residents of Lapland. The only concerns were related to the situation of the Sámi people in Enontekiö, as the education provided there seemed to better reach the Finnish members of the parish. Only a few of the Sámi people in Enontekiö were literate, which meant most could not teach Christianity to their children. Exceptions to this were a few reindeer-herding Sámi women who received almost the highest possible marks in examinations. However, they had problems with understanding Christianity (Kylli 2014, 40–41).

In the Sámi parish of Utsjoki, education had to be tailored to the needs of the Sámi people, as Finnish settlement in the parish area consisted of only a few civil servants, and the learning outcomes had been very impressive since the late nineteenth century. In a bishop's visitation carried out in Utsjoki in 1902, nearly everything was found to be praiseworthy; only the cleanliness of the homes and singing at church left a little to be desired. No indifference to Christianity was detected among the Sámi people of Utsjoki: of the young people confirmed in previous years who were invited to an examination on Christianity, all except one showed up, and that one person was unable to attend because of illness. The bishop of the diocese was delighted with the performance of the young people of the parish: "Far up here in the icy north, where nature is austere and the people are fighting hard for their living, it is delightful to see that the tough conditions are not preventing the sprit from being cultivated" (NA, OTA, Eb:138).

When visiting Utsjoki, the Russian diplomat D. N. Buharov (2010), who travelled in Lapland in the 1880s, was delighted to see that the local Sámi people were on the road to becoming civilised: they were abandoning their "primitive life" and beginning to form permanent settlements. As indicated by the outcomes of the visitation mentioned earlier, church documents reveal no remaining traces of the formerly "primitive" state of the residents of Lapland—at least not in terms of their level of Christianity (K. W. 1924). In other words, the education of the "savage" Sámi people had progressed and produced quite impressive results. At that time, the rest of Finland had already started to become secularised, but the Sámi people continued to be frequent churchgoers (NA, OTA, Eb:138).

Towards the end of the nineteenth century, writing became a highly necessary and valued skill, and many Sámi people learned to write in travelling schools conducted by Sámi catechists. According to Esko M. Laine and Tuija Laine (2010, 264–265), with regard to the history of Christian education in Finland, the increasing education and literacy in society created an entirely new type of individual: a person who could succeed in the world using information and wits acquired from books. The Sámi Aslak Laiti (1837–1895), who studied to become a primary school teacher in southern Finland, was a prime example (Kylli 2012a).

The change in Sámi society gained momentum towards the end of the nineteenth century, and no longer did all Sámi people need to choose between reindeer herding, fishing and cattle farming as livelihoods. Up until that point, their lives had depended more on the amount of fish or game caught or on successful reindeer herding, so in Lapland hunting skills had been appreciated more than an inclination for reading books. It was later said of Aslak Laiti that he was sent to herd cattle because, unlike his brothers, he had never learned how to use fishing tackle, a gun or an axe (Kylli 2012a). In the world of the nineteenth century, there were already other types of career options as well. Crippled or club-footed boys were taught to write because it was believed that although they would never grow into good workmen, writing skills would enable them to earn a living teaching children, for example (Rahikainen 2010, 331).

Aslak Laiti, who worked as a cattle herder, was more eager than his contemporaries to learn writing. He was taught by Anders Andelin, who became the vicar of the Utsjoki parish in 1854. In confirmation class, Andelin had taken note of Laiti—a Sámi boy adept at both reading and Christianity. Laiti became Andelin's work partner, helping the vicar with translations of Christian books into the Sámi language and translating *Logu-Luoittim Oappa-Kirji*, an arithmetic textbook published in 1862, into Sámi. The book had been created for the needs of the permanent school being planned for Utsjoki (Kylli 2012a). Laiti studied to become a primary school teacher at a time before the first teacher training colleges (or seminars). Nevertheless, his studies included "education skills", among other fields. His contemporaries hoped that, "through his education", he could affect the "education of the citizens" back home and bring "light and enlightenment to the gloomy homes of the north" (Kuopiosta 1861).

Aslak Laiti became the catechist of Utsjoki at a time when opinions within the Lutheran church had started to become more favourable towards education. In the latter half of the nineteenth century, church representatives began to believe more generally that Christian knowledge learned by rote would no longer be enough in the modern world. There were no teacher training seminars in the Sámi regions though, so Sámi people were forced to move south for an education. Towards the end of the nineteenth century, Sámi people were increasingly able to attain higher levels of education. Jooseppi Guttorm (1874–1936), who later worked as a teacher at the primary school in Outakoski, was able to attend the teacher training seminar established in Sortavala, thanks to the strong support from the church: Gustaf Johansson, the bishop responsible for Lapland, had stated the importance of educating a young Sámi man from Utsjoki to become a primary school teacher who knew the parishioners' language. Judging from church documents, Guttorm was talented and highly suited to work as a teacher (NA, OTA, Eb:138).

Just as it began to be possible for talented Sámi boys to embark on a career as a primary school teacher, it began to be possible for women also to gain an education and work in a profession. The first women catechists worked in Finnish Lapland during the last years of the nineteenth century, even though the work was regarded as difficult for women "because of the extensive traveling by reindeer", according to a statement written in 1898 (Kylli 2012b, 113). Laura Lehtola, born in 1902, worked as a catechist in Inari from 1919 to 1956. In her memoir, she described how writing equipment was essential for teachers working for the church in 1919: "The study material included a history of the Bible, a catechism, a primer, a nature book and a songbook with spiritual songs and hymns. Slates were used for elementary exercises. After the elementary exercises had been completed, pupils learned how to use paper. Pencils were new to them, as was paper" (Lehtola 1984, 16–17).

Conclusion

The religiousness of a people or language group is difficult to measure. However, this issue cannot be overlooked when creating a picture of the Sámi people. Here are a few assessments: 'The proportion of believers is definitely higher among the Sámi people than others. This is partly due to their closeness to nature. They have more time to think. They are more open to Christian ideas.' … 'God has blessed the Sámi people in particular, for where else can you find so many believers and preachers among such a small people.' … 'Whoever has a heart for religious life cannot help being fascinated by the genuine life of faith you find in various forms among the Sámi people. Seen in this light, the work of the church appears effective.'

In 1970, parish vicar Lauri Mustakallio—the writer of the above extract—published a report on the status of the Sámi people within the Evangelical Lutheran Church of Finland. He collected comparative material for his report in the Sámi areas of Sweden and Norway. Judging from the report, the Christian education of the Sámi people had produced good results in the three countries—even to the extent that it was difficult for Mustakallio to see the point of having special mission organisations for the Sámi in the twentieth century. In this article, I examined the developments in Finland that led to such a deep level of Christianity.

Finnish clergymen saw the Sámi residents of Lapland during the centuries as a pagan people who needed Christianisation, even when Sámi parishes seemed devoted Christians already during the first half of the eighteenth century—the time before Utsjoki and Inari gained its own priest and catechists. Sámi catechists, whose main concern was to teach the Sámi children to read and learn the main points of the Christian faith, knew Sámi language and culture, and all Finnish clergymen were also eager to learn Sámi language since the 1840s. The Sámi of Utsjoki and Inari were still during the early years of 1900s very faithful members of the Lutheran Church, despite the fact that the church had been the main instrument in Sámi assimilation. Christian education had produced good results among the Sámi people in general, but it was also very meaningful for individual people in many cases. Teaching offered many new opportunities for Sámi children with a passion for learning.

References

Archival Sources

National Archives (NA), Oulu.
OTA (Oulun Tuomiokapitulin arkisto, Archives of the Diocese of Oulu), Eb:138. Bishop's visitations, Utsjoki 1902–1907.
RA (Riksarkivet), Court records 1760, Inari. Svea Hovrätts arkiv, Norrbottens län. Vol. 40.
UKA (Utsjoen kirkonarkisto, Utsjoki Parish Archives), JI:1. HKM's letter to the Diocese of Kuopio, 20 February 1858.

Literature

Andelin, A. (1854, October 7). Lappalaisen waatteen muoto ja hinta. *Oulun Wiikko-Sanomia*, p. 3.
Andelin, A. (1858). Kertomus Utsjoen pitäjästä. *Suomi, Tidskrift i fosterländska ämnen.*
Anderzén, S. (1992). *Undervisningen i en Lappmarksförsamling Jukkasjärvi församling 1744–1820.* Stockholm: Almqvist & Wiksell International.
Anderzén, S. (1996). *Teaching and Church Tradition in the Kemi and Torne Laplands, Northern Scandinavia, in the 1700s* (Scriptum Nr 42). The Research Archives, Umeå University.
Buharov, D. N. (2010). *Matka Lapissa syksyllä 1883.* Helsinki: SKS.
Collingham, E. M. (2001). *Imperial Bodies: The Physical Experience of the Raj, c.1800–1947.* Oxford: Polity.
Hellander, A. (1857, March 28). Utsjoen Lapinmaalta. *Oulun Wiikko-Sanomia*, pp. 3–4.
Isaksson, P. (1995). *Degeneroituneesta rodusta kehitysjäänteeksi, verisukulaisesta ventovieraaksi.* Oulun yliopisto. Aate- ja oppihistorian lisensiaatintutkimus.
Jalava, M. (2011). Kansanopetuksen suuri murros ja 1860-luvun väittely kansakoulusta. In A. Heikkinen & P. Leino-Kaukiainen (Eds.), *Valistus ja koulunpenkki: kasvatus ja koulutus Suomessa 1860-luvulta 1960-luvulle. SKS:n toimituksia 1266:2* (pp. 74–86). Helsinki: SKS.
Johnson, C., & Coleman, A. (2012). The Internal Other: Exploring the Dialectical Relationship Between Regional Exclusion and the Construction

of National Identity. *Annals of the Association of American Geographers,* *102*(4), 863–880.

Kielioloista Lapissa. (1901, April 15). *Kaiku,* p. 1.

Kuopiosta. (1861, July 11). *Suomen Julkisia Sanomia,* p. 1.

K. W. (1924, April 30). Varhaisimmat toimenpiteet lappalaisten käännyttämiseksi kristinuskoon. *Alkuopetus,* p. 60.

Kylli, R. (2005). *Kirkon ja saamelaisten kohtaaminen Utsjoella ja Inarissa* *1742–1886.* Studia historica septentrionalia 47. Rovaniemi: Pohjois-Suomen historiallinen yhdistys.

Kylli, R. (2012a). Ei koskaan missään kotonaan? Suomalaistuva saamelainen Aslak Laiti. *Lähde – historiatieteellinen aikakauskirja.*

Kylli, R. (2012b). *Saamelaisten kaksi kääntymystä: Uskonnon muuttuminen* *Utsjoen ja Enontekiön lapinmailla 1602–1905.* Historiallisia tutkimuksia 259. Helsinki: SKS.

Kylli, R. (2014). Pois pakanallisesta pimeydestä. In P. Keskitalo, V. Lehtola, & M. Paksuniemi (Eds.), *Saamelaisten kansanopetuksen ja koulunkäynnin historia Suomessa* (pp. 30–43). Turku: Siirtolaisuusinstituutti.

Kylli, R., Salmi, A., Äikäs, T., & Aalto, S. (2019). "Not on Bread But on Fish and by Hunting": Food Culture in Early Modern Sápmi. In T. Äikäs & A. Salmi (Eds.), *The Sound of Silence: Indigenous Perspectives on the Historical* *Archaeology of Colonialism* (pp. 119–140). New York: Berghahn Books.

Laine, E. M., & Laine, T. (2010). Kirkollinen kansanopetus. In J. Hanska & K. Vainio-Korhonen (Ed.), *Huoneentaulun maailma: kasvatus ja koulutus Suomessa keskiajalta 1860-luvulle. SKS toim. 1266:1* (pp. 258–312). Helsinki: SKS.

Lappalainen, M. (1860, June 23). *Lapista.* Oulun Wiikko-Sanomia, p. 2.

Læstadius, P. (1977 [1831]). *Petrus Laestadius journaler. Faksimiletext och* *kommentar. 1, Journal för förstaåret af hans tjenstgöring såsom missionaire i* *Lappmarken.* Umeå: Skytteanska samf.

Lehtola, L. (1984). *Viimeinen katekeetta.* Porvoo: WSOY.

Lehtola, V.-P. (2014). Katekeettakouluista kansakouluihin – saamelaisten kouluhistoriaa 1900-luvun alkupuoliskolla. In P. Keskitalo, V.-P. Lehtola, & M. Paksuniemi (Eds.), *Saamelaisten kansanopetuksen ja koulunkäynnin* *historia Suomessa* (pp. 44–62). Turku: Siirtolaisuusinstituutti.

McCannon, J. (2012). *A History of the Arctic: Nature, Exploration and* *Exploitation.* London: Reaktion.

Mustakallio, L. (1970). *Kirkko saamelaisten parissa Pohjois-Skandinaviassa* *1970. Raportti,* p. 10.

3 Out of the "Pagan Darkness" ... 45

Nikunlassi -Lippo, L., & Nillukka, P. (1985). *Utsjoen kansakoululaitoksen synty ja kehittyminen vuosina 1878–1939.* Kasvatustieteen syventäviin opintoihin kuuluva tutkielma. Rovaniemi: Lapin Korkeakoulu.

Norlin, B., & Sjögren D. (2016). Kyrkan, utbildningspolitiken och den Sámiska skolundervisningen vid sekelskiftet 1900: Inflytande, vägval og konsekvenser? In D. Lindmark & O. Sundstöm (Ed.), *De historiska relationerna mellan Svenska kyrkan och samerna. En vetenskaplig antologi, Vol. 1* (pp. 414–420). Skellefteå: Artos.

Nurmi, V. (1995). *Suomen kansakoulunopettajaseminaarien historia.* Helsinki: Opetusalan ammattijärjestö OAJ.

Paulaharju, S. (1965 [1927]). *Taka-Lappia.* Porvoo: WSOY.

Paulaharju, J. (1966). *Äitini suvun tarina.* Helsinki: WSOY.

Rahikainen, M. (2010). Omat lapset, vieraat lapset, kerjäläislapset. In J. Hanska & K. Vainio-Korhonen (Ed.), *Huoneentaulun maailma: kasvatus ja koulutus Suomessa keskiajalta 1860-luvulle. SKS toim. 1266:1* (pp. 313–355). Helsinki: SKS.

Utsjoen Lapinmaalta. (1855, September 29). *Oulun Wiikko-Sanomia,* p. 3.

Walle, P. (1881, October 29). Inarista. *Pohjois-Suomi,* pp. 2–3.

4

Narratives of Sámi School History in Finland: Assimilation and Empowerment

Jukka Nyyssönen

Introduction

The aim of this article is to analyse and discuss narratives produced in the research of Sámi school history and the history of education in Finland. The choice of research material in this article covers studies on Sámi school history, the history of education and important recent studies on Sámi history dealing partly, but not solely, with aspects of school history. The range of studies varies from master theses to doctoral dissertations and scholarly monographs from the late 1980s to the present day. The choice is based on the recent increase in scholarly production and pluralisation of the research, which is due to the entrance of educationalists to the field, which also allows enough material for a comparison across disciplinary boundaries. I will examine six studies by historians and six pedagogical studies which focus on different narrative strategies.

J. Nyyssönen (✉)
The Arctic University Museum of Norway,
UiT—The Arctic University of Norway, Tromsø, Norway
e-mail: jukka.kalervo@uit.no

© The Author(s) 2019
O. Kortekangas et al. (eds.), *Sámi Educational History in a Comparative International Perspective*,
https://doi.org/10.1007/978-3-030-24112-4_4

47

48 J. Nyyssönen

To the best of our knowledge, no study of this sort has been made of this material, nor from this perspective. However, some historiographical work has been inspirational and used as a foundation for this study. In studies of the historiography of colonial education, a strong ideological foundation and early decolonising turn and ideological polarisation are detectable. Marxist criticism of education as a tool for empire building emerged in earnest in the UK in the 1970s. Studies have also revealed the ideologised debates of the gains from and problems embedded in colonial education (Whitehead 2005). More recently, studies of colonial education have engaged in the issue of colonial populations embracing the resources offered by the institution, indigenous support and gains from schooling (Whitehead 2005; Williamson 1997). Post-colonial scholarly production has discussed ways for education to be culturally sustainable, as a source of native health, achievement and empowerment (Smith 2013; Wilson 2013). As a sub-discipline of Sámi studies, emerging as part of the wider ethno-political awakening among the Sámi in Finland and the need to re- and self-interpret their history as well as the more general democratisation of historical inquiry and the choice of sources (Lehtola 2005a), the new genre of historical and pedagogical studies of Sámi school history resembles the anti-colonial scholarly production of colonial education in their stress on assimilation. The focus on shortcomings and cultural insensitivity has led to the dominance of victim-narratives. It is argued that Finnish studies belong to the critical vein and to some extent lack the international focus on the potential historical gains of receiving education (however, see the article by Ritva Kylli in this edition and Lehtola 2018).

With regard to the analysis of narratives, the typology of Jörn Rüsen was relied on, who considers that narratives mobilise the past in a way that makes it understandable and the future possible to form. Rüsen is interested in the functions of different narratives, what the narrative produced by a scholar *does*, in addition to what it is *saying*. The point of departure for Rüsen is the narrative's relation to tradition, and the function the tradition is intended to serve in the society that was contemporaneous to the writing historian. This makes it possible to study different political orientations in pedagogical and historical research. Rüsen first distinguishes *narratives of tradition*, which build continuity with the past and serve as a legitimation of contemporaneous identities and self-understanding. Second, *exemplary narratives* fortify abstract rules and principles in society and use history as a 'mentor of life'. Third, *critical narratives* create distance from tradition, which is deemed unwanted, pointing out a new and better action for the future. These counter-narratives strive to substitute one existing structure with another. A *genetic narrative* takes heed of historical change as such, without any normative judgement of the change, and reflects on the need for change in politics in tandem with actual historical change (Rüsen 2012). This last-mentioned stance resonates well with traditional epistemological and hermeneutical positions in the study of history, aiming for a sympathetic understanding of the object of study. It will be argued that this approach still has some merit and usage value, but on its own has come to a crisis in the field of Sámi studies, which is becoming increasingly instrumental in constructing its own critical narratives.

I will examine the following questions: How are narratives of Sámi school history constructed? How do the narratives produced under the new instrumental paradigm differ from the narratives produced by historians? Which functions are they meant to serve, critical or (mere) genetic? And, are there to be found different narratives, revealed in the international research, and how they might be possible to reveal?

The School Experience and Narratives of Assimilation

The tone in which Sámi school histories were written can be traced to a seminal linguistic—sociological work on the issue by Marjut Aikio, *Saamelaiset kielenvaihdon kierteessä* (1988, *The Sámi in the Thread of Language Shift*), which documented in great detail the linguistic assimilation and de facto language change which took place in much of the Sámi home region after the Second World War due to the policies followed in the school institution. The work is widely referred to and resulted in a focus on linguistic assimilation when the school institution was dealt with in research. It became typical to write about schools as 'fortresses of Finninisation' and attention was devoted to the variation of linguistic abilities and teachers' command over Sámi languages. Concerning the historical substance and construction of the narrative span, assimilation became the end-product in which the subjugation to the institution and historical processes led to. Catechists were approached from this angle as well and their success was implicitly or explicitly measured according to their command over Sámi languages (Lehtola 1999; Nyyssönen 2007; Rahkola 1999).

Catechist teaching is one debated issue of Sámi school history in Finland and to study it is tricky—the success in providing an education and achieving good results can be interpreted as an imposed cultural loss and the efforts of people with good intentions as harmful to the Sámi pupils. Esko I. Kähkönen (1988) balanced this problem by referring to plans to teach in Sámi, the existing literature in Sámi used in teaching, and Sámi pupils who already had a command of the Finnish language in a slightly apologetic manner. Kähkönen shows the difficulties in producing a coherent narrative of a history with numerous changes in policy between the use of Finnish and Sámi languages, with various actors and no lack of good intentions to provide pupils an education in Sámi. Kähkönen meant that Lutheran principles contributed to the fact that Sámi was used as the language of instruction in many of the catechists schools in early twentieth century northern Finland. Kähkönen built his narrative in a positive manner and depicted the catechists as bearers of the Sámi language through their teaching and as language instructors for written material published in Sámi during the nineteenth century. Kähkönen himself, as well as many of his actors, stress the inherent right to the mother tongue among the Sámi and denies claims of assimilative aims on the basis of legislation (identified as acts of good will), but in the end Kähkönen cannot deny the gradual erosion of command over Sámi languages even in Utsjoki, a municipality with a Sámi majority. The twentieth century was a period of erosion of command of and education in Sámi, due, for example, to hardening Finnish nationalist opinion; Kähkönen's narrative ends by pointing to the well-meaning catechists operating in an increasingly hostile environment, while 'holding the door open to their own (Sámi) culture'.

In her doctoral thesis on the church and priests in the Sámi region in the eighteenth and nineteenth centuries, Ritva Kylli (2005) disagrees with the common perception that catechist teaching would have been the form of education best suited to the conditions in Lapland. Instead, she relies on contemporaneous sources and depicts an institution in constant trouble due to the low number of teachers in the vast geographical area the catechists were meant to serve. Kylli strongly questions the language used for education; many priests demanded Finnish be used and education in Christianity took place with the help of Finnish literature. It is likely the catechists used both languages in their teaching, Kylli concludes, but the language barrier was a factor in poor learning results. The education provided was of low quality, the conditions unworthy and criticised as such by the contemporaneous teachers.

The texts, especially that of Kylli, can be read as genetic narratives, interested in historical developments and their changes as such. The texts are thematically framed with questions of language of instruction and linguistic assimilation, which serve as the looming end-product of the narrative formed around the institutional history. This is more evident with Kähkönen, who has some trouble fitting the end-product with his mild apologetic tendency to explain away the policies, while Kylli merely charts the numerous historical changes in education language policies. The complexity of the historical process, and the emerging genetic narrative revealed by her, make construction of any linear narrative a difficult task.

In historical research on twentieth-century school history, assimilation remains an element in the narrative strategy, as the actual linguistic change becomes more pressing in the Sámi homeland. Veli-Pekka Lehtola (2012) has depicted an institution striving to become culturally sensitive, but failing to do so due to a lack of governmental effort and poor allocation of human resources regarding Sámi languages. Jukka Nyyssönen (2007) has credited catechist teaching with creating room for the Sámi languages and lessening assimilative pressure, as the education given to pupils was of short duration and the teachers had in some cases command of Sámi languages. The narratives here are genetic ones of assimilation, the differences concern only the level, or depth of the actual assimilation. Whether the catechist institution is culture preserving or assimilative remains an open issue in the field.

Assimilation has also been approached from the perspective of school policies and whether there was a similar assimilative intention, as there was in Norway and Sweden. The theme is debated in Finnish school history. Nyyssönen (2011) stated that in the public sphere there was no such direct pressure towards cultural change as there was in Norway, and the assimilation could be compared to the county of Nordland in Norway, labelled as 'unintentional' due to the lack of programmatic assimilation policy and the location outside targeted areas, the coastal areas of Finnmark and Troms. In Finland, the public sphere was generally more 'Sámi-friendly' than in Scandinavian countries.

Sources produced in middle-level administration have revealed another kind of discourse. Veli-Pekka Lehtola (2012, 2015) is a proponent of a darker narrative, where the social evolutionist discourse of a 'dying people', the silencing of the special cultural needs of the Sámi and the inactivity of officials responsible for fulfilling the well-meaning, existing measures to provide Sámi pupils an education in Sámi resulted in linguistic assimilation and colonisation. The efforts in introducing Sámi as a language of instruction suffered from active resistance from within the Sámi communities (who wanted tuition in Finnish) and from state officials (who referred eagerly to the same desire). As the few Sámi teachers became early advocates of Sámi issues, as well as part of the civilised elite in the Sámi homeland, there were no positions available for them to work and promote their cause in the home-region or in their native language, due to the inactivity of state officials, which deepened the linguistic assimilation. Otso Kortekangas (2013) has proven that among the provincial school officials there was little willingness to fulfil the latent requirements in the legislation providing for education in the Sámi language, and even a readiness for assimilative measures. In summary, the historical studies show assimilation as the end-product of the narrative span.

The narrative has grown more critical concerning the history of the school institution and legislation in Finland. This narrative is detectable in charting the lack of will to implement legislation, a typical approach in Finnish educational policies well into the twentieth century.

The focus on and voice given to the Sámi actors, who pushed for change in vain, adds to the critical tone. This *narrative of unfulfilled rights*, of Sámi aspirations as well as Finnish goodwill and intentions, which did not materialise, written sometimes in a frustrated and ironic tone, has an emancipational and future-oriented aspect to it through the criticism of state policies (Kortekangas 2017a; Lehtola 2012), and gearing it towards critical narratives.

Narratives in Studies of Sámi Pedagogy

Educationalists, too, have produced narratives about assimilation. The studies have an instrumental and future-oriented side to them. They aim at reconciliation, decolonisation as well as revealing hidden narratives and troubled memories. The research has a strong instrumental side to it, meant to improve and sustain existing school structures and heal those having gone through the school experience. The narrative is one of assimilation as well, but instead of the end-product assimilation is taken as the starting point, the wrong produced in the history. Therefore, studies on the lack of cultural sensitivity and Sámi teaching have a challenging and empowering tone to them (e.g. Aikio-Puoskari 2006). The latest example is provided by Rauna Rahko-Ravantti (2016), showing the continuing success of the narrative of assimilation. According to Rahko-Ravantti, the school had a two-fold significance for the Sámi: (1) cultural and linguistic assimilation and weakening of contact with Sámi culture, and (2) the possibility for improvement in personal incomes.

Unlike historians, Sámi educationalists have taken a post-colonial perspective in their studies of the school institution, history and experience among Sámi pupils. This has deepened the critical narratives produced in pedagogical research. The assimilative wrongs of the past are corrected by healing in the schools through decolonisation and indigenising the teaching. This research vein and focus has engaged many scholars; Irja Seurujärvi-Kari (2012), herself having a long career in the international Indigenous Peoples movement, has studied the Sámi movement's engagement in a struggle against linguistic assimilation.

Rauna Rahko-Ravantti (2016) constructed a critical narrative from assimilation and colonisation to decolonisation by linking Sámi teaching to indigenous discourse and pedagogies. Pigga Keskitalo (2010) studied ways to build indigenous institutions (of education etc.) from the practices and values of the people themselves. What they all share is the aim to dispose of external, colonial structures and implement their own cultural models of modern structures through self-determination in educational issues. The assimilation frames the narrative and gives it both a substance and a starting-point, which must be removed. The effortless future orientation in pedagogy provides a better platform on which to construct critical narratives, since the temporary frames, including the future, examined in critical narratives and the quest of policy suggestions are available in its disciplinary tool-box, whereas History is not as well-equipped to achieve this.

This inherent 'lack' in history is less evident in multi-disciplinary studies on dormitory histories, which have emerged recently (Lehtola 1994; Länsman 2007; Magga 1997; Rasmus 2008). This internationally late emergence of research interest has revealed dark histories and experiences. The researchers have taken heed of the multiplicity of dormitory-experiences; they could be socialising, bearable or even fun, but often negative and traumatising elements. The dormitories were, according to many witnesses, places of fear, bullying and abuse, and the staff were considered emotionally cold and undermanned. The narrative of *trauma* is detectable, and the stress on cultural loss due to the breaks in inter-generational communication and the Finnish language used in the dormitories connects the genre to the narrative of assimilation. This genre has traits of a genetic narrative, in which histories are documented and revealed, but also a strong instrumental, future-oriented aspect, through the aim and desire to correct past wrongs materialising for example in the reconciliation commissions now active in Finland and in Norway.

From an identity politics and ethno-political perspective the narrative of assimilation possesses many strengths. It has proven to possess great political and identificational potential within the Sámi community in building narratives that set the Sámi apart from the rest of the population. For example, the narrative of assimilation has connected

Sámi authors and scholars in Finland to the global discourse of the ongoing struggle of Indigenous Peoples against colonialism and imperialism and for decolonisation. The narrative created legitimacy for the Sámi to access the Indigenous Peoples movement in its early phases. The shared dormitory histories are part of the discursive process of post-colonising the Nordic states, which has received legitimacy in the Finnish public sphere as well, but only lately. This is a major breakthrough in the context of the 'good' state, as Finland eagerly and traditionally has envisioned itself. This positive resonance is one of the most important features of the narrative and has led to tangible results in the schools, through improvements in teaching in and of Sámi languages, a seldom seen success in Sámi ethno-politics (Lehtola 2005b; Nyyssönen 2013, 2014a).

Although the reigning narrative, some problems exist. In identity politics, and in research as well, the narrative of assimilation is stingy in elements of positive self-image. Dominant narratives have a stunting effect on the variation of 'usable' histories and a silencing effect on less dramatic historical experiences. The experiences of identification with histories and narratives of assimilation and colonisation are not necessarily shared by all the Sámi, even though they have been turned into a political asset (Valkonen 2009). The narrative fails to see the schools as sites of cultural negotiation, resistance or as a source of personal empowerment (e.g. Williamson 1997). The narrative of assimilation has led to problems in explaining the Sámi's positive attitudes to receiving and providing education. These attitudes are another debated issue, and a Finnish dilemma in the Sámi school history. Now to address the issues contradicting the reigning narrative of assimilation.

Alternative Approach to Sámi School History

An example of such attitudes comes from Kolttaköngäs, located in Petsamo, Finland. A group of Skolt Sámi parents from Paaččjok *sij'dd* met on 5 July 1928 to discuss providing their children post-elementary education in the lower Skolt schools. The discussion had taken place during a special visitation day at the school. In the produced protocol, the claimants stated the following (translation, word for word, JN):

> The Skolt Sámi discussed in their own language under the leadership of Skolt Mikko Kalinin, on which way could further education of the children be organized after they have finished the lower Skolt school, after they receive school reports from the folk school. He (Kalinin) announced that the opinion of the Skolt was that a higher Folk school with a dormitory reserved exclusively to the Skolts is going to be asked for, and that the best equipped place is Kolttaköngäs, which is hoped/wished to be swelling into a great school—village for the Skolts.[1]

In all 42 Skolt Sámi signed the protocol, and Mikko Kalinin and Ontrei Titoff were chosen to be sent as deputies to meet the Minister, Mr. Tarjanne. It is not known if they ever visited the Ministry in Helsinki, but the school never came to be.[2]

This kind of opinion was not uncommon among the Sámi in Finland in the first half of the twentieth century. If one interprets the petition in light of the dominant perception of the school as an institution for assimilation the petition and rationality behind it appears irrational and damaging. The Skolt Sámi are reduced to actors of their own demise, catalysts of the narrative of victimhood and vanishing. Historians can reproach them for false consciousness, and deepen their victimhood.

Instead of focusing on disempowering victim narratives, a shift in tone towards externalities and the Sámi is needed. One example of such a methodological turn has been introduced by Lars Ivar Hansen (2010), whose aim is to chart local developments within demography, social conditions and resource utilisation as relational processes, without seeing the externalities only as a sign of aggressive and overwhelming intrusion. Instead, one can focus on how the local Sámi utilised the emerging structures and contacts as existing, accessible resource foundation at their disposition. One of the strengths of Hansen's highly contextual

---

[1] Minutes from a meeting in Kolttaköngäs. Letter from the folk school inspector in Petsamo, 10.11.1928, Folder 2, Box 18, Archive of Väinö Tanner, Archive of the Arctic University Museum of Norway.

[2] Ibid.

approach is consideration of the asymmetries in relations between the Sámi and stronger institutional actors, while avoiding the starting-point of Sámi lacking initiative and as passive actors, or solely as victims.

Seen from the perspective proposed by Hansen, the protocol can be used as a representative source of the hopes and rationality concerning the school institution among the Skolt Sámi. The Skolt Sámi petitioned actively for a culturally sensitive, protective institution, as citizens, in a context where their new mother-country had not yet managed to provide full education for their pupils, but which simultaneously constituted a societal-cultural problem for them and their subsistence (Petsamo and the Skolt Sámi villages were annexed to Finland in 1920). The Skolt Sámi had to seek jobs outside their *sijd'ds* (e.g. Lehtola 1999), and the proposed school would both improve opportunities for their children in Finnish society and labour markets, and sustain the traits of Skolt Sámi culture. The source is not explicit regarding the language of education, but does not convey any sign of a lack of cultural pride.

The protocol is not only an example of the strategic use of opportunities and structures which the Finnish annexation had created, but also of an effort to improve them to better serve the Skolt Sámi intentions and situation. Among the structures mentioned by Hansen, institutional structures can be added, which the Sámi thought they could employ for their benefit. The protocol can also be taken as a possible proof of dissatisfaction with the substance of the Finnish education given to the Skolt Sámi, the new citizens of Finland.

The new focus opens up studying and seeing education as *empowerment*, equipping the Sámi to claim their rights in Finnish society (Lehtola 2018, 275, 278) as well as integrate into the local/Finnish/Nordic/global society on an individual level. This has happened through improved opportunities to obtain employment, not an insignificant issue with the high unemployment rates in the Finnish northern peripheries. Many times this has meant leaving the Sámi home region or making a living in ways not sustaining the traditional means of living of the Sámi. The Sámi women boast a higher level of education, as well as a long history of emigration from the Sámi home region to more dynamic labour markets (Nyyssönen 2014b).

This approach offers an opportunity to focus on the Sámi leaping into modernity of their own initiative (Lehtola 2015, 30), as well as focus on Sámi strategies of integration by the numerous disappeared Sámi groups, i.e. those who have chosen or had to hide their ethnicity/ethnic identity. Concerning the well documented ethnic stigma, education might have provided easier access to urban and modern spheres, as well as escape from zones of stigma to zones of possibilities. These escapes happened at the cost of cultural loss. There are many histories of problems coping with ethnic stigma and hidden ethnicity, which is a living legacy in Northern Norway and Finland. Seen together, it would be possible to produce insights into the pathways to modernity and the genesis of hybrid Sámi identities.

In summary, the approach provides the possibility of reaching a more in-depth knowledge of the Sámi communities and Sámi history in their multiplicity and complexity (Lehtola 2015). One of the strengths of Hansen's approach is that it takes the asymmetries of the state-minority relationship seriously. This means that in depicting the empowering sides of the Sámi school experience, one does not, and indeed should not, forget, hide or silence the histories of assimilation and trauma, but not drown the Sámi historical agency. The approach allows one to look simultaneously at the assimilation, trauma, as well as leaps into the modern, which are all consequences of the Sámi history of education. The different fates experienced, strategies adopted and traumas suffered do not negate one another, but add to the multiplicity of the historical school experience of the Sámi.

Conclusions

The function of the narrative of assimilation has been to make histories visible, an important task as such. However, if one approaches the Sámi school history as a polyphonic field and takes the numerous voices seriously, it is possible to discern a multiplicity of narratives. In addition to the narrative of (linguistic) assimilation and the more sinister narrative of trauma, even a narrative of ethno-political victory is possible to be told. The narrative of empowerment, how the *Bildung* acquired in the school institution has emancipated individual Sámi to fulfil their potential and strengthened the communities (Ahonen and Rantala 2001, 11) is verified by the stratification and modernisation which has taken place in the Sámi domicile. Studied critically and avoiding mono-vocality, the narrative does not need to be turned into a triumphant one, praising the state project in correcting a 'handicap' among the minorities, i.e., a legitimising narrative of tradition. Instead, it can highlight the integrative pathways to majority societies as well as the building of Sámi societies and the problems encountered in these projects.

The agency of the Sámi actors could be restored by studying the individual strategies adopted to cope with, adapt to and redefine northern modernity on the basis of education received and taken. Strategies of opting-out of the modern, as well as parallel strategies within families/kins would also be possible to chart. The school as institution and education does not only build Finnish citizenship (Kortekangas 2017b), but Sámi agency and citizenship as well, in integrative, conflictual, complementary or parallel relationships to the Finnish variant. To recognise and acknowledge this multiplicity would open an in-depth view to the history of Sámi society in general through the varying positions and transformations which result from the different levels of education of the Sámi generations. A more exhaustive genetic narrative would be possible to produce, which could better inform those constructing other challenging critical narratives which aim for practical improvements in the school institution for the Sámi people.

References

Archival Sources

Minutes from a meeting in Kolttaköngäs, Letter from folk school inspector in Petsamo, 10.11.1928, Folder 2, Box 18, Archive of Väinö Tanner, Archive of the Arctic University Museum of Norway.

60   J. Nyyssönen

Literatures

Ahonen, S., & Rantala, J. (2001). Introduction: Norden's Present to the World. In S. Ahonen & J. Rantala (Eds.), *Nordic Lights, Education for Nation Civic Society in the Nordic Countries, 1850–2000* (pp. 9–28). Studia Fennica. Historica 1. Helsinki: SKS.

Aikio, M. (1988). *Saamelaiset kielenvaihdon kierteessä, Kielisosiologinen tutkimus viiden saamelaiskylän kielenvaihdosta 1910–1980*. Helsinki: SKS.

Aikio-Puoskari, U. (2006). *Raportti saamelaisopetuksesta Pohjoismaiden peruskouluissa, Pohjoismainen vertailu opetuksen perusedelletysten näkökulmasta*. Inari: Saamelainen Parlamentaarinen Neuvosto.

Hansen, L. I. (2010). Samene i lokalhistorien: Utfordringer og erfaringer. *Heimen, 47,* 315–340.

Kähkönen, E. I. (1988). *Katekeetat Suomen Lapissa 200 vuotta* (Lapin korkeakoulun kasvatustieteellisiä julkaisuja A 4). Rovaniemi: Lapin korkeakoulu.

Keskitalo, P. (2010). *Saamelaiskoulun kulttuurisensitiivisyyttä etsimässä kasvatusantropologian keinoin* (Dieđut 1/2010). Guovdageaidnu: Sámi Allaskuvla.

Kortekangas, O. (2013). *En nationell nödvändighet för allas bästa – utbildningsauktoriteternas diskurser om assimilering genom utbildning av ursprungsbefolkningarna i tidigt 1900-tals Finland och Peru i ett jämförande perspektiv* (Master's thesis). Åbo Akademi, Åbo.

Kortekangas, O. (2017a). *Tools of Teaching and Means of Managing, Educational and Sociopolitical Functions of Languages of Instruction in Elementary Schools with Sámi Pupils in Sweden, Finland and Norway 1900–1940 in Cross-National Perspective*. Turku: Iloinen tiede.

Kortekangas, O. (2017b). Useful Citizens, Useful Citizenship: Cultural Contexts of Sámi Education in Early Twentieth-Century Norway, Sweden and Finland. *Paedagogica Historica, 53,* 80–92. https://doi.org/10.1080/003 09230.2016.1276200.

Kylli, R. (2005). *Kirkon ja saamelaisten kohtaaminen Utsjoella ja Inarissa 1742–1886* (Studia Historica Septentrionalia 47). Rovaniemi: Pohjois-Suomen Historiallinen Yhdistys.

Länsman, A.-S. (2007). Saamelaislasten elämää 1960-luvun asuntolakoulussa - katkelmia ainekirjoitusvihkojen sivuilta. In J. Ylikoski & A. Aikio (Eds.), *Sámit, sánit, sátnehámit. Riepmočála Pekka Sammallahtii miessemánu 21. beaivve 2007* (pp. 269–278). Helsinki: Suomalais-Ugrilainen seura.

Lehtola, V.-P. (1994). *Saamelainen evakko, Rauhan kansa sodan jaloissa*. Helsinki: City-Sámit.

Lehtola, V.-P. (1999). Petsamon kolttasaamelaiset. In J. Vahtola & S. Onnela (Eds.), *Turjanmeren maa, Petsamon historia 1920–1944* (pp. 149–170). Rovaniemi: Petsamo-Seura.

Lehtola, V.-P. (2005a). 'The Right to One's Own Past': Sámi Cultural Heritage and Historical Awareness. In M. Lähteenmäki & P. Pihlaja (Eds.), *The North Calotte, Perspectives on the Histories and Cultures of Northernmost Europe* (pp. 83–94). Helsinki and Inari: Department of History, University of Helsinki, Kustannus-Puntsi.

Lehtola, V.-P. (2005b). *Saamelaisten parlamentti, Suomen saamelaisvaltuuskunta 1973–1995 ja Saamelaiskäräjät 1996–2003*. Inari: Saamelaiskäräjät.

Lehtola, V.-P. (2012). *Saamelaiset suomalaiset, Kohtaamisia 1896–1953*. Helsinki: SKS.

Lehtola, V.-P. (2015). Sámi Histories, Colonialism, and Finland. *Arctic Anthropology, 52,* 22–36.

Lehtola, V.-P. (2018). "Sielun olisi pitänyt ehtiä mukaan…", Jälleenrakennettu Saamenmaa. In M. Tuominen & M. Löfgren (Eds.), *Lappi palaa sodasta, Mielen hiljainen jälleenrakennus* (pp. 259–282). Tampere: Vastapaino.

Magga, B.-H. (1997). *Poropojat maailmalla, Tapaustutkimus koulun ja asuntolan vaikutuksesta porosaamelaisten perinteiseen elämänmuotoon* (Master's thesis). Lapin yliopisto, Faculty of Education, Rovaniemi.

Nyyssönen, J. (2007). *"Everybody Recognized That We Were Not White", Sami Identity Politics in Finland, 1945–1990* (Doctoral dissertation). University of Tromsø, Tromsø.

Nyyssönen, J. (2011). Principles and Practice in Finnish Policies Towards the Sámi People. In G. Minnerup & P. Solberg (Eds.), *First World, First Nations, Internal Colonialism and Indigenous Self-Determination in Northern Europe and Australia* (pp. 80–96). Eastbourne: Sussex Academic Press.

Nyyssönen, J. (2013). Sami Counter-Narratives of Colonial Finland: Articulation, Perception and the Boundaries of Politically Possible. *Acta Borealia, 30,* 101–121.

Nyyssönen, J. (2014a). Saamelaisten kouluolot 1900-luvulla. In P. Keskitalo, V.-P. Lehtola, & M. Paksuniemi (Eds.), *Saamelaisten kansanopetuksen ja koulunkäynnin historia Suomessa* (pp. 63–86). Tutkimuksia A 50. Turku: Siirtolaisuusinstituutti.

Nyyssönen, J. (2014b). Suomalainen koululaitos ja saamelaiskysymys. In P. Keskitalo, V.-P. Lehtola, & M. Paksuniemi (Eds.), *Saamelaisten kansanopetuksen ja koulunkäynnin historia Suomessa* (pp. 154–174). Tutkimuksia A 50. Turku: Siirtolaisuusinstituutti.

62   J. Nyyssönen

Rahkola, H. (1999). Petsamon kansakoulut. In J. Vahtola & S. Onnela (Eds.), *Turjanmeren maa, Petsamon historia 1920–1944* (pp. 373–400). Rovaniemi: Petsamo-Seura.

Rahko-Ravantti, R. (2016). *Saamelaisopetus Suomessa, Tutkimus saamalaisopettajien opetustyöstä suomalaiskouluissa* (Acta Universitatis Lapponiensis 332). Rovaniemi: University of Lapland.

Rasmus, M. (2008). *Bággu vuolgit, bággu birget, Sámemánáid ceavzinstrategiijat Suoma álbmotskuvlla ásodagain 1950–1960-logus* (Publications of Giellagas Institute NR 10). Oulu: Giellagas Institute.

Rüsen, J. (2012). Tradition: A Principle of Historical Sense-Generation and Its Logic and Effect in Historical Culture. *History & Theory, 51,* 45–59.

Seurujärvi-Kari, I. (2012). *Ale jaskot eatnigiella, Alkuperäiskansaliikkeen ja saamen kielen merkitys saamelaisten identiteetille* (Academic dissertation). Faculty of Arts, University of Helsinki.

Smith, M. S. (2013). Situating Indigenous Education in Canada. In M. S. Smith (Ed.), *Essays on Transforming the Academy, Indigenous Education, Knowledge and Relations* (pp. 10–13). Edmonton: University of Alberta. Retrieved from https://www.ualberta.ca/-/media/D2916F31E07E43B5 BFF8AF3FE2923920.

Valkonen, S. (2009). *Poliittinen saamelaisuus.* Tampere: Vastapaino.

Whitehead, C. (2005). The Historiography of British Imperial Education Policy, Part I: India. *History of Education, 34,* 315–329.

Williamson, A. (1997). Decolonizing Historiography of Colonial Education: Processes of Interaction in the Schooling of Torres Strait Islanders. *International Journal of Qualitative Studies in Education, 10,* 407–423.

Wilson, A. W. (2013). Indigenous Knowledge, Anticolonialism and Empowerment. In M. S. Smith (Ed.), *Essays on Transforming the Academy, Indigenous Education, Knowledge and Relations* (pp. 19–22). Edmonton: University of Alberta. Retrieved from https://www.ualberta.ca/-/media/ D2916F31E07E43B5BFF8AF3FE2923920.

5

Indigenous People, Vulnerability and the Security Dilemma: Sámi School Education on the Kola Peninsula, 1917–1991

Andrej Kotljarchuk

Introduction

The Kola Sámi are the indigenous people of Russia whose roots date back to medieval times (Sergejeva 2000; Wheelersburg and Gutsol 2008). Until the imperial edict of 1905, the Sámi reindeer herders were able to migrate freely across Fennoscandia from Sweden-Norway to the Grand Duchy of Finland and the Arkhangelsk region. Linguistically, the Russian Sámi are divided into five groups according to their dialects. The largest group are the Kildin Sámi; the next largest are the Skolt Sámi; and the smallest groups are the Ter-Jokanga, Akkala, and Filman Sámi. The majority of the Kola Sámi were reindeer herders. However, many of the Sámi fished in the Barents Sea and on the lakes and rivers of the peninsula. Almost all the Kola Sámi belonged to the Orthodox

A. Kotljarchuk (✉)
The School of Historical and Contemporary Studies,
Södertörn University, Huddinge, Sweden
e-mail: andrej.kotljarchuk@sh.se

© The Author(s) 2019
O. Kortekangas et al. (eds.), *Sámi Educational History in a Comparative International Perspective*,
https://doi.org/10.1007/978-3-030-24112-4_5

64   A. Kotljarchuk

Church and spoke Eastern Sámi dialects. However, the Filmans were Lutherans (Thorvaldsen 2011, 122–128). The 2002 census counted 1991 Sámi individuals in Russia, about 13% of them dealing with reindeer breeding and only 25% speaking their native language. This study aims to examine the reasons for the decrease.

Theoretical Frameworks, Method and Aims

Several threats to indigenous peoples in modern times show them to be vulnerable and endangered populations (Coates 2004). Per Axelsson and Peter Sköld note that research into the vulnerability of indigenous peoples to date has primarily been demographically oriented (Axelsson and Sköld 2006). This study will initially discuss the political aspects of vulnerability in the context of the Sámi education.

Another concept that is relevant for this study is that of security dilemma. The Sámi people are the only indigenous group in European Russia that live along a state border. The recent situation differs between the Kola Sámi and, for example, their neighbours the Nenets. Since the Great Terror, the Soviet state has perceived the semi-nomadic Sámi as a security problem. Scholars explain the Stalinist terror and the accompanying deportation of ethnic minorities based on the security dilemma in the border area, suggesting a need to secure the ethnic integrity of Soviet space vis-à-vis neighbouring capitalist enemy states in case of an invasion (Werth 2003; Mann 2005, 318–328). The results of previous studies show that the security dilemma has played an important role in political decision-making, prompting mass violence against the Sámi (Kotljarchuk 2012, 2014b). The second aim of this study is therefore to examine how the security dilemma affected State-Sámi relations in the sphere of school education.

Previous Research

Little is known about Sámi school education in the interwar Soviet Union because the leading scholars in the field were arrested during the Stalinist terror (Kuropiatnik 1999). The first surveys of the Sámi school education in Soviet Russia were published by David Zolotarev (1927) and Zakharii Cherniakov (1934). However, both scholars were arrested by the NKVD as alleged leaders of the "Sámi counter-revolutionary nationalistic movement" and sent to the Gulag. Zolotarev (Russian by birth) died in prison. Cherniakov (a Jew from Belarus) survived. His magnum opus *Essays on Sámi Ethnography* was published only posthumously (Cherniakov 1998). Cherniakov discusses the role of school education in the preservation of Kola-Sámi identity. He describes the fascinating experiment of early Soviet politics in establishing Sámi-language schools, using Latin script and special letters for the Sámi alphabet, a system that Cherniakov invented. According to the author, a modified version of Latin script is better for Sámi language speakers than Cyrillic because the Kola Sámi people perceive this alphabet as obviously non-Russian and closer to the native language. The author illustrates the decline of the Sámi school education in Russia with a small number of Kola Sámi who must share school and extra curricula education with local Russians.

Ethnographer Nikolai Volkov, who died in 1953 in the Gulag, prepared a manuscript on Sámi history that was never published in the Soviet Union. The monograph was printed only in 1996 with financial support from the Sámi Parliament of Sweden. Volkov did not mention the abolition of Sámi schools, but he was critical of the way in which the implementation of Sámi schools occurred in the early 1930s. According to Volkov, Sámi education was undermined by unreliable pedagogical professionals; most of the teachers were Russian by birth and were often young graduates unfamiliar with the Sámi culture (Volkov 1996, 101–102). Volkov praised the boarding schools established by the state for Sámi children (Volkov 1996, 101). However, recent research describes boarding schools as traumatic environments for Sámi children. Finally, in 2002, Nikolay Bogdanov published a short article titled "History of the school education of the Kola Sámi" in which he presented a survey of Sámi school education from the tsarist era to the present day. The author emphasized that the recent crisis in the Sámi school education has been caused by Stalinist political repressions (Bogdanov 2002).

Sámi Education in Leninist Nationalities Policy

About thirty small indigenous ethnic groups populated Soviet Russia, from the Sámi people on the Kola Peninsula to the Nivkh people in the basin of the Amur River and on Sakhalin. Practically all indigenous peoples in the Soviet Union had their own compact territories and achieved cultural and administrative autonomy. The ethnic policies of the Russian empire and the Soviet Union were completely different from each other. Tsarist Russia decided on the soft linguistic Russification of indigenous peoples; the Soviet state declared full support for cultural rights and administrative autonomy for indigenous peoples. While ethnic minorities faced discrimination around the world, the Soviet Union, in 1923, declared a policy of self-determination, with cultural and linguistic rights for all the country's minorities. The main aim of the Soviet nationalities policy in the Russian North was "to liberate indigenous peoples from the vestiges of the past" (Slezkine 1994, 220–221). The Bolsheviks regarded the reindeer herders positively as "primitive socialistic groups" (Leete 2004, 28–30; Kotljarchuk 2012). However, the remote Northern area was *terra incognita* for the Bolsheviks whose subjective knowledge was urban and linked to the industrialized context. Hence, with the help of advantageous school policy, the Bolsheviks wanted to attract the indigenous peoples to take their side (Toulouze 2005, 140–141). The new policy was named Leninist nationalities policy (*leninskaya natsionalnaya politika*), also referred to as the politics of indigenization.

Providing schools for ingenious peoples meant, in most cases, the implementation from scratch of a written language, nurturing of native pedagogical professionals and printing of textbooks. Achievement of these tasks demanded huge human and material resources, with the Bolsheviks expecting the reciprocal loyalty of the ingenious peoples to the new regime. The authorities also believed that schooling in the mother tongue would make the integration of the younger generation of reindeer herders into the socialist regime easier. The main aim of a new educational policy for the Sámi was "the elimination of the age-old backwardness", helping them to catch up with other, "more advanced" minorities, but at the same time reinforcing their ethnic identity (Natsionalnye menshinstva 1929, 35–36). According to Soviet ideology, the indigenous peoples were oppressed in the Russian Empire and were subjected to forced Russification (Kotljarchuk 2014b). Bolsheviks argued that the tsarist educational system had not covered all Sámi Children. There was only one Sámi school in Russia at the beginning of the twentieth century. In 1917 the number of Sámi schools increased to five. However, these schools did not work all year round and were, according to the Bolsheviks, a centre of religious propaganda (Alymov 1931). Therefore, the Communist party decided to build the secular school system for all indigenous children in the North and bring their education rapidly to the level of more advanced minorities (Sundström 2007, 130–135). On the one hand, the Murmansk authorities were to prioritize native-language schools to promote the ideas of socialism and to nurture a Sámi communist elite. On the other hand, the October Revolution mobilized a nationalist movement of Sámi people. In 1920 the demand for cultural autonomy was appealed by the national assembly of the Kola Sámi to the regional government in Murmansk (Dashchinskiy 1999, 21). The official nomenclature was changed, and the Soviet officials began to use the politically correct term Sámi (*saamy*) instead of Lapps (*lopari*).

Soviet reforms in Lapland started with a census based on ethnic criteria. The census of 1926 counted 1708 Sámi that constituted only 7.5% of the total population of the Peninsula (22,858 persons). Practically all the Sámi (99.4%) were involved at that time in reindeer herding and reindeer roamed across the vast area of the Kola Peninsula.[1] Before the Revolution, the Kola Peninsula was an uyezd (administrative district) of Archangelsk gubernia. Firstly, the Bolsheviks moved the administrative centre of the region from remote Archangelsk to Murmansk, the town that was founded in 1916. Secondly, the Murmansk district became, in 1927, a part of Leningrad Oblast. Therefore, Leningrad, the second capital of Russia, became an administrative centre for the Russian

---

[1]Calculated by the author from the 1926 All-Soviet census: http://demoscope.ru (accessed 1 October 2018).

Sámi. According to the indigenization plan, the Murmansk government was expected to establish cultural and administrative autonomy for the indigenous peoples of the region. In 1927, the Kola-Lappish National Rayon was formed. In 1931, the Murmansk authorities established the Lovozero Indigene Rayon (*Lovozerskii Tuzemnyi Rayon*) for the local Sámi, Nenets and Komi populations. According to Lenin, native cadres should be prioritized for administrative positions in the indigenous area. Already, in the mid-1930s, several educated Sámis occupied official positions in the Murmansk region. Among them were Yakov Osipov, the judge; Adrian Gerasimov, the head of Poluozero village administration; Nikon Gerasimov, the head of HR in Lovozero; Ivan Osipov, the university lecturer in the Sámi language and Fedor Arkhipov, the head of the Lapland National Reserve (Kotljarchuk 2012, 72). Scholars stated that new nationality policy had finally changed the negative demographic structures of the past and the Sámi population grew by 6% from 1926 to 1933 (Endiukovskii 1937, 126).

Native Textbooks and the Establishment of Sámi-Language Schools

The next stage was the opening of Sámi schools. A new educational reform was developed under the auspices of the State Committee of the North. The Murmansk division of the Committee of the North was established in 1924. Vasiliy Alymov, a prominent Bolshevik, headed the Murmansk Committee of the North.[2] An extensive study of the Sámi population was carried out between 1927 and 1933. A large amount of data regarding the Sámi dialects, resettlement and family structure was collected during scientific expeditions to Lapland (Kuropiatnik 1999).

---

[2]Vasiliy Alymov (1883–1938) was born in Ingria to a working-class family. A typographer by occupation, he joined the Russian Social-Democratic Party in 1905. From 1924 to 1935, he was the head of the Murmansk branch of the Committee of the North. He was arrested by the NKVD on 27 March 1938, accused of being "a President of the Sámi underground government" and shot on 22 October 1938 in Leningrad.

5 Indigenous People, Vulnerability and the Security Dilemma ... 69

In 1927 a new agency, the Committee of the New Alphabet, was established as a research department of the State Committee of the North. This branch of the Committee in Murmansk had been commissioned to invent a Sámi alphabet and a common written language. The research leader of the Murmansk branch of the Committee of the New Alphabet was a young scholar called Zakharii Cherniakov, also known by his Sámi pen-name Saxkri. The Committee of the North decided that, in contrast to tsarist Russia, Sámi was to be the language of instruction at primary schools for the Sámi. Thus, the Committee of the New Alphabet had to prepare new textbooks in the Sámi language. The textbooks that were published by the Orthodox Missionary Society for the Sámi and other indigenous peoples of the North before 1917 were perceived by Soviet scholars as harmful for numerous reasons (Bazanov 1936, 84–89). Firstly, the books were recognized by the authorities as a tool for religious propaganda that was unacceptable for a Soviet school (Bazanov and Kazanskii 1939, 42). Secondly, the absence of illustrations was a serious didactic gap. Thirdly, the quality of translation from Russian to native languages was extremely poor. For example, the contents of the alphabet book for the Mansi people (at that time known as the Voguls) was incomprehensible to students of Mansi origin (Bazanov 1936, 88). The 1894 Gospel of Matthew, based on the Skolt dialect included, according to the Kildin Sámi, many vulgar words. Finally, the alphabet of the imperial textbooks was based on the Cyrillic alphabet and considered to be unsuitable for the vocabulary of Finno-Ugric languages (Bazanov 1936, 89). Therefore, the written language was to be based on the Latin script with some specific Sámi letters adopted for the Sámi vocabulary. Karl Marx's idea of a world revolution played a key role in this decision. Bolsheviks saw the establishment of Sámi autonomy on the Kola Peninsula as necessary for the future socialist Sámi republic that would cover all the Sámi territory. Therefore, the state counted on the development of a common literary Sámi language that adopted vocabulary from different dialects and was based on Latin script that was, actually, less familiar to the Eastern Sámi than Cyrillic letters.

The enormous amount of linguistic data collected during the 1920s studies in the Murmansk region became the subject of scientific analysis in Leningrad. The main task was to invent a common written language that could be understood by all subgroups of the Sámi and an alphabet that could also be used by the Sámi in Scandinavia. Work on the written language was led by Cherniakov who inaugurated the Lappish Academic Seminar. There, he, Zolotarev and Alexander Endiukovskii consulted with Sámi students from the Institute for Peoples of the North regarding the new alphabet and written language, considering the phonemic structure of the Sámi language as well as the didactic perspective. The research group prepared several different versions of Sámi primers according to the basic dialects (Belenkin 1975).

The first Soviet alphabet book was printed in 1933 (Cerniakovin, *Saam bukvar*, 1933). This was not a translation from Russian, but an original primer edited by Cherniakov with the participation of four native students: Nikon Gerasimov, Irina Matrekhina, Anna Osipova and Yakov Osipov. The 1933 alphabet book is an illustrated textbook based on the traditional everyday experience of Sámi children. In 1933, Cherniakov also published *Guidelines for Teachers at Sámi Native Schools* to explain didactic principles for using the alphabet book (Cherniakov 1933). The written Sámi language was based on the Kildin dialect in which many other schoolbooks were printed in the 1930s (Endiukovskii 1937, 129). The publication of a Sámi primer was part of an extensive state-run project to produce native alphabet books for all the indigenous peoples of the Far North and the Far East (Akhemtova 2013, 52).

The intensive work of the Murmansk Committee of the New Alphabet is demonstrated by the protocols that discussed dozens of different issues, among them: the report on the work of the Sámi department at Murmansk pedagogical university college, the printing of new textbooks, the training of cultural workers for the adult population, the results of the first school year in Sámi-language schools, the output of academic research on the Sámi language, and the opening of new schools (Bogdanov 2002). By 1934, six schools (Jokanga, Kildin, Notozero, Voroninskii, Semiostrovskii and Lumbovskii pogosts) used only Sámi as the language of instruction, while other schools worked in both Sámi and Russian. The problem of different dialects remained; for example, the pupils in Jokanga had difficulty understanding the textbooks written in the Kildin dialect (Bazanov and Kazanskii 1939, 139).

In 1934, the Murmansk Committee of the New Alphabet reported on the activity of 17 Sámi schools with a total of 260 pupils (Chernavskii, 1934, 5).

The Nurturing of Native Pedagogic Cadres

The next task for the government was to nurture a body of native teaching professionals. As Eva Toulouze points out, the Soviet government had its own agenda in this campaign. The state needed to have mediators who were able to communicate between the state and indigenous peoples in order to transmit new socialist values (Toulouze 2005, 141). *Rabfak*, an educational establishment to prepare worker and peasant youth for higher education, was set up in Leningrad in 1924 for indigenous youth. In 1931, the training of Sámi educators was established at Murmansk pedagogical university college (*Murmanskii Pedtekhnikum* MPT). In 1934, 32 students (25 boys and 8 girls) studied in the Sámi department of MPT to be teachers at Sámi schools (Filippov 1934, 8–10). The Sámi department had both Russian and Sámi languages of instruction. The native language, geography and natural history were taught in Sámi; other subjects, in Russian. According to the staff of the Sámi department, they faced a number of problems. However, it was difficult to recruit Sámi youth to study in Murmansk, since "the parents did not want let children, especially girls, move to a completely strange town" (Filippov 1934, 8). The teachers visited the Sámi villages to convince parents of the great benefits of higher education for their children. According to a government report, the negative attitudes began to change and after two years the Sámi department became popular among Sámis. According to the authorities, other problems existed. The students had an unexpectedly poor knowledge of Russian, necessitating the establishment of an introductory course in the Russian language. Some students did not want to sleep in modern beds and preferred to use a *tul*, the traditional Kola-Sámi bed made of reindeer skins (Filippov 1934, 8). Besides the vulnerability of Sámi people, the official report illustrates many of the prejudices that were typical for the contemporary majority regarding indigenous peoples, such as the alleged "unwillingness of the Sámi students to visit the bath and dental office" (Filippov 1934, 8).

The students of Sámi origin were also invited to Leningrad, as part of a special quota, to study different subjects (pedagogy, herd management and law) at the Institute for Peoples of the North. The first Sámi who began studying at the Institute for Peoples of the North in 1925 was Ivan Osipov, a Skolt Sámi from Notozero. In 1927, the Institute for Peoples of the North accepted two female students of Sámi origin: Dunia Matrekhina and Nastia Matrekhina, both from Jokanga. Osipov was the first Sámi to graduate from the Institute and probably the first Sámi in modern history who became a university lecturer in the Sámi language. In addition to teaching, Osipov worked as an instructor for the elimination of illiteracy among the adult Sámi. He recorded old folk legends of the Notozero Sámi about the attacks on their lands made by so-called "Swedes" (Alymov 1930, 29–31). Many Sámi students were sent to Lapland to participate in the various information campaigns (Fillipov 1934, 9). The students were also the main contributors to a page in the Sámi language published by *Polarnaya Pravda* (Osipov 1933a, b).

At the same time, some students dropped out of higher education and returned to their native pogosts. Volkov explained this as being the result of the poor selection of candidates by the local authorities (Volkov 1996, 101–102). However, the departure of the Sámi students could be explained by the vulnerability of indigenous people in the modern urban milieu. Most graduates of the Institute for Peoples of the North returned from Leningrad to Murman.

Dramatic Turn: The Great Terror and the Abolition of Sámi Schools

In July 1933, Joseph Stalin visited the Kola Peninsula. At his instigation, the Northern Fleet, with 12,000 military personnel, was established on Sámi lands. Industrial development proceeded alongside the further militarization of the peninsula. For the first time the external exploitation of natural resources in the interests of the state security and

5 Indigenous People, Vulnerability and the Security Dilemma ... 73

the army was focused on Lapland. Over a short period of time, the Kola tundra was transformed from a nature reserve to a high-security military area (Shashkov 2000; Kotljarchuk 2014b).

The school policy changed dramatically when, in 1937, the secret police NKVD carried out a massive operation against influential members of the Sámi community (Rantala 2014). Altogether 68 Sámi were arrested between 1937 and 1938 and accused of being members of a fictitious underground paramilitary organization. The aim of the rebel organization would be to destroy the Soviet regime on the Kola Peninsula and to establish a Sámi republic under the protectorate of Finland—the great enemy of the Soviet Union in the North (Kotljarchuk 2012). The mass operation was one of the so-called national operations of the Soviet secret police. Altogether, 335,513 people of various ethnicities were arrested in several national operations and 247,157 of them were shot (Werth 2003, 232). In a short period of time, the Sámi minority decreased from 1841 individuals in 1937 to 1755 persons in 1939.[3] These population losses reflect the great purges. The indigenous peoples of the Murmansk region (Sámi, Komi and Nenets) amounted to 2.3% of the victims of the Great Terror whereas, among the entire provincial population, they amounted in 1939 to only 0.9% (Mikolyuk 2003, 66). A significant proportion of victims (11.5%) were representatives of a tiny group of Sámi intelligentsia (Kotljarchuk 2012, 72). The state-authorized terror destroyed also the Russian school of Sámi studies and the NKVD arrested practically all scholars dealing with the Sámi language and culture. Among the victims were Vasiliy Alymov, Zakharii Cherniakov, Alexander Endiukovskii, David Zolotarev, Fedor Ivanov-Diatlov, Vladimir Charnolusskii, Marta Palvadre, Vasiliy Meletiev and Nikolay Volkov.

Terry Martin has studied the link between the Great Terror and the eradication of the minority schools, as well as the increased role of the Russian language training in the curriculum for non-Russian schools in Russia (Martin 2001, 422–423). Indeed, during the Great Terror, on

---

[3]Calculated by the author from the 1937 to 1939 All-Soviet censuses: http://demoscope.ru (accessed 1 October 2018).

24 January 1938, the Central Committee of VKP (b) adopted a resolution "On the reorganization of native schools" in which it was stated that:

> The inspection found that the enemies of the people acting in regional Commissariats for Education opened native schools; German, Finnish, Polish, Latvian, Estonian, Ingrian, Vepsian and others, turning them into centres of bourgeois nationalist and anti–Soviet influence on schoolchildren. (Gatagova 2009, 342–343)

Sámi schools in this report were included under the category *the others*. The Politburo formed a commission on this issue headed by top politicians Andrey Zhdanov and Nikolay Bulganin. Native schools were to be reorganized into ordinary Russian-language schools. The liquidation of native schools in the Russian Soviet Federative Socialist Republic was to be started immediately and completed in record time, by 1 September 1938. The media began to present the politics of indigenization as the subversive activity of bourgeois nationalists. The central newspaper Izvestia published the headline *A New School Year* in which the government explained its reasons for the radical school reform:

> Enemies of the people established the native schools in which they sabotaged the teaching of the Russian language. Their aim was to separate the fraternal ethnic minorities of the Soviet Union from the Great Russian nation. Now it is time for the Soviet teaching staff to liquidate the results of this sabotage work. (Novyi uchebnyi god 1938)

Altogether 18 Sámi-language schools were closed on the Kola Peninsula in 1938, as well as the Sámi department at MPT that had nurtured native teaching staff. Simultaneously, the Kola-Finnish newspaper *Polarnoin kollektivisti* and the Sámi-language page in the regional newspaper *Polarnaya Pravda* were discontinued (Kotljarchuk 2017). In 1937 the Latin script of the Sámi language and textbooks was replaced by the Cyrillic alphabet (Endiukovskii 1937; Popova 1937), a new script reform that concerned all Finno-Ugric indigenous peoples in the Soviet Union. Moreover, the next year the Sámi textbooks, both in Latin and

Cyrillic scripts, were confiscated and destroyed, only a few copies being moved to the so-called *spetskhran* (special library deposit). The widespread state-authorized violence stopped the Sámi population from protesting regarding the elimination of native schools and prohibition of Sámi-language textbooks.

There is a connection between the abolition of native schools and the security dilemma. Stalin personally initiated a radical reform of native schools (Efimenko 2001, 43). The dictator explained that the need for non-Russian youth by security reasons, because the fighting capacity of Red Army depended on a perfect command of Russian (Gatagova 2009, 298–299). The transition to teaching in the non-mother tongue was accompanied by stigmatization of teachers and psychological stress for schoolchildren. Anna Sigalet (born 1931 in Gammalsvenskby) started in the first grade in a new school that opened instead of a Swedish school. Anna testifies that it was extremely difficult to learn in Russian and Ukrainian languages of which she had little knowledge (Kotljarchuk 2014a, 187). Roine Tuhkanen, a pupil of the Finnish school, recalls:

> When we returned from the winter holidays, we were stunned to see that the school had changed to Russian as the language of instruction, and the former teachers had disappeared; their places were taken by unknown Russian pedagogues. Our Russian was poor and this created difficulty in learning. In addition, the school had banned the use of the Finnish language by pupils even at breaks. (Kotljarchuk 2014a, 187)

The testimonies of Sigalet and Tuhkanen are typical of the dramatic situation in which the Sámi children found themselves. Prohibition of primary education in their native language disrupted the normal psychological development of children, opening the way for forced assimilation. The Sámi children therefore experienced double stress. Education in the native language was abolished and teachers spoke to them only Russian. In addition, most of the Sámi children were placed in regular boarding schools that existed only in large non-Sámi villages and therefore isolated them from their families and native environment.

76 A. Kotljarchuk

This ended in tragedy. In the winter of 1938, two Sámi children escaped from the boarding school in Belokamenka in a bid to return to their homes. A few days later, they were found frozen to death in the tundra and several local teachers were sentenced to prison for the crime of negligence (Sud nad vinovnikami 1938).

Some months later, the Party as usual claimed that the unacceptable approach of local officials in the school reform had to be corrected. In September 1938, the former Finnish school in Belokamenka (which many Sámi attended) became a Russian school. In January 1939, the new Russian teachers of the school were accused of "political errors in the education of Finnish pupils" (Nazrevshii vopros 1939). In particular, the rector told the teachers that "Finnish children are not able to be educated at all and could not ever be compared with Russian children" (Nazrevshii vopros 1939). The admission of some errors at the local level during the radical reforms led by the central authorities was a typical instrument of the Kremlin (Viola 1986, 26). The aim of such propagandist articles was to reassure the parents of native pupils (Kotljarchuk 2017).

Conclusion

One of the fallouts of the Cold War has been the rapid militarization of Russian Lapland. Due to the high-security regime of the borderland to Norway (member state of NATO), the Sámi were obliged to move to the central area of the peninsula. By 1965, over 90% of Russian Sámi were concentrated in four kolkhozes of Lovozero district (Gutsol et al. 2007). There, they herded 40,000 animals. As a result, a balance between economic and environmental sustainability was destroyed (Kol'skie saamy 2008, 21–24). In Lovozero, the different subgroups of Sámi people had to live, work and study alongside the Komi, the Nenets and the Russians. The result of this population mix was the increased vulnerability of the Sámi who were compelled to co-exist with non-Sámi majority. The small subgroups of Kola Sámi (Filman, Ter-Jokanga and Akkala) were never able to recover from the forced relocations and simply became extinct. About 80% of the Kola

Sámi born after the Second World War grew up in mixed families (Khelimskiy 2002). The use of the mother tongue was limited and was reduced to short speech practices in a few families where both parents were Sámi. Until Perestroika, the Sámi children were deprived of the opportunity to learn their native language at school and the prohibition of a native-language education opened the way for assimilation. Only with the start of democratization in the Soviet Union has the optional course of Sámi language been reintroduced in the schools of Lovozero. Textbooks and didactic materials were published in Sámi in Cyrillic script and the first Russian-Sámi-Russian lexicon was printed (Antonova 1982, 1990; Kert 1986; Kuruch et al. 1990). However, two generations of the Sámi people have never learned their native language at school. Thus, the teachers face a new problem; poor knowledge of the native language among the Sámi children. Today the school in Lovozero is the only school in Russia where there is possibility of learning the Sámi language. In 2014 only 21 pupils of Sámi origin learned their native language in Russia at school (Ivanishcheva 2016, 46–49), which is 12 times less than 80 years ago. Roza Rakhmaninova, a teacher of the native language in Lovozero, would like to see a state-sponsored school with Sámi as the language of instruction. However, only 23% of Sámi children support this teacher's opinion (Ivanishcheva 2016, 48–49).

Stalin's Terror against the Sámi people was the main factor behind the vulnerability of Sámi education. The terror was also a tool for achieving the elimination of native schools without any protest from the local population. After the death of Stalin, Sámi victims of the Great Terror were rehabilitated. However, this occurred only on an individual level. Stalin's crimes against the Sámi people were never recognized by the Soviet government. Therefore, the Lovozero Indigene Rayon was not re-established. The post-war history of Sámi cultural autonomy is similar to the Vepsian case, but different from that of the Nenets peoples.

Together with Nivkhs and Veps (other indigenous groups living in the borderland), the Sámi people are the most highly assimilated indigenous minority in Russia. The results of the study show that the security dilemma played a key role in defining the direction of state-determined education policy. The borderland position of Lapland could explain the difference between the Sámi and the Nenets cases. Unlike the Nenets people on the Yamal Peninsula, who were granted administrative autonomy and native classes after the death of Stalin, the Sámi lost everything. The Sámi minority have become victims of the Soviet state of exception. Being citizens of a totalitarian state, the Sámi were deprived to shape their own destiny. The abolition of native schools and native teacher training during the Great Terror interrupted the development of indigenous education. The high-security regime and militarization of Lapland was a final stage of the decline of Sámi education in Russia.

Acknowledgements This study was supported by the Foundation for Baltic and East European Studies as part of the research project Nordic Minorities and Ethnic Cleansing on the Kola Peninsula.

References

Published Sources

Alymov, V. (1930). Алымов, В. Живая лопарская старина. Исторические предания лопарей. *Karjalan Muurmannin Seutu, 1*, 29–30.

Alymov, V. (1931, January 20). Алымов, В. На основе ленинской нацирнальной политики. *Polarnaya Pravda.*

Antonova, A. A. (1982). Антонова, А. А. *Букварь для подготовительного класса саамской школы.* Ленинград: Просвещение.

Antonova, A. A. (1990). Антонова, А. А. *Букварь для подготовительного класса саамской школы.* Ленинград: Просвещение.

Bazanov, A. G. (1936). Базанов, А. Г. *Очерки по истории миссионерских школ на Крайнем Севере.* Ленинград: Институт Народов Севера.

Bazanov, A. G., & Kazanskii, N. G. (1939). Базанов, А. Г., & Казанский Н. Г. *Школа на Крайнем Севере.* Москва: Учпедгиз.

Cerniakovin, S. (1933). *Saam bukvar.* Moskva–Leningrat: Učpedgiz.

Cherniakov, Z. E. (1933). Черняков, З. Е. *В помощь учителю работающему с саамским (лопарским) букварем.* Ленинград: Коминтерн.

Endiukovskii, A. G. (1937a). Эндюковский, А. Г. *Саамь букваррь.* Ленинград–Москва: Учпедгиз.

Filippov, M. F. (1934). Филиппов, М. Ф. Саамское отделение Мурманского педтехникума. *Материалы по развитию языков и письменности народов Севера в Мурманском округе* (pp. 8–10). Мурманск: Комитет Нового Алфавита.

Gatagova, L. S. (2009). Гатагова, Л. С. (сост) *ЦК ВКП(б) и национальный вопрос*, Книга 2. Москва: Росспэн.

Kert, G. M. (1986). Керт, Г. М. *Словарь саамско-русский и русско-саамский: около 4000 слов: Пособие для учащихся начальной школы.* Ленинград: Просвещение.

Kuruch, R. D., et al. (1990). Куруч, Р. Д. *Методическое руководство по обучению саамскому языку в начальной школе.* Москва–Мурманск.

Natsionalnye menshinstva. (1929). *Национальные меньшинства Ленинградской области (сборник материалов).* Ленинград: Издательство Ленинградского облисполкома.

Nazrevshii vopros. (1939, January 1). Назревший вопрос. *Polarnoin kollektivisti.*

Novyi uchebnyi god. (1938, September 1). Новый учебный год. *Izvestiia.*

Osipov, O. O. (1933a, November 12). Səntəv saam opnəja. *Polarnaya Pravda.*

Osipov, E. U. (1933b, November 12). Saam di 16 Okţavr egk. *Polarnaya Pravda.*

Popova, N. S. (1934). *Arifmetika.* Leningrad: Učpedgiz.

Popova, N. S. (1937). Попова, Н. С. *Олкхэш школа варас арифметика опнуввэм книга.* Ленинград: Учпедгиз.

Sud nad vinovnikami. (1938, February 3). Суд на виновниками гибели белокаменских школьников. *Polarnoin kollektivisti.*

Literature

Akhmetova, A. V. (2013). Ахметова, А. В. *Власть и этнос: социальная политика советского государства в отношении коренных малочисленных народов Дальнего Восток, 1925–1985.* Владивосток: Дальнаука.

Axelsson, P., & Sköld, P. (2006). Indigenous Populations and Vulnerability: Characterizing Vulnerability in a Sami Context. *Annales de Demographie Historique, 111*(1), 115–132.

Belenkin, I. F. (1975). Беленкин, И. Ф. Саамские рукописные буквари. *Летопись Севера, 7*, 190–194.

Bogdanov, N. V. (2002). Богданов, Н. Б. *История становления системы образования Кольских саамов или этапы становления саамской педагогики.* www.sami.ru. Accessed 1 October 2018.

Cherniakov, Z. E. (1934). Черняков, З. Е. Отчёт о командировке в Полярный район Мурманского округа 1933 г. *Материалы по развитию языков и письменности народов Севера в Мурманском округе* (pp. 13–19). Мурманск: Комитет Нового Алфавита.

Cherniakov, Z. E. (1998). Черняков, З. Е. *Очерки саамской этнографии* (L. Rantala, Ed.). Rovaniemi: University of Lapland.

Coates, K. (2004). *A Global History of Indigenous Peoples: Struggle and Survival.* Hampshire: Palgrave Macmillan.

Dashchinskiy, S. (1999). Дащинский, С. *Президент Саамской Республики.* Мурманск: Мемориал.

Efimenko, G. G. (2001). Єфіменко, Г. Г. *Національно-культурна політика ВКП(б) щодо Радянської України (1932–1938).* Kyiv: Ukrainian Institute of History.

Endiukovskii, A. G. (1937b). Эндюковский, А. Г. Саамский (лопарский) язык, *Языки и письменность народов Севера* (pp. 125–162). Москва and Ленинград: Учпедгиз.

Gutsol, N. N., Vinogradova, S. N., & Samurokova, A. G. (2007). *Переселенные группы кольских саамов.* Apatity: Kola Research Centre RAN.

Ivanishcheva, O. N. (2016). Иванищева, О. Н. *Саамский язык: сохранение языка в эпоху глобализации.* Moscow–Berlin: DirectMedia.

Khelimskiy, E. A. (2002). Хелимский, Е. А. Саамский язык. *Языки народов России. Красная книга* (pp. 155–157). Москва: Энциклопедический словарь-справочник.

Kol'skie saamy. (2008). *Кольские саамы в меняющемся мире.* Под редакцией А. И. Козлова, Д. В. Лисицына, М. А. Козловой. Москва: Институт Наследия.

Kotljarchuk, A. (2012). Kola Sami in the Stalinist Terror: A Quantitative Analysis. *Journal of Northern Studies, 2,* 59–82.

Kotljarchuk, A. (2014a). *In Forge of Stalin: Swedish Colonists of Ukraine in the Totalitarian Experiments of the Twenties Century.* Södertörn Academic Studies 58. Huddinge: Södertörn Academic.

Kotljarchuk, A. (2014b). The Nordic Threat: Soviet Ethnic Cleansing on the Kola Peninsula. In N. Götz (Ed.), *The Sea of Identities: A Century of Baltic and East European Experiences with Nationality, Class, and Gender* (pp. 53–83). Stockholm: Elanders.

Kotljarchuk, A. (2017). Propaganda of Hatred in the Great Terror: A Nordic Approach. In *Ethnic and Religious Minorities in Stalin's Soviet Union New Dimensions of Research* (pp. 91–121). Södertörn Academic Studies 72. Huddinge: Södertörn Academic Studies.

Kuropiatnik, M. (1999). Expeditions to Sami Territories: A History of the Studies of the Kola Sami in the 1920s–1930s. *Acta Borealia, 16*(1), 117–125.

Leete, A. (2004). Леэте, А. *Казымская война. Восстание хантов и лесных ненцев против советской власти.* Tartu: Tartu University Press.

Mann, M. (2005). *The Dark Side of Democracy: Explaining Ethnic Cleansing.* New York: Cambridge University Press.

Martin, T. (2001). *The Affirmative Action Empire: Nations and Nationalism in the Soviet Union, 1923–1939.* Ithaca: Cornell University Press.

Mikolyuk, O. V. (2003). Миколюк, О. В. *Политические репрессии на Мурмане в 30-е годы XX века.* Мурманск: Мурманский государственный педагогический университет.

Rantala, L. (2014). *Kola-Samer som ble ofre for Stalins Terror.* Rovaniemi: University of Lapland.

Sergejeva, J. (2000). The Eastern Sámi: A Short Account of Their History and Identity. *Acta Borealia, 2,* 5–37.

Shashkov, V. Y. (2000). Шашков, В. Я. *Репрессии в СССР против крестьян и судьбы спецпереселенцев Карело-Мурманского края.* Мурманск: Мурманский государственный педагогический институт.

Slezkine, Y. (1994). *Arctic Mirrors: Russia and the Small Peoples of the North.* Ithaca, NY: Cornell University Press.

Sundström, O. (2007). *Kampen mot "schamanismen." Sovjetisk religionspolitik gentemot inhemska religioner i Sibirien och norra Ryssland.* Uppsala: Swedish Science Press.

Thorvaldsen, G. (2011). Household Structure in the Multiethnic Barents Region: A Local Case Study. In D. Anderson (Ed.), *The 1926/27 Soviet Polar Census Expeditions* (pp. 117–132). New York: Berghahn Books.

Toulouze, E. (2005). The Intellectuals from Russia's Peoples of the North: From Obedience to Resistance. In A. Leete & Ü. Valk (Eds.), *The Northern Peoples and States: Changing Relationships* (pp. 140–164). Studies in Folk Culture 5. Tartu: Tartu University Press.

Viola, L. (1986). Bab'i Bunty and Peasant Women's Protest During Collectivization. *The Russian Review, 45*(1), 23–42.

Volkov, N. N. (1996). Волков, Н. Н. *Российские саамы. Историко-этнографические очерки.* Leningrad: MAE RAN Kunstkamera.

Werth, N. (2003). The Mechanism of a Mass Crime: The Great Terror in the Soviet Union, 1937–38. In R. Gellately & B. Kiernan (Eds.), *The Specter of Genocide: Mass Murder in Historical Perspective* (pp. 215–239). Cambridge: Cambridge University Press.

Wheelersburg, R., & Gutsol, N. (2008). Babinski and Ekostrovski: Saami Pogosty on the Western Kola Peninsula, Russia from 1880 to 1940. *Arctic Anthropology, 45*(1), 79–96.

Zolotarev, D. A. (1927). Золотарев Д. А. Лопарская экспедиция 1927 года. Ленинград: Государственное Русское Географическое Общество.

6

The Perspective of Former Pupils: Indigenous Children and Boarding Schools on the Kola Peninsula, 1960s to 1980s

Lukas Allemann

Introduction

Together with former pupils, in this chapter I will look into the history of Soviet boarding schools in the Russian part of Sápmi. The testimonies and my interpretations emerged from a corpus of biographic oral history interviews created between 2013 and 2018.[1] The contributors have a Sámi, Komi, Russian or mixed background, and most of the testimonies stem from Lovozero, the administrative centre of the Lovozero district.

Three boarding schools will be discussed in this chapter, for which I will henceforth use the following abbreviations: The native boarding school in Lovozero (NBS; Russian: *natsional'naia shkola-internat*), the

---

[1] The interviews were undertaken as part of two projects funded by the Academy of Finland: ORHELIA (Oral History of Empires by Elders in the Arctic, 2011–2015, decision no. 251111), and WOLLIE (Live, Work or Leave? Youth-wellbeing and the viability of (post)-extractive Arctic industrial cities in Finland and Russia, 2018–2020, decision no. 314471).

L. Allemann (✉)
Arctic Centre, University of Lapland, Rovaniemi, Finland
e-mail: Lukas.Allemann@ulapland.fi

© The Author(s) 2019
O. Kortekangas et al. (eds.), *Sámi Educational History in a Comparative International Perspective*,
https://doi.org/10.1007/978-3-030-24112-4_6

83

remedial boarding school in Lovozero (RBS; Russian: *vspomogatel'naia shkola-internat*) and the boarding school in Gremikha (GBS; Russian: *shkola-internat*). Each section is followed by a set of testimonies about the respective boarding school.

After the closure and relocation of entire indigenous communities, from the 1960s onwards Lovozero became the artificial 'capital' of the Russian Sámi. Lovozero belonged to a category of planned villages for relocated indigenous people who had previously lived a nomadic or semi-nomadic life. Such villages were termed *compact dwelling settlement* (Russian: *mesto kompaktnogo prozhivaniia*, see Slezkine 1994, 340). In their new 'capital', however, the Sámi became a minority comprising about one-fifth of the population. The reasons behind the relocations included collectivisation, sedentarisation, economic rationalisation, industrial and infrastructural development, and the requirements of the military. It is beyond the scope of this text to go into more detail about such relocations; they are discussed by Konstantinov (2015, 96–196), Afanasyeva (2013), Allemann (2013), and Gutsol et al. (2007). The boarding school period discussed in this chapter mainly covers the 1960s to the 1980s.

While writing this contribution, I was guided by the thought that a historiography of boarding schools for indigenous children could only be created *together with* their former pupils and teachers: co-productive research views the interviewee as on par with the scholar (see Denzin 2009, 277–305; Allemann and Dudeck 2017). Co-creation should be a valid principle not only while creating the data, but also when it comes to using and displaying it. Allowing space for the collected testimonies to be displayed, without too many comments from an outside authorial position, is an effective way to realise and process what people experienced. It means acknowledging that my oral history interlocutors are not just raw data sources which I tap into and then interpret. Rather, it is primarily the interlocutors who actively interpret, analyse and theorise on their own lives (Bornat 2010), while my role as a scholar is to build my meta-interpretations on top of theirs. My intention with this chapter is to contribute to decolonising research, and I do so by breaking somewhat away from the conventions regarding the form of academic texts, leaving more space than usual for the *primary* interpretations given by the witnesses themselves, besides my *secondary* scholarly interpretations.

Present Discussions Among Former Boarding School Pupils

While positive and negative remembrances should not be seen as mutually exclusive, we can acknowledge that there is a need to talk about the boarding schools for indigenous children, as they massively changed the lives of individuals and communities, with the repercussions lasting to the present day. Overall, evaluations by former pupils of the boarding school system in Russia's and the Soviet Union's North tend to be highly ambivalent. People often praise the boarding schools for the chances they gave in terms of enabling individuals to climb the ladder in Soviet society to become doctors, engineers or boarding school teachers themselves. They also express feelings of gratitude and affection towards many of their former educators for their devotion and effort towards lowering the children's stress arising from being far from home. At the same time, former pupils inveigh against the system and some of the staff for stigmatising their social and ethnic background, pushing for assimilation and depriving them of parental love. Many children encountered psychological or physical violence.

In terms of traumatic experiences among former indigenous pupils, the RBS in Lovozero stands out, as many children were misdiagnosed as mentally disabled. However, being limited to the Kola Peninsula as a case study, and with little existing research on these schools, I was confronted with difficulties in assessing how widespread indigenous overrepresentation in these dooming schools was across the entire, immense Soviet North. A timely discussion on Facebook (Sulyandziga 2018), which I came across by chance, provided the answer. The author of the post condemned illegitimate indigenous overrepresentation in remedial schools in Russia's Far East. The commentators bore witness to the same practices I had heard about in my oral history research across the Russian North. This post showed that there was a need for an open discussion on the practices and consequences of these boarding schools.

The Native Boarding School in Lovozero

The NBS in Lovozero was the only school in the Murmansk Region with special ethnic profiling. This was a pan-Soviet school category designed to incorporate elements of the respective local non-Russian 'national cultures,' with 'national' in Soviet terminology meaning ethnic/native/indigenous (see Brubaker 2002, 178; Martin 1998). Such schools were meant for non-Russian children. The curricula of these schools, even in late Soviet times, remained faithful to what Stalin had already said in 1921: "The essence of the nationality question in the USSR consists of the need to eliminate the backwardness (economic, political and cultural) that the nationalities have inherited from the past, to allow the backward people to catch up with central Russia" (quoted in Slezkine 1994, 144). Ethnic segregation in education thus aimed at making indigenous people "catch up." Ultimately, those schools pursued a somewhat contradictory equality-through-segregation principle, being designed to offer indigenous children equal chances in Soviet society by mainly transmitting the Soviet majority society's forms of knowledge. With this type of education, indigeneity became firmly limited to cultural elements that were readily visible and understandable as such to outsiders. These included handicrafts, songs and sometimes native language tuition. The various nationalities were to develop their own intelligentsia, participate in Soviet life and limit their non-Soviet ethnic identity to the space offered by specific cultural institutions.

Between the 1950s and the 1980s, mainly Sámi and Komi children attended the NBS. Before the large-scale relocations, mainly children from far-away villages, which usually had only an elementary school, went to the boarding school in Lovozero after the fourth grade. From the 1960s onwards, after the mass relocations, also most Sámi children from relocated families attended the NBS, in spite of the fact that their parents lived in the same settlement (Afanasyeva 2019; Allemann 2018).

Under such conditions, being placed in the local boarding school instead of in the local daytime school looks, at a first glance, like a paradoxical situation. However, there were manifold, but not obvious, reasons for this, as I have shown previously (Allemann 2018). They included: Firstly, structural racism, resulting from a benevolent paternalistic policy mixed with vague but tenacious prejudices about the otherness and needs of the indigenous population, as shown in this sociological report to the Murmansk Regional Government about the living conditions of the indigenous population:

> Currently the indigenous people of the North [in the Murmansk Region] live in comfortable villages and settlements with modern conveniences: Lovozero, Revda [etc.], where the social infrastructure is well-developed: there are apartments with modern facilities, schools and kindergartens, shops, canteens, hospitals, health centres, Houses of Culture [Russian: doma kul'tury] and clubs. This guarantees the high level of adaptation of the indigenous population in the extreme conditions of the Kola North. (Balakshin 1985, 6)

The former headmaster of the NBS maintained the same kind of paternalistic attitude towards his pupils: "Our children whom we recruit to our boarding school have their own psychological peculiarities, they are slower, less developed, but they are not transgressors" (Commission on Under-age Affairs of the Lovozero District Executive Committee 1973). Secondly, the countrywide long-term goal to create a unified Soviet nation resulted, in practice, in a general policy of Russification, which, among non-Russian nations, was easier to inculcate through boarding schools. And thirdly, the most hidden and locally peculiar reason: a chronic housing shortage after the relocations that led to overcrowded flats and a generally difficult material and psychological situation of the relocated families. An easy way for the local authorities to—apparently—alleviate these problems and massage the housing statistics was to send the children of relocated families to the boarding school (Allemann 2018; Afanasyeva 2019, 191 f.).

The practice of placing children in the boarding school when their parents lived in the same village was phased out after the collapse of the Soviet Union. However, the school kept serving children from remote villages until its final closure in the early 2010s.

88   L. Allemann

Born in the 1960s, NBS[2]

There was no space to live [referring to the shortage of flats for the relocated families]. When I was visiting my mum [during boarding school leave on weekends], I saw how they lived there. My mum was happy, of course [that I visited her].

Born in the 1940s, elementary daytime school in Voron'e, then NBS, higher education

I hate this place, you know?

Lovozero?

Yes, Lovozero. It's for me … Well, can you imagine a child after … I don't remember now, were there four elementary school years? Yes. So, for the fifth grade I had to go to Lovozero [this was before the closure of the interviewee's native village; a few years later the village was closed down and the interviewee's parents were relocated to Lovozero, too]. They tore me away from my family and brought me to Lovozero, and they drilled us like soldiers in the boarding school. They forbade everything. When we went there, we spoke our native language. They forbade us to speak in our native language, only Russian. Imagine. And today, I can say that [[chuckling]] I basically forgot my mother tongue. […] And so, imagine, we arrived at this boarding school, small kids, where adults had command over us, taught us something, and they didn't allow us to speak in our language. So, we were forced to, when we would go to bed, to whisper between each other in our language, so that nobody else could hear us. That's how it was. And during the daytime we all tried to speak only in Russian. […] We were small, and we didn't understand anything of these political games. They prohibited it, and so we didn't speak. And when they finally said that we could speak, it was too late. Yes, we had already forgotten our language.

[…]

---

[2]Although many interviewees gave their general consent to publish their names, in this publication I opted for anonymising all quotations. My decision is due to the sensitivity of the topic up to this day and the mention of other peoples' names by the interviewees. Due to the potential ease of identifying individuals in this small community, I also refrained from indicating the sex and the precise year of birth. All names in the quotations have been changed to fictional ones.

6 The Perspective of Former Pupils: Indigenous Children ... 89

When we [the rest of the interviewee's family] moved to Lovozero we lived … they gave us a wooden hut. I don't remember. Either they gave it to us, or my parents had to rent it. There were two families living there: my parents' family and my mother's sister's family. The smallest kids lived with them, of course. But we, all the others, studied and lived at the boarding school because with only two small rooms [for both families] there was simply not enough space.

[…]

They always reminded us that the clothes that we wore must be clean, that you always needed to take care of the way you looked. […] All in all, I am very thankful that they taught me this in the boarding school. I don't know if I would have learned all this living at home. Although my parents, I must say, stood out for being very clean and neat people; they were always held up as an example.

[…]

I wouldn't say slow progress [about bad grades among pupils]. They were simply not interested at all in studying. Absolutely not interested. They just wanted to go home, to their parents, where they could be in their usual environment, where they could speak in their own language, where they didn't feel any interdictions. But we [my friend and I], when we came to the boarding school, we decided to study hard. Me and her, we finished [high] school. When we were already in about the seventh grade, we told each other: "Okay, we will study well. We will finish [high] school, and we will get a higher education, no matter what." We kind of swore it to each other. And we did it!

[…]

About the boarding school, I just remember this permanent homesickness. It was all the time, but at the same time, I want to say that the boarding school gave me very much, you know?

Born in the 1960s, NBS, higher education
There was some kind of dictate to get the children away from their families. That was really bad. Quintessentially, the boarding school should have been meant for kids whose parents were in the tundra, who were

not in the village. And that's how it was initially. Or for the children from remote settlements like Kanevka, Sosnovka and Krasnoshchel'e.

Yes-yes.

But then they introduced this rule that all kids should sleep at the boarding school. That was, of course, a bit on the heavy side.

Born in the 1950s, NBS, higher education

Of course, they used to shave our heads. But there were certain kids whom they wouldn't shave. They had to be A-graders, so this was like an incentive.

So, could you deserve not to be shaved?

Yes [[laughing]]! For example, Ira's sister, she always had the best grades, so they didn't shave her. But us, the eternal run-aways, they would shave us without hesitation.

[...]

For a child to visit home at the weekend, the parents had to apply for a certificate from the hygiene and disinfection department [Russian: *sanitarno-epidemiologicheskaia sluzhba*], confirming that the conditions at home were okay for the kids.

That was quite humiliating for the parents, wasn't it?

Well yes. It meant that they came to your home to check your bed linen, you know, those bugs in your hair. It all had to be done in due order. Although we were bald anyway! [...] And when the herders came back from the tundra, of course, we used to wash all the clothes, to boil them. Our people knew how to fight against this. Yes ... But the mentality of the others was that we were always full of bugs, dirty people, and so on. That's how they were brought up. My mum though, she was always saying: "They use the same bucket for washing their hair, their feet and the floor, while we have separate buckets for every task [[laughing]]."

[...]

But my [younger] brother, maybe the times had already changed a little bit, he successfully fought for his right to live at home. They were so fed up with him! [...] He would just go away, away from the village, where his mum was in the fields for the haymaking. Or in winter, he would take his boots and his hat and walk all the way, fifteen kilometres. And so finally they gave up, so the child wouldn't go completely ... [mad]. He was simply stubborn.

[...]

It's not that we just became resigned to it, no, I liked being there [at the NBS]. At home, you had to heat up the stove, bring water and collect the wood chips. Lots of duties [which we didn't have at the boarding school]. And they also fed you well. And yes, we all [the former pupils] don't like cooking, for us this is like ... I was in Russian families, and I can't imagine spending so much time cooking [[laughing]]. I'm not a good housewife. Only cleaning, that's not a problem, they taught us that [at school] [[chuckling]].

Born in the 1950s, NBS

I remember it very well, yes, when earlier we would have dancing parties at the House of Culture. Those evenings would last until eleven pm. We were in the ninth–tenth grade, and that was only on Saturdays. But inevitably, as soon as the clock struck ten, somebody from the boarding school would enter the hall and say: "Alright, all boarding school children [Russian: *vse internatskie*] back to the boarding school!" That was like a stab in the heart. That was so ... that was so humiliating.

So were the dancing evenings for all the teenagers from the whole settlement?

Yes, for the youth. "Alright, all boarding school children back to the boarding school!" And then you think "Oh my god." You leave, and there were all the teenagers from Revda [the neighbouring settlement]. "Look, there she goes," they would say. They called out to us: "The incubator kids [*batorskie*] are going". *Bator* [a slang abbreviation of *inkubator*].

The Remedial Boarding School in Lovozero

The RBS in Lovozero was opened in 1970. Remedial schools were special schools within the countrywide system for mentally 'deviant' children. On this pan-Soviet level, these schools were officially unrelated to the state's nationality policies and to ethnic markers. However, in Lovozero, the RBS was almost half as large as the district's boarding school for intellectually 'regular' children. Pupils of Sámi origin were transferred from the NBS to the RBS more often than average, ending up being heavily over-represented in the latter. While the school was also filled with mentally disabled non-indigenous children from all over the Murmansk Region, there was frequent misdiagnosing among the local indigenous children.

Such wrongful appointments to the RBS were mainly due to the indifferent application of Eurocentric norms about valid forms of knowledge and intellect—a colonial attitude, which has been criticised in relation to both 'Western' Arctic states and the USSR/Russia (Choate 2018; Arshavskii and Rotenberg 1991). In Lovozero, children recommended by teachers for transfer from the NBS to the RBS were tested via a countrywide, standardised assessment system enacted by groups of experts. These groups were called medical-pedagogical commissions. The forms of knowledge tested in order to assess the intellectual capacities of children presupposed a Soviet—meaning urbanised and Russianised—background; they were not locally adapted and hence not suitable for the indigenous children's knowledge systems and socio-cultural environment. For example, the task of describing a parrot or an oak could baffle a first-grader who had grown up mostly in the tundra without elements of the majority culture such as kindergarten tuition or television. While many children were afraid of and also threatened with being transferred to this school by teachers, there was also a strategy of making this school look attractive to children due to its easier curriculum and shorter lessons. Many misdiagnosed children had been brought to the commission unaccompanied by a parent or other guardian—which was against the rules. Besides that, the school's staff, who enjoyed higher salaries than in regular schools, had a self-interest in receiving a constant supply of pupils.

6 The Perspective of Former Pupils: Indigenous Children ... 95

if we were ... there was this commission that tested the children: "How heavy is the chicken if it stands on one leg and if it stands on two legs?" Those were the kinds of tests they were formally sticking to. Those who had put their hands up, they had to undergo these tests to check if they were intellectually suitable for the remedial school. I remember, the testing was in the teachers' room, there was a queue of kids, some were crying. There were also some who understood what that school was about. Not everybody was eager to be transferred there. [...] For example, Liuda [the interviewee's former classmate], she even got a higher education later. Those kids had to catch up in night school [as adults] because upon graduation from the remedial school, their educational level corresponded to the fifth or sixth grade. At that time, they had this kind of night school. And, after that, she went to college, graduated, and is now head of a kindergarten in [another city in Russia]. But she doesn't come here [to Lovozero]. She says: "How can I come, everybody remembers that I was in that school for morons." A whole generation was knocked out. [...] Such was the life of this generation. And those who managed to challenge this fate simply left for a place where people wouldn't know what kind of school they had been to [[sighing]], and basically they started a new life.

Born in the 1950s, NBS, higher education
I remember my sister came home and said: "You know what?" I said: "What? What happened?" She said: "I want to ... they told me that I could apply to go to the remedial school, and then I would leave earlier for the tundra [for summer holidays]!" We said: "Forget about this immediately!" She started to cry and left. I mean, you could just file an application [to be transferred to the RBS].

Born in the 1960s, daytime school in Revda, transferred to the RBS, later went to the night school
"Do you want to go to the boarding school [the RBS]? There are plenty of kids and toys, and you will always eat good food."—"Why are you asking, you'll send us there anyway." And so, they transferred us. That was in March 1971.

[...]

In our class [at the RBS] I was the only Russian. He [the interviewee's brother] at least had other Russian kids in his class. But I was the only Russian in my class, all the others were Sámi and Komi.

[...]

I and Kolia [the interviewee's brother], we often used to run away from the boarding school. Very often. We once even fled to Karelia. On freight wagons. Who would pay for our ticket! We would also hitchhike.

But it's not easy to get out of Lovozero [there is only one road], who would take you?

Yes, yes, as free-riders on the bus, or hitchhiking, whatever. Also walking. But what I wanted to say is that there were punishments for running away. With the girls, they were more merciful. Imagine, it's summer [holidays], you want to run around, have fun outside, but they strip you naked, damn, and you have to stick to your bed for a week or two. They'll only let you go to the toilet. Yes, there was such a thing.

Such a punishment?

Yes. But the boys! How many boys' lives they screwed up! Because of that my brother couldn't go to the army. They would send them [as a punishment] to Apatity [a nearby city] to the psychiatric hospital for two–three months. They were treated there, it would seem, with psycho-pharmaceuticals. Once they were back, it took them a long time to recover. Can you imagine what condition they were in?

They were sending kids to the psychiatric hospital?

Yes! Yes, yes. I don't know exactly what they were doing there with them, but some kind of experiment, it would seem. Later, when he [the interviewee's brother] would get drunk, my mum and I were very afraid of him. He did not know what he was doing.

[...]

They could also shave your head, "don't be a girl anymore". Imagine, girls, thirteen–fourteen years old, they played pranks, they would take them, of course, they wouldn't ask them. Imagine, she was a teenager, all of a sudden with a shaved head.

That was meant as humiliation.

Of course, of course.

Maybe under the pretext of hygienic measures?

Just to humiliate her and to discourage others.

[…]

Until May, our teacher [at the NBS] was Anna Alekseevna, she was the one who assigned us [to the RBS]. Half of the class she sent there, half! We were a huge class, classes were very big at the boarding school [the NBS]. […] And half of it she sent away [to the RBS], so that we were split into two classes of fifteen–sixteen people. […] And they took me, too.

The Nexus Between Boarding Schools and Post-relocation Social Despair

Placing children in boarding schools was a practice both welcomed and resisted by families relocated to Lovozero. It was partially welcomed, because the material conditions in the schools were better than the over-crowded conditions in relocated families' homes (Afanasyeva 2019, 191 f.). At the same time, if the state removed a child from a family and presented this as a solution to problems which had been created by that same state, this was perceived as a cynical and ignominious practice. It turned relocated parents into deficient parents.

The strengths or weaknesses of the parental background were a decisive factor in a child's educational path. Parents or other relatives who were aware of the situation, who enjoyed a secure social position and who were simply present in the village were more likely to successfully influence which school their child would be sent to. However, many of the relocated parents were limited in their possibilities to intervene, for several reasons: they still belonged to a generation with poor literacy; they were frequently absent for tundra work; additionally, after their relocation, many families were plagued by social issues such as a lack of

98 L. Allemann

acceptance by locals, chronic housing shortages, and a lack of suitable employment (see literature on relocations cited above). This led to widespread alcohol abuse and violence, with a more than twofold increase in violent deaths between pre-relocation and post-relocation times. Throughout the 1970s, the share of violent deaths was steadily above 50 per cent (Bogoiavlenskii and Kozlov 2008). While these social issues contributed to motivate the administrative separation of children from their families (Konstantinov 2015, 148f.), the separation itself in many cases contributed to the further social destitution of parents deprived of their children. As we can see from some of the quotations, following a typical transgenerational trauma pattern (Atkinson et al. 2010), social despair, including suicide and homicide, also spread to the relocated families' children.

Born in the 1960s, daytime school in Revda, transferred to the RBS, later went to the night school

We were 13–14 years old. We were already smokers. And so, she took us to her home; there were her drunken uncles. Her grandmother [...] was always at work, because she had to feed them, but those [uncles] didn't want to work, they drank. And so, they would give us drink. Well they were doing nothing else with us; they knew they could go to jail for that. But they were making fun of observing us when we became drunk. And all of a sudden there was somebody knocking at the door. We checked; it was the teachers. Our educators already knew where to look for us. They knocked: "Open this door, quickly, what's that, we have to fetch the children!" [[laughing]]. Finally, they opened the door, and we were drunk, imagine, drunken children. [...] And then, after the school years were over, they arrested Masha. She wasn't working anywhere and she was put to jail for being jobless.

Parasitism [Russian: *tuneiadstvo*]

By then [when Masha came out of the correction camp] her grandma had already died, Sasha [one of the drinking uncles] had hung himself, and Vasia [the other drinking uncle] had died from tuberculosis. And Masha ... it was very strict then about being registered [Russian: *propiska*, a permanent, official address], [...], three months without registration and they could arrest you. And so, she started living with an elderly man [...], he was over fifty then. But she had no choice, because of this registration, and she gave birth to a boy from him. [...] She was twenty-one when she came back from the camp. And one [day], they were drinking, and their boy was seven months old. And they went to check the [fishing] nets with the baby. And they all drowned. The baby was never found [...], but they found him and her. She was also Sámi. This kind of death was all around, imagine.

Yes, plenty.

Born in the 1930s, elementary daytime school in Varzino, GBS, higher education
[About her relatives in Lovozero:] In 1982, their son, Andrei, died. He hung himself, and in '82 Fedia was already dead, too, or maybe it was in '80–'81. And Anatolii hung himself in '82. In those years, Pasha also hung himself. Their entire family fell to pieces. I don't know why, maybe because the parents drank and let things slide. In Lovozero, you know, I can't really explain it, but there was a kind of tacit asperity, when there's physical violence among the kids towards each other. Beating each other up, and so badly that it hurt.

The kids among themselves or the parents towards the kids?

No-no, the kids among themselves. And I don't really understand the reasons, but Pasha was such a quiet boy, and he did this to himself.

The Boarding School in Gremikha

Gremikha, a settlement on the Barents Sea coast, stands apart from Lovozero not only geographically but also in terms of generally more positive boarding school experiences. Being an important military base, it had also a very different social composition and schooling history for its indigenous children. Before the closure of most of the smaller coastal villages, the GBS hosted many indigenous coastal children. However, according to my informants, placement in the GBS was not limited to indigenous children, as children from military families deployed to the North and from Russian coastal families attended it, too. Compared to the NBS in Lovozero, it lacked any specifically 'national' (i.e. non-Russian) features in its curriculum. This lack of formalised features in the curriculum directed towards the indigenousness of the children led to a less biased attitude by teachers. We can say that mixing the children independently of their provenience was in line with today's widely accepted paradigm that inclusion should always be favoured instead of segregation (Allemann-Ghionda 2015).

The GBS was closed down in the 1960s as there were no more distant villages left and—contrary to the 'ethnic' village of Lovozero—there was no practice of sending indigenous children to the boarding school when their parents lived in the same village. This can be explained by the fact that there was no special 'indigenous' profiling of the settlement and no housing shortage, as there was in Lovozero (see also Afanasyeva 2019, 27 f., 157 f., 183–185).

Born in the 1930s, elementary daytime school in Lumbovka, GBS, higher education, worked as a teacher in Gremikha
It was the influence. I don't remember speaking at the boarding school in our own language. Face to face, quietly, yes. But in public, no. What I knew I actually forgot. If I had lived in the village … Firstly, to Iokan'ga [a Sámi village, closed down in 1963], I only used to go there for the holidays. And, secondly, in the boarding school, I didn't hear our language, and so the language quietly disappeared from my mind.

[…]

Our educators [at the GBS] were very good. I remember several of them. They were remarkable people […], we had very good teachers. […] Our kids went for higher education to Moscow and St. Petersburg.

[…]

There we had also [military] officers' families, soldiers' families. Their kids were also at our boarding school. And not only natives went to this school but also Russian kids. Because in Lumbovka there were also Russian families […]. In every [pre-relocation] village there were also Russian families.

6 The Perspective of Former Pupils: Indigenous Children ... 101

Born in the 1930s, GBS, higher education, worked as a teacher in Lovozero
I warmly remember the Gremikha boarding school. Here [in Lovozero] they would have sent me to the nuthouse.

You mean the remedial school?

Yes, I told them once directly, during one of our teachers' meetings, I said if I had gone to school here, I, who spoke Sámi and almost no Russian, they would have sent me to the remedial school [laughing]. [...] Mainly children of reindeer herders were sent to the remedial school because their parents in the tundra had been speaking in Sámi to them.

Conclusion: Different Schools, Different Opportunities

While former pupils often warmly remember their devoted educators and teachers, and many appreciate the professional opportunities, which they got through their education, the symbolic violence (Bourdieu et al. 1991) exerted by the boarding school system should not be underestimated. In Lovozero, placement in the NBS, and, in many cases subsequently, in the RBS, was an effective mechanism for social exclusion and for the perpetuation of social hierarchies (Bourdieu and Champagne 1999); this chiefly concerned the families who were relocated to Lovozero from the villages that had been closed down—and these families were mostly of Sámi origin. In terms of boarding and remedial schooling, it was likelier for children from such families to fall prey to the system without being protected by any counter-force. However, the schools should not be seen as solely responsible for the ensuing social despondency, but rather as connected to the preceding mass relocations and as a factor exacerbating the negative consequences of these relocations.

In Gremikha, the GBS was not designed to account for the 'different' backgrounds of indigenous children. The lack of segregating affirmative action towards indigenous children reflects in consistently more positive feelings towards this school by its former pupils, as opposed to those who went to school in Lovozero. Speaking the Sámi language during lessons was, in practice, forbidden in all schools.

All schools were responsible for a drastic drop in the number of Sámi-language speakers. We can indeed speak of the "broken generation" (Vakhtin 1992, 18): children were pushed, and at times forced, not to use their indigenous language at school; at the same time, they faced difficulties in school because Russian was not their mother tongue.

However, within this frame of cultural assimilation, we can see a large number of ways in which pupils coped, depending on their own and their families' agency as well as on chance. These ways ranged from accommodating and using the offered opportunities for a successful education and professional life within the frames of the majority society, to being strongly limited by the system in terms of personal development and life opportunities.

References

Afanasyeva, A. (2013). *Forced Relocations of the Kola Sámi People: Background and Consequences* (Master thesis). University of Tromsø, Tromsø. http://munin.uit.no/handle/10037/5241.

Afanasyeva, A. (2019). *Boarding School Education of the Sami People in Soviet Union (1935–1989): Experiences of Three Generations* (Doctoral thesis). University of Tromsø, Tromsø. https://munin.uit.no/handle/10037/15101.

Allemann, L. (2013). *The Sami of the Kola Peninsula: About the Life of an Ethnic Minority in the Soviet Union.* Tromsø: Septentrio Academic Publishing. https://doi.org/10.7557/sss.2013.19.

Allemann, L. (2018). 'I Do Not Know If Mum Knew What Was Going On': Social Reproduction in Boarding Schools in Soviet Lapland. *Acta Borealia, 35*(2), 1–28. https://doi.org/10.1080/08003831.2018.1536115.

Allemann-Ghionda, C. (2015). Dealing with Diversity in Education: A Critical View on Goals and Outcomes. In T. Matejskova & M. Antonsich (Eds.), *Governing Through Diversity: Migration Societies in Post-multiculturalist Times* (pp. 125–142). New York: Palgrave Macmillan.

Allemann, L., & Dudeck, S. (2017). Sharing Oral History with Arctic Indigenous Communities: Ethical Implications of Bringing Back Research Results. *Qualitative Inquiry.* https://doi.org/10.1177/1077800417738800.

6 The Perspective of Former Pupils: Indigenous Children ... 103

Arshavskii, V. V., & Rotenberg, V. S. (1991). Pravo na 'pravopolusharnyi' obraz myslei. *Chelovek, 4,* 102–106.

Atkinson, J., Nelson, J., & Atkinson, C. (2010). Trauma, Transgenerational Transfer and Effects on Community Well-Being. In N. Purdie, P. Dudgeon, & R. Walker (Eds.), *Working Together: Aboriginal and Torres Strait Islander Mental Health and Wellbeing Principles and Practice* (pp. 135–144). Canberra: Australian Institute of Health and Welfare. http://aboriginal.telethonkids.org.au/media/54847/working_together_full_book.pdf.

Balakshin, Y. (1985). Perevod korennykh zhitelei Severa na osedlyi obraz zhizni—Aktual'naia zadacha partiinykh, Sovetskikh i khoziaistvennykh organov. In B. M. Levin, S. N. Batulin, & F. S. Donskoi (Eds.), *Sotsial'no-ekonomicheskie i demograficheskie problemy zaversheniia perevoda kochevogo naseleniia na osedlyi obraz zhizni* (pp. 3–6). Apatity: Akademiia nauk SSSR/ Murmanskii oblastnoi ispolnitel'nyi komitet.

Bogoiavlenskii, D. D., & Kozlov, A. I. (2008). Smertnost' ot vneshnikh prichin i otkloniaiushcheesia povedenie. In A. I. Kozlov, D. V. Lisitsyn, & M. A. Kozlova (Eds.), *Kol'skie Saamy v meniaiushchemsia mire* (pp. 78–85). Moscow: Institut naslediia. http://www.hse.ru/data/2012/12/17/1300811327/book.pdf.

Bornat, J. (2010). Remembering and Reworking Emotions: The Reanalysis of Emotion in an Interview. *Oral History, 38*(2), 43–52.

Bourdieu, P., & Champagne, P. (1999). Outcasts on the Inside. In P. Bourdieu (Ed.), *The Weight of the World: Social Suffering in Contemporary Society* (pp. 421–426). Cambridge: Polity Press.

Bourdieu, P., Thompson, J. B., Raymond, G., Adamson, M., & Thompson, J. B. (1991). *Language and Symbolic Power*. Cambridge: Polity Press.

Brubaker, R. (2002). Ethnicity Without Groups. *European Journal of Sociology/ Archives Européennes de Sociologie, 43*(2), 163–189. https://doi.org/10.1017/S0003975602001066.

Choate, P. (2018). *Assessment of Parental Capacity for Child Protection: Methodological, Cultural and Ethical Considerations in Respect of Indigenous Peoples* (Doctoral thesis). Kingston University, London.

Commission on Under-Age Affairs of the Lovozero District Executive Committee. (1973). *Protokol no. 4 zasedaniia komissii po delam nesovershennoletnikh pri Lovozerskom Raiispolkome.* Fund 146, list 5, file 193, sheet 22. State Archive of the Murmansk Region, Kirovsk.

Denzin, N. K. (2009). *Qualitative Inquiry Under Fire: Toward a New Paradigm Dialogue.* Walnut Creek: Left Coast Press.

Gutsol, N. N., Vinogradova, S. N., & Samorukova, A. G. (2007). *Pereselennye gruppy Kol'skikh saamov*. Apatity: Kol'skii nauchnyi tsentr RAN.

Konstantinov, Y. (2015). *Conversations with Power: Soviet and Post-Soviet Developments in the Reindeer Husbandry Part of the Kola Peninsula*. Uppsala: Acta Universitatis Upsaliensis. http://uu.diva-portal.org/smash/record.jsf?pid=diva2:865695.

Martin, T. (1998). The Origins of Soviet Ethnic Cleansing. *The Journal of Modern History, 70*(4), 813–861. https://doi.org/10.1086/235168.

Slezkine, Y. (1994). *Arctic Mirrors: Russia and the Small Peoples of the North*. Ithaca, NY: Cornell University Press.

Sulyandziga, P. (2018, March 7). *Post About Indigenous Children in Remedial Schools in Russia's North*. Facebook. https://www.facebook.com/pavel.sulyandziga/posts/10215675053209845.

Vakhtin, N. (1992). *Native Peoples of the Russian Far North*. London: Minority Rights Group International.

7

The Development of Sámi Children's Right to Learn Sámi in the Russian School Context

Ekaterina Zmyvalova and Hanna Outakoski

Introduction

In the year 2017, there was only one school in the Russian Federation (RF) where the children had the opportunity to learn the Sámi language as part of their formal education. This school is located in the village of Lovozero in the Murmansk Oblast (MO). The situation of formal Sámi language learning at this school, and elsewhere in the Russian Sápmi, is problematic for various reasons. This chapter focuses on the legal issues regarding this problematic situation, and the development and realization of the Sámi children's right to learn their mother tongue in school.

Our main method is the socio-legal method, which helps to understand functioning of law "in its social context" (Hydén and Wickenberg 2008, 7). Within the socio-legal method we employ the legal method and the method of document analysis of non-legal documents, that

E. Zmyvalova (✉) · H. Outakoski
Umeå University, Umeå, Sweden
e-mail: ekaterina.zmyvalova@umu.se

© The Author(s) 2019
O. Kortekangas et al. (eds.), *Sámi Educational History in a Comparative International Perspective*,
https://doi.org/10.1007/978-3-030-24112-4_7

both seek causal connections in the data. With the help of the legal analysis of the current situation, we show that there is a discrepancy between the legal regulation of the Sámi language teaching, and the reality in school.

The RF, through its participation in many international treaties, provides formal prerequisites for the right of Indigenous children to learn their mother tongue. Moreover, the national legislation also stipulates some additional support for this right. In practice, however, the legal provisions seem to have more of an aesthetic character because no educational obligations follow from the legal commitments, nor does there seem to be a political will to change the situation so as to ensure that the right to mother tongue education is respected.

The situation is further complicated due to the fact that the teaching of the language in the Lovozero School takes the form of an extracurricular after school activity. Besides being an extracurricular activity, the Sámi language learning is subsumed in a subject that rather focuses on the cultural and historic development of the Sámi people, than on language learning aspects. Current changes in learner demography and in the curricular content seem to coincide with diminished interest, or will, to attend the Sámi educational program.

In this article, we aim to define the contents of Indigenous children's right to learn their native language in Russian schools by analysing an integral regulatory framework that is based on the provisions of international law and the national legislation of Russia. We describe the trajectory of the Sámi language education in the Lovozero School from the end of nineteenth century to the organizational and attitudinal breaking point experienced during the school year 2016–2017. We also present an initial analysis of the reasons that have led to the organizational and attitudinal breaking point.

Following this introductory part, section "The Sámi in Russia" offers a brief summary of the current Sámi statistics in Russia. Section "Relevant International and National Legal Acts" explores briefly the most relevant sources of international and federal legislation regarding the right in focus, and it also determines the elements of this right. Section "The Sámi Language Teaching in the Lovozero School" presents a brief historic review on the Sámi language learning in the village of Lovozero and discusses the current situation in the last remaining Sámi school context in Russia. The final section provides concluding remarks.

The Sámi in Russia

The ancient and traditional land of the Sámi people spans a geographical area that is administrated and politically controlled by Russia, Sweden, Norway and Finland. Many Sámi live outside the traditional Sámi settlement area today. The population censuses and the official numbers of Sámi voters provided by the Sámi Parliaments imply that there are between 50,000 and 100,000 Sámi descendants in total. Another estimate is that roughly only every fifth Sámi still has a linguistic connection to their native Sámi language (Outakoski 2015, 7). Most of the active speakers of the Sámi language speak North Sámi, which is the largest of the nine surviving varieties.

According to the results of the latest Russian Population Census from the year 2010, there were 1771 Sámi residents in the RF (Federal State Statistics Service 2010). In Russia, the Sámi have traditionally inhabited the territory of the MO (Vinogradova = Виноградова 2005, 424). According to the latest census, 1599 Sámi residents still live in the Murmansk area, although some also live in the St. Petersburg area (Scheller 2011, 87). The MO includes different territorial entities. One of them is the Lovozero district, which in turn includes the urban settlement of Revda and the four villages of Lovozero, Kanevka, Krasnoshchelye, and Sosnovka (see Map 7.1).

According to Vinogradova (2005, 424) and the official statistics, the majority of the Russian Sámi population now lives in the village of Lovozero, which in 2010 had a total population of 3161 people. The centralization of the Sámi population to the Lovozero village is to a large extent due to the collectivization policy of the former Soviet Russia. To consolidate rural settlements, the peasant households of the Kildin Sámi and part of the Iokanga Sámi were relocated to Lovozero from different settlements on the Kola Peninsula (Galkina = Галкина et al. 2010, 35). Scheller (2011, 87) has described the Lovozero district

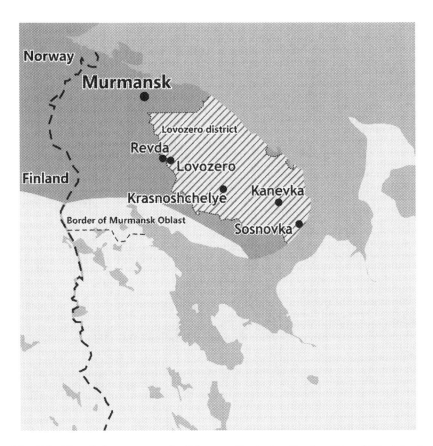

Map 7.1 The dark grey area in this map illustrates the traditional Sámi territory, Sápmi, which extends from Scandinavia over to the Kola Peninsula in the east. The dotted line in the Kola Peninsula marks the borders of the territory of the Lovozero district. The MO shares a national border with Norway in the north and with Finland further south. (Copyright granted by Aleksei Larionov)

as being a multi-ethnic community, and the latest population census from 2010 shows that the Sámi make up about 8% ($n=873$) of the entire district population, and 23% ($n=725$) of the Lovozero village population (Federal State Statistics Service 2010).

According to Scheller, "[t]he Kola Sami languages belong to the Eastern Sami group of the Finno-Ugric language family and are traditionally divided into Kildin, Ter, Skolt and Akkala Sami" (2013, 397).

Kildin Sámi is numerically the largest of the Kola Sámi languages. In 2013, approximately 700 people were estimated to have some knowledge of the Kildin Sámi language (Scheller 2013, 396). In 2013, Kildin Sámi was used actively by around 100 Sámi over the age of 60, and there were approximately 200 less frequent or dormant language users belonging to the generation of people between 30 and 60 years old. In 2013, some younger people still had good passive knowledge of Kildin Sámi, but very few fluent mother-tongue speakers existed who were younger than 60 years. However, Scheller (personal communication, 28 August 2017) points out that the language situation among Kildin speakers has changed dramatically since 2013. By 2018, several of the elder generation speakers have passed away causing severely diminished possibilities for remaining speakers to use the language actively. Scheller now estimates that there are between 20 and 30 elderly speakers who use Kildin Sámi actively in their everyday lives, and that the recent negative changes in the speaker demography are rapidly erasing language circuits and the connections that allow daily language usage between speakers. When linked to the Graded Intergenerational Disruption Scale (GIDS) (Fishman 1991, 81–121), it becomes clear that the language community is struggling against the odds as the eighth stage of the GIDS (Fishman 1991, 88–89), when the grandparents are the only active speakers, is rapidly evolving into a stage where no active speakers exist. From the educational point of view, the situation has been alarming for quite a while. Language speakers are getting older, which reduces the number of potential teachers, authors, school material producers and kindergarten workers who can still pass the language on to the young. We observe the consequences of these rapid speaker demographic changes in the Russian Sápmi, and the situation must be considered as critical.

Relevant International and National Legal Acts

There are both binding and non-binding sources of international law that proclaim the right of Indigenous children to learn their native language in school as a fundamental human right. Since the list of legal documents considered in this chapter is extensive, we have chosen to present the relevant sources in an attachment rather than in text (see Attachment 1).

Zmyvalova (2015) demonstrates that the sources of international law are interrelated and constitute an integral regulatory framework for the right in focus. The unity of the framework suggests the following core elements of the right in focus:

1. the right of Indigenous children to learn their native language in school must be guaranteed by the State,
2. the State should create the necessary basis for children to realize this right at all levels and forms of education,
3. the realization of this right must be carried out without discrimination,
4. this right must be realized in an effective way, and
5. the establishment and realization of this right must be carried out in such a way that the opinion of the Indigenous peoples is taken into consideration.

Many, although not all, of the international sources have been signed and ratified by the RF. However, this fact does not prove the RF's obligation to enforce all of the elements of the right that are listed here. International monitoring bodies, such as Human Rights Committee (CCPR) and Committee on the Rights of the Child (CRC), have repeatedly stated that the provisions of international law regarding the rights of Indigenous peoples are not fully implemented into the Russian legislation.

When the international law is not fully implemented in the Russian legislation, it is important to look at whether the national legislation has created the relevant framework for the realization of the right in focus. The legal regulation of the right of Indigenous children to learn their mother tongue in the RF is carried out at the federal, regional and local or school levels (see Attachment 1 for the relevant provisions at federal and regional levels). Federal laws create the framework, while federal executive bodies both specify and clarify the provisions of the federal legislation. Within the sphere of their competence, the subjects of the

Federation regulate the same issue to the extent it is not regulated by the federal legislation.

The educational sphere belongs to the joint competence of the RF and the subjects of the RF. Therefore, the legislation of the MO regulates those educational issues that are not regulated by the federal legislation. The state authorities of the MO adopt and implement state programs and departmental target programs. These programs can provide for the following: creating the necessary conditions in educational institutions for studying the native language of the indigenous small-numbered peoples; opening of small-scale schools in the areas of residence of the indigenous small-numbered peoples in the MO; providing the appropriate material and technical support to educational organizations that carry out native language teaching for the indigenous small-numbered peoples; preparing and publishing of curricula, textbooks, teaching, aids, and dictionaries; improving the systems of training pedagogical personnel for teaching the native language of the indigenous small-numbered peoples; and supporting the development of optimal forms of education for the children of the indigenous small-numbered peoples, including boarding schools that organize education for children by family type.

Currently, there is no law on the preservation of the Sámi language in the MO, although there have been plenty of initiatives for the adoption of such a law. In some other regions of the RF where Indigenous peoples reside, legislation has been established for the preservation of Indigenous peoples' languages. For example, there is the law on the preservation of the Nenets language in the NAO. Despite the fact that there is no law on the preservation of the Sámi language, the analysis above shows that the formal legal basis for the preservation of the Indigenous languages, Sámi included, has been created and that the basic framework should in theory support the right of Sámi children to learn their mother tongue in school in the MO.

We argue, that for effective realization of the right, there must be legal guarantees in the national legislation at federal and local levels. The federal provisions contain the first four elements of the right in focus (Zmyvalova 2015, 160). The fifth element concerning the establishment and realization of the right in focus given the opinion of the

Indigenous peoples, is partly touched upon in the federal legislation, and is also included partly in the regional legislation. Therefore it can be said that all five elements of the right in focus are present in the national legislation, thus fulfilling the prerequisite for the effective realization of the right.

Close reading of the legal provisions shows, however, that the legislator makes a reservation for the executive bodies to depart from this responsibility whenever the realization of the right is not deemed practically possible. An example of this can be a situation in which the community needs an educated language teacher for the mother tongue tuition, but such a specialist is not available. The state can in practice support language community initiatives, but since there is no obligation to assist in organizing teacher-training programs or in-service education, the state can use the lack of teachers as an excuse to depart from its legal obligations. Also, only two laws regulate languages in the RF (the laws of 25.10.1991 N 1807-1 and 01.06.2005 N 53-FZ, see Attachment 1). There are no explicit provisions on the languages of indigenous small-numbered peoples in these laws. Instead, these two laws provide a substantial basis to support the status of the Russian language in most educational and social spheres, and the non-mentioning of Indigenous languages renders them invisible in this important legal context.

There are three educational levels in Russian schools that are regulated by a separate ministerial order (Article 10 (4) of the FL 'On Education in the RF', see Attachment 1). These are:

1. primary general education (*nachal'noe obshchee obrazovanie*);
2. basic general education (*osnovnoe obshchee obrazovanie*); and
3. secondary general education (*srednee obshchee obrazovanie*).

Of these three, only the first level is of relevance when it comes to education of Sámi children in their heritage language, since the extracurricular Sámi classes end already after the fourth grade in primary school.

The Russian educational system suggests that Indigenous children or other minorities can receive one of three kinds of tuition forms. In the first form everything is taught in Russian and there are no separate lessons for the minority group in their heritage language nor in their own culture. In some autonomic parts of RF, the language of tuition can also be the language of the people in that autonomic state, but this is only an option in a few cases. The formal tuition for Sámi children in Lovozero is organized in Russian. Teaching in the minority language and culture is organized as an extracurricular after school activity that takes place when regular lessons are finished, and the program is titled "Language and its history, culture and folklore of the Sámi people".

The Sámi Language Teaching in the Lovozero School

The previous section has described the contents of the Sámi children's right to their mother tongue in school according to international law and the Russian national legislation. Now we will turn to the description of the Sámi language teaching in the Lovozero School because it reflects the realization of the right. The Lovozero School is at present the only Russian state school that offers Sámi language education to Sámi children. This section starts with a description of the trajectory of the Lovozero School and the Sámi education there, and it continues with an initial analysis of changes in the curricular content of the Sámi subject. Although explanatory research in this area is one of our main goals in the future, the following section is to a large part descriptive rather than analytical.

The Trajectory of Sámi Education in Lovozero

The first school in Lovozero was opened in November 1890 (Arkhangelsk 1890, 104–105), and the main language of tuition in this school was Russian. According to the information published in the *Arkhangelskie Eparkhialnye Vedomosti* (Arkhangelsk Eparchial Journal) in 1904, Lovozero was a central Sámi village and therefore a "convenient place to open a grammar school" (Rozov = Розов 1904, 593).

Two years after the school's opening, the priest who was the first teacher at the school left Lovozero, and the school closed

(Tupitskaya = Тупицкая 2015, 3). However, a year later the school was reopened, and Ivanov, a first-grade student at the theological seminary, became the teacher at the school. A lot later, in his novel *Kolskaya Zemlya* (The Kola Land), Ivan Ushakov (1972, 462) describes the Lovozero School as a very rustic and small-sized building. Due to the shortcomings of the initial school building, all school activities were later moved to the church lounge (Rozov = Розов 1904, 596). In 1896 the entire church property burnt down, and the inhabitants opened a new grammar school themselves. The lessons were held in the new church lounge by a local psalm-reader (Rozov = Розов 1904, 595), and later in his apartment (Tupitskaya = Тупицкая 2015).

In 1898 the school was expanded to include a classroom, a teacher's apartment, a kitchen (which was also used as a bedroom for pupils), and a small room for the night guard and domestic animals. That same year the school obtained the status of a parish school. The length of the school year depended on when the pupil population was in Lovozero. Due to the nomadic lifestyle of the residents, this ranged between 94 and 125 days. Classes began in autumn when the people came from the lakes to stay over the winter in the central Sámi villages (Kharuzin = Харузин 1890, 98). Classes finished in April when the Sámi left for the tundra.

Nikolai Kozmin described the ethnic composition of the school as a mix of Sámi, Samoyeds, two Russians, and 19 Zyrians. In the same passage, Kozmin also asserted that the reason for the low number of Sámi pupils was believed to be a feud between the Sámi and the Zyrians (Kozmin 1912, 21). In 1917 the school was renamed a primary school, and 70 children studied there. In 1922 the school began also to teach the adult population. In 1929, the Lovozero primary school was transformed into a seven-year school.

In 1960, the officials in Lovozero adopted a decision to open an eight-year boarding school in Lovozero with 180 places for the children whose parents roamed the tundra. The boarding school was opened in October 1960. Since that same year, there existed two schools in Lovozero—a boarding school and a secondary school. Later, the boarding school was made into a regional school, which meant that not only children of Lovozero parents who roamed the tundra studied there, but

7 The Development of Sámi Children's Right to Learn Sámi ... 115

also all the teenagers who did not have an opportunity to go to school in their home residence.

Very little is known about the teaching in Sámi language in the earlier history of the school. Initially, Sámi language may have played a role of a support language for those children who did not know Russian when they came to school, although the language of tuition has for most part been Russian. During the Soviet era, however, Sámi language was not taught in the Lovozero boarding school. Bolshakova (2005, 178) remarks that "[i]n 1976 the Lovozero boarding school got permission to resume the Sámi language teaching". This decision was put into force in 1977 (Bolshakova = Большакова 2005, 234).

In 1994 the Lovozero boarding school was renamed the Lovozero National Secondary Boarding School. The school had this status until 31 December 2002. According to Bolshakova, the Sámi language was being taught only in the primary school of the Lovozero boarding school (Bolshakova = Большакова 2005, 178). The Sámi language was also taught as a facultative subject at the school. From the 1990s until 2013 the Sámi language was taught as an extracurricular educational activity, and the course was named "The Sámi language", thus having a clear linguistic or language learning orientation.

The Period Between 2010 and Today

In 2010, the schools for Sámi pupils in the Lovozero area were united into one single school. For three years, the new school had the status of a boarding school, and since 2014 it has had the status of a general municipal school carrying the official name Lovozero Secondary General Educational School.

In the school year 2013–2014, the Sámi educational activity received the name "Language and its history, culture and folklore of the Sámi people". Currently, the new subject is taught at this school as an extracurricular activity for a maximum of 45 minutes per week. This activity is not included into the school curriculum and is not part of the obligatory educational program (See Table 7.1).

116 E. Zmyvalova and H. Outakoski

Table 7.1 Provision of the Sámi language and culture teaching in the Lovozero School from 2009 to 2017 showing the change in the content of the extra-curricular subject and in the school form that changed from a boarding school to a municipal school

Extra-curricular activity (*kruzhok*) "The Sámi language"			Extra-curricular activity (*kruzhok*) "Language and its history, culture and folklore of the Sámi people"	
2009–2010	2010–2013		2013–2014	2014–2017
Lovozero boarding school	Lovozero boarding school		Municipal school	
Municipal school				

In the Lovozero School, the tuition is carried out only in the Russian language. The Sámi language is taught as an extracurricular educational activity. However, during this activity the main language of instruction is Russian, and Sámi is used only occasionally.

The number of pupils who attend the Sámi classes is typically low, as shown in Table 7.2. At the Lovozero School, the extracurricular Sámi activity is proposed for pupils from grade one to four. The year 2010–2011 was an exception as four pupils in the fifth grade attended the Sámi class. Ten pupils in the second grade and 12 pupils in the mixed class group of third and fourth graders attended the extracurricular Sámi activity in the school year 2016–2017. Mixed classes mean that the teaching of the first and the second grades, or the third and the fourth grades, is carried out jointly. This is a common model also in the smaller Sámi schools in Nordic Countries, and is often applied since the number of children who want to learn the Sámi language varies from year to year. Joint classes are thus not a unique solution only in the Russian Sámi context. In smaller schools, mixed grades allow a more effective and economic use of teacher resources.

The year 2016–2017 deviates from the rest in one important respect. This was the first year when no first-grade pupils chose to attend the additional class "Language and its history, culture and folklore of the Sámi people". We believe that the numbers in Table 7.2 are a strong

7 The Development of Sámi Children's Right to Learn Sámi ...   117

Table 7.2 Pupils learning the Sámi language in the Lovozero School (2009–2017)

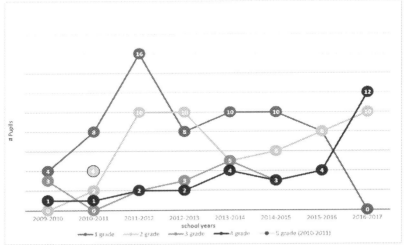

indicator of a breaking point for Sámi education and language education in Russian Sápmi. We can also see that in the school year 2011–2012, there was a peak in the number of new pupils attending the school as 16 pupils in the first grade were enrolled. However, 30% of these pupils did not attend this activity during the next school year.

In order to determine the reasons for this, a more elaborated study is needed. However, the preliminary observations from a visit to the Lovozero School together with personal communication with Elisabeth Scheller indicate that the situation is rather desperate. We have found that the school has problems finding willing and competent teachers. In addition, the status of the Sámi activity is low because it is arranged as an extracurricular subject. The program targets the youngest learners, but the late after-school hours do not attract this group of pupils. Furthermore, English is seen as potentially more beneficial than the native language. Finally, the changes in the content of the curriculum seem to go along with the diminishing interest in the Sámi subject as the subject has gone from being primarily a language subject into a subject with very little focus on the language.

Changing Curricular Content

The curricular breaking point for the Sámi subject in Russia can be traced back to the year 2014, when the initial "Sámi language" program was replaced by a program called "The language and its history, culture and folklore of the Sámi people". The first educational program that was in use until 2014, focused on the Sámi language as such. After finishing program, the pupils were expected to, for example, receive and understand instructions in Sámi, to produce speech and to participate in dialogues, and to read and write Sámi with the help of a dictionary.

In the program for the subject "The language and its history, culture and folklore of the Sámi people" that replaced the language subject in 2014, language receives a more peripheral role. Sámi language is now subsumed in a larger package that includes history, culture and folklore. Thus, the pupils in the class use their 45 minutes a week on many different tasks of which only few include linguistic, oral or textual stimuli. The linguistic contents of the new course include vocabulary knowledge of common topics and some limited conversational skills.

We observe and point out that there has occurred a shift from a linguistically oriented subject to a more culturally oriented subject. The language teaching part of the course has changed from a more holistic language subject to a limited training of vocabulary and oral skills. The changes in the curricular content coincide with the changes in pupil numbers as the number of pupils attending the extracurricular activity has decreased since 2014 when the new curricular subject was adopted at the school.

Taking into account that the Sámi language subject is non-obligatory, and the children do not always attend the classes, it seems hardly possible to achieve the expected learning outcomes in the current educational program. There is very little time for language learning, but the cultural content that is important for the development of a cultural identity also receives too little attention when the different aspects of the educational content are left to compete over the very limited time. At the best, the Sámi pupils receive around 40 hours of teaching in this subject per year (45 minutes per week). We estimate that less than half of the time is used for language learning. The actual learning outcomes of such a program cannot come anywhere near the outcomes of a program designed to strengthen and give a child a mother tongue. Furthermore, the contents of the educational program for Sámi learners are the same for all four grades, that is, there are no separated learning outcomes for different grades. Thus, although the calendar-thematic planning for each grade may be different, the learning outcomes are described for the entire program. Due to the fact that no separate learning outcomes are stated for different grades, it is hard to evaluate what level of knowledge children of different grades should have and how they should be assessed in different grades.

We conclude that although the legal analysis demonstrates that Indigenous children in Russia, Sámi children included, have legal guarantees to learn their mother tongue, the school practice shows that the provided learning opportunities do not contribute to the realization of these legal guarantees. We have also seen that the states, in this case Russia, are able to depart from the responsibilities that the legal framework places on them by playing a passive role in the revitalization of the threatened languages. This is done, for example, by not contributing to the expansion of linguistic and cultural programs in schools, and by not arranging teacher education for the communities that are in need of such educational support.

Concluding Remarks

The analysis conducted in this chapter shows a discrepancy between the legal regulation of the Sámi language teaching and the real situation at the Lovozero School. The Sámi languages in Russian Sápmi are at their final breaking point, and the analysis of the current educational situation shows that without governmental support and community initiatives the breaking point will take us beyond a point of no return. We concur with the monitoring bodies and claim that passive attitudes often equal aggressive attitudes when we are talking about Indigenous minorities here and elsewhere in the world.

Attachment 1: The Relevant Sources of International, Federal and Regional Law

International Law

The following are the relevant binding sources:

- Article 5 (1.c) of the United Nations Educational, Scientific and Cultural Organization (UNESCO) Convention Against Discrimination in Education (1960, entered into force May 22, 1962);
- Article 7 of the United Nations (UN) International Convention on the Elimination of All Forms of Racial Discrimination (1965, entered into force April 4, 1969);
- Article 27 of the UN International Covenant on Civil and Political Rights—ICCPR (1966, entered into force March 23, 1976);
- Articles 28, 29, 30 of the UN Convention on the Rights of the Child—CRC (1989, entered into force September 2, 1990);
- Article 28 (1) of the Convention Concerning Indigenous and Tribal Peoples in Independent Countries—ILO 169 (1989, entered into force September 5, 1991);
- Article 14 of the Framework Convention for the Protection of National Minorities by the Council of Europe (1995, entered into force February 1, 1998);
- Article 8 of the European Charter for Regional or Minority Languages by the Council of Europe (1992, entered into force March 3, 1998).

The most relevant non-binding international sources are as follows:

- Article 4 (3) of the UN Declaration on the Rights of Persons Belonging to National or Ethnic, Religious and Linguistic Minorities (December 18, 1992);
- Article 14 (2, 3) of the UN Declaration on the Rights of Indigenous Peoples – UNDRIP (September 13, 2007).

Federal Legislation

- Articles 26 (2) and 68 of the Constitution;
- Articles 3 (1, 2) and 3 (1, 7) of the FL of 29.12.2012 N 273-FZ 'On Education in the RF';
- Article 9 of the FL of 24.07.1998 N 124-FZ 'On Basic Guarantees of the Rights of the Child';
- Article 10 of the FL of 30.04.1999 N 82-FZ 'On Guarantees of the Rights of Indigenous Small-Numbered Peoples of the RF';
- Article 10 of the FL 17.06.1996 N 74-FZ 'On National-Cultural Autonomy';
- Article 2 of the law of 25.10.1991 N 1807-1 'On Languages of the People of the RF'.

Regional Legislation

- the Charter of the MO;
- the Law of the MO (2013) of 28.06.2013 N 1649-01-ZMO 'On Education in the MO';
- the Law of the MO (2008) of 20.06.2008 N 984-01-ZMO 'On the State Support for the Indigenous Small-Numbered Peoples of the North of the MO that Carry out Traditional Economic Activities'.

References

Arkhangelsk, E. (1890). Школьный отдел [Educational Department]. *Архангельские Епархиальные Ведомости* [Arkhangelsk Eparchial Journal], 104–105.

Bolshakova = Большакова, N. (2005). *Жизнь, обычаи и мифы кольских саамов в прошлом и настоящем* [Life, Customs and Myth of the Kola Sámi in the Past and the Present]. Murmansk: Мурманское областное книжное издательство [Murmansk Regional Publishing House].

CCPR = Concluding Observations of the Human Rights Committee. Russian Federation (CCPR/C/RUS/CO/6).

CRC = Concluding Observations on the Combined Fourth and Fifth Periodic Reports of the Russian Federation (CRC/C/RUS/CO/4-5).

Federal State Statistics Service. (2010). Информационные материалы об окончательных итогах Всероссийской переписи населения 2010 года, Приложение № 7, Национальный состав населения Российской Федерации [Information Materials on the Final Results of the Russian Population Census 2010, Appendix 7, National Composition of the Population of the RF].

Fishman, J. A. (1991). *Reversing Language Shift*. Clevedon, UK: Multilingual Matters.

Galkina = Галкина, E. A., Sharshina = Шаршина, N. S., Maksimenko = Максименко, O. A., Ушакова, Н. С., Данилова, С. С., Медведева, М. Г., et al. (2010). Пути развития языков коренных малочисленных народов Севера [The Ways of Development of the Languages of Indigenous Small-Numbered Peoples of the North]. *Science and Business in Murman, 69*, 35–44.

Hydén, H., & Wickenberg, P. (2008). *Contributions in Sociology of Law: Remarks from a Swedish Horizon*. Lund: Lund Studies of Sociology of Law.

Kharuzin = Харузин, N. (1890). *Русские лопари (очерки прошлого и современного быта)* [The Russian Sámi (The Essays of the Past and the Modern Life)]. Moscow: Высочайше утвержденное Товарищество скоропечатни А. А. Левенсон [The Imperially Approved Partnership Printing House of A. A. Levingston].

Kozmin = Козмин, N. (1912). *По школам Лапландии (Дневник наблюдателя)* [Around the Schools of Lapland (The Diary of the Observer)]. St. Petersburg: синодальная типография [The Synodal Printing House].

Outakoski, H.(2015). *Multilingual Literacy Among Young Learners of North Sámi: Contexts, Complexity and Writing in Sápmi* (Doctoral dissertation). Umeå University, Umeå.

Rozov = Розов, P. (1904). Ловозерская миссионерская церковно-приходская школа (краткие исторические сведения) [The Lovozero Missionary Parish School (Brief Historical Information)]. *Архангельские Епархиальные Ведомости* [Arkhangelsk Eparchial Journal], 593–598.

Scheller, E. (2011). Samisk språkrevitalisering i Ryssland: möjligheter och utmaningar. *NOA Norsk Som Andrespråk, 27*(1), 86–119.

Scheller, E. (2013). Kola Sami Language Revitalization—Opportunities and Challenges. In K. Andersson (Ed.), *L'Image Du Sápmi II: Études Compares* (pp. 392–421). Örebro: Örebro University.

7 The Development of Sámi Children's Right to Learn Sámi ...

Tupitskaya = Тупицкая, Т. (2015). Ловозерской школе – 125! [The Lovozero School Is 125 Years Old!]. Ловозерская Правда Lovozerskaya Pravda 3.

Ushakov = Ушаков, I. (1972). *Кольская земля: Очерки истории Мурманской области в дооктябрьский период* [The Kola Land: Essays on the History of the Murmansk Oblast in the Pre October Period]. Murmansk: Кн. изд-во [Murmansk Publishing House].

Vinogradova = Виноградова, S. (2005). Саамы Кольского полуострова: основные тенденции современной жизни [The Sámi of the Kola Peninsula: The Main Tendencies of the Contemporary Life]. In Kalinnikova = V. Калинникова and Vinogradova = S. Виноградова (Eds.), *Формирование Основ Современной Стратегии Природопользования в Евро-Арктическом Регионе* [Formation of the Basis of the Modern Strategy of Nature Use in Euro-Arctic Region]. Апатиты [Apatity]: Изд. КНЦ РАН [KSC RAS Publishing House].

Zmyvalova, E. (2015). Indigenous Children's Right to Learn Their Mother Tongue at School: Implementation and Realization in Russia. *Arctic Review on Law and Politics, 6,* 151–174.

8

Sámi Issues in Norwegian Curricula: A Historical Overview

Torjer A. Olsen

If you are to be a teacher in Norway, you have to have knowledge—and be able to teach—about Sámi and indigenous issues. In fact, the most recent overarching part of the national curriculum states that all students within the Norwegian school system should have an indigenous perspective integrated in their understanding of democracy. Part of the rationale for this is Norway's obligation to national law and international treaties on the rights of indigenous people.

In societies where the states have committed themselves through national law, treaties, constitution, and/or international declarations like ILO-169 (International Labour Organization, Treaty on the rights of indigenous and tribal peoples) or the UN Declaration on the Rights of Indigenous Peoples (UNDRIP), there is a supposed guarantee for Indigenous people to be recognized and have an education on their own premises. Using the mainstreaming approach, I argue that the legal foundation and

T. A. Olsen (✉)
Centre for Sámi Studies,
UiT the Arctic University of Norway, Tromsø, Norway
e-mail: torjer.olsen@uit.no

© The Author(s) 2019
O. Kortekangas et al. (eds.), *Sámi Educational History in a Comparative International Perspective*,
https://doi.org/10.1007/978-3-030-24112-4_8

recognition should imply that also the majority society can learn from and needs knowledge of Indigenous people and minorities in general, and of Indigenous people and minorities in or related to the community.

This recognition of the rights of Indigenous people and of the right to education has not always been the case. Until the 1970s, the role of the educational system in Norway had mainly been to take part in a system of colonization and assimilation.

In this article, I present an overview of the different national curricula for Early Childhood Education (ECE), primary school, and secondary school, focusing on Sámi and indigenous issues. My aim is to look at the curricular representation of Sámi and indigenous issues, as well as at how this has changed over the years. My first task is to look for dominant trends and major changes from 1974 to 2017. My second task is to discuss how the different curricula deal with and treat Sámi and indigenous issues today. My third task is to discuss whether today's situation and policy represent a complete makeover within Norwegian educational policy on Sámi and indigenous issues. The overview is based on the more specific analyses done in previous works (Andreassen and Olsen 2017; Olsen and Andreassen 2017, 2018; Olsen et al. 2017). Combining the analysis of the different curricula has not been done earlier, neither by me nor other scholars.

The methods used are mainly curriculum analysis (cf. Goodlad 1979; Gundem 1990), inspired by discourse analysis (Buras and Apple 2006; Olsen and Andreassen 2017). I seek to analyze the discourse of the Sámi and indigenous people in the curricula as they appear in related documents within one particular sector of public domain. This means looking for which concepts are used, any collocations with other terms and concepts, and the connections to broader discourses. I look for broader tendencies and potentially changing discourses. At the same time, I realize that I may miss some of the finer points of each curriculum.

I argue that there are three main periods relevant for the scope of this article. The first period goes from the early 1970s to 1987, and covers the first national curricula, the ECE act of 1975 and the national curriculum of 1987. The second period goes from 1988 to 1997, and starts out outside the curricular discourse per se, as it refers to the constitutional changes and the ratification of ILO-169. It moves on to the second ECE Act and the first ECE curriculum of 1995, as well as to the curriculum for upper secondary school from 1994 and the new national curriculum in 1997, which for the first time included a Sámi curriculum. The final period covers the ratification of the European Council's treaty on national minorities, moves on to the curricula of 2006, and goes all the way to the new general part of the curriculum of 2017.

There is not a lot of research on these issues. The national curricula in their particular outlooks and contexts are well studied. However, when it comes to Sámi issues, not much is done. The research on Sámi issues in ECE has focused on practice (cf. Storjord 2008), and has not looked into the curricula (except for Olsen and Andreassen 2016, 2017). The school curriculum is more researched. I lean to and look into the research of Keskitalo et al. (2013), Andreassen and Olsen (2015, 2017), Olsen and Andreassen (2018), Folkenborg (2008), Gjerpe (2017), Hirvonen (2004), and Solstad et al. (2012). Research combining ECE and school curricula is rare. Bergland (2001) is an exception.

Grand Narrative

The Sámi hold a status as an Indigenous people in Norway. This means that the Norwegian state has recognized the Sámi as a people that lives and dwells—and historically has lived and dwelled—in the same areas since before the current state borders were made. Further, in this understanding of Indigenous peoples that is found in international conventions, the Sámi are in a minority situation and have a language and a culture that distinguish them from the majority population.

Such an understanding of Indigenous peoples is to some extent contrary to a more common understanding of what being an Indigenous people means. In public debate on anything related to the Sámi in Norway, the question is often raised about who came first. In other regions around the world with Indigenous people, this is a rather easy question to answer. The many Native American groups, Indians or First Nations in the Americas clearly came before the Europeans. As did the Māori of Aotearoa/New Zealand and the Aboriginals and Torres Strait Islanders of Australia. In a Nordic and Sámi context, the case is more complex. People

128   T. A. Olsen

have lived in many parts of what is today Sápmi/Sábme/Saepmie (here, the three official Sámi languages Northern Sámi, Lule Sámi and Southern Sámi are used to name the land of the Sámi), Norway, Sweden, Finland and Russia in more than 10,000 years. However, we do not know which ethnic identity/-ies these first inhabitants had. Strictly speaking, it does not even matter much for the understanding of Indigenous peoples.

An important side of history is no matter what that if you are to talk about colonization in a Sámi and Nordic context, it would have to be done in somewhat different forms and words than colonization as known in the aforementioned other contexts. To the Americas, Australia and Aotearoa/New Zealand, colonizers arrived at certain points of time in ships from Europe. In various ways and different scales, they aimed to take control of land, resources and people, leading to centuries of history of oppression, war and some places even genocide. For centuries in Sápmi/Sábme/Saepmie, people from different groups and ethnicities have been living side by side with each other, in neighbouring villages, areas and houses. Some places, like Målselv and Bardu, Norwegian settlers arrived in Sámi areas during the eighteenth and nineteenth centuries. Other places, people have wandered, as the Finnish or Kven coming to several places in the north, and as the Marka Sámi, moving from the Swedish to the Norwegian side of Sápmi/Sábme/Saepmie.

The recognition of the Sámi as a people living on the land since time immemorial was explicit in the Norway/Sweden border negotiation in the middle of the eighteenth century, manifested in the Lap Codicil. This clearly points towards what appears to have been a common way of looking at the Sámi and the relation to other peoples at the time (Pedersen 2008). However, this did not stop the Norwegian state (and the other states) to move on to colonize Sápmi/Sábme/Saepmie.

The Sámi of Norway and Educational History Until 1975

Schools—and entire educational systems—are excellent arenas for the implementation of state policy, especially when it comes to minorities and indigenous peoples (Smith 2017, 82). Schools are the state's tools to provide its inhabitants with the knowledge and ways of getting knowledge that are defined as the most important. Thus, schools and education are tools for reproduction of ideology and for making policies come into reality. The experiences of indigenous peoples tell about challenges both on local and global levels. Educational systems tend to be based on the majorities, on the mainstream. The experiences of indigenous peoples worldwide clearly tell the story of school and education as main arenas for colonization, assimilation and the communication of states' monocultural ideologies. In recent years, however, schools seem also to have the potential for being arenas of decolonization and revitalization. I will return to this.

History: Precolonization, Colonization, Assimilation

In Norway, history has shown several great changes since the beginning of the public school. The School Act of 1739 made it compulsory for all children to go to school. A main rationale for this was making all citizens able to read—the Bible. This coincides with the intensified colonization policy towards the Sámi, the indigenous people of the Nordic countries. A major part of colonization was Christian mission, with school as an important dimension. A century later, the school became the most efficient and important tool for the implementation of the assimilation (Norwegianization) policy that sought to make all minorities abandon their ethnic (and religiously dissident) identity and become Norwegian (and Christian). From the middle of the nineteenth century, the Sámi were one of several minorities who were more or less forbidden to speak their native tongue or learn about their own culture and history in school.

By the end of the second world war, the Norwegianization policy had primarily come to an end. The end of the war was in itself a catastrophe for the Sámi in the northernmost part of Norway. The losing German forces left the area using the scorched grounds tactic, leaving nothing but ruins behind. For many Sámi and Kven, this meant that their material culture was left in ruins. This clearly made it easier for many to follow the pressure from Norwegianization and become Norwegians. Thus, the Sámi societies went through major changes.

On a national level in Norway, assimilation policy had turned Norway into more of a unitary state getting more or less rid of the "problematic" minorities. The Sámi had become marginalized and exoticized, as shown in popular representations and textbooks. The diversity of the Sámi communities had, in the eyes of the public, turned into a reindeer herding culture that was almost part of nature. Within the national school, the Sámi seem to have had no place.

At the same time, there were forces within the Sámi communities working for the rights of the Sámi. The first wave of Sámi politics occurred in the beginning of the twentieth century, and crossed the borders of the states. The same happened with the second wave of Sámi politics, with the establishment of the Nordic Sámi Council in 1956. This was a factor when Sámi activists took part in the beginning of international Indigenism from the 1970s onwards. Within the school system, traces of the impact of Sámi activism can be seen in the first national curricula as the pressure given by politicians of the Parliament (Olsen and Andreassen 2018). Within educational research on Sámi issues, there is a movement towards creating and articulating a Sámi pedagogy, which is culture-sensitive and takes the life and experiences of Sámi children as a starting point (Keskitalo et al. 2013).

1970–1987: From Ignorance to Inclusion

In 1974, Norway made its first official national curriculum. New versions of the national curriculum came in 1987, 1994, 1997 and 2006. In 2017, the core curriculum, or the introduction or "overarching part", of a new curriculum was ratified, with a completely new curriculum coming in 2020. All the curricula have had a core. This part is directed towards the ideological and value-based basis of the curriculum. Thus, it is highly relevant as a source to knowledge about the state's official policy and ideas about different issues. As an ideological text, the core curriculum reflects society and social changes.

The preface of the 1974 curriculum gives an insight into the process of making the curriculum, and states that issues related to Sámi society have been discussed on top national level. The covering of Sámi culture and history was strengthened throughout the plan because of requests from the Parliament (Stortinget) (Curriculum of 1974, 4). This can be seen as a change in the political climate regarding Sámi issues, and as a sign of the impact of Sámi activism. However, the Sámi are still mainly marginalized throughout the curriculum.

When talking about Sámi issues, the curriculum mainly talks about Sámi students as students living and attending school in "mixed language districts" (språkblandingsdistrikter, my translation). This could potentially cover students from several groups, but from the context it is clearly the case that it deals with Sámi students. The situation for these students is described as challenging on several levels: Many students have to live in boarding schools, many are not used to books, they can be afraid of using two languages, and they may have bigger contact issues than other students. To face these challenges, the school is described as a key (Curriculum of 1974, 18).

Throughout the 1974 curriculum, the covering of Sámi issues is mainly related to the situation of Sámi students in school. The curriculum says hardly anything about the need for majority students to learn about Sámi issues. With one exception, that is: In the social studies syllabus for year 8, there is one point stating that the students should learn about generational conflicts in Sámi homes caused by the Norwegianization of the young ones (Curriculum of 1974, 186). This rather specific statement is interesting both because it is directed towards all students and because it brings in the bigger narrative of Norwegianization and its effects (Folkenborg 2008, 45).

In 1975, Norway launched its first ECE Act as a result of the rapid growth in the number of kindergartens. This first ECE Act said nothing about Sámi issues, the Sámi communities or Sámi children.

Between 1974 and 1987, the Norwegian society went through big changes of continuous modernization and urbanization, institutionalized immigration, and on the financial side. Changes did also occur when it comes to the Norwegian policy towards the Sámi.

The Alta case (1979–1981), the building of a power dam in a Sámi area, led to huge protests from both environmentalists and Sámi activists. In the aftermath of this conflict, big changes were made in Norway (Minde 2003). In the decades following the Alta conflict, Norway went through a rather radical change in its politics towards the Sámi and minorities. The Sámi Act of 1987 made Sámi an official language. The Sámi Article was introduced to the Norwegian Constitution in 1988, stating that Norway is obligated to ensure that the Sámi people can keep and develop their language, culture and society. The Sámi Parliament opened in 1989. In 1990, Norway ratified the ILO Convention 169 about the rights of indigenous and tribal peoples, thereby recognizing the Sámi as an Indigenous people. Of the countries with a Sámi population, Norway is the only one that has ratified ILO's agreement on indigenous peoples.

In the 1980s, the Norwegian school system went through a massive overhaul. As part of this, a new curriculum came in 1987. The new curriculum reflected the changes in society, and intended to lead to pluralist integration, an approach clearly enabled by the increasingly diverse society.

The 1987 curriculum maintains a strong focus on Sámi students and their rights to be taught on basis of Sámi language and culture. The school is said to have a particular responsibility to take care of language and traditions. The curriculum further opens up a new curricular idea of mainstreaming, stating that all students should receive knowledge about Sámi culture (Olsen and Andreassen 2018).

As part of this bigger emphasis on Sámi issues, the core curriculum includes a chapter of its own on Sámi issues. This curriculum provides a recognition of the Sámi that is new within curricular contexts: "The Sámi hold a special position amongst the ethnic minorities of our land" (M-87, 18). This statement is interesting and has three main elements: First, there are several "ethnic minorities" in Norway. Second, the Sámi hold a special position amongst these. Third, the Sámi belongs to the group of ethnic minorities, which implies that the Sámi is not to be recognized as an indigenous people.

Following this, the 1987 curriculum expresses the presence of several ethnic groups in Norway, stating that Norwegian society is part of a global community. Describing Norwegian heritage, the curriculum adds that minority groups need to have a place in school. "Ethnic minority" is a key word here, and includes groups that later will be labelled indigenous people, national minorities and cultural minorities. At the same time, the concept of "language minorities" is still in use, alongside the term "immigrant".

From 1974 to 1987, "immigrants" replaced "Alien workers" as a term. In dealing with this category, the 1987 curriculum uses a resource perspective (Olsen and Andreassen 2018). Those coming from other cultures and other parts of the world are presented as someone who can teach us something important. Thus, "immigrant students" are presented as a resource that can serve the common good. Further, this implies an important distinction between "us" and "the others", between the Norwegian community and those coming from the outside. Immigrant students, despite being part of the school system, are not included fully in the curriculum version of Norwegian community.

The 1987 curriculum, with its emphasis on the others coming both from the outside and from within state borders, is a text of quite outspoken Othering. Othering implies presenting a group of people as fundamentally different than another. As process or strategy, Othering implies the reproduction and accumulation of power structures (Moreton-Robinson 2000). When a curriculum is Othering different minority groups, it is a powerful expression of the hegemonic discourse of a state struggling with what to do with diversity (Olsen and Andreassen 2018).

1988–1997: Towards a Sámi Curriculum

The 1990s also included a curricular reform. The core curriculum was introduced in 1993, and was to become the core curriculum to both upper secondary school curriculum (1994) and the primary school curriculum (1997). This text is a highly ideological document with an ambitious (and slightly pretentious) style. The seven parts of the document all refer to a "human type" and look into different dimensions of Norwegian school and society.

Sámi issues are mentioned in one of the seven, "The spiritual human being". Here, Sámi language and culture are located as part of the shared national heritage, for which Norway has a special responsibility. Later, the mainstreaming dimension is repeated, stating that all primary school students should have knowledge about Sámi culture and society.

In 1995, a new ECE Act was made, including the first national ECE curriculum. This brought ECE fully into the educational system. Regarding indigenous issues, the 1995 Curriculum stated that Norway has a special responsibility for its own indigenous group of people ("urbefolkningsgruppe", our translation), based on the Sámi Act and the ILO-169. The curriculum added a new concept of "Sámi kindergarten", meaning kindergartens for Sámi children in Sámi municipalities. The paragraph on Norway's responsibility for the Sámi was mainly related to the Sámi kindergartens, not to mainstream society.

The multicultural society is an important aspect of the 1995 Curriculum. The Sámi culture was talked of as a minority culture alongside other minorities. When it comes to the challenges of multicultural society, the Sámi were described as having a particular competence and responsibility: "Because the Sámi have an experience of being in a minority situation, they have a particular competence and responsibility for ensuring that other minority cultures in Norway have their cultural heritage safe-guarded and developed" (The Ministry of Education 1995, 105, my translation). Thus, the Sámi's experience and status as minority supposedly gives them a responsibility beyond that of other citizens. The state seems to attempt to transfer part of its obligation to support minority cultures to the Sámi. A statement of this kind clearly shows that the curriculum is including indigenous issues on the premises of majority society. There is an echo of Othering to be heard here: The different Others in Norwegian society must be able to learn from each other from the basic fact of being Others. In the process, they repeatedly redefined as The Other in Norwegian society. The 1995 curriculum clearly shows that the majority population's perspective, experience, and history are privileged (Buras and Apple 2006).

The concepts used in the 1995 ECE Curriculum highlight that Norway's recognition of the Sámi as indigenous is not fully mirrored in the curriculum. The concept of indigenous people ("urfolk") is not used despite the foundation in Acts and the ILO-169. This leaves an impression of ambiguity: Sámi culture is referred to as a part of Norwegian national heritage, and respect and tolerance towards the Sámi is a central value. Being an expression of recognition, this is at the same time an expression coming from the majority side. Including the Sámi in Norwegian national heritage is a way of communicating an asymmetrical relationship.

In 1997, a new national curriculum for the primary school was launched. This curriculum can be seen as an implementation of the ambitious ideology and goals of the 1993 core curriculum. The most noticeable when it comes to Sámi and minority issues was of course the creation of a parallel and equal Sámi curriculum in 1997, written in the North Sámi language. This was to be used by Sámi schools and Sámi students, that is, schools in municipalities within the Sámi administrative area. This was a major step for the recognition of Sámi rights and of huge political and symbolic importance. Finally, the Sámi could take a step outside of the shadow of marginalization and absence on the educational arena. In practice, a Sámi curriculum was not entirely different from the national curriculum. The core curriculum was the same. Some subjects had a particular curriculum or syllabus within the Sámi curriculum, making parts of the subjects different.

However, there is a question raised whether this led to something missing in the majority school curriculum. Kajsa Kemi Gjerpe (2017) argues that the majority curriculum seems to have less about Sámi issues than what could be expected when a particularly Sámi curriculum is launched at the same time. Mainly, it follows along the same lines as the 1987 curriculum. Further, there were quite a few Sámi children who would not be covered by the Sámi curriculum as they were going to school outside the area of the Sámi schools.

In the mainstream national curriculum of 1997, the words used about the diverse society changed from 1987. Instead of "immigrants", the 1993/1997 curriculum talks of "Norwegians with a different cultural background". In addition, the term diversity enters, reflecting a change of perspective to a more descriptive and less normative one. Thus, the resource dimension is downplayed.

1998–2017: Diversity and Indigenization

In 1999, Norway ratified the European Council's convention about the protection of national minorities, announcing the official status as national minority for the Forest Finns, the Kvens/Norwegian Finns, the Roma people, the travellers and the Jews. This institutionalized the differences between the different groups of people within the Norwegian society. The recognition of the Sámi as indigenous put them higher up on the ladder of rights than the National minorities, who were all granted rights.

Norway's ratification of the European Council's convention on the protection of the rights of national minorities was reflected in the curriculum. However, it took some time. When a new curriculum was launched in 2006, neither "indigenous people" nor "national minorities" were found in the short introduction added to the existing core curriculum of 1993. Thus, I will not dwell in 2006s primary school curriculum for long, only long enough to see the continuing tendency of a focus on cultural diversity and the multicultural society. There is more going on in the ECE sector.

In 2006, the government launched a new ECE curriculum. Some minor adjustments were made in 2011. I refer to the 2011 edition in the following. As in 1995, the Sámi are given a central mention in the beginning of the curriculum of 2011. This time around, the position of the Sámi is even stronger: "Norwegian society consists, in addition to the majority population, of the indigenous Sámi, the national minorities, and the immigrant minorities" (The Ministry of Education 2011, 8, my translation). This statement adds to the introductory claims that ECE is to be based on the Sámi Act and the ILO-169. The distinction between indigenous people, national minorities, and immigrant minorities shows a certain development since the 1995 curriculum. An aspect of this is a much clearer basis in treaties and a more precise terminology. In 2011, the Sámi is talked of unequivocally as an indigenous people and distinguished from the national and immigrant minorities.

The multicultural society is equally important in 2011 as in the previous edition of the ECE curriculum. However, the Sámi's particular experience and responsibility is not talked of any longer. Another important change from 1995 to 2011 is found with regards to mainstreaming. The responsibility to consider and take care of the interests of Sámi children and parents is now presented as valid no matter where the family lives (The Ministry of Education 2011, 24). Preserving and enabling the further development of the Sámi languages is noted as particularly important. In addition to the responsibility for Sámi children, the kindergarten also has a function for providing knowledge for the majority population. All children going to kindergarten should "[...] learn to know that the Sámi are the indigenous people of Norway, and get some knowledge of Sámi stories, tales, and other parts of Sámi culture and everyday life" (The Ministry of Education 2011, 47). This is an ambitious statement making it the responsibility of the whole ECE sector to provide knowledge about the Sámi to children regardless of where they live or go to kindergarten. It is easy to see this as a way of highlighting the implications of acts passed and treaties ratified. The Sámi's indigenous status commits the Norwegian state, as expressed in UNDRIP, ILO-169, and national law. The ECE sector is a part of this commitment with its institution and teachers (Olsen and Andreassen 2017).

In 2017, a completely new ECE curriculum was launched. Even though it is considered a complete makeover of the curriculum and the ECE sector as such, the changes concerning the Sámi are small. The curriculum represents a further institutionalization of the privileged position of the Sámi as indigenous, of the rights of Sámi children, and of the obligation of the Norwegian system to provide knowledge and attitudes related to the Sámi within the majority population.

In 2017, Norway also launched a new core curriculum for the school system as the first step in a process of a complete makeover of the national curriculum. Here, the groundwork and the principles of the coming curriculum were laid out, in a language and style quite different from its 1993 predecessor. The most remarkable change from previous curricula, from my point of view, is expressed through the way the Sámi and minorities are described and categorized. For the first time in the core of a national curriculum, the Sámi are explicitly recognized as an indigenous people with special rights as stated in the ILO-169 and the Constitution. In addition, the national minorities are for the first time on a curricular level recognized as such.

The Sámi's status as an Indigenous people is expressed and implied several places in the core curriculum. Sámi culture is a part of Norway's national heritage. The Constitution secures the rights of the Sámi to maintain and develop language, culture and society. To add to this rights dimension, there is also a mainstream or majority dimension. Through the school, the students should receive insight into and knowledge about the diverse history, culture, knowledge and rights of the indigenous Sámi people. This is quite an expansion of earlier goals set by a national curriculum. So is the citizenship dimension that the curriculum presents regarding democracy teaching: "A democratic society also defends indigenous peoples and minorities. An indigenous perspective is a part of what students should learn about democracy" (O-17, 9). This last statement implies moving on from knowledge to perspective as a goal. The ambition is high: All students of the Norwegian school system, regardless of where they go to school, should receive both knowledge about the Sámi as well as an ability to see and understand society from the position and/or viewpoint of an indigenous people (Olsen and Andreassen 2018).

Tendencies

A result of colonialism is that minorities are made and—further down the road—silenced, put into the margins, and even left out. The school system provides an arena for this—as it provides an arena for revisiting, revitalizing and retelling of what was marginalized and made invisible. For the Sámi in the Norwegian school system, both strategies or acts are seen.

In my analysis of how Sámi and indigenous issues are presented in Norwegian curricula, I see a tendency of Othering and silencing. Nonetheless, there have clearly been changes. This goes from absence and marginalization shown in early curricula, via active inclusion and indigenization in later curricula.

The national curricula for ECE and the school system are sources from which the state's policy on the Sámi can be found. As such, the slow changes of this policy are also made visible through a diachronic reading of 40 years of curricula. In 1974, the school curriculum talks of students in mixed language districts. The 1987 curriculum is launched

8 Sámi Issues in Norwegian Curricula: A Historical Overview   139

the same year as the Sámi Act and (but) shows (only) parts of this political shift. The legal, constitutional and internationally treaty-based changes of the late 1980s do take some time to be integrated into the curricula.

Looking at the ECE case, it is easy to see the changes made from 1996 to 2006, from the first to the second curriculum. The explicit commitment to recognize the Sámi as indigenous through the mainstream ECE curriculum dimension can be seen as an expression of indigenization. This is shown through the central positioning of Sámi and indigenous issues and through the basis in the Sámi Act and the ILO-169. The 2011 curriculum is made much more on the premises of the Sámi than was its predecessor: The Sámi people are explicitly talked of as indigenous, and there is an equally explicit recognition of Sámi language and knowledge as important. The ECE Curriculum is part of a bigger tendency of Norway's policy towards the Sámi. Even more concretely, the curriculum is part of the implementation of state policy.

Concepts used in curricula matter. Used in a national curriculum, a concept becomes fixated and institutionalized. Sámi students have been termed "students in mixed language districts", "ethnic minority", "Sámi students", and "indigenous".

The Norwegian school policy can be seen as having gone from a politics of integration to a politics of recognition (Seland 2013; Olsen and Andreassen 2018). The first is characteristic of the 1974 primary school curriculum, with the idea of the school as an arena for evening out social inequalities. From 1987 on, there is more of a politics of recognition, with its roots in multiculturalism. The current curricula for all levels are, however, more of a return to the politics of integration through their unifying diversity perspective and the claim to include an indigenous perspective for all. In further research and pedagogical development, I argue that there is a need to combine such perspectives and reflections with the growing body of Sámi pedagogy (Keskitalo et al. 2013).

140 T. A. Olsen

References

Andreassen, B.-O., & Olsen, T. A. (2015). Religionsfaget i videregående skole. En læreplanhistorisk gjennomgang 1976–2006. *Prismet 2*, 65–79.

Andreassen, B.-O., & Olsen, T. A. (2017). Hva skal vi med samisk innhold i læreplanene for religionsfagene? In S. Undheim & M. von der Lippe (Eds.), *Religion i skolen. Didaktiske perspektiver på religions- og livssynsfaget* (pp. 70–86). Oslo: Universitetsforlaget.

Bergland, E. (2001). *Samisk skole og samfunn. Plattform for pedagogisk utviklingsarbeid 4/2001*. Guovdageaidnu: Sámi instituhtta.

Buras, K. L., & Apple, A. (2006). The Subaltern Speak: Curriculum, Power, and Educational Struggles. In K. L. Buras & M. Apple (Eds.), *The Subaltern Speak: Curriculum, Power, and Educational Struggles* (pp. 1–42). New York: Routledge.

Folkenborg, H. R. (2008). *Nasjonal identitetsskaping i skolen. En regional og etnisk problematisering*. Tromsø: Eureka Forlag.

Gjerpe, K. K. (2017). Samisk læreplanverk – en symbolsk forpliktelse? *Nordic Studies in Education, 3–4*, 150–165.

Goodlad, J. I. (Ed.). (1979). *Curriculum Inquiry: The Study of Curriculum Practice*. New York: McGraw-Hill Book.

Gundem, B. B. (1990). *Læreplanpraksis og læreplanteori: en introduksjon til læreplanområdet*. Oslo: Universitetsforlaget.

Hirvonen, V. (2004). *Samisk skole i plan og praksis. Hvordan møte utfordingene i L97S? Evaluering av Reform 97*. Kárášjohka: Sámi allaskuvla.

Keskitalo, P., Määttä, K., & Uusiautti, S. (2013). *Sámi Education*. Frankfurt am Main: Peter Lang.

Minde, H. (2003). The Challenge of Indigenism: The Struggle for Sámi Land Rights and Self Government in Norway 1960–1990. In S. Jentoft, H. Minde, & R. Nilsen (Eds.), *Indigenous Peoples: Resource Management and Global Rights*. Delft: Eburon.

Ministry of Church and Education. (1974). *Mønsterplan for grunnskolen* [Primary School Curriculum]. Oslo: Aschehoug.

Ministry of Church and Education. (1987). *Mønsterplan for grunnskolen* [Primary School Curriculum]. Oslo: Aschehoug

Ministry of Education. (2017). *Overordnet del av læreplanen* [The General Part of the Curriculum]. Oslo: Aschehoug.

Moreton-Robinson, A. (2000). *Talkin' Up to the White Woman: Indigenous Women and Feminism*. St Lucia: University of Queensland Press.

8 Sámi Issues in Norwegian Curricula: A Historical Overview   141

Olsen, T. A., & Andreassen, B.-O. (2016). Ansvar, hensyn og forpliktelse. Urfolk og samiske forhold i barnehagens rammeplaner. In N. Askeland & B. Aamotsbakken (Eds.), *Folk uten land? Å gi stemme og status til urfolk og nasjonale minoriteter.* Kristiansand: Portal Forlag.

Olsen, T. A., & Andreassen, B.-O. (2017). Indigenous Issues in Early Childhood Education Curricula in Norway and Aoteoroa/New Zealand. *New Zealand Journal of Educational Studies, 52*(1), 255–270.

Olsen, T. A., & Andreassen, B.-O. (2018). "Urfolk" og "mangfold" i skolens læreplaner. *FLEKS Scandinavian Journal of Intercultural Theory and Practice, 5*(1). https://doi.org/10.7577/fleks.2248.

Olsen, T. A., Sollid, H., & Johansen, Å. M. (2017). Kunnskap om samiske forhold som integrert del av lærerutdanningene. *Acta Didactica Norge, 11*(2), 1–15.

Pedersen, S. (2008). *Lappekodisillen i nord 1751–1859. Fra grenseavtale og sikring av samenes rettigheter til grensesperring og samisk ulykke. Diedut 2.*

Seland, I. (2013). Fellesskap for utjevning – Norsk skolepolitikk for en flerreligiøs og flerspråklig elevmasse etter 1970. *Tidsskrift for samfunnsforskning, 54*(2), 188–214.

Smith, G. H. (2017). Kaupapa Māori Theory: Indigenous Transforming of Education. In T. K. Hoskins & A. Jones (Eds.), *Critical Conversations in Kaupapa Māori* (pp. 79–94). Wellington: Huia.

Solstad, K. J., Nygaard, V., & Solstad, M. (2012). *Kunnskapsløftet 2006 Samisk. Mot en likeverdig skole? Sluttrapport fra evalueringsarbeidet av Kunnskapsløftet Samisk (LK06S) 1/2012.* Bodø: Nordlandsforskning.

Storjord, M. (2008). *Barnehagebarns liv i en samisk kontekst. En arena for kulturell meningsskaping* (PhD thesis). University of Tromsø, Tromsø.

The Ministry of Education. (1995). *Early Childhood Education Curriculum.* Oslo.

The Ministry of Education. (2011). *Early Childhood Education Curriculum.* Oslo.

9

The History of the Sámi Upper Secondary School in Guovdageaidnu: Language Policy Development

Inker-Anni Linkola-Aikio

Introduction

This chapter presents the history and language policy in the Sámi upper secondary education. The development of the Sámi secondary education is described first as a special act towards a minority group and later as an equivalent to the Norwegian educational system as well as an indigenous educational institute. The chapter especially highlights the language policy guidelines during the education history. The status of the Sámi language in the institution reflects the national and local language policy. This chapter is based on the author's doctoral thesis on the Sámi linguistic landscape (Linkola 2014). The development of language policy in the Sámi education and the power relationships as a key in developing indigenous schools (e.g. the Sámi Upper Secondary School in Guovdageaidnu) will also be explored. Developing indigenous secondary and vocational education is essential for equal rights and opportunities in education; it

I.-A. Linkola-Aikio (✉)
Sámi University of Applied Sciences, Kautokeino, Norway

© The Author(s) 2019
O. Kortekangas et al. (eds.), *Sámi Educational History in a Comparative International Perspective*,
https://doi.org/10.1007/978-3-030-24112-4_9

143

is part of the societal development towards equality and pluralism where the ideology rests on appreciating multiculturalism as a resource (Baker 2011/1993; García 2009; Ruiz 1984).

The history of the Sámi education in Norway has been presented in a book series on the Sámi school memories collected by Svein Lund and Brock Johansen. This series offers a complete picture of the Sámi education in Norway from coastal areas to the inland and from the primary to vocational and university education. The Sámi education and pedagogy have been studied by Asta Balto (1997), research on its curricula has been conducted by Vuokko Hirvonen (2003), Jan Henry Keskitalo (2009), and Pigga Keskitalo (2010), and the Sámi early education and kindergarten history in Norway has been compiled by Marianne Storjord (2008). The writings on the Sámi education in Norway illustrate a history filled with efforts to silence the indigenous language and forcefully assimilate children into the Norwegian culture and way of living (Minde 2005; Balto 1997). Thus, one of the key questions in the Sámi politics has been concerned with achieving equality in education and developing the Sámi education for the Sámi children.

Very few studies have been carried out into the Sámi upper secondary education (e.g. Graff 2016; Hætta Klemetsen 2019; Linkola 2014; Lund 2002; Nystad 2003). According to Lund (2002), the Norwegian educational system allocates limited space to the Sámi curricular areas of interest at the secondary education level. Linkola (2014) found that there are challenges in promoting the use of the Sámi language in education, mainly because of the socio-historical status of the Sámi language. Due to the existence of language hierarchy in education, awareness of systematic language planning is required to support the Sámi language.

The theoretical background of this research is informed by language policy in education. Research on language policy can be used to explore the role of power relations by highlighting linguistic behaviour in education (Johnson 2013). Language is a key prerequisite for education, because it allows communication between the student and the teacher; in addition, it is an essential tool for knowledge formation (Reagan 2002). Language practices and rights are key elements when developing the indigenous education and reflecting on the colonial power

(King and Schielman 2004). In order to promote equality for indigenous peoples in education, the history of the existing practices and developments should be subject to scrutiny, backed by empirical research. Research on the position of the Sámi language in education as an indigenous language can reveal the challenges and offer solutions to developing indigenous education. The position of the Sámi language in education has been one of the pivotal elements in the Sámi political struggle for over a century (Hirvonen 2004).

Overall Picture of the Sámi Education in Norway

The Sámi language has played a central role in developing the Sámi education. In 1989, Norway ratified the ILO's Indigenous Peoples Convention No. 169. The agreement contained an article on the education of indigenous peoples, which assured indigenous peoples equal opportunities for education. Further, the state was required to co-operate with indigenous peoples on developing and implementing educational institutions (Kommunal- og moderniseringsdepartementet 2018).

Historically, the development of the Sámi language in education in Norway can be divided into five eras: (1) the missionaries' era from the eighteenth to the late nineteenth century; (2) the time of Norwegianisation from the nineteenth century to the late 1960s, when the use of the Sámi language was forbidden; (3) the use of the Sámi language as a subsidiary language from the Second World War to the 1980s; (4) the 1980s when the Sámi language became a subject at school; and (5) the Sámi language was declared an official language in the 1990s (Balto 1997). Today in the Sámi districts, every primary school child is entitled to be educated in the Sámi language. Outside the Sámi districts, students also have the right to education in the Sámi language, although their rights are somewhat more limited than in the Sámi districts. Alternative forms of education such as distance learning may be offered when teaching cannot be provided by the school's own teaching staff (Opplæringslova 1998).

The basic education system in Norway consists of a 10-year comprehensive school and subsequent secondary education. This includes the primary school (Barneskole), lower secondary school (Ungdomsskole) and upper secondary school (Videregående skole). After compulsory education, students have the right to a five-year secondary education. The governance of the comprehensive school is the responsibility of the municipality, whereas financing and governing upper secondary education usually fall within the remit of the county (fylkeskommune) (Government 2018). Some upper secondary schools are state owned, such as the two Sámi upper secondary schools: Sámi Secondary School and Reindeer Husbandry School in Guovdageaidnu and Sámi Upper Secondary School in Kárášjohka. For secondary education, the Sámi students in Norway are entitled to receive instruction in the Sámi language (Opplæringslova 1998). In the following chapter, I will introduce the history and language policy pertaining to the Sámi secondary education in Guovdageaidnu.

Sámi Secondary Education in Guovdageaidnu

Sámi Upper Secondary School and Reindeer Husbandry School have the special task of educating the Sámi youth. The school is situated in Guovdageaidnu in Northern Norway. Guovdageaidnu is often seen as a leading Sámi municipality in Norway, mainly because 90% of its residents speak the Sámi language as their first language (Kautokeino kommune 2019). Today Guovdageaidnu has approximately 2900 inhabitants and the municipality (out of 422) is the largest by area in Norway (Statistisk sentralbyrå 2017). The most important source of living in Guovdageaidnu is reindeer husbandry (Kautokeino kommune 2019) which together with fishing constitute one of the main traditional Sámi sources of livelihood. Many Sámi institutions are located in Guovdageaidnu, such as the Sámi upper secondary educational institution, Sámi university of applied sciences, National Sámi theatre, Sámi archives and the education department of Sámi parliament in Norway, the International Centre for Reindeer Husbandry and Duodji (Sámi handicraft) Institute as well as the Sámi Department of the Norwegian Institute for Human Rights,

9 The History of the Sámi Upper Secondary School ... 147

among others (Kautokeino kommune 2019). Most of the students in the Sámi secondary education in Guovdageaidnu come from Guovdageaidnu or the nearby areas, to whom we can add students from other parts of Norway and neighbouring countries; the majority of the students speak the Sámi language.

The history of the Sámi secondary education in Guovdageaidnu dates back to the end of the Second World War. The idea of a separate vocational school for the Sámi youth was raised during the reconstruction plans in the aftermath of the war. At that time, the Norwegian government raised the question of education for the Sámi youth. In 1947, the school director of Finnmark decided to explore special educational needs in multilingual Finnmark. After 1948, the Board of the Ministry of Church and Education suggested that the Sámi-speaking students be taught in the Sámi language, which meant that more Sámi-speaking teachers and textbooks would be needed. The board also suggested that the education of the Sámi youth should be the responsibility of the state. In 1951, a committee was set up to draft a plan for a practice-oriented school for the Sámi youth (Hætta Eriksen 2002; Nordby 2007).

The secondary school in Guovdageaidnu was first established as a temporary domestic vocational school for the Sámi students, and the first course was funded by the Ministry of Agriculture in Norway in 1952. A school called *Statens Heimyrkeskole for Samer* was founded permanently in the autumn of 1953. The school pursued the aim of teaching the Sámi students, who depended on reindeer husbandry and agriculture for their livelihood. At that time, the school offered three courses (metalworking, woodworking and weaving and sewing) (Lund 2003). *Duodji*, a Sámi craft, was among the first subjects. In addition to duodji, the students studied the Sámi language orally and in its written form. Students also took a written exam in the Norwegian language. Other school subjects included the Sámi history and bookkeeping (Hætta Eriksen 2002).

In 1968, the school's name was changed to *Den samiske yrkes- og husflidsskole, Kautokeino* (Sámi Vocational and Crafts School, Kautokeino). At that time, the school had three departments: metalworking, woodworking and sewing and weaving. In 1970, more courses were added: the HVAC (plumber) and the construction programmes, to which reindeer

148   I.-A. Linkola-Aikio

husbandry and snowmobile repairing courses were subsequently added. In 1975, the school achieved the status of an upper secondary school (videregående skole) and, by order of the Guovdageaidnu School Board, it was renamed 'Sámi joatkkaskuvla' in the Sámi language (Hætta Eriksen 2002).

In 1981, the state reindeer husbandry school was moved from Borkenes to Guovdageaidnu. At first, it operated as a separate school but later joined the Sámi joatkkaskuvla in 1988. At that time, the name of the school was changed to what it is today, that is *Sámi joatkka- ja boazodoalloskuvla, Guovdageaidnu* (Sámi Upper Secondary School and Reindeer Husbandry School, Guovdageaidnu) (Lund 2003; Hætta Eriksen 2002) (Table 9.1).

Today the Sámi Secondary School and Reindeer Husbandry School in Guovdageaidnu are state owned and offer education to students all over Norway and internationally. The school has five different study programmes, two of which are the Sámi programmes and include hand-icraft (*duodji*) and reindeer husbandry; the school has a national respon-sibility for these programmes. The school also offers distance education in the North Sámi language. The school's aim is to develop the Sámi secondary education with the Sámi values and culture and to educate the Sámi youth by strengthening their Sámi identity, language and cultural knowledge to enable the youth to live and work in the Sámi, Norwegian and international societies (Samisk videregående 2019). The school has been recognised as an indigenous secondary school, as it is part of the WINHEC (World Indigenous Nations Higher Education Consortium) network. While providing students with knowledge

Table 9.1 Names of the school in different periods

Names	Years
Statens heimeyrkeskole for samer/Stáhta ruovttofidnoskuvla sámiide	1952–1968
Den samiske yrkes- og husflidsskole – Kautokeino/Sámi fitnodat- ja duodjeskuvla – Guovdageaidnu	1968–1976
Sámi joatkkaskuvla/Samisk videregående skole	1976–1988
Sámi joatkka- ja boazodoalloskuvla/Samisk videregående skole og reindriftskole	1988–present

in the Sámi language and culture, the school is also obliged to offer upper secondary education according to the Norwegian national standards for secondary education and under the supervision and in cooperation with the Norwegian Director of Education and Ministry of Education (Utdanningsdirektoratet 2018; also see Lund 2002).

Language Policy Development in the Sámi Secondary Education

In addition to the language of instruction a school's language policy means language choices outside the formal teaching contexts, including the language used in joint events, during breaks or in communications sent to parents. The social status of the language has often influenced its position in schools. Indigenous languages often have to struggle to gain a status as an accepted language in education. The concept of language policy was developed by Bernard Spolsky (2004) and was further refined by Elana Shohamy (2006). It has been used to examine the relationship between language, power and inequality and solve, among other things, the problems created by colonisation. The education language policy reflects attitudes towards the home and foreign languages as well as decisions on which language should be used for the medium of instruction and on other occasions. The language policy in education also includes decisions on methods, teaching materials, teacher qualifications and tests. The language policy can also be unofficially recognised practices which can impact language use at school (Johnson 2013; Shohamy 2006; Tollefson 2002). Expressions of language policy include official documents and actual language practices. These different facets of language policy can be called 'open' and 'covert' or 'de jure' and 'de facto'. The de jure language policy refers to the official documents that aim to regulate linguistic behaviour. Practical (de facto) language policy means real language practices, that is the language used and the language choices made in practical situations and outside the actual teaching context (Shohamy 2006; Spolsky 2004).

150 I.-A. Linkola-Aikio

When the school was founded in 1952, the language of instruction was initially Norwegian, although instruction in the Sámi language was also given as a school subject. In 1959, the school board developed a curriculum making the Sámi language and history common subjects across all the educational programmes. Thus, the Sámi language was taught in upper secondary education 15 years earlier than in primary education in Guovdageaidnu (Lund 2003).

The board of *Statens Heimyrkesskole* for Samer in 1967 (see Table 2.1) made it compulsory to use the Sámi language for two weeks for metalworking and woodworking. However, for several years in the 1970s, courses in the Sámi language were only given for sewing and weaving. In 1974, it was possible to have the Sámi language taught in the sewing and weaving study programme. However, because the classes in the Sámi language were organised in the evenings, all the students in the school had the opportunity to attend them. At that time, none of the teachers in the school were competent enough to teach and write in the Sámi language; therefore, the teachers for these classes were borrowed from the primary school. The Sámi language was offered as an optional subject for some classes in the late 1970s, whereas the vocational education classes did not yet have the Sámi language as a subject. The reindeer husbandry courses were taught in the Sámi language after the Reindeer Husbandry School was moved to Guovdageaidnu and joined the Secondary School in 1981. The Sámi language was a school subject in two other programmes too. Only in 1989 did the Sámi language become a compulsory subject for all study programmes. 1988—1994 the school organised also language courses and terminology developing projects for teachers (Lund 2002, 2003).

The majority of the school's students have always been Sámi speakers. The Sámi-speaking teachers have used the Sámi language to guide individual students, even if the classes were taught in Norwegian according to the curriculum. In the late 1980s, the Sámi-speaking students and teachers began to demand that the Sámi language be recognised as the language of instruction in the school. The school board aimed for a Sámi-speaking school, although some of the school teachers opposed the decision. In order to improve the Sámi language skills of the teaching staff, it was proposed that teachers' assignments should at least have

9   The History of the Sámi Upper Secondary School ...   151

the Sámi as a foreign language. This decision was opposed by some teachers who were worried for the Norwegian-speaking students; the Ministry of Church and Education (*Kirke- og Utdannings departementet*) also disagreed with this decision. Thus, in practice, teaching continued to be mostly in Norwegian (Lund 2002).

In the twenty-first century, the aim of the Sámi secondary school is to offer students excellent Sámi language teaching and increase the use of the Sámi language during all classes (Styret for samiske videregående skolene 2009). According to the board's strategic plan, the school strives to achieve this goal by teaching all the students at different levels in the Sámi language and motivating them to use the language at school. In 2017, the school organised language courses in five different levels and in three different Sámi languages. The school also aims to improve the language skills of its staff through language courses. The school's strategic plan specifies that the school should aim to offer the Sámi-speaking students the opportunity to complete their exams in the Sámi language. The strategic plan states that the Sámi language should be an inherent feature of the school administration, the prime example of which is the practice of giving all internal and external information in two languages (Styret for samiske videregående skolene 2009; Samisk videregående skole 2018). The Sámi language is a part of the school's educational and identity strategy to give students from all over Sápmi (even across the state borders) a solid Sámi identity and knowledge in language and culture (Samisk videregående 2019).

According to the school's statistics in the academic years 2009–2010 and 2010–2011, between 81 and 90% of the students (slightly varying per academic year) studied the Sámi language as their first language (Gran 2011); this figure was 80% in 2017 (Samisk videregående skole 2018). The students' views on their own language skills show that they mostly feel confident in both languages (i.e. Sámi and Norwegian) as well as about being bilingual. Students study the Sámi language as a compulsory subject at school and believe that studying this language is important. A key motivational factor in language learning is that students feel that knowledge in the Sámi language is an important tool for integration into the local community where the Sámi language is the language of daily communication. Further, the Sámi language skills are seen as a way to self-expression, and language in general is seen to be valuable which can and should be transmitted to the future generations. The Sámi language skills are also seen to have an instrumental value, because they help in finding work and obtaining study scholarships (Linkola 2014).

In the 2010s, there were 42 teachers in the school. Teachers' language proficiency tends to vary more than the students' linguistic background. The number of teachers who have no or limited knowledge in the Sámi language is higher than the number of students who do not speak the Sámi language. Of the teaching staff, 36% have the oral Sámi language skills but without official qualifications (i.e. a certificate in the Sámi language skills). This mostly applies to the elder teachers who are actually native Sámi speakers who have not had the opportunity to study the Sámi language as part of their education due to earlier language education policies in Norway. In 2017, 78% of the teaching staff can use oral Sámi language but they don't have a formal qualification. 31% of the teaching staff have both a formal Sámi language qualification and a pedagogical qualification, but most of them are teachers in Sámi language or work in the administration. This leaves only four teachers that have a formal qualification in oral and written Sámi and teacher qualification in other subjects than language (Samisk videregående skole 2018).

The school's main strategy is to provide parallel study groups in Sámi and Norwegian in so-called identity building school subjects like social science, history and natural science. Otherwise, teachers use different language choices and strategies when teaching bilingual groups. The first strategy is that they speak one language but show the PowerPoints or use other materials in the other language. The second difference is that the teachers use both languages orally and in their written forms. The third strategy is that the teacher mainly uses one language when teaching but can advise the individual students in the other language. The fourth different strategy is that they use one language in front of the class but use both languages for discussions. The final difference is that the teachers use only one language but the students use the other language (or both languages) for classroom discussions. Occasionally, the two-teacher system is also used in the classroom where one teacher uses one and the other teacher uses the other language. The language choice in the classroom depends on the teachers' and students' language skills as well as the materials used and the subject taught (Linkola observations 17–21 January 2011). It seems that there is no common strategy or guideline for using certain methods in bilingual education at the research school. My observations show that the teachers know or think they know their students' linguistic backgrounds and decide on their own language strategies on the spot. The teachers can address the needs of different students in different languages in the same classroom in order to engage the students in class interactions or make teaching interesting and understandable. While many of the teachers are willing to use two languages orally during the lessons, they find translating the teaching materials in both languages a demanding task (Linkola, Research diary 20 January 2011). In the 1990s, some textbooks in the Sámi language for the second grade were first published; however, limitations in the Sámi-language textbooks persist in many subjects in the twenty-first century (Lund 2002; Samisk videregående skole og Reindriftsskole 2018).

Sámi Language in the School's Linguistic Landscape

The linguistic landscape can be seen as a means of implementing the language policy. The linguistic landscape refers to the written language that can be seen in a public place (Landry and Bourhis 1997). It is part of the linguistic reality of the school. Research on the linguistic landscape of an institution gives information about the hierarchy of languages in education (Hertting and Alerby 2009), mainly because the visibility of a language reflects its position in society (Landry and Bourhis 1997). In this review, I use 'linguistic landscape' as an example of the position of the Sámi language in the school in the twenty-first century.

As mentioned earlier, the Sámi Secondary School is located in a community where the Sámi language is widely spoken by the majority of the inhabitants. In the school, the majority of the students and staff speak the Sámi language. Although the spoken Sámi language is the main language for communication, the Norwegian monolingual texts dominated the linguistic landscape of the Sámi upper secondary education between 2009–2013 when the research was conducted. The monolingual Norwegian texts constituted over half (52%) of the texts in the linguistic landscape, whereas the texts in Northern Sámi constituted only one fifth (21%) of the texts in the linguistic landscape. Bilingual texts (Norwegian Sámi) constitute 19% of the linguistic landscape (Linkola Digital Photos). The research results also show that the linguistic landscape of the Sámi Upper Secondary School was not only influenced by the language choices within the school but also by the texts produced by the third parties outside the school. The texts produced outside the school were mostly in Norwegian, whereas the school staff and students also used the Sámi language in the linguistic landscape. Although the majority of the texts produced within the school (i.e. texts produced by staff and students) were in Norwegian, the proportion of the Sámi and bilingual texts was considerable. Most of the texts that were written in the Sámi language were produced for teaching or during the classes as part of the teaching materials. Using bilingual texts in the linguistic landscape was also quite popular among the students and staff (Linkola 2014).

The rationale behind using the Sámi language in the linguistic landscape was to highlight the Sámi identity of the school. The Sámi language was highly valued in the Sámi school. Since there was no linguistic landscape plan in the school, the students and staff made personal language choices. Although the Sámi language is a language for daily communication, it is not necessity for the transmission of information in the linguistic landscape, mainly because everybody knows the Norwegian language, reducing the amount of writing in the Sámi language. Using bilingual texts in the linguistic landscape was also considered a way of taking into account the non-Sámi-speaking students and staff in the school. Bilingual texts were most often equally bilingual so that readers could choose the language they liked. The Sámi language was considered the first language in most bilingual texts, emphasising the importance of the Sámi language in the educational institution. The school's linguistic landscape was also influenced by the lower status of the Sámi language as a language of literacy in Norway. This can be seen as a shortcoming in the Sámi language learning materials and choices made by the external organisations (Linkola 2014).

Language Policy in Guovdageaidnu Sámi Secondary School

Throughout the school's history, the position of the Sámi language in the school has changed. The school planned for the Sámi language teaching earlier in the primary school, due to the special status of the Sámi-led vocational education institution. However, the Sámi language has been in a weak position as a teaching language due to the socio-historical status of the Sámi language as a minority language and a language of low status. The weak legal status of the Sámi language in education until the 1980s is still noticeable in the twenty-first century as the lack of textbooks, materials and the use of the Sámi language in official documents and administration persists. The school has also been affected by a shortage of competent Sámi-speaking teaching staff. It has also led to the solution that the Sámi language skills cannot be demanded of the teachers. Moreover, using the Sámi language has also been seen to give the Norwegian staff and students an unequal status. The vast majority of the students in the school have been Sámi speakers throughout the history of the school. Lack of the teachers, materials have prevented the students from receiving instruction in their native language (Linkola 2014; Lund 2003).

Since the outset, the school has tried to offer education in the Sámi language. The Sámi language in teaching has been included in the school's plans, and it has been pursued in a variety of ways. In the beginning, the Sámi language was considered one of the school subjects, which was rare at that time. In the 1960s and 1970s, classes in the Sámi language were organised occasionally but not supported by the national education policy. From the 1980s, the Sámi language as a language of instruction has had a central position in the school board's language policy. One of the challenges facing the board has been the school staff and students who come from outside the central Sámi areas and do not know the Sámi language. Moreover, due to a lack of support from the national education policy, the shortage of study books and teaching materials in the Sámi language has been a problem for the Sámi secondary education and has had a negative impact on the indigenous minority's language use in the secondary education (Linkola 2014; Lund 2003).

In the twenty-first century, the Sámi Upper Secondary School is evolving. The school has set itself the goal of supporting the students' Sámi identity and knowledge in the Sámi language and culture (Samisk videregående 2019). The school has been consistently working towards becoming an indigenous school. Despite the school's efforts to provide education fully in the Sámi language, it is still far from success. Practical language choices and teaching strategies vary according to the language skills of the teachers and student groups (Linkola Research Diary 2011). These choices are made by individual teachers depending on their language skills and those of the student groups; the school plans are only guidelines (Linkola 2014).

Conclusion

In this chapter, I reviewed the 60-year history of the language practices and policies in the Sámi secondary education in Norway. I elaborated the developments and challenges affecting the indigenous education in Norway by giving Sámi upper secondary school and reindeer husbandry school as an example of Sámi education.

Although the Sámi secondary school has been continuously striving for a complete Sámi-language medium of instruction, more effort is still required to this end. This chapter shows that, throughout its history, the position of the Sámi language has varied in the Sámi secondary education. The students' linguistic needs and preferences have not always informed the choice of language at the school. The language policy for secondary education is formulated by the national language policy and ideology. In practice, the choice of language has been influenced by the language knowledge and interests of the school staff. The state language policy has barely supported the language ideology and interests of the students and the local community, whereas the school board and staff have tried to apply their minority language policies whenever possible.

The language policies and practices in schools reflect the reproduction of power. The socio-economic status of a group usually determines whether or not the group governs the education system. The education system determines who will benefit most from education. Thus, education reproduces the power structures in society. School's language policies are should be examined in relation to the general social life, where it is dependent on the political, economic and social power relations (Cummins 2002; García 2009, 91–103; Kroskrity 2000, 8; Shohamy 2006, 76–77; Tollefson 2002, 8). The education policy in Norway is closely linked to the national politics, resulting in educational reforms that are controlled by politicians (Afdal 2012).

Education is vital for the future of the Sámi language. In education, positive attitudes towards the indigenous language, multilingualism and language planning are vital for successful Sámi and indigenous education. Thus, if the minority language speakers perceive their own language as unnecessary or even harmful at school, this leads to language shame and abandonment of their own language and linguistic background. The colonialist schools particularly give grounds to one being ashamed of his/her own linguistic background (McCarty et al. 2011, 32–43). Awareness of language practices in education is important to support minority languages and promote linguistic equality in education and society. In order to develop the indigenous schools and promote equal opportunities in education language policies and practices, all inequalities should be removed.

References

Sources

– Digital Photos of Sámi joatkkaskuvla ja boazodoalloskuvla, Linkola, Inker-Anni 201 Photos.
– Gran, Lisbeth. Inspector 1. Sámi joatkkaskuvla ja boazodoalloskuvla. E-Mail. 27 May 2011.

158   I.-A. Linkola-Aikio

– Observations, Linkola, Inker-Anni 20 April 2010, 17–21 January 2011.
– Research Diary. Linkola, Inker-Anni 2009 – 2013.

Literatures

Afdal, H. W. (2012). *Constructing Knowledge for the Teaching Profession. A Comparative Analysis of Policy Making, Curricula Content and Novice Teachers' Knowledge Relations in the Case of Finland and Norway* (PhD). Olso: Universitetet i Oslo. Det utdanningsvitenskaplige fakultetet.

Baker, C. (2011/1993). *Foundations of Bilingual Education and Bilingualism* (5th ed.). Clevedon: Multilingual Matters.

Balto, A. (1997). *Samisk skolehistorie: en kort innføring. SA-Oahpahusčálus/Sámi allaskuvla—nr 1(1996).* Guovdageaidnu: Sámi allaskuvla.

Cummins, J. (2002). Rights and Responsabilities of Educators of Bilingual-Bicultural Children. In L. D. Soto (Ed.), *Making a Difference in the Lives of Bilingual/Bicultural Learners* (pp. 195–210). New York: Peter Lang.

García, O. (2009). *Bilingual Education in 21st Century: A Global Perpective.* Oxford: Blackwell.

Government. (2018). *The Education System.* https://www.regjeringen.no/en/topics/education/school/the-norwegian-education-system/id445118/. (Referred 24.7.2019).

Graff, O. (2016). *Joikeforbudet i Kautokeino.* Kárášjohka: Davvi Girji.

Hætta Eriksen, E. (2002). Árbevierut lávkkas. In L. Gran, L. R. Haldorsen, E. Eriksen Hætta, & A. L. Dahl (Eds.), *Árbevieruin ja oahpuin boahtteáigái/ Med tradisjon og i inn Kunnskap framtiden: Sámi joatkkaskuvla ja boazodoal- loskuvla/Sami Videregående skole og reindriftskole 1952–2002* (pp. 13–21). Alta: Fagtrykk.

Hætta Klemetsen, M. A. 2019. *Luodda šaddá gálidettiin: Motivašuvdna sámegiela čállinoahpahusas joatkkaskuvllas fidnofágasuorggis.* Master. Guovdageaidnu: Sámi allaskuvla.

Hertting, K., & Alerby, E. (2009). Learning Without Boundaries: To Voice Indignous Children's Experiences of Learning Places. *The International Journal of Learning, 16*(6), 633–648.

Hirvonen, V. (2003). *Mo sámáidahttit skuvlla? Reforpma 97 evalueren.* Kárášjohka: ČálliidLágádus.

Hirvonen, V. (2004). *Sámi Culture and the School: Reflections by Sámi Teachers and the Realization of the Sámi School.* Norsk forskningsråd, Samisk høgskole og ČálliidLágádus.

9 The History of the Sámi Upper Secondary School ... 159

Johnson, D. C. (2013). *Language Policy*. Basingstoke, UK: Palgrave Macmillan.

Kautokeino kommune. (2019, April 2). https://www.kautokeino.kommune. no/politihkka-ja-halddahus/suohkana-birra/da-lea-guovdageainnu-suohkan/.

Keskitalo, J. H. (2009). Sámi máhttu ja sámi skuvlamáhttu: teorehtalaš geahčastat. *Sámi diedalaš áigečála*.

Keskitalo, P. (2010). *Saamelaiskoulun kulttuurisensitiivisyyttä etsimässä kasvatusantropologian keinoin*. Dieđut 1/2010 (PhD). Guovdageaidnu: Sámi allaskuvla.

King, L., & Schielmann, S. (2004). *The Challenge of Indigenous Education: Practice and Perspectives* (pp. 40–44). Paris: UNESCO Pub. https://unesdoc.unesco. org/in/documentViewer.xhtml?v=2.1.196&id=p::usmarcdef_0000134773&-file=/in/rest/annotationSVC/DownloadWatermarkedAttachment/attach_ import_81be2a9d-1b4a-40ce-8e12-3deb65b11c73%3F_%3D134773eng. pdf&locale=en&multi=true&ark=/ark:/48223/pf0000134773/ PDF/134773eng.pdf#%5B%7B%22num%22%3A186%2C%22gen%22%3 A0%7D%2C%7B%22name%22%3A%22XYZ%22%7D%2C-293%2C768 %2C0%5D. 2 April 2019.

Kommunal- og moderniseringsdepartementet. (2018). *ILO-konvesjon om urfolks rettigheter*. https://www.regjeringen.no/no/tema/urfolk-og-minoriteter/urfolkry-ddemappe/ilo-konvensjonen-om-urfolks-rettigheter-/id487963/. 3 April 2019.

Kroskrity, P. (2000). Regimenting Languages: Language Ideological Perspectives. In P. V. Kroskrity (Ed.), *Regimes of Language: Ideologies, Polities and Identities* (pp. 1–34). Santa Fe, NM: School of American Research Press.

Landry, R., & Bourhis, R. Y. (1997). Linguistic Landscape and Ethnolinguistic Vitality: An Empirical Study. *Journal of Language and Social Psychology, 16*(1), 23–49.

Linkola, I.-A. (2014). *Saamelaisen koulun kielimaisema -etnografinen tutkimus saamen kielestä toisen asteen oppilaitoksessa* (Academic dissertation). Dieđut 2/2014. Faculty of Education, The University of Lapland. Guovdageaidnu: Sámi allaskuvla.

Lund, S. (2002). Riikka joatkkaskuvllaid vuogádahkii. In L. Gran, L. R. Haldorsen, E. Eriksen Hætta, A. L. Dahl (Eds.), *Árbevieruin and oahpuin boahtteáigái/Med tradisjon og i inn Kunnskap framtiden: Sámi joatkkaskuvla and boazodoalloskuvla/Sami Videregående skole og reindriftskole* 1952–2002 (pp. 25–39). Alta: Fagtrykk.

Lund, S. (2003). *Sámi skuvla vai "Norsk Standard"? Norgga skuvlaodastusat ja sámi oahpahus*. Karasjohka: Davvi Girji.

McCarty, T., Romero-Little, M. E., Warhol, L., & Zepeda, O. (2011). Chritical Ethnography and Indigenous Langue Survival: Some New Directions in Language Policy Research and Praxis. In T. McCarty (Ed.),

160   I.-A. Linkola-Aikio

Ethnography and Language Policy (pp. 31–52). New York and London: Routledge.

Minde, H. (2005). Fornorskninga av samene – hvorfor, hvordan og hvilke følger? i *Gáldu Cála*, nr. 3/2005. Guovdageaidnu: Gáldu.

Nordby, R. (2007). Praktisk skule for samar i Noreg. In E. Lund & S. Boine Broch Johansen (Eds.), *Sámi skuvlahistorjá 2- Ártihkkalat and muittut skuvlaeallimis* SAMIS (pp. 142–165). Karasjohka: Davvi girji.

Nystad, I. M. K. (2003). *Mannen mellom myte og modernitet.* Vett og Viten AS.

Opplæringslova. (1998, July 17). *LOV-1998-07-17-61: Lov om grunnskolen og the vidaregående opplæringa.* Kunnskapsdepartementet. nr. 61. http://www.lovdata.no/all/tl-19980717-061-007.html. #6-3

Reagan, T. (2002). *Language, Education and Ideology: Mapping the Linguistic Landscape of U.S. Schools.* Westport, CT and London: Praeger.

Ruiz, R. (1984). Orientations in Language Planning. *Journal of the National Association for Bilingual, Education, 8,* 15–34.

Samisk Videregående. (2019, April 2). *Skuvlla birra. Kautokeino: Samisk Videregående skole og reindriftsskole.* http://www.samisk.vgs.no/.

Samisk videregående skole. (2018). *Årsrapport.*

Samisk videregående skole og Reindriftsskole. (2018). *Tilstandsrapport for Samisk videregående skole og rendriftsskole 2016–2017.* Kautokeino: Samisk videregående skole og reindriftsskole.

Shohamy, E. (2006). *Language Policy: Hidden Agendas and New Approaches.* London and New York, NY: Routledge.

Spolsky, B. (2004). *Language Policy.* Cambridge: Cambridge University Press.

Statistisk sentralbyrå. (2017). *Table: 06913: Population 1 January and Population Changes During the Calendar Year (M).*

Storjord, M. (2008). *Barnehagebarns liv i samisk kontekst: En arena for kulturell meningsskaping* (PhD). Tromsø: Universitetet i Tromsø.

Styret for de Sami Videregående skolen. (2009). *Langsiktig Plan.* Høringsutkast.

Tollefson, J. W. (2002). Critical Issues in Educational Language Policy. In J. W. Tollefson (Ed.), *Language Policies in Education: Critical Issues* (pp. 3–19). Mahwah, NJ: Lawrence Erlbaum Associates.

Utdanningsdirektoratet. (2018). *Tildelingsbrev til Styret for De Ssamiske videregående skoler i Kautokeino og Karasjok.* Oslo: Udir.no.

10

Christian Morality and Enlightenment to the Natural Child: Third-Sector Education in a Children's Home in Northern Finland (1907–1947)

Merja Paksuniemi and Pigga Keskitalo

Introduction

In the 1900s, children's homes were established throughout the world. This article particularly concerns out-of-home care and the history of institutionalised education as it affected indigenous children. This discussion is part of an international scientific debate on the nature of children's homes with regard to the circumstances of indigenous children. In international research, children's homes have been connected to various well-known phenomena, and a great deal of research has been done on indigenous children living in institutions. The term 'Stolen Generations' refers to Australian Aboriginal and Torres Strait Islander peoples of

---

M. Paksuniemi (✉) · P. Keskitalo
Department of Education, University of Lapland, Rovaniemi, Finland
e-mail: Merja.Paksuniemi@ulapland.fi

P. Keskitalo
e-mail: pigga.keskitalo@ulapland.fi

© The Author(s) 2019
O. Kortekangas et al. (eds.), *Sámi Educational History in a Comparative International Perspective*,
https://doi.org/10.1007/978-3-030-24112-4_10

161

mixed-race descent who were removed from their families by Australian Federal and State government agencies and church missionaries between 1905 and the 1970s (Marten 2002, 229) and treated as half-caste children (Read 2006). The act of taking these children away from their cultural heritage had tremendous impact; as they grew older, the removed Aboriginal people were less likely to complete a secondary education, three times as likely to have a police record and twice as likely to use illicit drugs compared to Aboriginal people who grew up in their ethnic communities. The only notable advantage associated with Aboriginal people being removed from their communities as children was receiving a higher-than-average income as adults. However, there is little evidence that mixed-race Aborigines who were removed from their homes were successful in gaining better work, even in urbanised areas (Bereson 1989). On the other side of the world, in Canada, about 150,000 First Nations children went through the church-run residential school system, which ran from the 1870s until the 1990s. In many cases, indigenous children were forced to attend these schools under a deliberate federal policy of 'civilising' the indigenous peoples of the country. Many of these children were physically, mentally and sexually abused. Some committed suicide, while others died while attempting to flee their schools (Bennet et al. 2005). Although the above-mentioned reformatory schools were part of the government policies, the forced removals through institutions, including third-sector ones, created the stolen generations in general around the world. As a result, this out-of-home care caused trauma and cultural genocide in many cases (see, e.g. Evershed and Allam 2018; Sjögren 2010).

In northern Finland, as part of the rise of the childcare system in Finland in which the third sector took part, indigenous Sámi children were mainly settled in the Riutula Children's Home. This article focuses on the Home, which was named for the village it was located in, Riutula, in the municipality of Inari in northern Finland. The Home operated from 1907 to 1979 and was run by the Lutheran Young Women's Christian Association (YWCA), a third-sector association. This Home's situation differs from those of similar institutions in Australia and Canada: as a YWCA children's home, it was a private non-governmental institution. Because of that, we want to note that the Riutula Children's Home cannot be compared to similar Australian and

Canadian residential school systems because it took in both Finnish and Sámi children. What can be compared among the three contexts are the measures, ways and the how and why out-of-home care of indigenous children was conducted in different parts of the world and the wider significance the YWCA's actions. These questions are important in order to reveal the histories of vulnerable children, whose experiences would otherwise remain hidden.

Some research and other writings on the Riutula Children's Home have already been published. Tiina Saukko studied the Home's archives, focusing on its establishment and describing the activities of the residence and provider of primary education set up in connection with it (Saukko 2010, 2011, 45–59). The research of Veli-Pekka Lehtola (2003, 340–341) and Teuvo Lehtola (1998, 327), as well as other non-academic writings, have also described the Riutula Children's Home (Inari-Media 1995, 18–21; Korppila 1996, 8–11; Manninen 2017). V. A. Mansikka-aho's detailed memoir is based on his personal experiences of being a child at the Home (Mansikka-aho 1994). According to study, life in the Home differed from the daily life of the inhabitants of the village of Riutula in terms of lifestyle and nutrition (Korppila and Airamo 1999). Knowledge of daily life in the Riutula Children's Home can also be gathered from the YWCA's journals, which published messages from the Home's employees.

Institutionalised childhood and the treatment and experiences of the residents of such homes have become the subject of an ongoing national debate in Finland. According to Marjo Laitala and Vesa Puuronen, it was not unusual for reformatory children to face violence, lack basic needs, food and healthcare and to suffer many other forms of humiliation, such as physical and sexual harassment (Laitala and Puuronen 2016). Mistreatment was perpetrated both by adults and other children and was an intrinsic part of the children's day-to-day lives. These experiences undoubtedly influenced the children's self-esteem and overall development (see Hytönen et al. 2016; Laitala and Puuronen 2016; Svanfeldt-Winter 2016). The punishments were common educational measures employed in children's homes in the 1950s, especially in boarding schools. The disciplinary measures were meant to be good for the children, but sometimes they proved to be overwhelming.

It is estimated that between 1937 and 1983, approximately 150,000 children were in foster care in Finland. Each of these children has his or her own story, many of which are sad. Biographical material and child welfare research both contain indications that there have been problems and negligence in the care of these children. Although there were rules, no one actually worked to ensure that they were followed (Hytönen et al. 2016). The general idea was that children were not meant to be independent but instead should depend on the nurses (Talja-Larrivoire 1976). Research conducted in Sweden produced similar results (Sjögren 2010; Socialdepartementet 2011): David Sjögren (2010) stated that in Sweden, 'Swedishness' was articulated as a norm for the national minority groups. Complicated justification processes for identification, sorting and implementation of a separative education were conducted.

The above-mentioned national and international research concentrated mostly on the experiences of children. This article, however, concentrates on the employees of a specific institution. Our goal is to analyse the practice and aims of the Riutula Children's Home in order to understand the ideas promulgated by the association that owned and oversaw it, the YWCA, whose personnel were in charge during the period under investigation (1907–1947). The unseen and hidden procedures children were subjected to may become apparent through the extant descriptions of daily practices and written histories. This article contemplates the former knowledge of the history of education of the children of northern Finland by describing the effect of institutionalised out-of-home care on indigenous children (see Erkkilä and Estola 2014, 263–269; Itkonen 1941; Keskitalo et al. 2016; Kylli 2012, 2014a; Lassila 2001a, b; Lehtola 2004; Paksuniemi et al. 2015, 67–75; Rasmus 2008).

The primary data source for this article was the Riutula Archives, which are stored in the National Archives of Finland in Helsinki. The data consists of Annual Reports, Lists of children and of personnel maintained by the employees of the Riutula Children's Home, and a summary of the vicissitudes of the Riutula Children's Home compiled in 1957 by several writers who either worked there or took notes during or after visits to the Home. The writings of the personnel of the Riutula Children's Home in journals published by the YWCA (*Betlehemin tähti, Kotia kohti, Mot hemmet*) were also studied closely.

Overall, the article analyses how child protection measures were implemented during the first part of the twentieth century in northern Finland. The main goal of this article is to examine ideas and conduct of the Riutula Children's Home as a third-sector out-of-home education institution whose mission was to take care of and educate children in northern Finland. This was assessed using two research questions:

1. What was the significance of the Riutula Children's Home as part of the child protection programme in Finland?
2. How were ideological measures implemented in the education provided by the Riutula Children's Home?

The Home was part of the rise of the Finnish child protection initiatives. In this article, 'child' protection refers to laws and reports produced by the government and other national agencies which affected the founding of the Riutula Children's Home. In addition, the term 'education' refers to various aspects of the education provided to the children, such as skills, manners and behaviour. We assume that the YWCA's ideology was reflected in the Home's educational programme in many ways. As such, most of the descriptions included in the Riutula Home's archives were provided by the institution's personnel and express the ideas of their employer, the YWCA.

The Context of Child Welfare in Finland During the Period Under Investigation

Research on childhood history is relevant precisely because the decisions made in one era tend to have an impact on future generations (Eeklaar 2004, 178–194). This is particularly important with regard to vulnerable children, orphans and indigenous children, and the changes in their societies and families which the YWCA took part in causing. From the 1800s until the early twentieth century, life in Finland was limited to one's village and family communities, with three generations—children, parents and grandparents—usually living in each household.

Finland was a dominantly agricultural country in which children were collectively raised by the community as a whole, with the primary responsibility for childrearing being placed on women and servants.

According to Hämäläinen (2007), child protection as a concept emerged in Finland in the mid-1800s when various activities and institutions drew attention to children's growth environment. Social, educational and health-related themes became particularly significant. The modernisation, which occurred in the nineteenth and twentieth centuries led to some families and communities no longer being able to care for and raise their children. This led to dysfunctional socialisation, neglect and even the abuse of children. Child welfare came to be seen as a state responsibility and thus required government funding (Hämäläinen 2007).

In Finland the idea of liberalism emerged in the 1860s with the establishment of mercantile regulations. This in turn contributed to a new social policy, based on which money was allocated for social welfare. On the other hand, the famine of the 1860s put the country in poor financial straits. In the background was also the 1852 Child Care Regulation, which recognised poverty as a social problem. Although at the time poverty management was largely the responsibility of parishes and municipalities, in the 1850s charity work and civic activity became important in cities. Bourgeois women's associations and similar actors shared grants with those in need. Several nurseries, kindergartens and educational institutions were set up as private establishments as well. Social policy was seen as an important part of the control system, and at the beginning of the twentieth century poverty management was based on rigorous needs assessments and control. Those who were able to work had to take care of themselves independently, and the social safety net was largely based on the traditional family and community. The invalidity or death of a guardian was very problematic for a family. In such cases, it became the duty of the local government to take care of the children and the invalids, which was felt to put a strain on municipal finances and increase taxation. All of these measures were hampered by poor management and implementation. There was no separate agency to manage child protection; it was simply a part of the general welfare management and thus under the control of the municipalities. Disadvantaged children were found to be weak-minded and uncivilised and were generally placed in the care of foster families, whose attitudes towards their situations varied greatly (Satka 2007, 47–51). Gustav Adolf Helsingius (1855–1934) served as an inspector for the care of the poor and launched control and inspection guidelines for the large-scale construction of paediatric homes and nursing care facilities established by the municipalities (Harjula 2000, 25–27). He argued that because the law obligates municipalities to take care of their distressed residents, it also gives the government the right to ensure that these laws are monitored (Helsingius 1899, 262).

The number of child deaths was quite high in the countryside. For instance, during the period 1901–1905, approximately 13 out of 100 children died before the age of 1. The reasons for these deaths were mostly epidemics and poxes; however, the low standard of hygiene and lack of knowledge were also seen as contributing factors (Harjula 2000, 25–27). The Civil War in 1918 added new pressures to child protection and welfare. The consequences of the war accelerated development, because the municipalities were too weak to respond to the needs of childcare and child protection. Child welfare organisations were set up to help fulfil this demand in the 1920s. As a result of the war, a growing effort was made to establish national child welfare organisations. According to current estimates, the Civil War and its devastating aftermath caused the deaths of approximately 40,000 people, mostly in southern Finland. The various multiplier effects of the war, both in the form of mental suffering and the scarcity of basic necessities, were extensive. War led to fundamental shifts in culture and society. People became used to suffering in silence, facing guilt and shame or experiencing bitterness, which manifested over time in various negative ways. The consequences of the war and the strong ideological currents of the time disrupted the organisational field as well (Paksuniemi 2014). Large national organisations soon became involved in the development of childcare programmes and social services for children and young people (Pulma and Turpeinen 1987).

168 M. Paksuniemi and P. Keskitalo

Wartime in Finland was tough and affected the lives of the Finnish people for many years thereafter. At the time, a large number of people were living in poor conditions and something needed to be done to improve their situation. On 28 April 1922, a law to take care of the poor (*Köyhäinhoitolaki*) was passed and went into effect in 1923. According to this law, the poor and needy were divided into three categories: old and sick people, children and those who needed work. Special care facilities and homes were planned for each group, with more children's homes being established, thereby raising children's standard of living (Government of Finland 1922). This most likely reduced the number of child deaths during the period 1936–1939, when approximately seven children out of every 100 died before the age of 1year (Harjula 2000).

The establishment of the Children's Protection Law in 1936 was a landmark event. For the first time, children and youth became the responsibility of society, which enhanced the possibilities to improve child protection. According to the law, a child could be taken into protection in the following cases: being orphaned; suffering from physical or mental illness; parents being unable to provide care and education; being abused or having their health threatened; not going to school; behaving badly; not having a residence; or being involved in felonies (Government of Finland 1936). The Committee Report of 1947 included a new stipulation: when children who had been taken into care turned 16, they would have the choice to move away from their home if they had been sufficiently educated and would be able to manage in society alone. If, however, they wished to remain in their home after turning 16, this was possible following approval by a social board (Government of Finland 1947).

The organisation which is the focus of this essay, the YWCA, represented the third sector. The third sector was part of the national care network and complemented the state care network. The role of third-sector institutions as caretakers and child protectors was quite common during early 1900s; they became increasingly involved in providing education during the course of the first decade of the twentieth century.

The Establishment of the Riutula Children's Home in Inari, Northern Finland

The purpose of children's homes in the 1900s was not just to provide shelter for children but also to give them a moral upbringing (Vehkalahti 2008, 36–39). In the early 1900s, the YWCA, decided to set up a children's home in Inari in northern Finland to accommodate the children in the area. The need for a better approach to childcare in northern Finland was highlighted by Ida Lilius, an elementary school teacher who had some experience with Swedish Sámi missionary work. Lilius introduced her idea in 1900 at a YWCA conference, after which the Porvoo City Deacon, noblewoman Naëmi von Bonsdorff, expressed her willingness to help. In the same year, Lilius and von Bonsdorff left for Lapland and ended up in Inari, where Lilius worked as a primary school teacher and von Bonsdorff served as a deaconess (Kerkkonen 1915, 3–9). In their work, they sometimes struggled with feelings of despair; for example, with regard to children's education, von Bonsdorff said: 'It is probably a mistake for the Lappish people, that those who are so undeveloped and mentally poor have to learn the same knowledge as other children. They cannot do that'. The hygiene level of Sámi homes also worried the missionaries (von Bonsdorff 1915, 4–5). In her work as a deaconess, von Bonsdorff stated that there was a great need to set up a home for Sámi children. According to her, the Sámi children received clothes and food, but no home education (von Bonsdorff 1904, 29).

In 1903, von Bonsdorff was consulted about a farm for sale, located about 13 kilometres from the church in Inari on the banks of Lake Muddusjärvi: 'One Lappish had allowed the farm to decay and wanted to sell it'. Von Bonsdorff travelled to the farm and ended up buying it with her own money for a price of FIM 2000. She then donated the farm to the YWCA along with additional funds for building materials and household goods. The state assisted by contributing FIM 10,000 to the project (NA, RA, RL, 9). The aim was to set up a missionary station that could provide care for both the elderly and children.

The missionaries seemed to be worried about the welfare of the Sámi, as they lacked a Christian upbringing. In 1907, von Bonsdorff described the Sámi as people who had none of the characteristics of enlightened people; the effort to 'enlighten' those they cared for became a secondary (though significant) goal of the care system created in northern Finland, and was an explicit part of the mission of the Riutula Children's Home. The Sámi were represented as being *other*—as childish, underdeveloped, unenlightened and different:

> You seem to have gone back about a century, namely meaning here people's enlightenment. The mind becomes depressed when acquainted with both their mental and sacred immaturity. But sometimes it is a refreshing thing to keep in touch with that natural child… Even though Lapland is part of our country, [the] Sámi people don't really feel [a] connection with it […] half of the population here in Inari parish are real Sámi, half Finnish who have maintained their own habits, and the Sámi have kept their own. (von Bonsdorff 1907b, 8)

This picture of a primitive and backward population enabled differentiation and othering. Indigenous peoples were denigrated as 'less than human', thereby reinforcing white supremacy, and as part of a trend of distinguishing differences between races since the 1700s (Moreton-Robinson 2011 [2004], 76–77). The programme and practise of the Riutula Children's Home became entangled with Christianity and the mission to educate diligent citizens. The rise of modernism made the universalism of humanness paradoxical, as it allowed people to emphasise, exaggerate and even fabricate racial differences (see Moreton-Robinson 2011 [2004]). Colonialist practices were characterised by Jean-Paul Sartre (1978, 8) as follows: 'your humanism claims we are at one with the rest of humanity but your racist methods set us apart'. In the case of the Riutula Children's Home, colonialism was realised through missionary work. Overall, colonialism can be understood as a domestic or foreign policy designed to retain and extend the authority of one country over a specific people or territory (Veracini 2010, 5). As von Bonsdorff stated that it was the YWCA's purpose to spread Christianity among the Sámi people under the aegis of the Riutula Missionary Centre, which was at that time under construction, colonialism was therefore practised through Christianity and caring: '[their] intention was to provide a home for poor, insecure, hard-working, old, sick and children, where they can feel Christian love and be under Christian influence' (von Bonsdorff 1907b, 9). Such transactions are described as 'caring power', which was spawned by the combined discourses of humanitarian sensibility and evangelical Protestantism. The motivation for caring for those deemed to be other was both humanitarian and religious. In the process children were trained in a specific direction, for instance to adopt a new identity or ideology (van Drenth and de Haan 1999).

A good home was seen as the foundation of a good society. Society could only be healthy when homes were able to mentally and physically nurture healthy citizens, which was considered to be closely related to people's living standards and society as a whole (Saarikangas 2005). The importance of hygiene began to be addressed at the beginning of the 1900s. Good living standards and high levels of hygiene positively influenced people's physical and mental welfare, according to this idea.

For the YWCA, the establishment of the Riutula Children's Home seemed to be a significant event, as it was mentioned in several publications, for instance, in the *Kotia Kohti* journal in 1904. A call for more help in Inari was published so that the Home could be opened in time. The floor plan of the facility was also revealed to the public for the first time: it included a common room, a meeting room, a room for the female administrators, two rooms for sick older people and one room for the children (S. F. 1904, 59).

The Riutula Children's Home began operations in 1907, beginning with six elderly people and nine children. Combining the living spaces of the elderly and the children on the same premises was challenging, however, because of the wide age gap—the oldest inhabitant was about 90 years old and the youngest was one and a half years old (von Bonsdorff 1907a, 41). Over the years the Home's parent organisation, YWCA stopped taking in elderly individuals and the institution became solely a children's home (NA, RA, RL, 9). Because more children were arriving in Riutula as the century progressed, in 1925 the premises were expanded to include 20 rooms in the main building, three rooms in the house across the yard, a cowshed and a sauna. Altogether, the Home could accommodate 32 children. A cabin was built 2 kilometres away for the employees to 'relax their nerves' (NA, RA, RL, 14). There are many reports about the difficult circumstances at the Home, and many of the Finnish employees living and working there were under a great deal of stress. Despite this, its missionary work and child welfare goals prompted many women to continue working there for long or short periods.

The managers of the Riutula Children's Home were sophisticated women from Southern Finland. The fact that the upper-class women were active in such a process was not unusual (Markkola 2006, 21–22). Altogether, the Home had 14 different managers between 1907 and 1950 (NA, RA, B:2). These women were called 'mothers' of the Home and were often described as being self-sacrificing and caring people (Na, RA, RL, 138–139). A rather interesting fact is that the managers (except for one) did not have any special training in working with children nor in managing a home according to bourgeois values: 'They have with the desire of their hearts and sacrificing love tended to guide and educate children of Lapland to be God-fearing and hardworking members of the society' (NA, RA, RL, 28. Also NA; RA, B:2). Markkola stated that the Finnish women working there were practicing the Biblical concept of 'loving one's neighbour', a sentiment also believed to be connected to the Christian role of a woman in various voluntary and charity organisations (Markkola 2006).

Most of the personnel were Finnish, as the Sámi people were not considered to be qualified to take care of children: 'The home has a Lappish maid but since she has been raised in Lapland she cannot influence on children or [in any way] mentally control [them]. Therefore, Sister Naëmi has sacrificed as much time as possible for the children' (M. C. 1904, 13–14). This was also mentioned in the following passage, which discusses the difficulty in finding suitable personnel for the Riutula Children's Home:

> The children of nature who have been raised in Lapland are shown to be untidy and feisty personalities and therefore unsuitable to be employees of Riutula. However it is hard to get employees from southern Finland since most of them are afraid about the reality what working in Lapland requires. (NA, RA, RL, 28)

10 Christian Morality and Enlightenment to the Natural Child ...

Most of the male employees, however, were Sámi, as were some of the women who took care of the kitchen, probably because they had the most appropriate knowledge and skills for the job. They mainly did the outdoor and indoor work and also guided the male employees in different tasks (NA, RA, RL, 29).

A 'Haven' for the Children of Northern Finland

The majority of the children who arrived at the Riutula Children's Home between 1907 and 1947 were from Sámi families (NA, RA, AR, 1936; 1939; 1949; 1941; 1946; NA, RA, B:1). For example, in 1922 there were 17 Sámi children and eight Finnish children; in 1931, there were 15 Sámi children and four Finnish children (Saukko 2011, 49); and in 1946, the home had a total of 18 children who spoke Sámi and nine who spoke Finnish (e.g. NA, RA, AR, 1946). Some of the children were given by their families to employees of the Home when they visited Sámi communities and residences. The following excerpt is about a four-year-old girl: 'The mother was joyful like a child when I promised to take one of her children with me because she knew that the daughter would get a better life' (Unknown Author 1909, 96–96). According to the archives, from 1907 to 1920, the children living in the Riutula Children's Home were usually orphans or belonged to poor families who could not provide them with decent living conditions. Most of them were from Sámi families (NA, RA, B:1).

According to the data, moving to the Home and living there was hard for some of the children who missed their parents, family homes and siblings. When they had the opportunity to visit their family homes, coming back to the Home was quite hard, as they had to leave their parents and siblings again. However, in some cases, more than one child from a single family moved to the Home, which gave the siblings the opportunity to be raised in the same environment and not miss each other (NA, RA, B:1).

When the children first arrived at the Riutula Children's Home, they were described as being in need of a bath and new clothes: 'Almost all of them arrived dirty and [with] mess[ed] up hair, wearing torn and even borrowed clothes'. They were usually first taken to the sauna and given new clothes. A lady was appointed to sew traditional Sámi clothes for them, 'since most of them were Lappish and they felt weird and sad to get Finnish clothes'. As a greater number of children began to enter the Home, they began to wear Finnish clothes which were donated by the citizens of southern Finland (von Bonsdorff 1907a, 40–41). Altogether, almost half of the population of Inari were Sámi. Two-thirds of them were Sámi who made a living by fishing, reindeer herding and farming. One-third of them were Sámi who made a living mainly through reindeer herding (Itkonen 1984, 122–126).

In 1917–1918, Finland went through a civil war. Like most war-torn countries, Finland also faced a lack of basic supplies during this time. This problem also affected Riutula (Lehmusvirta 1918, 158). The following personnel record describes the harsh living conditions: 'For six months we haven't seen other bread than which we received from our friends from Tampere, two 10 kilos packages [...] once we lived a whole week...eating only potatoes' (B. R. 1919, 43). However, the number of children living at the Riutula Children's Home remained constant (NA, RA, B:1).

In early 1920, the Spanish influenza arrived in Inari: 'In the past weeks...a pestilence...[called] Spanish influenza [has] raged in Inari [...] Many houses have become uninhabited and the number of orphans has increased. ...The number of deaths is [approximately] 300 in Inari, which had altogether 1,700 inhabitants' (Unknown Author 1920, 76). Statistics show that 9.8% of the population died, most of whom were Sámi women. The influenza also left 120 children orphans, 63 of whom were 0–10 years old, 24 who were 11–15 years old and 33 who were over 15 years of age. Finding a home for these children became a major problem for the region (Linnanmäki 2005, 114–126). As a result, the Riutula Children's Home took in more children (NA, RA, B:1). The influenza reached the Home as well—most of the staff and children got ill and five children died (Unknown Author 1920, 77).

Even though the law in 1936 listed new reasons for children being taken into care (Children's Protection Law 1936), these reasons were

10 Christian Morality and Enlightenment to the Natural Child ...   175

never cited in the Riutula Children's Home archival data. Children continued to be sent to Riutula for the same reasons they had been in previous years: poor families being unable to raise their children (NA, RA, B:1). Children were also sent there when most of their relatives had died and there was no one left to take care of them. Furthermore, it seems that it was fairly easy to recruit children to live in the Riutula Children's Home, as the general sense was that the facility had enough food and would be good for the children—facts that appealed to poor families who were unable to take care of their children. It was also believed that when a child had any serious illness, he or she would be better taken care of in Riutula.

From 1939–1945, WW2 severely affected Finland. Altogether, Lapland faced three different wars: The Winter War from 1939 to 1940, the Continuation War from 1941 to 1944 and the Lapland War from 1944 to 1945. The effects of the war years can be seen in the Riutula Children's Home statistics. Some children were sent to the Home when a new stepfather would not allow their predecessor's children to reside in the same house. Several children whose fathers were German soldiers (NA, RA, Bb:1) were also sent to Riutula, as having a child of the enemy was a social stigma (see Wendisch 2006); mothers therefore decided to send such children away, which was the best solution at the time. Another reason for sending a child to the Home was that one of his or her parents had died and the remaining parent had to give the child or children away in order to get paying work (NA, RA, B:1). Having a job in the post-war years was extremely important, as the country was still recovering economically. Some children were sent away to Oulu to get help for their problems. Children in auxiliary schools were found to slow down other children and disturb the workers (Svanfeldt-Winter 2016).

Approximately 20–30 children lived in the Riutula Children's Home at a time; when the older ones moved away, new ones were taken in. After leaving the Home, the children got jobs or continued their studies in a different part of Finland (NA, RA, B:1).

Measures for Educating Civilised Citizens

This section discusses what the Home's 'mission to civilise' meant in practical terms. Living in the Home not only provided children with a residence but also the opportunity to learn skills for the future: 'With careful upbringing they are aimed to be educated as individuals who [will be] fit for...society' (NA, RA, RL, 25).

The younger children took care of laundry and learnt textile work—the girls in particular were taught how to do housework, cook and take care of cattle, as seen in this excerpt about a 17-year-old girl: '[She] is involved with animal husbandry, sewing and taking care of the younger children' (NA, RA, RA, 1936). The boys practised fishing, hunting, timber work and making fishing nets, while both girls and boys took care of the garden (NA, RA, AR, 1922; 1929; 1939). It was also the children's responsibility to keep their rooms tidy and take turns helping in the kitchen (e.g. NA; RA, AR, 1946). All the work had to be done during their spare time, as children aged 7–12 years attended school on weekdays.

According to the data, the children were also educated in Sámi culture. A yearbook from 1929 mentions that the boys took care of the reindeer (NA, RA, AR, 1929), which is an example of a skill that Sámi boys would need to know later in their lives. One teenager was described as 'a typical Sámi boy who has reindeer herding in his blood' (NA, RA, B:1). The number of farm animals and reindeer at the Home increased over the years—in 1937, the Home had two horses, 30 reindeer, eight cows (including one heifer and one bull), seven chickens and four sheep (NA, RA, AR, 1937). The following passage was written about a ten-year-old boy: '[He] joyfully takes care of the sheep and helps in the barn and elsewhere. [He] is really careful and hardworking' (NA, RA, B:1). Using children as workers was quite common in children's homes located in the countryside: They were first educated on how to perform various tasks by themselves and then to serve as productive and free labour in the home (Hytönen et al. 2016, 142; Leino and Viitanen 2003, 187–198).

Farming and caring for farm animals were particularly important activities in Riutula because of the village's location. Subsistence

10 Christian Morality and Enlightenment to the Natural Child ...   177

farming was the only way to guarantee food supplies throughout the year. An article published in 1907 described this necessity:

> Why do you need to do farming and keep farm animals in Riutula, some may wonder. And we answer: the circumstances in the [far] North requires that. We cannot buy milk anywhere and it will be really expensive to by reindeer meat for everyone [...] this is why we have 8–10 cattle [...] and do farming. (R. W. D. 1907, 14)

These skills were learnt as by-products of the children's daily life in the Home.

Life in the Riutula Children's Home was well-planned and followed a homelike daily schedule. Younger children woke up at 0600 hours and older children at 0630 hours. Bedtime for the younger children started at 1800 hours and for older ones at 2100 hours. The home provided breakfast, lunch, dinner and a late snack every day. Each child had regular doctor's appointments, usually twice a year, and more frequent check-ups with nurses (NA, RA, AR, 1942). Overall, the children were in good health, with some brief epidemics mentioned in certain years (e.g. NA, RA, AR, 1922; 1929; 1937; 1942). They went to a Finnish sauna twice a week and went swimming almost daily during the summer. The sauna was located near the lake and because running water was installed only at the end of the 1950s, the children carried their bath water from the lake; their drinking water was drawn from a well (NA, RA, RL, 30).

If the children did not obey the rules or misbehaved, there were consequences such as physical discipline or special punishments intended to ostracise them. This can be seen in the following excerpt: 'In a few cases the children had physical punishment with [a] birch [switch]. It seems to be a huge benefit [to] the child's mindset'. The 1929 yearbook mentioned younger children being physically punished and other kinds of punishment being used on older children which were described as having been 'successful and productive' (NA, RA, AR, 1929). After the 1930s, such references to punishment were no longer included in the yearbooks. One reason is that during the 1930s, the personnel wrote down yearly information on a blank sheet of paper, whereas previously they had used a particular form; also, in 1947, a Committee Report indicated that children should be disciplined through kind advice and warnings rather than physical punishment (Committee Report 1947). Overall, the children were cared for and loved, at least according to the archives, as seen in the following excerpt about a three-year-old: 'A cute little girl [...] wants to have a goodnight kiss on cheek every evening' (NA, RA, B:1).

Some children did not know Finnish at all, or understood it but could not communicate in Finnish, as seen in this excerpt: '...they [three boys] are Lappish. They understand some Finnish but don't speak it yet' (von Bonsdorff 1907a, 42). The Finnish language was the primary form of communication used in the Riutula Children's Home and after living there for a while all the children learnt to use it daily. The following excerpt is about a three-year-old child: 'Dark-eyed, lively and cute boy, spoke only Lappish [Sámi] [...] imitates other children's talk, has [quickly learned] to speak Finnish' (NA, RA, B:1). Some of the children also continued to use their mother tongue Sámi, as the following description shows: 'A young Sámi girl who got a doll as a Christmas present used Sámi word *olmmoš* when playing with the doll' (von Bonsdorff 1905, 45).

As the residents of the home reached the age of compulsory education, they attended classes in the Home: 'The children are enjoying school teaching and [do] other work during their spare time' (Kerkkonen 1915, 3–9). Their teachers were employees of the Home rather than strangers brought in from further away. When the Home had a higher number of children aged at least seven years old, it became necessary to construct an elementary school because the primary school in Inari was too far away. In 1915, a primary school was built 300 metres from Riutula. Other children in the region who lived in the dormitory also attended this school—they were described as being from poor families and Sámi children from the mountain region (NA, RA, RL, 14). That same year, according to the *Teacher's Journal*, the elementary school inspector of Lapland brought up the possibility of also arranging upper elementary school education. However, he decided that there was no need for such an educational project, as there were only a few children living in the area (Vihtori 1915, 370). In 1916, the topic was brought up again and, after several years, an upper elementary school was commenced in the same building (Leinto 1916, 18).

The changes in society and lack of food supplies in 1917 resulted in the dorm for the children attending elementary school being shut down and the children being sent home. The school continued to function, however, and the children of the Riutula Children's Home attended it regularly. It even took in five younger children who were under the age of compulsory education as extra pupils (Lehmusvirta 1918, 158). Without the subsistence economy, the years 1917–1918 would have been difficult for the Home.

The school-going children spent six days a week and most of their daily hours in the school. According to previous studies, the Finnish school system quite strongly highlighted 'Finnishness' from its establishment up until the 1950s (Keskitalo et al. 2016; Paksuniemi 2009). Riutula's elementary school followed the same curriculum as schools in other parts of Finland, whose aim was to educate citizens to live in Finnish society. The teaching was also therefore conducted in Finnish: 'A thorough description has to be done for everything. Every object needed to [be] shown [because] they don't understand the explanation. Some of them don't know letters, others don't know the language' (Lehtola 1915, 89–90). However, according to the archives, the children did quite well and most graduated from primary school.

Discussion

In the effort to build the concept of Finnish nationhood, the country's minorities' and indigenous peoples' (that is, the Sámis') education, language and needs were not given any particularly culturally sensitive attention: The focus was instead on the national Finnish language and the culture of 'Finnishood' (Keskitalo et al. 2014; Paksuniemi 2009). Cultural sensitivity would have required that special measures be taken in the Sámi language, incorporating the Sámi worldview and be planned, conducted and led by the Sámi people. The same criticism has been made of out-of-home care conducted for indigenous children throughout the world.

Most of the children in the Riutula Children's Home were Sámi, but there were also a few Finnish children. Unlike other places in the world, where indigenous children were placed in dormitory schools as a government policy, the purpose of which was to eradicate their language and culture (e.g. Evershed and Allam 2018), the measures which were implemented and the ideologies which highlighted Christian morality in the Riutula Children's Home were familiar to the Finnish children living there. As a side-effect of this policy, Sámi children lost their mother tongue. The Riutula Children's Home had many tasks, such as practicing Christian morality and caring for the children. The political view of the Sámi was not treated as an absolute, but it was combined with the Fennoman ideology by the missionary women. YWCA personnel sought to highlight Finnishood and their written texts underline this concept of white supremacy.

In the effort to take care of the poor, the Riutula Children's Home probably had a positive influence. Education had positive results as well, although at the same time it was culturally discriminatory. Many are now examining the nature of othering and the teaching of colonial Christianity during this period. The Sámi communities at this time were already quite religious (Laestadian), and so on; Christianity itself was not new to the children (Kylli 2014b). However, the YWCA employees included Christian morality in the measures they implemented in the Riutula Children's Home. In addition to the humanitarian and religious motivation for the care provided, this included a new identity and new ideology (see van Drenth and de Haan 1999) of Finnishness and the Finnish language. Smith (2009), who studied boarding schools for indigenous children, noted that the aim of civilising the children was to integrate the indigenous people into mainstream society. This work was conducted by different Christian organisations. The main idea behind this was that a citizen was a whole unit after the cultural aspects of his/her personality were stripped away: 'For Native people to become fully "human", they would have to lose their Native cultures' (Smith 2009, 18–29).

Our data does not delve into the experiences of children. In international and national research in Finland, indigenous children and children in general were treated badly in institutions according to our

10 Christian Morality and Enlightenment to the Natural Child ... 181

values today. We need to ask what kind of treatment Sámi children were subjected to in the Riutula Children's Home; our data tells us only what the employees wrote. These texts give a hint that the circumstances were not easy, either for children or employees. Physical punishment was documented. It is also a fact that orphans and children left to children's homes were doubly marginalised because of their ethnic background. They were poor, orphans and rejected by society; Sámi children in particular were treated and described as inferiors.

Eeklaar (2004) stated that decisions made in the past influence the future. In this light, the Riutula Children's Home acquires even greater significance. The Sámi children in Riutula were living between two cultures—Sámi and Finnish. Little by little, however, the cultural aspects of the dominant Finnish culture became stronger. This influenced not only the lives of the individuals but also their families and descendants.

References

Archival References

Annual Reports (AR), 1909–1947.
Lists of Children (B:1).
Lists of Personnel (B:2).
Riutula Archives (RA).
Riutulan lastenkoti täyttänyt v. 1957 loppiaisena 50 vuotta, (RL) 1957.
The National Archives (NA), Helsinki.

Printed Sources

B. R. (1919).Tervehdys Riutulasta. *Kotia Kohti, 3*, 43.
Government of Finland. (1922). *The Law of Taking Care of the Poor*. Helsinki.
Government of Finland. (1936). *Children's Protection Law*. Helsinki.
Government of Finland. (1947). *Committee Report*. Helsinki.
Helsingius, G. A. (1899). *Handbok i fattigvård*. Helsingfors: Simelii arfvingar.
Itkonen, T. I. (1941). Lappalaisten leikit ja ajanvietot. *Lapin sivistysseuran julkaisuja, 9*.

182 M. Paksuniemi and P. Keskitalo

Kerkkonen, K. (1915). Mikä on Riutula? In *Lapin muistoja Riutulan hyväksi, ystäviltä yhteistoimin,* YWCA. Helsinki: Suomalaisen Kirjallisuuden Seuran Kirjapaino osakeyhtiö.

Lehmusvirta, I. (1918). Kertomus työstä Riutulan kodista w.1917. *Kotia Kohti, 10,* 158.

Lehtola, I. (1915). Muistoja. In *Lapin muistoja Riutulan hyväksi. Ystäviltä yhteistoimin,* YWCA. Helsinki: Suomalaisen Kirjallisuuden Seuran Kirjapaino Osakeyhtiö.

Leinto. (1916). Kansakoulu-uutisia Lapista. *Opettajain lehti, 2,* 17–18.

M. C. (1904). L. N. T. *Kotia Kohti, 1,* 12–14.

R. W. D. (1907). Lapinmaa. *Kotia Kohti, 1,* 14.

S. F. (1904). Tietoja L .N. T:stä. *Kotia Kohti, 4,* 58.

Unknown Author. (1909). Kotilähetys. *Kotia Kohti, 11,* 96–97.

Unknown Author. (1920). Lähetysaloiltamme, Inarista. *Kotia Kohti, 5,* 76.

Vihtori. (1915). Inarin Riutulan ylemmän kansakoulun perustamishanke. *Opettajain lehti, 32,* 370.

von Bonsdorff, N. (1904). Kirje Lapista. *Kohti, 2,* 27–30.

von Bonsdorff, N. (1905). I Herren, kära! *Mot Hemmet, 3,* 45–47.

von Bonsdorff, N. (1907a). Tervehdys Lapista. *Kotia Kohti, 3,* 41.

von Bonsdorff, N. (1907b). Kuvaus Lapin Oloista. *Betlehemin Tähti, 12,* 7–8.

von Bonsdorff, N. (1915). Kuvaus Lapin Oloista. *Betlehemin Tähti, 12,* 4–5.

Literatures

Bennet, M., Blackstock, C., & De La Ronde, R. (2005). *A Literature Review and Annotated Bibliography on Aspects of Aboriginal Child Welfare in Canada* (2nd ed.). Winnipeg: The First Nations Research Site of the Centre of Excellence for Child Welfare and The First Nations Child and Family Caring Society of Canada.

Bereson, I. (1989). *Decades of Change: Australia in the Twentieth Century.* Richmond, VIC: Heinemann Educational Australia.

Eeklaar, J. (2004). Children Between Cultures. *International Journal of Law, Policy and the Family, 2,* 178–194.

Erkkilä, R., & Estola, E. (2014). Pitkä koulumatka—Saamelaislapsen Muistoja Kansakoulun Aloittamisesta 1960-luvulla. In P. Keskitalo, V.-P. Lehtola, & M. Paksuniemi (Eds.), *Saamelaisten kansanopetuksen ja koulunkäynnin historia Suomessa* (pp. 263–269). Turku: Siirtolaisuusinstituutti.

10 Christian Morality and Enlightenment to the Natural Child ... 183

Evershed, N., & Allam, L. (2018, May 25). Indigenous Children's Removal on the Rise 21 Years After Bringing Them Home. *The Guardian.*

Harjula, M. (2000). *Terveyden jäljillä: suomalainen terveyspolitiikka 1900-luvulla.* Tampere: University of Tampere.

Hämäläinen, J. (2007). *Lastensuojelun kehityslinjoja: tutkimus Suomen lastensuojelun aatepohjasta ja oppihistoriasta.* Snellman-instituutti.

Hytönen, K.-M., Malinen, A., Salenius, P., Haikari, J., Markkola, P., Kuronen, M., et al. (2016). *Lastensuojelun sijaishuollon epäkohdat ja lasten kaltoinkohtelu 1937–1983.* Jyväskylä: University Digital Archive.

Inari Media. (1995). Inarin joulu. *Inarilaisen joululehti* (pp. 18–21). Ivalo.

Itkonen, T. I. (1941). Lappalaisten leikit ja ajanvietot. *Lapin sivistysseuran julkaisuja, 9.*

Itkonen, T. I. (1984). *Suomen lappalaiset vuoteen 1945. II osa.* Helsinki-Juva: WSOY.

Keskitalo, P., Lehtola, V.-P., & Paksuniemi, M. (Eds.). (2014). *Saamelaisten kansanopetuksen ja kouluhistoria Suomessa.* Turku: Siirtolaisuusinstituutti.

Keskitalo, P., Nyyssönen, J., Linkola, I.-A., Paksuniemi, M., Turunen, T., & McIntosh, L. (2016). Saamelaisten ja Australian alkuperäiskansojen kouluhistorian erityispiirteet. *Ennen ja Nyt: Historian Tietosanomat, 3.* http://www.ennenjanyt.net/2016/09/saamelaisten-ja-australian-alkuperaiskansojen-kouluhistorian-erityispiirteet/.

Korppila, M. (1996). *Talouskoulussa—Kaisa Kitti muistelee. Inarilainen 1996 vuosikirja* (pp. 8–11). Inari: Ukko-Media.

Korppila, M., & Airamo, T. (1999). *Luontaistaloudesta eläneen kylän perinteen kerääminen ja tallentaminen. Viilipytystä purkkimaitoon ja ajohärjästä peltipailakkaan.* Helsinki: Maa- ja metsätalousministeriö. Maatalousosasto.

Kylli, R. (2012). *Saamelaisten kaksi kääntymystä—uskonnon muuttuminen Utsjoen ja Enontekiön lapinmailla* Helsinki: SKS.

Kylli, R. (2014a). Kolmen pitäjän kuolinsyyt paikallisyhteisön kuvastajina 1700- ja 1800-luvun Pohjois-Suomessa. *Ennen ja nyt. Historian tietosanomat, 4.* http://www.ennenjanyt.net/2014/11/kolmen-pitajan-kuolinsyyt-paikallisyhteison-kuvastajina-1700-ja-1800-luvun-pohjois-suomessa/.

Kylli, R. (2014b). Pois pakanallisesta pimeydestä. In P. Keskitalo, V.-P. Lehtola, & M. Paksuniemi (Eds.), *Saamelaisten kansanopetuksen ja koulunkäynnin historia Suomessa* (pp. 30–43). Turku: Siirtolaisuusinstituutti.

Laitala, M., & Puuronen, V. (2016). *Yhteiskunnan tahra. Koulukotien kasvattien vaietut kokemukset.* Tampere: Vastapaino.

184 M. Paksuniemi and P. Keskitalo

Lassila, J. (2001a). *Lapin koulutushistoria – kirkollinen alkuopetus, kansa-, perus- ja oppikoulut, osa 1.* Oulu: University of Oulu.

Lassila, J. (2001b). *Lapin koulutushistoria – kirkollinen alkuopetus, kansa-, perus- ja oppikoulut, osa 2.* Oulu: University of Oulu.

Lehtola, T. (1998). *Kolmen kuninkaan maa.* Inari: Kustannus Puntsi.

Lehtola, V.-P. (2003). Elämää riutulassa. In V.-P. Lehtola (Ed.), *Inari-Aanar: Inarin historia jääkaudesta nykypäivään* (pp. 340–341). Oulu: Painotalo Suomenmaa.

Lehtola, V.-P. (2004). *Saamelainen evakko.* Helsinki: SKS.

Leino, M., & Viitanen, K. (2003). Aikuiseksi kasvaminen suomalaisessa maalaisperheessä 1940–1950-luvuilla. In S. Aapola & M. Kaarninen (Eds.), *Nuoruuden vuosisata. Suomalaisen nuorison historia.* Helsinki: SKS.

Linnanmäki, E. (2005). *Espanjantauti Suomessa. Influenssaepidemia 1918–1920.* Helsinki: SKS.

Manninen, R. (2017). *Raudna Aikio—ilon ja surun vuoristoradalla. Naisten ääni.* Suomi Finland 100. Suomalainen naisliitto ry. http://www.naistenaani.fi/raunda-aikio-ilon-ja-surun-vuoristoradalla/.

Mansikka-aho, V. A. (1994). *Riutula ikirakkaus.* Jyväskylä: Gummerus.

Markkola, P. (2006). *Synti ja siveys: naiset, uskonto ja sosiaalinen työ Suomessa 1860–1920.* Helsinki: University of Helsinki.

Marten, J. A. (2002). *Children and War: A Historical Anthology.* New York: NYU Press.

Moreton-Robinson, A. (2011 [2004]). Whiteness, Epistemology and Indigenous Representation. In A. Moreton-Robinson (Ed.), *Essays in Social and Cultural Criticism: Whitening Race* (pp. 75–88). Canberra: Aboriginal Studies Press.

Paksuniemi, M. (2009). *Tornion alakansakoulunopettajaseminaarin opettajakuva lukuvuosina 1921–1945 rajautuen oppilasvalintoihin, oppikirjoihin ja oheistoimintaan.* Rovaniemi: University of Lapland.

Paksuniemi, M. (2014). *Vahvoiksi kasvaneet. Lapin lapset sodan jaloissa.* Turku: Siirtolaisuusinstituutti.

Paksuniemi, M., Turunen, T., & Keskitalo, P. (2015). Coping with Separation in Childhood—Finnish War Children's Recollections About Swedish Foster Families. *Procedia—Social and Behavioral Sciences, 185*(13), 67–75.

Pulma, P., & Turpeinen, O. (1987). *Suomen lastensuojelun historia.* Helsinki: Lastensuojelun keskusliitto ry.

Rasmus, M. (2008). *Bággu vuolgit, bággu birget. Sámemánáid ceavzinstrategijat Suoma Álbmotskuvlla ásodagain 1950–1960-logus.* Oulu: University of Oulu, Giellagas-institute.

Read, P. (2006). *The Stolen Generations: The Removal of Aboriginal Children in New South Wales 1883 to 1969* (p. 200). Surry Hills, NSW: Aboriginal Affairs (1st pub. 1982).

Saarikangas, K. (2005). *Suomalaisen kodin likaiset paikat: hygienia ja modernin asunnon muotoutuminen.* Helsinki: University of Helsinki.

Sartre, J.-P. (1978). *Sartre by Himself.* New York: Urizen Books.

Satka, M. (2007). Huoltotyöstä sosiaalityöksi, kotikäynneiltä toimistoon. In M. Satka, A. Auvinen, S. Aho, & H. Jaakkola (Eds.), *Kokemuksia ja sattumuksia sosiaalialan vuosikymmeniltä* (pp. 47–52). Jyväskylä: PS-kustannus.

Saukko, T. (2010). *Lapsia ja Jumalan valtakuntaa varten. NNKY:n ulkolähetystyö Inarissa vuosina 1902–1938 ja Riutulan lastenkoti.* MA dissertation. Oulu: University of Oulu.

Saukko, T. (2011). Riutulan lastenkoti ja saamelaisten suomalaistaminen Inarissa 1900-luvun alussa. *Faravid, 35,* 45–59.

Sjögren, D. (2010). *Den säkra zonen: Motiv, åtgärdsförslag och verskamhet i den särskiljande utbildningspolitiken för inhemska minoriteter 1913–1962.* Umeå: University Press.

Smith, A. (2009). *Indigenous Peoples and Boarding Schools: A Comparative Study.* Paper Secretariat of the United Nations Permanent Forum on Indigenous Issues. New York: UN.

Socialdepartementet. *Vanvård i social barnavård – slutrapport.* SOU 2011:61. www.regeringen.se/sb/d/14017/a/176670.

Svanfeldt-Winter, L. (2016). Kansakouluun sopimattomiksi katsotut oppilaat Turussa 1921–1939: Apukoulusiirtojen perustelut sukupuoli- ja luokkanäkökulmasta. *Ennen ja nyt. Historian tietosanomat, 2.* http://www. ennenjanyt.net/2016/09/kansakouluun-sopimattomiksi-katsotut-oppilaat-turussa-1921-1939-apukoulusiirtojen-perustelut-sukupuoli-ja-luokkanakokulmasta/.

Talja-Larrivoire, S. (1976). *Älä unohda minua!.* Helsinki: WSOY.

van Drenth, A., & de Haan, F. (1999). *The Rise of Caring Power: Elizabeth Fry and Jopsephine Butler in Britain and Netherlands.* Amsterdam: Amsterdam University Press.

Vehkalahti, K. (2008). *Daughters of Penitence—Vuorela State Reform School and the Construction of Reformatory Identity, 1893–1923.* Turku: University of Turku.

Veracini, L. (2010). *Settler Colonialism: A Theoretical Overview.* New York: Palgrave Macmillan.

Wendisch, I. (2006). *Salatut Lapset.* Helsinki: Gummerus.

11

History of Early Childhood Education in the Sámi Language in Finland

Marikaisa Laiti

Introduction

This chapter describes a study on the history of early childhood education organised in one of the Sámi languages spoken in Finland. This is a new and less studied perspective of the history of Finnish early education. The study concentrates on the beginning of Sámi early education and the matters that have influenced its' further development. The development of Sámi early education will be approached from two perspectives; first, the legal direction and other influential documents, and second, its implementation at the everyday level. Following Lujala (1999, 55), the study contributes to the history of education. In particular, I have focused on the social-historical study of Sámi early education, meaning that the micro level everyday events are seen as part of a larger historical and societal development (Rinne et al. 2004, 75).

M. Laiti (✉)
Loijakkakieppi 7, Inari, Finland

© The Author(s) 2019
O. Kortekangas et al. (eds.), *Sámi Educational History in a Comparative International Perspective*,
https://doi.org/10.1007/978-3-030-24112-4_11

187

According to Kortekangas (2014, 352), broader and comparative research is needed, since education is always part of larger systems and worldwide trends and does not exist in isolation.

Many researchers (Alila and Kinos 2014; Hänninen and Valli 1986; Lujala 1999; Niiranen and Kinos 2001) have studied the history of early education in Finland focusing on the development of pedagogy, changes in the ideological basis, and development of institutions within Finnish society. Välimäki and Rauhala (2000) in Finland and Pukk (2015) in Estonia noticed that the day-care system and its organisation are tightly connected to changes within society. Moreover, day care has always followed the needs of the society (Välimäki and Rauhala 2000, 402).

Early education settings play an important role in children's lives, and in Finland around 76% of children participate in early education on a daily basis (THL 2017). Early education provided in the Sámi language clearly supports the continuation of this language, its cultural heritage and Sámi children's identities. Most Sámi children live in urban and semi-urban settings, where the Sámi culture cannot be approached directly. This separation is a challenge for indigenous peoples and their children, as fewer language experiences are connected with participation in cultural activities. Moreover, children are seldom able to follow grown-ups performing their traditional work and tasks. Therefore, the role and meaning of early education is of crucial importance (Lehtola and Ruotsala 2017). The successful revitalisation of the Aanaar Sámi language and culture provides a good example of the importance of early childhood education for the Sámi people (Olthuis et al. 2013; Pasanen 2015).

Two important documents that currently set the norms for early education are the "Act of Early Education" (Varhaiskasvatuslaki 2018) and a binding norm called the "Curriculum Guidelines on ECEC" (Varhaiskasvatussuunnitelman perusteet) (OPH 2016). These two documents guide the organisation and implementation of early education in Finland. Through them, the organisation and practice of Sámi early education is tightly connected to the contents and pedagogy of main culture early education (Lehtola 2015; OPH 2016; see also Keskitalo 2010; Rahko-Ravantti 2016).

However, there are some points in the directives that are connected to Sámi children. The Act of Early Education (Varhaiskasvatuslaki 2018, 8§) states that all Sámi children have the right to receive early education in their mother tongue, which is the Sámi language. The Curriculum guidelines on ECEC in Finland (OPH 2016) reinforce that early education for all Sámi children has a special goal to strengthen their Sámi identity and awareness of their own culture. When early education for Sámi children is organised in one of the Sámi languages, the main goal is to strengthen their understanding and usage of the language (OPH 2016, 47–48).

Currently, around 200 children are receiving Sámi language early education in Finland. More than half of these children are in mother tongue groups, with the rest in language nests or language immersion groups (Lehtola and Ruotsala 2017). According to legislation, early education is organised either in early education centres or in family day-care groups (OPH 2016, 14). Other forms, such as language nests or language immersion groups are not official forms of early education and are not part of the children's rights. However, they are mentioned as a possible work orientation.

The development of Sámi early education was studied with the help of the following question: What are the milestones of Sámi early education on guiding, frame-setting and on a practical level in Finland?

Methods

My approach in this study was to identify the main events in the development and implementation of Sámi language early education. In addition, the main phases were reflected by the experiences of early educators working in Sámi language groups and units. I have used the content analysis method to analyse the material in this study (Latvala and Vanhanen–Nuutinen 2001; Mayring 2004; Patton 2002; Tuomi and Sarajärvi 2018). The material was analysed according to its relevance for the development of Sámi early education.

In this study, I interviewed 23 Sámi early educators about their everyday life experiences in Sámi early education. I noticed that many of them shared their experiences regarding how they had been involved in or even initiated the establishment of the Sámi language groups themselves. These stories are used as reflectors of the historical development. Combining the documentation and research interview data could be called an abductive method of analysis, as it forms a dialogue between guidance and practice (Kinos 1999; Pukk 2015). The citations have been translated by the author from Finnish to the English language.

Historical studies always present a restricted perspective on the studied phenomena. Pihlainen (2011) and Lehtola (1997) remind us of the critical usage of historical information. They emphasise the importance of the contextualisation and careful consideration of the acquired information. Knowledge represents only one perspective and researchers of the history must be aware of these limitations (Lujala 1999, 57). One of my own limitations is that I am a representative of the majority culture and interpret the material from this perspective.

The materials analysed consist of relevant laws ($n=1$), acts ($n=2$), decrees ($n=1$), committee reports ($n=1$), Sámi Parliament documents, reports and publications ($n=8$), the norms ($n=1$) and research literature ($n=4$). In Finland, there is a law and several acts regarding Sámi early education. Since 1981, the Day Care Act has recognised Sámi children (Laki lasten päivähoidosta 1973, 875/1981, 11§). This Act was supported by the amendment to the Decree of Day Care in 1994 (Asetus lasten päivähoidosta 1973, 1336/1994, 1a§). The decree was replaced by a new one in 2018 which no longer recognised the need for Sámi children's early education. The Day Care Act was changed to the Early Education Act in 2018 (Varhaiskasvatuslaki 2018), with the same rights for the Sámi children as earlier. The Finnish government gave Indigenous status to the Sámi people in 1999 in Finnish Constitution 17.3§ (Suomen perustuslaki 1999).

The Sámi Parliament represents the Sámi people in Finland. It has made several commitments and verdicts (Saamelaiskäräjät 2007, 2008, 2014, 2015c, d) concerning Sámi day care and early childhood education. It has also prepared and implemented use of the supporting pedagogical material (Saamelaiskäräjät 2009, 2013, 2015a, b).

Documents about the establishment of Sámi language units and groups were mostly resources such as early education curriculums (Inarin kunta 2017; Utsjoen kunta 2018), reports (Lehtola 2015; Lehtola and Ruotsala 2017; Länsman 2008), research publication (Pasanen 2015) or statements (Saamelaiskäräjät 2008) and Sámi association pages (Saaminuett 2010).

Some master lever studies, for example Helander (1994) and Lehtola (2015), and doctoral dissertations by Äärelä (2016) and Laiti (2018), focus on the establishment and implementation of early education in Sámi languages. They approach Sámi early education from the parents', workers' and language perspectives. Guttorm (1984), Guttorm (1986), Lehtola and Ruotsala (2017), OKM (2012), Pasanen (2016), and Vuolab (1983) have all reported on the situation of early education in Sámi languages in different time periods.

When researching the legislation, documents and literature connected to the development of Sámi language early education, I identified three different phases (see Keskitalo et al. 2013, 10–11, periods for school development). I named the first period as the proceeding phase of institutional Sámi language early education. The second phase is formed by the establishment and expansion of Sámi early education, and the third phase represents the increase in pedagogical interest. Following Rowan (2007), these are seen to form the developmental frames for Sámi language early education. These three phases partly overlap in time and each has its own legislative and other influencing basis. The practical implementation of these phases will be presented next.

The Three Phases of Sámi Language Early Education

The Proceeding Phase: Before the First Experimentations

Finnish society experienced drastic changes because of World War II. This influenced the Sámi community both during and after wartime.

The Sámi people were living mostly in the northern part of Finland before the war and practised a nature-bound economy. However, two remarkable things happened: evacuation of the inhabitants from Lapland to the western part of Finland in 1944 and the rebuilding of Lapland later when these people returned (Lehtola 2004; Vuolab 1983). These events caused gradual changes in the Sámi community and their daily life. Lehtola (2004, 168–169) describes how the main way of life changed to become a new, alternative model for life and how the meaning of the Sámi nature-bound life declined. An exchange economy was introduced and multi-economical livelihoods increased. Parents could now work for a salary, meaning that fewer children could observe the daily activities of adults as much as before (Vuolab 1983, 10). Keskitalo et al. (2013, 10) mentioned that these changes weakened school-age children in particular because institutionalised education had started for all children over 7 years earlier in 1947.

By that time, many people started to think that the Sámi language had no future, and the Finnish language was largely used with children even in Sámi speaking homes. Due to this assimilative practice, the loss of the Sámi language began. There are examples of workers in Sámi early education who have experienced this disconnection with their mother tongue and needed language lessons to regain these language skills. One such as interviewee spoke about her experience.

> Well, I had worked for 30 years as family day care worker. Then I… well…got an idea to learn Sámi. My mother is Sámi, she spoke Sámi in those times, but not with us children. Then, after that language course, I came to work here. (Ed 16)

Before the first Sámi language experimental activities for young children were established, Sámi children under school age used to spend their time within their home communities (Balto, 1997; Päivänsalo 1953; Saamelaiskäräjät 2009, 11; Seitamo 1991; Storjord 2009). They continued to share the home environments until the 1980s (Lehtola and Ruotsala 2017; Vuolab 1983). Some of the interviewees spoke about their childhood experiences, for example the sharing of everyday chores and having responsibilities within their Sámi communities.

I must have always taken care of my younger brother… from early on. It's usual…, one child takes care of another. (Ed 21)

The rights of Sámi children became an issue when the Sámi Delegation (the predecessor of Sámi Parliament) was established in 1973 and raised educational questions concerning Sámi children (Lehtola 1997). However, this did not have an immediate influence on the first Law of Child Care, which was issued in Finland in 1973. There was no reference to the Sámi children's position or right to day care in their own language in this law. Until the 1990s, even in the Sámi Homeland area, Sámi children participated in Finnish language day care (Helander 1994).

At state level, early education began gradually in Finland in the nineteenth century. According to Välimäki and Rauhala (2000, 402), Finnish early education was a new phenomenon, and its massive development began only in the 1970s. From the beginning, there has been two, partly competing, approaches to early education, namely social and educational. The social tasks focused on supporting poor families to raise their children, while educational tasks focused on children and their development based on Fröbelian pedagogy (Niiranen and Kinos 2001, 62). Before the first Law of Early Education was passed in 1973, education was marked mostly by social welfare support for poor families and working parents. Urbanisation, the need for a women's workforce and moving away from relatives were the reasons why Finnish society had to consider supporting families with a general day-care system. The First Law of Day Care (Laki lasten päivähoidosta 1973) led to better economical and administrative approaches for children's public day care services.

Establishment of Sámi Language Day Care and Its Expansion from Utsjoki to Helsinki

Initially, institutionalised day care created a context for the establishment of Sámi language early education facilities. The actual history of institutionalised Sámi language early education began in 1981 in

Utsjoki, the northernmost municipality in Finland. This was much later than in Norway where the first activity was established in 1969 (Storjord 2009). In the case of Sweden, Sámi language under school-age activities were established at the same time as in Finland (Sarri and Kuhmunen 2008, 4).

Parents of Sámi children demanded day care in the North Sámi language in Utsjoki (Guttorm 1986; Komiteanmietintö 1985; Vuolab 1983). They pointed out that the day care of Sámi children was mostly provided in the Finnish language (Komiteanmietintö 1985, 204). The initial demand was made to ensure that the language remained alive and is transferred to the next generations. This resulted in a circulating group day-care experiment from November 1981 until May 1983 (Guttorm 1984; Vuolab 1983). The event was the start of the history and establishment phase and gradual expansion of Sámi language early education.

It is remarkable that the first Sámi language day-care initiative took place just before the Child Day Care Act was renewed in December 1981 (Laki lasten päivähoidosta 1973, 875/1981). According to acts' 11§, the availability of Sámi mother tongue child care became compulsory everywhere in Finland. The same sentence is included in the present Act of early education, which states that "municipalities have in addition to take care that child day care be provided in the child's mother tongue, Finnish, Swedish or the Sámi language" (Varhaiskasvatuslaki 2018, 11§). This was the first time that Sámi children's right to mother tongue child day care was recognised in Finnish legislative history. However, despite this, most Sámi children still enter Finnish language day care, specially outside the Sámi Homeland area (Lehtola and Ruotsala 2017; Saamelaiskäräjät 2008).

The Report of the Sámi Culture Committee (Komiteanmietintö 1985) deals extensively with the cultural life of the Sámi people, including early childhood education. It was mentioned in this report that Sámi day care is such a new phenomenon that it misses its own model (Komiteanmietintö 1985, 205). The report presented practical ideas for development and organising Sámi day care, including for example 100% state support, establishment of day-care groups for the bigger

11 History of Early Childhood Education ...   195

population centres in the Sámi Homeland area[1] and state support for material production (Komiteanmietintö 1985, 388–389).

Despite post-war changes in the society, and first day-care experimentations in Utsjoki, Sámi children under school age largely continued to have the same everyday life as adults. Some of the interviewees talked about their experiences of everyday life with their parents or other relatives and how they learned to practice and value the Sámi way of life. They felt that this is their strength in their present working life.

> Then of course... my own childhood memories like using reindeer fur for a toboggan slide... now we do it here with children. And then... what I learned in my childhood too are the traditional skills, I try to teach them for children here... like catching willow grouses. I used to do it with my father. Now we have made some traps in the nearby forest with the older children. (Ed4)

This study shows that Sámi language groups gradually increased in number from 1995 onwards, first in the Sámi Homeland area and then expanding from the end of the 1990s on into other parts of Finland. From the 1990s on, expansion of Sámi language services became necessary due to the increasing movement of the Sámi people outside the Sámi Homeland area. In fact, by the beginning of 2000, more than 50% of Sámi children were living in other parts of Finland. What they lacked there was provision of early education in the Sámi language (Länsman 2008, 8–11).

The expansion of Sámi language services started right after the amendment to the Decree of Day Care in 1994. This amendment clarified that one of the educational goals was to provide cultural and language support for Sámi children in collaboration with the representatives of the culture. In 1999, the status of the Sámi people was written into the Constitution Law of Finland (Suomen perustuslaki 1999,

---

[1] The Sámi Homeland area comprises the three northernmost municipalities of Finland (Utsjoki, Inari and Enontekiö) and the area of the Lapland Reindeer Herding Association in the municipality of Sodankylä. It is defined in the Sámi Parliament Act of 1995 (Laki Saamelaiskäräjistä 1995).

196 M. Laiti

17§3), which again strengthened the Sámi peoples' right to maintain and develop their own language and culture. This was a clear sign of the important position of Sámi people within Finnish society. These two events in legislation seem to have been important for the establishment of Sámi day-care groups and units, since most of the present time groups were established after these events.

How the Establishment of Units and Groups Was Realised

It wasn't until the mid-1990s that early educational activities in all of three Sámi languages in the Sámi Homeland area municipalities were seen. All of the activities had some breaks at the beginning before becoming more permanent and receiving regular financing. From the start, the language used in these groups has been one of the Sámi languages.

When collecting and transcribing the research material, the novelty/ newness of Sámi language units and groups became clear since many of the early educators interviewed shared their experiences of establishing them. The following example is a typical story of how the initiation and establishment of these units and groups has taken place:

> Mk: Would you tell me, how have you come to work in Sámi early education?
> Ed20: Yes... well it was like... that when people awakened to idea that... if now nothing happens... the language will disappear. They were aware of Maori language bathing principles and thought that "Why wouldn't it work here, if it has worked there.... Let's try." Then these locals, they started to ask me, since they knew I've been working with children for a long time. They said "... and then you begin ... we will start a new group and you need to apply for it".

The research materials show the importance of active individuals in the initiation and establishment of these units. In fact, their role has been crucial throughout this history (Laiti 2014; Länsman 2008). In the conversation below, one early educator shares her experience of the initiation and later establishment of one day-care unit. This example illustrates the importance of local activity.

> Mk: How did it all start here, how did you come to think about establishing a Sámi language unit here?
> Ed1: ... Sámi people themselves were active for it for a long time... I myself was also collecting names for the list... two different times. But somehow it remained in some politician's drawer, it didn't proceed then... to the state level. But then, well one local politician on a municipality level, made again a new initiation in year 2006 or so, and again started the settlement of the need... and some two years later I started a new Sámi language group with a small number of children... soon we needed a second worker.

Nowadays, most early education units using the Sámi language are located in the Sámi Homeland area villages and population centres, and in the biggest towns in other parts of Finland (Lehtola and Ruotsala 2017). Most of the early education is organised in the North Sámi language and in the form of language nests. According to Lehtola and Ruotsala (2017), there were 13 units in the Sámi Homeland area and six units and one integrated group in other parts of Finland. Out of these Sámi Homeland area units, five were mother tongue groups (in North Sámi) and the rest of the units were language nest groups. Again, in other parts of Finland, there were two mother tongue groups (in North Sámi) and four groups/units were language nest groups. Aanaar and Skolt Sámi language nests can be found only in the Inari municipality.

Pedagogical Interest in Sámi Language Early Education

The first two decades, 1980s and 1990s, of Sámi language early education were labelled as times of establishment and expansion. The use of Sámi languages and their maintenance was the ultimate reason and main focus during these decades. This is well described by one educator who said:

198   M. Laiti

...there has not actually been anything else but the struggle with language all of the 36 years that I've been working... so... not a great proceeding. (Ed13)

Finnish early education was initially established to take care of children while parents worked (Hänninen and Valli 1986). Until 1996, the right for public services was connected to parent's employment, and from then on early education has been the subjective right of a child (Alila and Kinos 2014). This approach was still strong by the time the first Sámi day-care groups were established in the 1980s. Pedagogical questions were not central at that time either in the Finnish day-care discussions (Niiranen and Kinos 2001) or in the Sámi ones (Saamelaiskäräjät 2008).

Pedagogical and content aspects of Sámi early education became an issue in the 2000s when it was noticed that the number of children entering Sámi language services was continuously increasing. Another reason was the understanding that children had less and less daily contact with Sámi languages and culture, and the threat of these disappearing was more real than ever before. This meant that these issues needed more explicit attention. The third phase is therefore named the pedagogical phase.

One reason for the greater attention to content and increased pedagogical interest was mentioned in the Sámi Parliament Report in 2008. The report highlighted that Sámi day-care practices were based on the Finnish system of values and practices in an assimilative and integrative manner. It also mentioned that Sámi children were being directed more towards Finnish society than the Sámi community. As a result, a day-care system that would be based on Sámi beliefs, values and attitudes was demanded (Saamelaiskäräjät 2008).

An increasing number of children had less contact with the Sámi culture and languages and the main cultural basis for Sámi early education was due to the pedagogical demand. Soon after, most of the present-day Sámi day-care units were established in Finland and the Sámi Parliament demanded day care based on the Sámi culture in 2008. The first Sámi early education curriculum was published in 2009 (Saamelaiskäräjät 2009). The purpose of this curriculum was to ensure the quality of Sámi early education and its content and pedagogical implementation. The curriculum also aimed to ensure equality in Sámi early education services (Saamelaiskäräjät 2009, 43). Later, this curriculum was followed by guidelines for everyday practices (Saamelaiskäräjät 2013), which aimed to make the culture-based practices more visible and concrete. It is notable that neither of these documents has official status in the Finnish educational system.

One of the important changes supporting the pedagogical approach in Sámi early education can be seen in Finnish early education in general. This was the administrative shift at state level. In the year 2013, responsibility for early education moved from the Ministry of Social Welfare to the Ministry of Education. In addition, the emphasis on early education shifted from the social to pedagogical approach.

Conclusion

According to this study, four events can be considered as milestones in Sámi early education in Finland. The first was the Renewed Law of Day Care 1981, which resulted in all Sámi children in Finland having the right to Sámi language day care. Next, in 1994, the Decree of Day Care was added with a new goal of upbringing to support Sámi children's own culture and language. In 1999, the Sámi people in Finland were given the status of indigenous people, which was the third important milestone. This status increased the demand for Sámi language early education. Lastly, in 2008, the Sámi Parliament called for more pedagogical activity for Sámi day care, which led to the pedagogical discussion and implementation of Sámi early education. This received support from the state and norm-setting changes were made in 2013 when the Ministry of Education took over responsibility for early education.

Sámi day-care units (in all three Sámi languages) were first established in the Sámi Homeland area of Finland. From the year 2000 onwards, they expanded to other parts of country. It is interesting that, in spite of commitments from municipalities to organise Sámi language day care since 1981, the local communities and parents must have played a role in realising the service. Their activity has particularly supported the expansion of Sámi early education from Utsjoki to Helsinki over the past 40 years (Helander 1994; Komiteanmietintö 1985, 386; Lehtola 2015; Länsman 2008, 10).

Following the change in the ministry responsible for early education, the pedagogical approach has been strongly emphasised in the national Curriculum Guidelines on ECEC (OPH 2016). There is also a growing understanding that indigenous pedagogy needs to be established into cultural ways of child-rearing, teaching and learning (Keskitalo et al. 2013; Laiti 2018; Nãone and Au 2010). However, according to the report by the Sámi culture committee, the official and legitimised Sámi early education pedagogy, as a collected and summarised set of educational practices, failed to achieve its aims by 1985 (Komiteanmietintö 1985, 205). Indeed, a well-established model for Sámi pedagogy for schools has been achieved only recently (Keskitalo et al. 2013), suggesting that the education is based on culturally sensitive Sámi values (see also Saamelaiskäräjät 2008).

According to this study, Sámi early education has developed gradually with the help of local activity and supportive legislation. The history of Sámi language early education could be called a story of victories and success. Saarikivi (2014, 349) sees it as positive that Sámi language early education now has an official status all over Finland. On the other hand, it is a short story of complex and sporadic development. Sámi early education has developed within the Finnish legislative and institutional system in an invisible and quiet way. This has meant that it lacks a model or organisation of its own, and does not have its own legal, officially accepted and binding core curricula. Furthermore, its task as the revitaliser and transmitter of the Sámi languages and culture is not clearly recognised within the Finnish system of early education. Sámi early education was also weakened when the goals of upbringing were moved from the Decree of Day Care to the Core Curriculum of ECE (OPH 2016). In this curriculum, the goals for Sámi children's upbringing were removed.

The organisation and implementation of Sámi early education still needs to develop further to meet the needs of the Sámi people (Keskitalo 2010; Laiti 2018; Saamelaiskäräjät 2014, 2015d). The institutions also have a societal task to raise children within their surrounding society (Tudge 2008, 1). I hope we can learn from the history and work harder in a co-operative (Heikkilä et al. 2013) and community-based (Gruenewald and Smith 2008) way to ensure the implementation of a coherent and coordinated Sámi early education model. This should help to maintain a strong connection between indigenous generations and decolonise children's early education.

References

Äärelä, R. (2016). *"Dat ii leat dušše dat giella"- "Se ei ole vain se kieli"* [It's Not Just the Language]. Rovaniemi: Lapin yliopisto.

Alila, K., & Kinos, J. (2014). Katsaus varhaiskasvatuksen historiaan. [Review in History of Early Education]. In K. Alila, M. Eskelinen, E. Estola, T. Kahiluoto, J. Kinos, H.-M. Pekuri, et al. (Eds.), *Varhaiskasvatuksen historia, nykytila ja kehittämisen suuntalinjat* [History, Present and Future Lines of Early Education]. Opetus-ja kulttuuriministeriön työryhmämuistioita ja selvityksiä 2014:12.

Asetus lasten päivähoidosta. (1973). *Degree of Child Day-Care.* Retrieved from https://www.finlex.fi/fi/laki/ajantasa/1973/19730239.

Balto, A. (1997). *Sámisk barneoppdragelse i endring* [Sámi Childrearing in Change]. Grovik: Ad Notam Gyldendal AS.

Gruenewald, D. A., & Smith, G. A. (Eds.). (2008). *Place-Based Education in the Global Age: Local Diversity.* New York: LEA.

Guttorm, H. (1984). *Avoimen kiertävän päiväkodin saamen kielen ja kulttuurin opetuskokeilu Utsjoen kunnassa* [The Teaching Experiment of Sámi Language and Culture in Open and Circulating Day-Care in Utsjoki]. Utsjoki: Utsjoen kunta.

Guttorm, J. (1986). *Alle kouluikäisten saamelaisten kasvuolosuhteet ja niiden kehittämismahdollisuudet Utsjoen kunnassa* [Under School-Age Sámi Children Circumstances and Development of Them in Utsjoki]. Helsinki: Valtion painatuskeskus.

Hänninen, S.-L., & Valli, S. (1986). *Suomen lastentarhatyön ja varhaiskasvatuksen historia* [History of Kindergarten Work and Early Education in Finland]. Keuruu: Otava.

Heikkilä, L., Laiti-Hedemäki, E., & Pohjola, A. (2013). *Saamelaisten hyvä elämä ja hyvinvointipalvelut* [Sámi Peoples' Good Life and Well-Fare Services]. Rovaniemi: Lapin yliopistokustannus.

Helander, P. (1994). *Saamenkielinen päivähoito Utsjoen, Inarin ja Enontekön kunnisssa* [Sámi Language Day-Care in Utsjoki, Inari and Enontekiö]. Jyväskylä: Jyväskylän yliopisto.

Inarin kunta. (2017). *Inarin kunnan varhaiskasvatussuunntelma* [Core Curriculum of Inari Municipality]. Retrieved from http://www.inari.fi/media/tiedostot-2017/sivistysosasto-2017/varhaiskasvatus//vasu-suomenkielinen-kommentointia-varten.pdf.

Keskitalo, P. (2010). *Saamelaiskoulun kulttuurisensitiivisyyttä etsimässä kasvatusantropologian keinoin* [Cultural Sensitivity in the Sámi School Through Educational Antropology]. Diedut 1/2010. Guovdageaidnu: Sámi Allaskuvla.

Keskitalo, P., Määttä, K., & Uusiautti, S. (2013). *Sámi Education*. Frankfurt am Main: Peter Lang.

Kinos, J. (1999). Vuoropuhelua lähihistorian dokumenttien kanssa [Dialogue with Near-History Documents]. In I. Ruoppila, E. Hujala, K. Karila, J. Kinos, P. Niiranen, & M. Ojala (Eds.), *Varhaiskasvatuksen tutkimusmenetelmiä* [Research Methods in Early Education] (pp. 73–88). Jyväskylä: Atena.

Komiteanmietintö. (1985). *Saamelaiskulttuuritoimikunnan mietintö* [Report of Sámi Culture Committee]. Komiteanmietintö 1985:66. Helsinki: Sisäasiainministeriö.

Kortekangas, O. (2014). Uusia suuntia, vanhoja rajoja - saamelaisten kouluhistorian moniääninen tulevaisuus [New Direction, Old Borders—The Multivocal Future of Sámi Peoples School History]. In P. Keskitalo, V.-P. Lehtola, & M. Paksuniemi (Eds.), *Saamelaisen kansanopetuksen ja koulunkäynnin historia Suomessa* [The History of Sámi Folk Education and School Attendance in Finland] (pp. 351–357). Turku: Siirtolaisinstituutti.

Laki lasten päivähoidosta. (1973). *Act of Child Day-Care*. Retrieved from https://www.finlex.fi/fi/laki/alkup/1973/19730036.

Laki Saamelaiskäräjistä. (1995). *Act of Sámi Parliament*. Retrieved from https://www.finlex.fi/fi/laki/ajantasa/1995/19950974.

Laiti, M. (2014). Arki, kulttuuri ja kasvatuskumppanuus. In P. Keskitalo, S. Uusiautti, E. Sarivaara, & K. Määttä (Eds.), *Saamelaispedagogiikan ydinkysymysten äärellä* (pp. 111–124). Rovaniemi: Lapin yliopistokustannus.

Laiti, M. (2018). *Saamelaisen varhaiskasvatuksen toteutus Suomessa* [The Implementation of Sámi Early Childhood Education in Finland]. Acta Universitatis Lapponiensis 376. Rovaniemi: Lapin Yliopisto.

Länsman, A. (2008). *Saamen kieli pääkaupunkiseudulla* [Sámi Language in the Capital Area]. Vähemmistövaltuutetun Julkaisusarja 5. Helsinki: Edita.

Latvala, E., & Vanhanen–Nuutinen, L. (2001). Laadullisen hoitotieteellisen tutkimuksen perusprosessi: sisällönanalyysi [The Basic Process of Qualitative Nursing Science Research: Content Analysis]. In S. Janhonen & M. Nikkonen (Eds.), *Laadulliset tutkimusmenetelmät hoitotieteessä* [Qualitative Methods in Nursing Science] (pp. 81–115). Helsinki: WSOY.

Lehtola, R. (2015). *Saamenkielinen päivähoito kieli- ja kulttuurikasvattajana* [Sámi Language Day-Care as Language and Culture Educator]. Pro gradu –tutkielma. Oulu: Oulun yliopisto.

Lehtola, R., & Ruotsala, P. (2017). *Saamenkielisten palveluiden nykytilakartoitus* [Survey of Sámi Language Services in Present] Inari: Saamelaiskäräjät.

Lehtola, V.-P. (1997). *Saamelaiset. Historia, yhteiskunta, taide* [Sámi Peoples: History, Society, Art] Inari: Kustannus-Puntsi.

Lehtola, V.-P. (2004). *Saamelainen evakko* [Sámi Evacuee]. Inari: Kustannus-Puntsi.

Lujala, E. (1999). Historian tutkimuksesta paikallisen päivähoidon vaiheisiin [From History Research to Phases of Local Day-Care]. In I. Ruoppila, E. Hujala, K. Karila, J. Kinos, P. Niiranen, & M. Ojala (Eds.), *Varhaiskasvatuksen tutkimusmenetelmiä* [Research Methods in Early Education] (pp. 55–72). Jyväskylä: Atena.

Mayring, P. (2004). Qualitative Content Analysis. In U. Flick, E. von Kardoff, & I. Steinke (Eds.), *A Companion to Qualitative Research* (pp. 266–269). London: Sage.

Nãone, C. K., & Au, K. (2010). Culture as a Framework Versus Ingredient in Early Childhood Education: A Native Hawaiian Perspective. In O. N. Saracho & B. Spodek (Eds.), *Contemporary Perspectives on Language and Cultural Diversity in Early Childhood Education* (pp. 147–165). Charlotte, NC: IAP Information Age Publishing.

Niiranen, P., & Kinos, J. (2001). Suomalaisen lastentarha- ja päiväkotipedagogiikan jäljillä [On Steps of Finnish Kindergarten Pedagogy]. In K. Karila, J. Kinos, & J. Virtanen (Eds.), *Varhaiskasvatuksen teoriasuuntauksia* (pp. 58–85) Juva: WSOY.

OKM. (2012). *Toimenpideohjelma saamen kielten elvyttämiseksi* [Operational Program for Revitalizing Sámi Languages]. Opetus- ja kulttuuriministeriön työryhmämuistioita ja selvityksiä 2012:7. Retrieved from http://urn.fi/URN :ISBN:978-952-263-121-3.

Olthuis, M.-L., Kivelä, S., & Skutnabb-Kangas, T. (2013). *Revitalising Indigenous Languages: How to Recreate a Lost Generation*. Bristol: Multilingual Matters.

OPH. (2016). *Varhaiskasvatussuunnitelman perusteet* [Core Curriculum of Early Education]. Määräykset ja ohjeet 2016:17. Retrieved from

204   M. Laiti

http://www.oph.fi/download/179349_varhaiskasvatussuunnitelman_perusteet_2016.pdf.

Päivänsalo, P. (1953). *Lappalaisten lastenhoito- ja kasvatustavoista* [Lappish Child Care and Child-Rearing Practices]. Helsinki: Suomen kasvatus-sosiologinen yhdistys.

Pasanen, A. (2015). *Kuávsui ja peeivicuová. 'Sarastus ja päivänvalo'.* Inarinsaamen kielen revitalisaatio [Dawn and Daylight: The Revitalization of Aanar Sámi Language]. Uralica Helsingiensia 9. Helsinki: Unigrafia Oy.

Pasanen, A. (2016). *Saamebarometri* [Sámi Barometer]. Oikeusministeriön julkaisu 39/2016. Helsinki. Retrieved from http://urn.fi/URN:I SBN:978-952-259-530-0.

Patton, M. Q. (2002). *Qualitative Research and Evaluation Methods.* Thousand Oaks, CA: Sage.

Pihlainen, K. (2011). Historia, historiatietoisuus ja menneisyyden käyttö. [History, History Consciousness and Usage of Past]. *Kasvatus & Aika, 5*(3), 5–17.

Pukk, M. (2015). *Varhaiskasvatus Virossa – Aikalaiskuvauksia lastentarhatoiminnan alkuajoista nykypäivään* [Early Childhood Education in Estonia— Contemporary Descriptions of the Kindergarten Practices from the Early Days to the Present]. Tampere: Tampereen yliopisto.

Rahko-Ravantti, R. (2016). *Saamelaisopetus Suomessa* [Sámi Education in Finland]. Rovaniemi: Lapin yliopisto.

Rinne, R., Kivirauma, J., & Lehtinen, E. (2004). *Johdatus kasvatustieteisiin* [Introduction on Educational Sciences]. Helsinki: WSOY.

Rowan, M. C. (2007). Considering the Framework for Inuit Child Care. *Canadian Journal of Native Education, 30*(1), 52–61.

Saamelaiskäräjät. (2007). *Lausunto luonnoksesta valtioneuvoston lapsi-ja nuorisopolitiikan kehittämisohjelmaksi* [Proportion of Cabinets Child and Youth Political Draft for Developmental Program].

Saamelaiskäräjät. (2008). *Saamelaisten lasten kielellisten ja kulttuuristen oikeuksien turvaaminen päivähoidossa* [Ensuring the Language and Cultural Rights of Sámi Children in Day-Care]. Saamelaiskäräjät kannanotto [Sámi Parliament Statement].

Saamelaiskäjärät. (2009). *Saamelainen varhaiskasvatussuunnitelma* [Core Curriculum of Sámi Early Education]. Inari: Inarin kunta. Retrieved from http://www.inari.fi/media/files/sote_savasusuomenkielinen.pdf.

Saamelaiskäräjät. (2013). *Saamelaisen varhaiskasvatuksen arjen käytäntöjen opas* [Guidelines for Implementation of Sámi Early Education]. SaKaste-Saamelaisten sosiaali- ja terveyspalvelujen kehittäminen – hanke.

11 History of Early Childhood Education … 205

Saamelaiskäräjät. (2014). *Saamelaisten perus- ja ihmisoikeuksien toteutuminen saamenkielisessä päivähoidossa* [The Implementation of Basic and Human Rights of Sámi Children in Sámi Language Day-Care]. Kannanotto [Statement].

Saamelaiskäräjät. (2015a). *Menetelmäopas kielipesätyöntekijöille* [Guidelines for Workers in Language-Nest]. Inari: Saamelaiskäräjät. Retrieved from http://www.kuati.fi/media/.materials/o_1a0ekcn6d2e089b118ge0s16eb10.pdf.

Saamelaiskäräjät. (2015b). *Opas kielipesälasten vanhemmille* [Guidelines for Language-Nest Children's Parents]. Inari: Saamelaiskäräjät. Retrieved from http://www.kuati.fi/media/.materials/o_1a0eka43u1u6s1l8q1n4h191thpc10.pdf.

Saamelaiskäräjät. (2015c). *Lausunto hallituksen esityksestä varhaiskasvatuslaiksi* [Statement of Governmental Proposition for Law of Early Education].

Saamelaiskäräjät. (2015d). *Esitys saamelaisten varhaiskasvatuspalvelujen, kulttuurin ja kielipesätoiminnan turvaamiseksi ja kehittämiseksi vuonna 2017* [Proposition for Ensuring and Developing the Sámi Early Education Services, Culture and Language-Nest Activities Year 2017].

Saaminuett. (2010). *Koltasaamen kielipesä Sevettijärvellä* [Skolt Sámi Language-Nest in Sevettijärvi]. Retrieved from http://www.saaminuett.fi/saami-nuett-ry/toiminnan-kulmakivet/koltansaamen-kielipesae-sevettijaervellae.html.

Saarikivi, J. (2014). Vähemmistökielten suojelu ja vähemmistökielinen koulutus saamelaiskontekstissa [The Protection of Minority Languages and Minority Language Schooling in Sámi Context]. In P. Keskitalo, V.-P. Lehtola, & M. Paksuniemi (Eds.), *Saamelaisen kansanopetuksen ja koulunkäynnin historia Suomessa* (pp. 340–350). Turku: Siirtolaisinstituutti.

Sarri, C., & Kuhmunen, G. (2008). *Kan samisk traditionell kunskap överföras till en ny tid i den samiska förskolan, och i så fall hur?* [Is It Possible to Shift Traditional Knowledge to the Present Sámi Early Education, and How?]. Luleå: Luleå Tekniska Universitet. Retrieved from https://www.ltu.se/cms_fs/1.4622!/kunskapsöverföring.pdf.

Seitamo, L. (1991). *Psychological Development in Arctic Cultures: A Comparative Study of Skolt Saami and Finnish Children in the North of Finland Within the Frame of Reference of Ecological Psychology.* Oulu: Oulun yliopisto.

Storjord, M. H. (2009). *Sámi mánáidgárddiid historijá* [History of Sámi Kindergartens]. Karasjohka: Davvi Girjji. Retrieved from http://skuvla.info/skolehist/storjord-s.htm.

Suomen perustuslaki. (1999). *The Constitution of Finland.* Retrieved from http://www.finlex.fi/fi/laki/ajantasa/1999/19990731#L2P17.

206 M. Laiti

THL. (2017). *Varhaiskasvatus 2016. Tilastoraportti 29/2017* [Early Childhood Education 2016. Statistical Report 29/2017]. Retrieved from http://www.julkari.fi/bitstream/handle/10024/135183/Tr29_17_vuositilasto.pdf?sequence=5&isAllowed=y.

Tudge, J. (2008). *The Everyday Lives of Young Children*. New York: Cambridge University Press.

Tuomi, J., & Sarajärvi, A. (2018). *Laadullinen tutkimus ja sisällönanalyysi* [Qualitative Research and Content Analysis]. Helsinki: Tammi.

Utsjoen kunta. (2018). *Utsjoen kunnan varhaiskasvatussuunnitelma* [Core Curriculum of Utsjoki Municipality]. Retrieved from http://www.utsjoki.fi/media/Sivistystoimi/Varhaiskasvatus/.8.2018.pdf.

Välimäki, A.-L., & Rauhala, P. (2000). Lasten päivähoidon taipuminen yhteiskunnallisiin murroksiin Suomessa [The Yielding of Children's Day-Care for Societal Changes in Finland]. *Yhteiskuntapolitiikka, 65*(5), 387–405.

Varhaiskasvatuslaki. (2018). *Act of Early Education*. Retrieved from https://www.finlex.fi/fi/laki/ajantasa/1973/19730036#L2P1.

Vuolab, K. (1983). *Raportti saamen kielen ja kulttuurin opetuksen kokeilusta Utsjoella* [The Report of Experiment of Sámi Language and Culture Teaching in Utsjoki]. Utsjoki: Utsjoen kunta.

12

A Historical Perspective of Indigenous Education Policy in Japan: The Case of Ainu Schools

Yoko Tanabe

Introduction

In the late nineteenth century, Japan underwent drastic political, social and economic changes. Following the Meiji Restoration of 1868 (the political revolution which ended the regime of the Tokugawa Shogun and restored the Emperor to supreme power), Japan pursued vigorous efforts to build a modern nation-state. As part of the government's modernization policy, Ezochi, the northern island which was inhabited by the indigenous Ainu people, was renamed Hokkaido and incorporated into Japan under the doctrine of *terra nullius* (Siddle 1996). By the provisions of the *Family Register Act of 1871*, the Meiji government nominally granted Japanese citizenship to the Ainu people as *heimin* (commoners). However, the Ainu were required to register themselves with a Japanese family name and were treated as little more than second-class citizens. In addition, traditional Ainu culture and customs,

Y. Tanabe (✉)
UCL Institute of Education, London, UK
e-mail: y.tanabe.14@ucl.ac.uk

© The Author(s) 2019
O. Kortekangas et al. (eds.), *Sámi Educational History in a Comparative International Perspective*,
https://doi.org/10.1007/978-3-030-24112-4_12

207

such as women's tattoos and men's earrings, were considered uncivilized and were banned. When it came to education, two different schooling systems for the Ainu coexisted in the Meiji era (1868–1912): government-operated elementary schools and those run by the Church Missionary Society (CMS)—an Anglican mission society established in London in 1799.

Recent decades have witnessed a distinct shift in perspectives on Ainu historiography (see, for example, Emori 2007; Hirose 1996; Iwasaki 1998; Kaiho 1992; Nakamura 1991; Ogawa 1997; Takegahara 2008a, b). As Howell (2008) has demonstrated, there has been a growing number of studies on Ainu-centred histories seen through various theoretical lenses "to overcome the nation-state's centrality in discourses about the Japanese archipelago" (p. 123). Ogawa (1997) was one of the first to carry out a systematic study of the modern Ainu education system. Moreover, there has been a renewal of interest in the CMS Ainu schools and missionary works among Japanese scholars in recent decades (Nakamura 2003, 2005, 2008; Ogawa 2015; Shimoda 2013). Of particular significance among English-language scholarship on the topic is Frey's dissertation (2007), which traces the CMS Ainu schools' history using CMS archive materials and illuminates overlooked aspects of Japan's indigenous policy vis-a-vis CMS Ainu schools in the late nineteenth century. Despite these recent efforts, however, relatively little comparative research has been done to date on the two above-mentioned education systems.

The purpose of this chapter is to give an overview of Japan's Indigenous education policy in the late nineteenth and the mid-twentieth century, with special emphasis on the comparison between the two different education systems: the government Ainu schools and those run by the CMS. This chapter aims to contribute to the existing body of knowledge by shedding new light on two hitherto under analysed topics: firstly, the education provided by the Japanese government and foreign missionaries towards the Ainu, and secondly the school experiences of the Ainu under the *Hokkaido Former Aborigines Protection Act of 1899*. The first two sections review the two education systems individually, followed by a case study of the "CMS Hakodate Ainu Training School". This Ainu school was significant, if compared to the other CMS schools, for being the first and last board-ing school run particularly for the Ainu youth. In the final section, discussions regarding the government's assimilation policy towards the Ainu in the late nineteenth and the mid-twentieth century are drawn, along with a brief comparison of the Norwegianization of the Sámi.

The Hokkaido Former Aborigines Protection Act and Ainu Elementary Schools

Traditionally, the Ainu pursued fishing and hunting for their livelihood in *iwor* (traditional livelihood space) and coexisted harmoniously with nature and *kamuy* (Ainu deities). In the Ainu worldview, *kamuy* exist everywhere around humans, including in natural phenomena, animals, plants and tools. For instance, *apehuci kamuy* (the deity of fire) is the most familiar and well-respected deity in a house. The Ainu worship things which are indispensable to their lives are beyond the control of humans (Fitzhugh & Dubreuil 1999).

In May 1869, the Emperor issued the *Ezochi Kaitaku Gokamon-sho* (Emperor's written inquiry regarding development of Ezochi). Following the Emperor's order, the *Kaitakushi* (Hokkaido Development Commission) was established in July 1869, and Ezochi was renamed Hokkaido. After the official annexation of Hokkaido in 1869, the Ainu became consider-ably outnumbered due to the influx of *Wajin*, the ethnic Japanese of the mainland. While Hokkaido's total population quadrupled from 252,952 in 1883 to 1,077,280 in 1903, the Ainu population remained almost unchanged at roughly 17,800 (Emori 2007, p. 127). Also, as contact between new settlers and the Ainu increased, epidemic diseases spread rap-idly and devastated the Ainu community. By the end of the nineteenth cen-tury, a considerable number of Ainu were faced with extreme poverty due to the requisitioning of their lands and the prohibition of traditional fish-ing and hunting practices. Against this background, the *Hokkaido Former Aborigines Protection Act* was promulgated by the Imperial Diet in March 1899. It marked a turning point in the history of Ainu education.

The 1899 Protection Act was enacted with the aim of "safeguarding" the Ainu and solving the poverty that long plagued the Ainu. The Act dealt with education, and contained other measures regarding private land ownership, medical care, and communal property. However, it did little to ameliorate the lives of most Ainu. Instead, it played an important role in their increasing "Japanization". Momose (1994) mentions that the Protection Act had the following two goals: (1) to encourage the Ainu to practice settled agriculture; and (2) to assimilate the Ainu into the dominant Japanese culture and society. Education was considered a means through which to achieve the second goal. Hence, in accordance with Article 9 of the Protection Act, the government set out a plan to establish state-funded *Former Aborigines Schools* across Hokkaido and twenty-five separate elementary schools for Ainu children were established between 1901 and 1910.

The plan's implementation was followed by the enactment of the *Regulations for the Education of Former Aboriginal Children of 1901* (the 1901 Regulations). Ainu children's years of mandatory schooling was set for four years by the Protection Act, just the same as the ones for the Wajin children. However, educational standards and attainment targets differed between the two ethnic groups. The 1901 Regulation affirmed that the content covered by Ainu children over four years of schooling should have already been covered by Wajin students after their third year (Table 12.1).

Shortly after the promulgation of the *1907 Elementary School Order* by the central government, the Hokkaido regional government enacted

Table 12.1 The 1901 school curriculum for government Ainu schools

Subject	Grade 1 (hours/week)	Grade 2 (hours/week)	Grade 3 (hours/week)	Grade 4 (hours/week)
Moral education	2	2	2	2
Japanese language	8	12	14	14
Arithmetic	5	6	6	6
Physical education	3	3	3	3
Sewing			Girl 2	Girl 2
Farming			Boy 2	Boy 2
Total hours	18	23	27	27

Regulations for the Education of Former Aboriginal Children (March 31, 1901)

12 A Historical Perspective of Indigenous Education Policy ...   211

the new 1908 Regulations for Ainu children. Ainu schooling was duly extended from four to six years in 1908, and now included the teaching of additional subjects such as Japanese history, geography, science and agriculture. In 1910, roughly one-third of school-age Ainu children were enrolled at government Ainu schools, and the remaining two-thirds at other institutions (Ogawa 1997). Nonetheless, the government's inconsistent approach to the Ainu meant the measure was short-lived. In 1916, the Hokkaido government enacted *the Regulations for the Education of Former Aboriginal Children* (the 1916 Regulations), shortened the total length of Ainu schooling to four years, and removed the recently added subjects from the curriculum.

Little is known about the reasoning behind these policy shifts. However, they reflect the fact the Japanese authorities lacked a coherent Ainu education policy and consistently maintained a sense of racial superiority and prejudice towards the Ainu. The separate levels of instruction enshrined in the 1916 Regulations reaffirmed the belief that Ainu and Wajin students were civilized to differing degrees: the total number of years at school was reduced for the Ainu because it was assumed they could not follow the same pace of physical and intellectual development as Wajin students. The total amount of teaching received by Wajin students was one-and-a-half times greater than that received by their Ainu counterparts (six years compared to four). In addition, the 1916 Regulations postponed the school starting age for Ainu children to seven, whereas Wajin children continued to start school at the age of six. This revision was a change for worse, largely reverting to the 1901 curriculum. The only difference between the two curricula for the Ainu was that under the 1916 curriculum, they were spending three more hours per week learning Japanese.

Ainu School Experiences Under the Protection Act

After the abolition of the Ainu schools in 1937, Ainu students attended ordinary elementary schools along with Japanese students. Nevertheless, both overt and covert discrimination towards the Ainu persisted.

For instance, Sato Washiya who studied at both Anecha Ainu Elementary School and Nofuka Ordinary Elementary School had contrasting school experiences. Having been born in Urakawa, Southern Hokkaido, she first went to Anecha Ainu School, which was established in 1904, and was then transferred to Nofuka Ordinary School when she was in the fifth grade:

> Wajin students laughed at us whatever we did. They laughed at every single thing Ainu children did. When we raised our hand to answer a question, when we said 'good morning', when we ate our lunch, they burst into laughing. They definitely didn't see us as human beings. We were animals to them. So it was funny for them that we acted as human being.... I enjoyed my school life before, but that feeling disappeared in a flash (after transferring to Nofuka Ordinary School) and I came to thoroughly hate going to school. (Washiya 1975, pp. 22–23)

As Washiya testified, Wajin students showed discriminatory attitudes towards transferred Ainu students. Their sense of supremacy over the Ainu probably mirrored the common attitudes among Wajin settlers, which could often result in insidious bullying at school. After transferring to Nofuka Ordinary School, Washiya suffered from school anxiety and the school became a battlefield to her. The Anecha school, in fact, remained a truly "Ainu school"—without the enrolment of a single Wajin student—until its closure in June 1937 (Society of Historical Research of Education 1988). Therefore, the Ainu-only Anecha School provided Washiya with a safety zone as an institution outside of Japanese hegemony.

In short, Japan's indigenous policy was predicated on *dōka* (assimilation) and *kōminka* (imperialization). Hence, the schooling Ainu children received was principally assimilation-oriented, with a special emphasis on *shūshin* (moral education) and Japanese language. A corollary of Japan's indigenous policy was the largely irreparable destruction of traditional Ainu culture and society. That said, the 1916 Regulations was promulgated in the Taishō era (1912–1926), which was characterized by a flowering of political liberalism, known as *Taishō Democracy*. In the light of the unprecedented liberal climate, the Regulations drew

12 A Historical Perspective of Indigenous Education Policy ... 213

strong criticism from the Ainu on one level, resulting in the emergence of political and civic engagement of the Ainu.

On another level, having faced Japan's racial and equity issues, Ainu people made considerable efforts to catch up educationally with the Wajin. This is evident from the fact that levels of school enrolment among Ainu children steadily increased after the introduction of the government Ainu schools, from 44.6% in 1901 to 96.6% in 1916 (Emori 2007). In 1937, being convinced that the assimilation process had been completed, the authorities abolished government-run Ainu schools and racial segregation technically ended. However, the move meant that the Ainu rapidly began to deliberately abandon their native language and culture in order to gain equal status in Japanese society. So far, this chapter has focused on the government Indigenous policy and the Ainu schools under the 1899 Protection Act. The following section offers a brief overview of the private Ainu schools run by the CMS in the Meiji period.

The Church Missionary Society and Ainu Schools

The Church Missionary Society (today known as the *Church Mission Society*) is an Anglican mission society established in London in 1799. The Meiji government lifted the ban of Christianity in 1873, and various Catholic, Protestant and Russian Orthodox churches subsequently sent numbers of foreign missionaries to Japan. The first CMS missionary sent to Japan was the Reverend George Ensor who arrived at Nagasaki in 1869. It was not until the summer of 1874 that a CMS missionary—the Reverend Walter Denning—first set foot on Hokkaido, entering the port of Hakodate. After the opening of its port in 1859, Hakodate became the northernmost commercial town in Japan. After landing in 1874, Denning opened the CMS's first "preaching place" in Hakodate and began his evangelical works (Committee on Historiography of the Anglican-Episcopal Church in Japan 1966). Not only did Denning begin the CMS Hokkaido Mission, but he was also a pioneer in works carried out for the Ainu. Nevertheless, despite a promising start, the CMS Hakodate Mission faced a great deal of disruption in 1882 due to Denning's abrupt resignation.

The Ainu Mission was eventually taken over by the Reverend Walter Andrews and John Batchelor, who initially came to Hakodate in 1877 as a lay helper. After being ordained as a deacon in 1887 and then a priest in 1889, he made distinguished contributions to improving the lives and well-being of the Ainu for over four decades. His major works include establishing the first CMS Ainu school in Hokkaido, opening the Ainu "hospital rest" in Sapporo, publishing both an Ainu-Japanese-English dictionary and English books on Ainu folklore, and translating Christian prayers and the Gospels into Ainu. This led to him being dubbed 'the father of the Ainu' (Nitami 1963). Unlike the other Christian churches, which concentrated on the Wajin, the CMS were engaged in evangelical and benevolent works for both Wajin and Ainu populations in the fields of education, medical care, and social welfare. As a consequence, the number of Anglican Ainu rapidly increased and even outnumbered Anglican Wajin in Hokkaido: Ainu only made up 3% of Anglicans in Hokkaido in 1885, yet by 1898 this number had increased to approximately 60% (Frey 2007). This demonstrates that the Ainu Mission came to hold a prominent position in the evangelical works of the CMS missionaries in Hokkaido.

The CMS Ainu Schools in Hokkaido (1888–1906)

The CMS ran more than 10 Ainu schools between 1888 and 1906, mostly in southern Hokkaido. The first CMS Ainu school was opened in Horobetsu in 1888, through the joint efforts of Batchelor and local Ainu people. As Frey (2007) underscored, it was the first "Christian charity school" (p. 194) of this kind established for Ainu children by foreign missionaries. Although detail cannot be gone into due to space limitations, some of the CMS Ainu schools began due to the efforts and zeal of local Ainu chiefs. In general, CMS Ainu schools were relatively small in scale and operated as day schools. There were no tuition fees and school materials were provided at no cost, as contrasted to government schools where students needed to purchase their own school materials (Ogawa 2015). As a rule, the schools were established primarily for Ainu children and classes were taught in both Ainu and Japanese. Hence, it was anticipated that Ainu students would make up the great majority of students, although Japanese students were also allowed to enrol in some cases (Frey 2007). This majority-Ainu environment would have created a more conducive learning environment for Ainu students. Much of the curriculum taught at CMS schools mirrored the government's curriculum.

Translating the Bible was one of the methods the CMS applied for spreading the Gospels to "Heathen(s)" (Stock 1898). The Ainu language never had a writing system; therefore, Batchelor used the Roman Alphabets to transcribe the Ainu words phonetically. In 1897, Batchelor completed a translation of the *New Testament* in the Ainu language. The use of the Ainu tongue at schools must have facilitated smooth communication and easier relationships between the CMS and the Ainu. In the following section, the curriculum and students' school life at the Hakodate Ainu School is reviewed with reference to the CMS Archive. The Hakodate Ainu School is significant for being the first and only Ainu boarding school established by the CMS.

The Hakodate Ainu Training School

The *Hakodate Ainu Training School* (hereafter, "Hakodate Ainu School") was opened in the spring of 1893, with Charles Nettleship as superintendent. As described in the previous section, the CMS Ainu schools were founded for the philanthropic purpose of providing basic schooling to Ainu children and youths. In contrast, the mission of the Hakodate School was to educate bright young Ainu who could themselves carry out missionary work in their home communities in the future. According to Nettleship's report (1895b), there were 21 students at the Hakodate Ainu school as of January 1, 1895 (19 boys and two girls). Among them, 14 were baptized and four were with physical disabilities. It can be assumed that the Hakodate Ainu School accepted and took care of these physically challenged students in the spirit of Christian charity.

216   Y. Tanabe

The students came from various Ainu villages; the furthest amongst them was Kushiro, approximately 500 km away from Hakodate. The oldest student was 25 years old, and the youngest was nine years old. According to the examination results of June 1895 (Nettleship 1895a), 19 students took exams in arithmetic and in Japanese reading and writing, as well as sitting exams in Ainu-language reading, writing and dictation. Examinations were also held on the Scripture. However, the 1900 exams indicate that Japanese had become the only language of examination: 16 students took examinations on Scripture, reading, composition, arithmetic and writing—all in Japanese. It is not certain if the school taught subjects in the Ainu language around the turn of the century, but this fact signalled that Japanese had already become the dominant language among the Ainu.

Nettleship also attached the school's 1895 timetable and listed subject hours (see Table 12.2). During weekdays, students began the day with morning prayer at 5:45, followed by breakfast at 6:00. Morning classes were from 7:00 till 12:00, and afternoon classes were from 13:00 to 17:30. In the afternoon, there were also periods for farm work and industrial activities, such as sandal making. After supper and prayers, students had singing or music classes several days a week. Bedtime

Table 12.2 Analysis of Hakodate Ainu training school timetable 1895 (Nettleship 1895c)

Subjects	Hours (per week)
New Testament	5
Old Testament	3
Prayer book	2
Catechism	3
Model lesson	2
Composition	2
Elementary science	2
Reading Ainu	3
Reading Japan	5
Dictation Ainu	2
Writing Japan	5
Arithmetic	5
Singing	1
Music	2
Total	42

12 A Historical Perspective of Indigenous Education Policy ...

was 21:00. On Saturday, there were no classes, but the day began in the same way as weekdays. After breakfast, the children cleaned the school in the morning and did recreational activities or other chores in the afternoon. On Sunday, students attended the Divine service at the school, which was held alternatively in Ainu or Japanese. In the afternoon, all students (except for one disabled student who could not walk at all) participated in regular Japanese Sunday school and the Divine service at the CMS church along with Wajin Christians. Considering the racial division and discrimination towards the Ainu during the era, the inclusiveness displayed by Wajin Christians should be underscored.

The subjects to be taught in ordinary, non-Ainu elementary schools were stipulated in the *Elementary School Order of 1890* as follows: moral education, reading, composition, calligraphy, arithmetic and physical education. However, students at the Hakodate Ainu School took classes both in Ainu and Japanese languages, alongside Bible study and other related

Image 12.1   Ainu School. (n.d.). Hakodate City Central Library

subjects. Furthermore, it should be noted that the total of 42 teaching hours at the Hakodate Ainu school was much greater than in ordinary government elementary schools (though if one simply adds up the total subject-hours in the timetable, it should have been 46 hours). The government set the maximum number of teaching hours at less than 30 hours per week for ordinary elementary schools and 36 hours per week for higher elementary schools. As can be imagined, Ainu students in such a boarding school had hectic schedules with very limited free time (Image 12.1).

The Closing of the CMS Ainu Schools

Throughout this period, government-run Ainu schools and CMS Ainu schools never operated in close geographical proximity, with only one exception at Shiranuka. As Batchelor argued early on, "the Japanese Government has provided these (Ainu schools) for the people, and we can never compete with them" (Batchelor 1894). CMS missionaries were seemingly aware of potential government interference in their work. This concern proved justified, as all CMS schools either became "public" or were closed by the end of 1906. The once flourishing Hakodate Ainu Training School was closed in June 1905 (*Hakodate Mainichi Newspaper* 1906).

There were multiple reasons behind the school closings. Firstly, the emergence of government Ainu schools made a tremendous impact on Ainu schooling. Figure 12.1 shows the huge leap in the Ainu school enrolment ratio after 1900. The rate of school participation increased by roughly 60% between the enactment of the Protection Act in 1899 and the closing of the last Ainu school in 1906. Secondly, the *Private School Order of 1899* stipulated that school-age children should generally not be enrolled in private schools. In addition, the Ministry of Education issued *Directive No. 12 of 1899*, which prohibited all religious teaching at schools, except in "miscellaneous schools".

Nakamura (2008) points out that the Reverend Lang, who was in charge of the Kushiro region, also decided that the Harutori Ainu School would close if the Japanese government established its own Ainu schools nearby. Hence, it is fair to say that the closing of the CMS

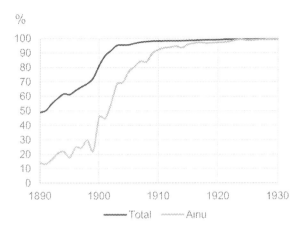

Fig. 12.1 Elementary school enrolment rate in Japan (1890–1930). *Source* Ministry of Education (1972, p. 497), Ogawa (1997, p. 10)

Ainu schools primarily resulted from the Private School Order of 1899 and the emergence of government Ainu schools in the early twentieth century. As far as the Ainu Mission is concerned, Batchelor made tremendous contributions for over half a century, even after he resigned as a CMS missionary in 1923. However, the CMS Hokkaido Mission lacked funds, employees and Ainu catechists to fully carry out evangelical works in Japan (Committee on Historiography of the Anglican-Episcopal Church in Japan 1974). As a result, many Ainu churches and preaching places were abandoned, and native Japanese churches took greater initiative.

Discussion

Cole (2011) discusses how Indigenous peoples are, in many cases, regarded as a formidable obstacle to fledgling nation-states. This is because those new states seek to simultaneously strengthen sovereignty over their territories and forge a strong national identity. The government-run Ainu schools functioned as a tool through which to turn the Ainu into loyal subjects of the emperor and to inculcate Japanese civic values, including manners and hygiene practices. In particular, emperor-centered moral education became one of the central pillars of Japanese early modern education, thanks to the passing of the 1890 *Imperial rescript on Education*. Emperor worship was inextricably linked to the forced cultural assimilation of the colonized.

As highlighted in the previous sections, there were significant differences in terms of school curriculum, teaching methods, and legacies between government and CMS Ainu schools. At government schools, the use of Ainu was discouraged, leading to a sharp decline in the number of those speaking the language. In contrast, at CMS Ainu schools, CMS missionaries recognized and utilized the language's potential, teaching some subjects in Ainu with the Roman alphabet. It was ironic that CMS Ainu schools became a substantial threat to government schools in the late 1880s and 1890s, which led to the establishment of government-run Ainu schools and compulsory attendance of school-age Ainu children. Due to the rapid decrease in student enrolments, not a single CMS Ainu school survived after 1906 and Christianity gradually lost its influence among the Ainu. This resulted in the further integration of the Ainu into the hegemony of imperialist Japan.

That being said, the government and CMS Ainu school systems represented two sides of the same coin, in the way they downgraded Ainu religious beliefs and ways of life. The ultimate purpose of both CMS and government Ainu schooling was to "civilize" indigenous people, albeit through different faiths and ideologies. While CMS missionaries aimed to spread the Gospel to the Ainu and convert them to Christianity, Japanese authorities imposed state Shintōism. In other words, both the CMS and the Japanese government aimed to eliminate indigenous religion and culture so that they could impose their own religious and moral beliefs on the Ainu. Therefore, it can be said that both school systems were parts of colonial projects.

Drawing a parallel to the Ainu case, the mid-nineteenth century witnessed the beginning of the Norwegianization of the Sámi (Minde 2003). Based on the strong belief in social Darwinism, Indigenous peoples were considered "backwards" and "barriers" for national development. As argued by Lehtola (2002), the Norwegianization policies were characterized by the following two tendencies: "One was the settlement and livelihood policy…The other was the language and education policy" (p. 194). In a similar vein, the Japanization policy for the Ainu started in full swing after the Meiji restoration of 1868 and continued at least until the late 1990s. In particular, education and language policies played a crucial role in terms of Indigenous identity and culture both in Japan and Norway. Although the Japanese government did not introduce boarding school system to assimilate Ainu children in Hokkaido, partly due to financial constraints, schools functioned as an apparatus for primarily "enlightening" the Ainu. It can therefore be assumed that both Ainu and Sámi people share parallel experiences in the process of social, political and cultural assimilation into a dominant society.

Conclusion

This chapter has looked critically at historical trajectories and the effects the government's indigenous education policy had on Ainu society. As summarized here, rapid modernization, growing nationalism, and hegemonic discourse on race and ethnicity during the nineteenth and early twentieth centuries in Japan significantly affected the government's indigenous policy as well as the CMS Ainu Mission's works. Although it is beyond the scope of this chapter, it should be noted that after the co-education of Ainu and Wajin students officially began at ordinary elementary schools in 1937, school attendance rates among the Ainu dropped and remained low, even into the post-war period (Ogawa 1997). Multiple factors caused this decrease, including social discrimination and financial difficulties. Lower levels of educational attainment among the Ainu has persisted up until today, mostly due to socioeconomical factors (Nozaki 2011).

On May 24, 2019, *Act on the Promotion of Policy Measures for Realizing a Society that Respects the Pride of the Ainu* (the new Ainu Act) came into force. One of the significances of this Act is that the Japanese government legally recognized the Ainu as an indigenous people of Japan. In addition, Article 4 prohibits discrimination or any other act that violates the interests of or the rights of Ainu people. Overall, however, the Act falls short of providing measures to redress intergenerational injustices and inequalities that the Ainu people have suffered for centuries. As Morris-Suzuki (2018) proclaims, Japan's Ainu policy lacks "any explicit recognition of the group rights of indigenous communities" (p. 3); therefore, the Act does not adhere to the basic principles of the *United Nations Declaration on the Rights of Indigenous Peoples*. Several of the new policy measures stipulated in the Act would benefit certain industry sectors, such as the tourism industry, yet the path to achieve genuine reconciliation, social justice and equity remains long and difficult.

References

Batchelor, J. (1894, April 11). [Letter to C.C. Fenn]. Church Missionary Archive (G1 J/O/1894/117), Birmingham, UK.

Cole, W. (2011). *Uncommon schools: The global rise of postsecondary institutions for indigenous peoples*. Stanford, CA: Stanford University Press.

Committee on Historiography of the Anglican-Episcopal Church in Japan. (1966). *Kyōku 90 nen shi: Nihon Sei Ko Kai Hokkaido Kyōku* [90 years' history of the Diocese: Diocese of Hokkaido, the Anglican Episcopal Church in Japan]. Sapporo, Japan: Diocese of Hokkaido, the Anglican-Episcopal Church in Japan.

Committee on Historiography of the Anglican-Episcopal Church in Japan. (1974). *Akashibito tachi: Nippon Seikō Kai jinbutsu shi* [Witnesses: Historical Biographies of Notable People in the Anglican-Episcopal Church of Japan]. Tokyo, Japan: Nippon Seikō Kai Press.

Emori, S. (2007). *Ainu minzoku no rekishi* [The history of the Ainu]. Urayasu, Japan: Sōfu Kan.

Fitzhugh, W. W., & Dubreuil, C. O. (1999). *Ainu: Spirit of a northern people*. Washington, D.C.: Arctic Studies Center, National Museum of Natural History, Smithsonian Institution in association with University of Washington Press.

Frey, C. J. (2007). *Ainu schools and education policy in 19th-Century Hokkaido, Japan*. Bloomington, IN: Indiana University.

Hakodate Otsushi Sōshi (Year Review of 1905). (1906, January 1). *Hakodate Mainichi Newspaper*. Hakodate, Japan.

Hirose, K. (1996). Hokkaidō karigakkō fuzoku hokkaidō dojin kycikusho to kaitakushi kan-en e no Ainu no kyōsei shūgaku ni kansuru kenkyū' [A study on how Ainu youth were forced to attend Kaitakushi Ainu school and national farms in Tokyo]. *The Annual Reports on Educational Science, 72,* 89–119.

Howell, D. L. (2008, June). Is "Ainu history" "Japanese history"? *Journal of Northeast Asian History, 5*(1), 121–142.

Iwasaki, N. (1998). *Nihon kinsei no Ainu shakai* [Ainu society in the early-modern period of Japan]. Tokyo, Japan: Azekura Shobo.

Kaiho, Y. (1992). *Kindai hoppō shi-Ainu minzoku to jyosei to* [The Japanese northern history in the modern period—The Ainu and women]. Tokyo, Japan: San-ichi Shobō.

Lehtola, V. P. (2002). The Sami siida and the Nordic states from the Middle Ages to the beginning of the 1900s. In K. Kristina & E. Johan (Eds.), *Conflict and Cooperation in the North* (pp. 183–194). Umeå: Norrlands Universitetsförlag.

Minde, H. (2003). Assimilation of the Sami-implementation and consequences. *Acta Borealia, 2,* 121–146.

Ministry of Education, Science and Culture, Government of Japan. (1972). *Gakusei Hyakune Shi* [Japan's modern educational system: A history of the first hundred years]. Tokyo, Japan: Teikoku Chihō Gyosei Gakkai.

Momose, H. (1994). Hokkaido kyūdojin hogohō no seiritu to hensen no gaiyō [An overview of the enactment and revisions of the Hokkaido Former Aborigines Protection Act]. *Shi'en: The Journal of Historical Studies, Rikkyo University, 55*(1), 64–86.

Morris-Suzuki, T. (2018). Performing ethnic harmony: The Japanese government's plans for a new Ainu law. *The Asia-Pacific Journal, 16*(21), 1–18.

Nakamura, K. (1991). *Nagakubo Hidejirō no kenkyū* [Research on Nagakubo Hidejirō]. Kushiro, Japan: Kushiro City.

Nakamura, K. (2003). 19 seiki matu-20 seiki shotō Miss Bryant no Biratori ni okeru Ainu minzoku e no dendō (1)-CMS nenji shokan o tōshite [Missionary works of Miss Bryant among the Ainu in Biratori (1)-Through the CMS annual letters]. *Women's History in Hokkaido, 1,* 55–73.

Nakamura, K. (2005). Miss Bryant no Biratori ni okeru Ainu minzoku e no dendō (2) 1911–1922-CMS shiryō o tōshite [Missionary works of Miss Bryant among the Ainu in Biratori (2) 1911–1922-Through CMS Archives]. *Women's History in Hokkaido, 2,* 160–174.

Nakamura, K. (2008). 19 seiki matu-20 seiki shotō Miss Lucy Payne no kita Indo to Hokkaido ni okeru senkyō no kiseki [The trajectory of missionary works of Miss Lucy Payne in Northern India and Hokkaido]. *Women's History in Hokkaido, 3,* 63–95.

Nettleship, C. (1895a, July 31). *Examination for the half year ending 30th June.* Church Missionary Society Archives (G1 J/O/1895/199), Birmingham, UK.

Nettleship, C. (1895b, July 31). *Report of the Hakodate Ainu training school.* Church Missionary Society Archives (G1 J/O/1895/200), Birmingham, UK.

Nettleship, C. (1895c, July 31). *Hakodate Ainu training school timetable.* Church Missionary Society Archives (G1 J/O/1895/203), Birmingham, UK.

Nitami, I. (1963). *Ainu no chichi John Batchelor* [John Batchelor, the Father of the Ainu]. Sapporo, Japan: Nirenoki Shobō.

Nozaki, Y. (2011). Current situation of educational inequality and awareness. *Report on the Hokkaido Ainu living conditions survey (English Version), 1,* 65–78.

Ogawa, M. (1997). *Kindai Ainu kyōiku seido shi kenkyū* [Research on the history of the modern Ainu education system]. Sapporo, Japan: Hokkaido University Press.

Ogawa, M. (2015). Hakodate to kindai Ainu kyōiku shi-Yachigashira ni atta Ainu gakkō no rekishi [Hakodate and the history of the modern Ainu education: The history of the Ainu school existed in Yachigashira]. *The Bulletin of Hakodate City Museum, 25,* 1–21.

Shimoda, T. (2013). John Batchelor ga nokoshita mono: Asahikawa ni okeru baiburu ūman no sokuseki [The lagacy of John Batchelor: footsteps of Bible women in Asahikawa]. *Studium Christianitatis, 48,* 36–40.

Siddle, R. M. (1996). *Race, resistance and the Ainu of Japan.* London, UK: Routledge.

Society of Historical Research of Education. (1988). Ainu kyōiku shi: Kyōiku shi gakkai korokiumu 'Ainu kyōiku shi' no kiroku [The history of education for the Ainu: Presentations at a colloquium of the Society of Historical Research of Education]. *The Annual Reports on Educational Science, 51,* 89–134.

Stock, E. (1898). *Japan and the Japan Mission of the Church Missionary Society.* London, UK: Church Missionary Society.

Takegahara, Y. (2008a). *Kindai Hokkaido shi o torae naosu* [Revisiting the modern history of Hokkaido]. Tokyo, Japan: Shakai Hyōron Sha.

Takegahara, Y. (2008b). *Kyōiku no naka no Ainu minzoku* [The Ainu in education]. Tokyo, Japan: Shakai Hyōron Sha.

Washiya, S. (1975). Tada Hitasurani Ningen o Shinjite [Trusting in human beings with all my heart]. In M. Gōnai & M. Wakabayashi (Eds.), *Asu ni mukatte: Ainu no hitobito wa uttaeru* [Towards tomorrow: Ainu people make an appeal] (pp. 19–36). Tokyo, Japan: Alice Kan Publishing.

13

Indigenous in Japan? The Reluctance of the Japanese State to Acknowledge Indigenous Peoples and Their Need for Education

Madoka Hammine

Introduction

Japan's self-image as an ethnically, linguistically, and culturally homogeneous nation is shared by most Japanese and outsiders. This is partly because Japanese policy has rarely acknowledged the presence of indigenous peoples, languages, and cultures within the Japanese state (e.g., Hanks 2017; Heinrich 2012; Liddlecoat 2013; Maruyama 2014; among others). In fact, Japan, in terms of the protection of linguistic, ethnic, and cultural minorities, is categorised as "a third world nation" by human rights standards (Lewallen 2008; as cited in Heinrich and Galan 2011). Churchill (1986) states that "linguistic and cultural minorities have emerged as a central concern for educational policy in almost all the Organisation for Economic Cooperation and Development (OECD) countries, with the sole exception of Japan".

Previous research has criticised Japan's lack of policy support for indigenous peoples and the lack of education that is designed to meet

M. Hammine (✉)
Faculty of Education, University of Lapland, Rovaniemi, Finland

© The Author(s) 2019
O. Kortekangas et al. (eds.), *Sámi Educational History in a Comparative International Perspective*,
https://doi.org/10.1007/978-3-030-24112-4_13

225

the needs of indigenous peoples (e.g., Gayman 2011; Liddlecoat 2013; Maher 1997; Maruyama 2014; Ogawa 1997; Uemura and Gayman 2018; Yokota 2015). However, previous research has not explored the extent to which indigenous groups in Japan can or cannot choose to build or pursue their identities in current Japanese society. Moreover, there is a criticism that most research on indigenous peoples in Japan has been predominantly conducted by non-indigenous Japanese or foreign researchers (see, e.g., Shinya 2015). In the existing indigenous studies research, especially that conducted by non-indigenous researchers among indigenous people, there is often a failure to appreciate how one's own viewpoint is biased by, and reflects, dominant perspectives (e.g., Smith 1999); this is an important ethical issue. Although it is important to reflect on such dominant viewpoints when conducting research on indigenous people (e.g., Smith 1999; Lee 2005), it is not yet commonly accepted by many researchers in Japan. Although the importance of Ainu-centred perspectives is mentioned in recent work by some researchers (e.g., Emori 2007; Hirose 1996; Iwasaki 1998; Takegahara 2008), decolonisation is often used only as a metaphor without real, concrete implications. This chapter demonstrates the importance of taking indigenous viewpoints in research on indigenous groups in Japan.

Indigenous Peoples in Japan

According to the definition in the UNDRIP,[1] the United Nations Declaration on the Rights of Indigenous Peoples, there are two groups in Japan that could be identified as indigenous. The Ainu are the only nationally recognised indigenous people in the Ainu territories (Hokkaido, the Kuril Islands, and Sakhalin), in what is now the

---

[1]The United Nations human rights bodies have dealt with the Ainu people as an indigenous people since 1987 and have accepted Okinawan delegations as members of the community of indigenous peoples since 1996 (Uemura 2003). There are several other names to call this group, including Uchinaanchu and Okinawans. I use "Ryūkyūan" in order to also include inhabitants on the smaller islands of the archipelago.

northern part of Japan and the northeastern part of Russia. Okinawans or Ryūkyūans are on the Ryūkyū Islands, which make up the current Okinawa Prefecture and a part of Kagoshima prefecture (see, e.g., Uemura 2003; Uemura and Gayman 2018; Yokota 2015). Ryūkyūans have not yet been officially recognised by the Japanese government as an indigenous people of Japan. The concept of indigenous peoples was introduced into Japan in the late 1970s, mainly from North America and Europe, where there had been recognition and political movements on behalf of indigenous peoples since the 1970s (e.g., Minde 1996; Lee 2005). However, the recognition of the indigenous peoples of Japan emerged as a topic of discussion only after the 1980s. Until then, indigenous peoples were not an issue for the government, as in 1980 the Japanese government told the UN such minorities "did not exist in Japan" (Siddle 1996; Emori 2015).

Despite Japan's reluctance to acknowledge indigenous peoples and their rights, Ainu people started to participate in the UN in the 1980s and Japan recognised the Ainu as an indigenous people in 2008, which gave inspiration to the Ryūkyūans, who started to participate in the UN in the 1990s (see Yokota 2015). Despite international pressure from the UN, the Japanese government recognised the Ainu as an indigenous people only in 2008 and it has not recognised the Okinawans or Ryūkyūans as an indigenous people. Although the Japanese government adopted the UNDRIP in 2007, it does not recognise the unconditional right to self-determination of indigenous peoples and the government has not ratified ILO Convention 169[2] (Maruyama 2014).

The Situation of the Ryūkyūans and Other Indigenous Peoples in Japan

Ryūkyūan people are internationally considered as an indigenous group. However, the Japanese government does not recognise them as an Indigenous population (see more in Yokota 2015 and in Uemura and

---

[2]For a detailed analysis of indigenous rights and education for the Ainu, see Gayman (2011).

Gayman 2018). Although Ryūkyūans often consider themselves as a separate people or nation, or, at the very least, an ethnic minority, other Ryūkyūans maintain pride in their cultural and historic legacy within their sense of belonging to a larger Japanese community (Siddle 2002; Tanji 2006; Yokota 2015).

In 2016, on Okinawa Main Island, a riot police officer dispatched from Osaka to help local police respond to an anti-US-base movement in Okinawa Prefecture hurled an ethnic slur at protesters, calling them *dojin*, meaning "aboriginal" or "native", which provoked anger among local inhabitants. Here, the important question is whether the local inhabitants, including the protesters, were angry because the word "aboriginal" implies "inferior" to the Japanese, or rather because their "Japaneseness" was denied by the Japanese. This incident mirrors the struggle that Ryūkyūans have faced for a long time, their struggle to define their identities (see also Takahashi 2015). Although no problem has required the Japanese government to confirm the indigeneity of the Ryūkyūan people, the so-called "Okinawa problem" has been an issue since the annexation of the Ryūkyū Kingdom (see Tanji 2006; Yokota 2017).

Indigenous rights for Ryūkyūans have been ignored completely in Japan's current legislation. The independent Ryūkyū Kingdom was established in the fifteenth century and it prospered through trading with other Asian countries. The kingdom was conquered and came under the control of the *Satsuma han*, [the Satsuma domain] in 1609, which created a triangular relationship between China and Japan. Japan formally annexed the Ryūkyū Kingdom in 1879, which is known as the *Ryūkyū Shobun*, [the disposal of the Ryūkyūs] (Kerr 2000; Uemura 2003). The Japanese state renamed the islands as Okinawa Prefecture and part of the islands were integrated into Kagoshima Prefecture. The Battle of Okinawa during World War II cast a shadow of militarism over the archipelago and, until their reversion to Japan in 1972, the Ryūkyū islands were under US military governance. The base complex is still there (78% of US military facilities in Japan are concentrated in Okinawa's 0.6% of the national territory; see also McCormack 2017; Yokota 2015, 2017).

13 Indigenous in Japan? The Reluctance of the Japanese State ...

On the other hand, the Ainu have lived in Russia and in *Ainu Mosir*, "Ainu land", which is now a part of Japan, for centuries. As part of the Meiji Restoration of Japan in 1869, the authorities renamed Ainu land *Hokkaido*. The Meiji period (1868–1912) signifies the first systematic legal attack on the Ainu. In 1899, the Japanese government passed the *Hokkaido Kyūdojin Hogohō* [the Hokkaido Former Native Protection Act]. The term translated here as "aborigine or native", *dojin*, refers to a person of the land, while *kyū*, "old" or "former", implies an understanding of the Ainu as people of the past. The designation of the Ainu as former natives at this period constructed the ideology of the Ainu as being at a more primitive stage of cultural evolution, something that could be overcome by cultural assimilation to the more evolved mainstream Japanese (see more in Siddle 1996; Ogawa 1997; Liddlecoat 2013). In 1997, the *Ainu Bunka Shinkōhō* [the Ainu Culture Promotion Act] replaced the former Act [the Hokkaido Former Native Protection Act] and it was expected to emancipate the Ainu from the sufferings caused by the assimilation policies. Yet it stipulated neither Ainu indigeneity nor Ainu linguistic and cultural rights (see also Maruyama 2014). There is still no policy explicitly permitting the use of the Ainu language or an implementation of indigenous Ainu knowledge in public education.

The devaluation of indigeneity and the lack of policies in support of indigenous peoples in Japan might be the reasons why the inhabitants in the Ryūkyūs do not want to identify themselves as indigenous[3] and why they seek to be considered as Japanese. In other words, no one would wish to be indigenous if they experience devaluation or discrimination after they claim their indigenous identity. In the following, I examine how educational policies have contributed to the devaluation of indigenous rights and have influenced the "invisible" indigenous identities in Japan.

---

[3]Kaizawa (1993) and Kayano (1994) describe their own experience as Ainu in Japan. In 1994, Shigeru Kayano gave a speech in the Ainu language and then in Japanese in the National Diet, which was the first and the last time that occurred up until now.

Indigenous Education in Japan

Let us look at how education has contributed to the indigenous groups' lack of education in Japan and to mainstream lack of awareness of the existence of indigenous group in Japan. The Japanisation of the indigenous population through assimilative policies happened simultaneously in the north, in Ainu land and in the South in the Ryūkyūs. Under the ideology of monoethnicity as "Japanese", non-Japanese identities and indigenous identities have been assimilated through means such as the assignment of Japanese names, use of the Japanese language, construction of *shinto*[4] shrines on indigenous land and adoption of Japanese customs (Howell 2004; Oguma 1998). The goal of these policies was always assimilation, because it was not possible to achieve the ideology of a monoethnic, mono-cultural, and monolingual nation with the presence of non-Japanese (Ainu and Ryūkyūans/Okinawans) peoples (see also Weiner 1997). The following discussion shows that education policies were and still are integral to assimilating the attitudes and behaviours of the indigenous population to those of the dominant Japanese mainstream both in the Ryūkyūs and in Ainu land.

The Ryūkyūs and Education

The rights of the Ryūkyūan peoples to their own language, culture, and identity as Ryūkyūans have been downplayed. Education was key to assimilating the inhabitants of the Ryūkyū Islands into the Japanese mainstream, not only to strengthen national defence but also to govern the smaller islands (Oguma 1998; Clarke 2015). Japanese[5] officers came to Okinawa Island to implement the Japanese educational system and educational policies; they were assigned to work in the newly built Okinawa prefectural government building. The first governor of Okinawa prefecture was a Japanese, *Naosugi Nabeshima,* who wrote:

---

[4]Shinto is a state religion of Japan.
[5]In the Okinawan language, people call the Japanese *yamatonchu.*

13 Indigenous in Japan? The Reluctance of the Japanese State …

> The most important assignment for governing Okinawa prefecture is to make the languages and customs the same as those in mainland Japan. In order to do so, education is the key. (as cited in Kondo 1993: translated by the author)

The Japanese government started to build schools on the Ryūkyūs after the disposal of the Kingdom in 1879, initially on Okinawa Main Island and later on smaller islands in the archipelago, including Yaeyama, Miyako, Amami, and other smaller islands. There were three types of school: namely, elementary schools, junior high schools, and conversation schools. Conversation schools were especially built only on the Ryūkyūs in order to change local languages and customs to be more like those of mainstream Japanese and to educate Ryūkyūans to be teachers in Japanese schools. There, conversation schools were later called *shihan gakkō*[6] [normal school] and served as schools for pupils who were to be teachers. In these conversation schools, students were taught in Japanese, using textbooks written in both Okinawan and Japanese. These schools were based on Japanese legislation, and educational policies were considered as the most important for "Japanising" the local populations (Kondo 1993; Oguma 1998).

In 1881 the government built 19 elementary schools and in 1882 the number increased to 51 schools. Although the number of schools increased, it the beginning it was difficult to increase the number of Ryūkyūan[12] children who attended school. In the 1880s, for instance, the school attendance rate of children in the Ryūkyūs was only 3%, whereas the average attendance rate of children in mainland Japan was 40% (Oguma 1998, p. 39). Moreover, the officials forced Ryūkyūan children to attend schools. The schools were called *yamatoya* [the Japanese House] by Ryūkyūan people, who were afraid of losing their children to mainland Japan if their children learned *yamato gakumon* [the scholarship of the Japanese] (Kondo 1993; Oguma 1998, p. 38).

In a similar manner to the education policies for Ainu children, the education in the Ryūkyūs was assimilationist. The schools also

---

[6]*shihan gakkō* served as a type of school for pupils who became teachers.

promoted programmes aimed at improving the sanitation and living habits of the community because the Ryūkyūan people were considered not clean and their habits were considered backward (Oguma 1998). In order to eliminate the so-called backwardness of the Ryūkyūans, school policies encouraged the Ryūkyūans to change their dress and their customs of female tattoos and of male hairdressing to the Japanese ways (Oguma 1998). Importantly, education policies avoided the use of the term *wafuku* [Japanese dress] but instead used the term *futsūfuku* [normal dress]. Similarly, the policies intentionally avoided the use of the term "Japanese language" but promoted the use of the term *futsūgo* [normal language] or *kokugo* [national language] (Oguma 1998). In this way, policies of assimilation in the Ryūkyūs created the norm that Japanese dress was the normal dress and that the Japanese language was the normal language, leaving those of Ryūkyūans with no space to be normal. Based on these policies in schools, the so-called *hōgen-fuda*, or "dialect tag" worn around the neck, was used to punish children who used indigenous languages, which encouraged the spread of the Japanese language in the Ryūkyūs (e.g., Hokama 1971; Kondo 2008, among others).

In March 1945, with the onset of the Battle of Okinawa[7] at the end of World War II, the administrative power of the Japanese government over the territory of the former Ryūkyū Kingdom was terminated and this territory came under US military administration until its reversion to Japan in 1972 (Uemura and Gayman 2018). During American rule, the US Military government sought to facilitate American control by encouraging territorial autonomy, encouraging the Ryūkyūan people to keep their identity separate from that of Japan by promoting the use of Ryūkyūan languages rather than Japanese, and by encouraging them to have Ryūkyūan ethnic identities (Clarke 2015). The US government provided compulsory education in the Ryūkyū Islands starting in 1945, with the purpose of separating its system from that of mainland Japan. For Ryūkyūan children, education was based on the system of one year of pre-school, eight years of elementary school, and four years of high

---

[7]The Battle of Okinawa was a major battle of the Pacific War fought on the Okinawa island.

13 Indigenous in Japan? The Reluctance of the Japanese State …

school. However, in the next year, in 1946, the Japanese educational system was introduced in Ryūkyū Islands, with six years of elementary school and three years of high school.

Since 1972, Okinawa has been one of the Japanese prefectures, but essentially a semi-colonial territory dominated jointly by the United States and Japan, still partly occupied by the United States (McCormack 2017, p. 119). Up until now, there have been neither systematic language learning opportunities to learn any of Ryūkyūan languages in public school nor a cultural Ryūkyūan-based school curriculum in the Ryūkyūs, despite much research demonstrating the powerful role that education can play in establishing the well-being of indigenous peoples (e.g., Hornberger 2008; Skutnubb-Kangas 2010). Recently, however, a number of language revitalisation efforts have been reported in the Ryūkyūs, in different parts of the archipelago (Ishihara 2016; Hammine, in press; Heinrich 2018), which gives a hope of indigenous language revitalisation in the Ryūkyūs for the future.

The Ainu and Education

Under Japan's colonisation of Ainu lands (Hokkaido, the Kuril Islands, and Sakhalin), the Ainu were assimilated into the dominant Japanese[8] by education and deprived of their language and culture by regulations (Maruyama 2014). Already in the 1870s, Japanese officials, the *Kaitakushi*[9] (often translated as "the Colonisation Commission"), started to separate Ainu children from their families for so-called educational purposes (Ogawa 1997). In 1872, 36 Ainu children were sent to *Kaitakushi Kari Gakkō* [the Provisional Native School] in Tokyo to learn Japanese and agriculture, while 15 Ainu children were forced to study in Sapporo based on the assumption that the process of assimilation would be better and easier when separated from their culture, their

---

[8]Ainu call the Japanese "*wajin*" or "*shamo*."

[9]*Kaitaku* translates from the Japanese into English as "cultivation" or "pioneer", but in the context of Ainu land, I use the translation "Colonisation Commission", as used by others. See, e.g., Siddle (2003).

communities and their parents (Ogawa 1997). Although these schools did not last for a long time, the idea of segregating Ainu children from their families already existed in this period and it developed further later.

Two laws established the Ainu education system: the *Hokkaido Kyūdojin Hogohō* [the Hokkaido Former Native Protection Act] in 1899 and the *Kyūdojin Kyōiku Kitei* the Hokkaido Former Native Protection Act [the Regulations for the Education of Former Native Children] of 1901. Under these laws, education for Ainu people was segregated from the Japanese; where large communities existed, *Kyūdojin Gakkō* [Schools for Former Natives] were built with central government funding under Article Nine of the Protection Act, or existing schools were brought under the Act (Siddle 1996; Ogawa 1997). Some 24 schools were established in total, although a small number lasted only a few years (Siddle 1996). In other areas with smaller Ainu populations, Ainu children attended Japanese schools but were taught in separate classes under the above regulations. These regulations not only segregated Ainu children from Japanese children but also prohibited the use of the Ainu language. These regulations excluded the Ainu from learning history, geography, and science, on account of the Ainu people's alleged "emotional and intellectual immaturity" (Maher 1997).

The school attendance rate of Ainu children rose dramatically over a decade, from 17.9% in 1985 to 84.2% in 1907 (Maher 1997). By 1928, 99.2% of Ainu children were attending elementary school (Maher 1994). However, the education these children received was of inferior quality and shorter duration compared to that of Japanese children: compulsory education was six years long for the Japanese, but it was only four years long for the Ainu (Maher 1997; Ogawa 1997). To be more specific, from 1916, the curriculum for Ainu children was fixed at four years, starting at age seven, in contrast to Japanese children, who started at age six and continued for six years. In this system, the first year for Ainu children was devoted to acquiring the Japanese language, and there were also non-academic subjects, such as farming and sewing. Such non-academic education for Ainu children was, again, justified as appropriate, given the so-called backwardness of Ainu children and it implied that they were not expected to continue on to further education

(Liddlecoat 2013; Siddle 1996). Hence, the assimilationist education system, providing an inferior curriculum for Ainu children to learn, did not give the Ainu any route to consolidate their sense of being a distinct community, which might affirm their language heritage and identity as Ainu.[10]

The 1901 *Kyūdojin Jidō Kyōiku Kitei* [Regulations for the Education of Former Native Children] aimed at the complete linguistic conformity of the Ainu and at the elimination of the Ainu language (see more in Maher 1997). In 1911, the Revised Regulations of Education for Former Native Children further reinforced the disparity between the Ainu and Japanese people's access to the same education (Maher 1997; Ogawa 1997). The reason that the revised regulation gave for this was that "the development of the Ainu is slower than that of Japanese both mentally and physically" (Siddle 1996). The use of the Ainu language began to decline sharply.

Similarly to the situation in the Ryūkyūs, school teachers were often the first Japanese to live in Ainu communities and teach the Ainu. The Japanese schoolmaster coming from the Japanese mainland was an important figure in the *kotan* (group settlement). The school itself functioned as a focal point during national holidays and other imperial celebrations that adult Ainu were required to attend. The school also promoted programmes aimed at improving the sanitation and living habits of the community since those of the Ainu were considered backward, a condition which continued until at least the year 2004 (Jeff Gayman, personal communication). The inferior curriculum for Ainu children was dropped in 1922, and separate Ainu schooling was finally abandoned in 1937 (Siddle 1996). Although the separate system was dropped, policies based on suppressing and assimilating the Ainu language and culture to the Japanese language and culture are still in effect. Up until now, Ainu children have been taught mainly in Japanese, with Ainu as supplemental language lessons in school.

---

[10]Kaizawa (1993) wrote of his own experience of trying hard to be recognised as Japanese, due to the state policies of assimilation.

From the 1980s onwards, crucial efforts have been made to increase the cultural vitality of the Ainu in the forms of revival of traditional rituals, development of teaching materials, language classes in community centres and some universities, and a body of Ainu-sponsored political proposals that touch upon language maintenance (Maher 1994). In 1983, the first Ainu language school was established by Shigeru Kayano in the Ainu community. For many years, language learning classes have been held privately in the Nibutani area[11] and these have been augmented by other Ainu language classes started by local community groups in community centres in Hokkaido, for example, in Sapporo, Asahikawa, Obihiro, Chitose, and elsewhere (Maher 1994; Martin 2011). Municipal funding for the classrooms in Biratori (i.e., the Nibutani Classroom) and Ashikawa commenced in 1987.

There appears to be a strong desire in Ainu communities to learn the language. However, the number of students in Ainu language classes still remains low due to discrimination from the mainstream society and the lack of socioeconomic advantages in learning the language (Martin 2011). Moreover, due to the lack of teachers and staff who could deliver lessons, several Ainu language classes stopped delivering lessons (Kayano 2017). This is because teachers and staff members of these classes often work for almost no pay. As of 2017, in the Nibutani Elementary School, for example, Ainu language lessons are conducted currently only about ten times per year. These classes are conducted for students in all grades, from first to sixth grade. For the third, fourth, fifth, and sixth graders, the classes use official curriculum hours called *sōgō tekina gakushyū no jikan* [integrated learning hour]. For the first and second graders, the class uses official curriculum hours of normal subjects by negotiating with classroom teachers.

In addition, there are some high schools in Hokkaido that offer Ainu language classes, but these classes are for students who already know which universities they will attend after graduation. For those students,

---

[11]In the Nibutani Valley area, Ainu language lessons were started by Shigeru Kayano in 1983.

13 Indigenous in Japan? The Reluctance of the Japanese State ... 237

it is unproblematic to teach the Ainu language (John Smith, email communication).

This shows that the Ainu language does not have the same status in the official curriculum as does the dominant language, Japanese, and that the implementation of Ainu language lessons depends strongly on individual teachers' and local initiatives. The Ainu language lessons are conducted only as local initiatives without a concrete teaching curriculum (Kenji Sekine, email communication). Teaching the Ainu language is a concept that needs to echo the practice of teaching indigenous languages in other parts of the world, elsewhere, indigenous languages can be learned as languages throughout the formal education system from elementary school up to university, not as supplementary subjects only for those who have time to learn them (see, e.g., Hornberger 2010b).

At present, the Ainu and the Ryūkyūans possess neither rights nor guarantees to establish or control their own education at any educational level, from pre-school through to tertiary education. Their rights that they have not been granted include developing and implementing a culturally based curriculum, culturally based Ainu or Ryūkyūan pedagogical methods, and the use of their own language in schooling (Gayman 2011; Hammine, in press; McCarty and Lee 2014). The systematisation and institutionalisation of education do not yet exist for indigenous culture and language. At present, despite an increasing trend for schools with Ainu students to implement education for intercultural understanding, multicultural education, and human rights education, Ainu students at these schools receive no special ethnic recognition or distinct educational opportunities based upon their ethnicity. In other words, they receive the standard Japanese curriculum (Gayman 2011). In the Ryūkyūs, similarly, despite the local desire to teach indigenous languages and cultures, there are no educational opportunities supported by the official curriculum to pursue indigenous languages or culture (Ishihara 2010; Hammine, in press). In both cases, education systems based on dominant Japanese values have fed continuing racism and discrimination, often socially excluding, if not ignoring, indigenous groups, cultures and languages in Japan (see also Takayanagi and Shimomura 2013).

Indigenous in Japan?

I have discussed the history of assimilation through education for both the Ryūkyūans and the Ainu in Japan. How can indigenous individuals pursue their indigenous identities in Japan? According to statistics from the Hokkaido government, the Ainu are approximately 0.02% of the total population of Japan and their numbers are extremely small; only around 13,000 people officially identify themselves as Ainu. It is difficult to estimate the exact number, both because many Ainu try to hide their ethnic backgrounds or ancestry out of fear of discrimination and because of substantial intermarriage over many generations (Takayanagi and Shimomura 2013; Emori 2015). There are many young Ainu individuals who do not affirm their Ainu identity and heritage due to the negative attitudes to their Ainu heritage and ethnicity that their parents and ancestors experienced.[12]

In the Ryūkyūs, Japan's assimilation policy of encouraging people to speak Japanese discouraged people from speaking their local languages (see Oguma 1998; Ishihara 2016, among others). Until now, none of the Ryūkyūan languages has been taught as a subject at school. Ryūkyūans also identify themselves as Japanese since their ancestors made efforts to be Japanese by studying Japanese to achieve success in mainstream society. Although a strong desire to learn the Ryūkyūan languages and culture is reported (Ishihara 2010; Hammine, in press), there is not yet systematic education which recognises the need for indigenous language and cultural transmission in the Ryūkyūs.

In addition, I examined one case of revitalisation of the Yaeyaman language (one of the Ryūkyūan languages spoken on and around Ishigaki Island), and I found the phenomenon of internalised oppression among Ryūkyūan language speakers (Hammine, in press). The speakers of Ryūkyūan languages themselves devalued their own

---

[12]In December 2017, I met Ms. Sayaka Mizuki (has Sayaka-san given her permission for you to use her name in this context? If not, then you should quickly get her permission, or otherwise keep her name anonymous), who told me her own experience of growing up not knowing she was actually Ainu.

13 Indigenous in Japan? The Reluctance of the Japanese State ...

language and culture due to the history of assimilation in the past, and they believe their language is dirty. This kind of internalised psychological colonialism is a phenomenon often reported in other indigenous groups all over the world (see, e.g., Ngugi 1986; Hornberger 2008).

Since there is a lack of awareness of Indigeneity in Japanese society, there is little awareness of cultural appropriation in Japan. On Ainu land, visitors today encounter Ainu people primarily within the context of tourist villages that convey the impression of the relics of the Ainu as "a not quite dead culture" (Siddle 1996). On the Ryūkyūs, tourists encounter *shīsā*[13] sold as commodities and there are even workshops run by Japanese people on making handmade craft objects that convey the impression of the relaxing Okinawan way of life. To recognise the ethical problem of using indigenous culture in this type of tourism seems to be difficult for the Ainu and Ryūkyūans themselves. Yet the problem is deeper: with a monolingual, monocultural ideology, the Ainu and Ryūkyūan themselves are made to believe their own heritage, culture, and languages are inferior to those of Japanese.

There is a need to consider the question: why has it been difficult for indigenous groups in Japan to notice and identify these problems? Educational policies in the past and present have fed ignorance among the majority of Japanese citizens of Japan's multilingual, multiethnic, and multicultural reality, and they have also fed the reluctance of indigenous groups to affirm their own heritage and identities in Japan (see, e.g., Maher 1997; Gayman 2011; and Yokota 2015).

Decolonisation is a concept that is necessary in the field of education for indigenous peoples in Japan to ensure their access to indigenous languages, culture, and knowledge, a concept that will enable them to restore or choose their identities and instil positive self-esteem (Skutnabb-Kangas 2010; Smith 1999). In order to give individuals a choice to have an indigenous identity and to instil positive self-esteem of indigenous populations in Japan, indigenous peoples themselves need

---

[13]*Shīsā* is a traditional Ryūkyūan decoration from Okinawan mythology, resembling a cross between a lion and a dog.

240 M. Hammine

to be ensured that there is a choice to be an indigenous or minority in Japan. Hence, there is a need to re-evaluate the monolingual, monocultural, and monoethnic policy prevailing in the Japanese education system; since it crucially feeds the negative self-esteem of indigenous peoples.

Conclusion

I agree with Gayman (2011) that the status of groups as indigenous minorities has been downplayed, compared to the international standard set in the UNDRIP[16]. The principles of UNDRIP, in particular, Articles 13, 14, and 15 on education and cultural transmission, are: (1) the notion of indigenous knowledge, (2) the recognition of the devastating effects of colonisation on indigenous knowledge systems, especially through schooling, (3) the simultaneous recognition of the need for modern education to achieve the political and economic aims of indigenous peoples to further their own autonomy and self-determination, and (4) the recognition of the need and desire to bring more congruence between traditional ways of knowing and modern knowledge practices, as epitomised by the school (Gayman 2011). These principles are not taken into consideration in current education policies in Japan, for both Ryūkyūans and Ainu. Their indigenous rights to education, including the appreciation of indigenous knowledge, recognition of theyoko indigenous knowledge systems, and recognition of the right to a simultaneously modern education, are as yet unrealised in the Japanese educational system.

In order to decolonise indigenous research in Japan, first, there is an urgent need to improve education and professional training by focusing on multilingualism and multiculturalism for future teachers and researchers who possess indigenous language abilities and indigenous backgrounds, including the Ainu and Ryūkyūan in Japan (e.g., Hornberger 2014). In order to include more teachers, educators, and researchers with these backgrounds, the educational system needs to change. There is a lack of a multilingual, multicultural foundation for a system of education that would recognise the rights of indigenous peoples in Japan; this lack has persisted through the educational policies in the past up to the present. There is a need to recognise the multiple linguistic, cultural, and ethnic resources that exist in Japan; this recognition will enable individuals from indigenous communities to make the choice to construct their indigenous identities comfortably in the modern world (e.g., Cummins 2001; Hornberger 2008). In such cases, multicultural, multilingual educational policy based on the multicultural, multilingual reality of the different regions in Japan would enable indigenous individuals both to choose to construct indigenous identities comfortably and to achieve success in a society where dominant values prevail. In other words, policy based on the multicultural, multiethnic, and multilingual reality of the nation could be a solution; being indigenous could become a real choice in Japan.

Acknowledgements The author would like to thank Sayaka Mizuki, Utae Ehara, Adriana Dobanda Shiro Kayano, Kenji Sekine, Jeffry Gayman, Hiroshi Maruyama, Hideaki Uemura, Robert Duckworth for providing encouragement, and for giving constructive feedback during the writing process.

References

Churchill, S. (1986). *The Education of Linguistic and Cultural Minorities in the OECD Countries*. London: Multilingual Matter.

Clarke, H. (2015). Language and Identity in Okinawa and Amami. In P. Heinrich, M. Shimoji, & M. Shinsyou (Eds.), *Handbook of the Ryukyuan Languages*. Berlin: Mouton de Gruyter.

Cummins, J. (2001). *Negotiating Identities: Education for Empowerment in a Diverse Society*. Los Angels: California Association for Bilingual Education.

Emori, S. (2007). *Ainu Minzoku no Rekishi* [The History of the Ainu]. Urayasu, Japan: Sofukan.

Emori, S. (2015). *Ainu Minzoku no Rekishi* [History of Ainu people]. Tokyo: Saifukan.

Gayman, J. (2011). Ainu Right to Education and Ainu Practice of "Education": Current Situation and Imminent Issues in Light of Indigenous Education Rights and Theory. *Intercultural Education, 22*(1), 15–27. https://doi.org/10.1080/14675986.2011.549642.

Hammine, M. (in press). Educated Not to Speak Our Language -Language Attitudes and Newspeakerness in the Yaeyaman Language-. *International Journal of Identity, Language and Education.*

Hanks, D. (2017). Policy Barriers to Ainu Language Revitalization in Japan: When Globalization Means English. *Working Papers in Educational Lingusitics, 32*(1), 91–101.

Heinrich, P. (2012). *The Making of Monolingual Japan: Language Ideology and Japanese Modernity.* Bristol: Multilingual Matters.

Heinrich, P. (2018). Revitalization of the Ryukyuan Languages. In L. Hinton, L. Huss, & G. Roche (Eds.), *The Routledge Handbook of Language Revitalization* (pp. 455–463). New York: Routledge.

Heinrich, P., & Galan, C. (Eds.). (2011). *Language Life in Japan: Transformation and Prospects.* New York: Routledge.

Hirose, K. (1996). Hokkaidō karigakkō fuzoku hokkaidō dojin kyōikusho to kaitakushi kan-en e no Ainu no kyōsei shūgaku ni kansuru kenkyū [A Study on How Ainu Youth Were Forced to Attend Kaitakushi Ainu School and National Farms in Tokyo]. *The Annual Reports on Educational Science, 72,* 89–119.

Hokama, S. (1971). *Okinawa no gengo-shi* [Language History of Okinawa]. Tokyo: Hōsei Daigaku Shuppan.

Hornberger, N. H. (2008). *Encyclopedia of Language and Education.* Springer Reference. https://doi.org/10.1007/978-0-387-30424-3.

Hornberger, N. H. (2010a). Language and Education: A Limpopo Lens. In N. H. Hornberger & S. L. McKay (Eds.), *Sociolinguistics and Language Education* (pp. 549–564). Bristol, UK: Multilingual Matters.

Hornberger, N. H. (2010b, January). *Multilingual Education Policy and Practice: Lessons from Indigenous Experience.* Center for Applied Linguistics, pp. 40–43.

Hornberger, N. H. (2014). "Until I Became a Professional, I Was Not, Consciously, Indigenous": One Intercultural Bilingual Educator's Trajectory in Indigenous Language Revitalization. *Journal of Language, Identity and Education, 13*(4), 283–299. https://doi.org/10.1080/15348458.2014.939028.

Howell, D. L. (2004). Making " Useful Citizens" of Ainu Subjects in Early Twentieth-Century Japan. *The Journal of Asian Studies, 63*(1), 5–29.

Ishihara, M. (2010). Ryūkyūgo no sonzokusei to kikido -gyakkōteki gengo shi-huto wa kanō-ka [Survival and Endangerment of Ryukyuan language - Is Reversing Language Shift possible? -]. In P. Heinrich & S. Matsuo (Eds.), *Higashi ajia ni okeru gengo fukkou [Language revitalization in East Asia]* (pp. 111–149). Tokyo: Sangensha.

Ishihara, M. (2016). Language Revitalization Efforts in the Ryukyus. In M. Ishihara, E. Hoshino, & Y. Fujita (Eds.), *Self-Determinable Development of Small Islands* (pp. 67–82). Singapore: Springer.

Iwasaki, N. (1998). *Nihon kinsei no Ainu shakai* [Ainu Society in the Early-Modern Period of Japan]. Tokyo, Japan: Azekura Shobo.

Kaizawa, T. (1993). *Ainu waga jinsei* [Ainu My Life]. Tokyo: Iwanami Shoten.

Kayano, S. (1994). *Our Land was a Forest: An Ainu Memoir* (M. Selden, Trans.). London: Routledge.

Kayano, S. (2017, November). *The Right of Ainu People to Learn the Ainu Language.* Paper presented at the International Conference on Policy towards Indigenous Peoples: Lesson to be learned, Sapporo: Hokkaido.

Kerr, G. (2000). *Okinawa: The History of Island People.* North Clarendon: Tuttle Publishing.

Keskitalo, P., & Sarivaara, E. (2017). Sámi Language for All: Transformed Futures through Mediative Education. In E. McKinley & L. T. Smith (Eds.), *Handbook of Indigenous Education.* Singapore: Springer.

Kondo, K. (1993). Gakkō ga yamatoya to yobareta koro: Ryukyu shobun chokugo no okinawa ni okeru gakkō [A Study on the Schools in Okinawa Immediately after the Close of the Ryukyu Court]. *Annual Report on Educational Science, 68*, 161–175. Sapporo: Hokkdaido University.

Kondo, K. (2008). *Hōgenfuda—kotobatokarada* [Diarect Tag—Language and Body]. Tokyo: Shakaihyōronsha.

Lee, B. R. (2005). Twenty-First Century Indigenism. *Anthropological Theory, 6*(4), 455–479.

Lewallen, A. (2008). Indigenous At Last! Ainu Grassroots Organizing and the Indigenous Peoples Summit in Ainu Mosir. *The Asia-Pacific Journal,* Vol. 48-6-08,

Liddlecoat, A. (2013). Langauges in the Education of Indigenous People. In *Language-in-Education Policies: The Discursive Construction of Intercultural Relations* (pp. 150–171). Bristol: Multilingual Matters.

Maher, J. (1994). *Atarashii Nihonkan Sekaikan ni mukatte—nihon ni okeru gengo to bunka no tayosei-* [Towards New View of Japan, View of the World—Linguistic and Cultural Diversity in Japan-]. Tokyo: Kokusai Shoin.

Maher, J. (1997). Linguistic Minorities and Education in Japan. *Educational Review, 49*(2), 115–127. https://doi.org/10.1080/0013191970490203.

Martin, K. (2011). Ainu Itak: On the Road to Ainu Language Revitalization. *Media and Communication Studies, 60*, 57–93. Hokkaido University.

Maruyama, H. (2014). Japan's Policies Towards the Ainu Language and Culture with Special Reference to North Fennoscandian Sami Policies. *Acta Borealia*. https://doi.org/10.1080/08003831.2014.967980.

McCarty, T., & Lee, T. (2014). Critical Culturally Sustaining/Revitalizing Pedagogy and Indigenous Education Sovereignty. *Harvard Educational Review, 84*(1). Policies, *3831* (June 2016). https://doi.org/10.1080/08003 831.2014.967980.

McCormack, G. (2017). Ryūkyū/Okinawa's Trajetory: From Periphery to Centre, 1600–2015. In S. Saaler & C. Szpilmann (Eds.), *Routledge Handbook of Modern Japanese History* (pp. 118–133). Abingdon: Routledge.

Minde, H. (1996). The Making of an International Movement of Indigenous Peoples. *Scandinavian Journal of History, 21*(3), 221–246. https://doi.org/10.1080/03468759608579326.

Ngugi, W. T. (1986). *Decolonizing the Mind: The Politics of Language in African Literature*. London: James Currey.

Ogawa, M. (1997). *Ainu Kyōiku Seisakushi* [History of Ainu Education Policy]. Sapporo: Hokkaido University Publication.

Oguma, E. (1998). *"Nihonjin" no kyōkai: Okinawa, Ainu, Taiwan, Chōsen*, shokuminchi shihai kara fukki undō made [The Boundary of "Japanese": Okinawa, Ainu Taiwan, Korea from colonization to the Return Movement]. Tokyo: Shinyosha.

Pietikäinen, S., Huss, L., Laihiala-Kankainen, S., Aikio-Puoskari, U., & Lane, P. (2010). Regulating Multilingualism in the North Calotte: The Case of Kven, Meänkieli and Sámi Languages. *Acta Borealia, 27*(1), 1–23. https://doi.org/10.1080/08003831.2010.486923.

Shinya, G. (2015). *Ainu minzoku teikō shi* [The history of Ainu Resistance]. Tokyo: Kawade shobō.

Siddle, R. (1996). *Race, Resistance, and the Ainu of Japan*. London: Routledge.

Siddle, R. (1998). Colonialism and Identity in Okinawa Before 1945. *Japanese Studies, 18*(2), 117–133. https://doi.org/10.1080/10371399808727647.

Siddle, R. (2002). Return to Uchina⁻: The Politics of Identity in Contemporary Okinawa. In G. Hook & R. Siddle (Eds.), *Japan and Okinawa Structure and Subjectivity* (pp. 133–147). London: RoutledgeCurzon.

Siddle, R. (2003). The Limits to Citizenship in Japan: Multiculturalism, Indigenous Rights and the Ainu. *Citizenship Studies, 7*(4), 447–462. https://doi.org/10.1080/1362102032000134976.

Skutnabb-Kangas, T. (2010). Education of Indigenous and Minority Children. In J. A. Fishman & O. Garcia (Eds.), *Handbook of Language and Ethnic Identity* (pp. 186–204). Oxford: Oxford University Press.

Smith, L. T. (1999). *Decolonizing Methodologies: Research and Indigenous Peoples*. New York: University of Otago Press.

Takahashi, S. (2015). *Regionalizing the Local, Localizing the Region: The Okinawa Struggle and Place-Based Identity*. PhD thesis, Australian National University.

Takayanagi, T., & Shimomura, T. (2013). Indigenous Women Facing Educational Disadvantages: The Case of the Ainu in Japan. *Prospects, 43*(3), 347–360. https://doi.org/10.1007/s11125-013-9273-y.

Takegahara, Y. (2008). *Kindai Hokkaido shi o torae naosu* [Revisiting the Modern History of Hokkaido]. Tokyo, Japan: Shakai Hyōron Sha.

Tanji, M. (2006). *Myth, Protest, and Struggle in Okinawa Sheffield Centre for Japanese Studies/Routledge Series* (G. D. Hook, Ed.). New York: Routledge.

Uemura, H. (2003). The Colonial Annexation of Okinawa and the Logic of International Law: The Formation of an "Indigenous People" in East Asia. *Japanese Studies, 23*(2), 213–222. https://doi.org/10.1080/1037139032000154867.

Uemura, H., & Gayman, J. (2018). Rethinking Japan's Constitution from the Perspective of the Ainu and Ryūkyū Peoples. *The Asia-Pacific Journal, 16*(5), 1–18.

Weiner, M. (1997). *Japan's Minorities: The Illusion of Homogeneity*. London: Routledge.

Yokota, R. M. (2015). The Okinawan (Uchinanchu) Indigenous Movement and Its Implications for Intentional/International Action. *Amerasia Journal, 41*(1), 55–73.

Yokota, R. M. (2017). Reversion-Era Proposals for Okinawa: Regional Autonomy. In P. Iacobelli & H. Matsuda (Eds.), *Rethinking Postwar Okinawa Beyond American Occupation* (pp. 59–79). New York: Lexington Books.

14

School Histories in Amazonia: Education and Schooling in Apurinã Lands

Pirjo Kristiina Virtanen and Francisco Apurinã

In Brazilian Amazonia, a significant number of Indigenous children and youth are born in Indigenous reserves and settlements located at several days' river journey from the nearest urban areas. This rainforest environment differs from those Indigenous settlements and demarcated Indigenous territories that are only a few minutes' distance from nearby urban areas. Many Indigenous families live in cities for generations, but their visits to their home villages can be frequent.

All of the above-mentioned cases apply to the Apurinã, but most of the Apurinã live in demarcated or rural areas. They are one of Brazil's approximately 305 Indigenous groups, numbering almost 900,000 people in total. Indigenous groups in Brazil can be classified according to their language families—Tupi, Carib, Ge, and

---

P. K. Virtanen (✉)
University of Helsinki, Helsinki, Finland
e-mail: pirjo.virtanen@helsinki.fi

F. Apurinã
University of Brasília, Brasília, Brazil

© The Author(s) 2019
O. Kortekangas et al. (eds.), *Sámi Educational History
in a Comparative International Perspective*,
https://doi.org/10.1007/978-3-030-24112-4_14

Arawak being the biggest ones (Funai 2019). The special requirements to develop Indigenous schooling have principally been studied from the perspectives of anthropology, education, and linguistics (see, e.g., Cabral et al. 1987; Monte 1996; da Silva and Ferreira 2001), and today both Indigenous and non-Indigenous scholars are contributing to this Indigenization (e.g. Weber 2006; Tassinari and Cohn 2009; Luciano 2013). In this chapter, we are interested in exploring how the first schools were set up in Southwestern Amazonia and how the participation in state schools has been experienced. Our case is the history of Apurinã schools from the perspective of the Apurinã themselves. Arawak-speaking Apurinã live along the Purus River, in the state of Amazonas, but also in Rondônia and in many urban areas of Acre, Brazil.

In exploring the kinds of education that Apurinã children have experienced, we first look at Apurinã traditional education, and then the historical and structural changes in their national and political contexts. Finally, we discuss the recent changes in education as well as the challenges encountered in sustaining the Apurinã in their education processes. Our focus is on elementary school students, as there are no high schools in the current demarcated territories for the Apurinã.

Examining schooling in the Apurinã context, our methods have been ethnography, collaborative work, and reviewing historical records. The first author has worked in Southwestern Amazonia since 2003. The second author is an Apurinã scholar, originally from the Camicuá (Kamikuã) reserve in southern Amazonas state, and therefore one of our examples is from there. Ethnography and local Indigenous experiences are used especially in analyzing traditional Apurinã education and memories, as well as attitudes toward schooling. Then we draw on the first historical records on the arrival of state schooling in Apurinã lands. Brazilian Indigenous education policies are also presented to contextualize Apurinã schooling in the past as well as today. Our research, combining local and larger views, contributes to studies on local school histories, and it is the first to present school history from an Apurinã perspective.

Traditional Apurinã Education

The Apurinã have been oppressed by state powers, rubber patrons, settlers, nut-collectors, merchants, and others. For a long time, they have been told to abandon their mother tongue or traditions (see Schiel 1999; Facundes 2000). Today, in order to claim their Indigenous rights, they are however, asked to show and prove their cultural difference. The task is difficult for many people, especially for those whose parents had close interactions with non-Indians, and who, in order to survive, had to speak only Portuguese to their children. Due to harsh assimilation politics, most of the Apurinã people no longer speak their Indigenous language fluently. Having said that, knowledge of Apurinã language is still strong in some villages and Apurinãs learn about their history through their parents, as well as through natural medicine, chants, dances, and oral histories. In this particular part of Brazil, Indigenous youth living in villages have a deep knowledge of their local environments and know how to live in the forest.

For the Apurinã, history starts with the myth of Tsura, who is responsible for the creation of the world and everything that exists in it. The existence, presence, and role of the *mỹyty*, generally known as a shaman, are also significant for the Apurinã. Shamanic principles construct the world, and in order to understand it, one needs to comprehend how the body and the person are, according to Apurinã knowledge, produced in interrelation. The *mỹyty* are undoubtedly the most important persons for the well-being of the Apurinã collective, since they are the holders of fundamental knowledge that allow them to heal, to predict things, and whose ontological knowledge reaches the domain of the codes by which they communicate with the world of spirits and the inhabitants of other lands.

Apurinã social organization also explains their ways of being. Apurinã society is divided into exogamous moieties with social and political functions, and these define the right to consume or restrict certain types of food, the right to marry, and generally the social rules of the people. These patrilineal moieties are called *meetymanety* and *xiwapurynyry*. They are traditionally represented by the *atukatxi* (the sun) and *kasiri* (the moon), or the figures of *kyãty* and *wainhamary* cobras.

"Small children receive Apurinã education at home following the principles of Apurinã socio-philosophies." Since the age of four, children accompany and learn from their parents the daily activities, which make them human subjects as Apurinã. Young men and boys are typically capable of undertaking various kinds of activities, such as preparing slash-burn swiddens, planting, clearing a plantation, house building, and fishing, while the young women and girls know how to gather, prepare 'traditional' food, and prepare several objects from their natural environment. The second author of this chapter, Francisco (*Ywmunyry*), for instance, has accompanied his father on his long excursions to collect wild fruits, such as *kinhary* and *kitxiti* palm trees, and their *upu* and *txükinhiky* worms. His father also took him hunting and fishing, so that he learned how to handle a bow and arrow, as well as other instruments. He also learned how to make and take care of plantations of banana, yam, inhame, cará, cassava, and other staples that are part of the Apurinã diet. This offered him rich land and place-specific environmental knowledge.

According to Francisco's father, Katáwyry, in this way it is possible to be a person who can represent the Apurinã people well, as well as be admired by one's future father-in-law. On the other hand, if a boy is a liar, or lazy and fearful, he will have little respect within the village, and will die a bachelor, as no father would want to have a son-in-law like this. Nor can such a person become a wise person. The same goes for girls.

Francisco learned myths and oral histories about the creation of the cosmos from his grandparents. Gradually, he learned the words and actions that allowed him to connect with the other agencies of the environment, including the respect the Apurinã should have for each living being that makes up what non-Indigenous people call "nature." For the Apurinã, every living species has a function on the earth, and must be respected by humans. In this way, an individual can be a guardian who protects the environment and biodiversity. As Francisco's father said:

> We Apurinã are on the earth since the beginning of the world, as my father told me, as his grandfather had told him, as my great-grandfather had told my grandfather [...]. Tsura, our creator gave life to our people and everything that exists in the world: those who live on the earth, those

who live in the forest, those who live in the water and even those who live in the air. Since then, we have learned to take care of the things that he left from the first day, taking from nature only what is necessary, as he taught us; respecting his creation, because even the animals talk to us and deserve respect. Many of these animals are our own kin, but Tsura also gave the Apurinãs the knowledge that allows them to know which animals we can kill to serve as food, and which ones we should respect as our relative. That is why everything that is harmful to our culture also does harm to the law of Tsura.

Normally, when the Apurinã return from a hunting or fishing trip, they share with their relatives what they managed to capture. They kill only what is enough for them to eat that day. If unsustainable actions happen, the person is considered severely to be punished by the spirits that protect the forest, which are usually Apurinã ancestors who have transformed into animals (see Virtanen 2015; Apurinã 2017). Moral education, not only related to humans but also-non humans, is present in Apurinã practices.

Looking at the Past: The First Schools in the Purus River

If we move from ethnography to colonial historical documents, we find that the Purus River is mentioned in the reports of Francisco Orellana's expedition, the first written source on Latin America. The Southern Amazonas state was one of the last places in Brazil to receive missionaries and colonizers, as well as adventurers. The first historical records mentioning the Apurinã in the lower and central Purus River are, among others, the reports by Coutinho (1862), Chandless (1866), and Labre (1872), which mention the region to be rich in cacao, natural oils, cotton, nuts, herbs, and rubber. In fact, the report of Coronel Labre's (1889, 501) journey along the Purus River toward the Madre de Dios River ends by mentioning that an Apurinã chief had given Labre three young men to assist him in exploring the Ituxi River, and in a compensation Labre had taught them to read and write.

The rubber boom changed the history of Amazonia, as it brought many settlers to work in the area, which led to the enslavement of various Indigenous peoples, including some Apurinã, forcing them to work in rubber collection, on farms, or in other services. Until the end of the nineteenth century, the Apurinã could live in their traditional lands, and after that they experienced violence, even massacres by new settlers, whose aim was to turn them into a workforce or use them to exploit the natural resources of their territories (Schiel 1999).

Most of the historical records mention the Apurinã as strong people, although they are also represented as savages, ignorant, barbarians, violent, and without manners, and this attitude from the non-Indigenous population still persists today. The positivist views of the state concurred that for "progress" to take place, the Indigenous population had to be assimilated into the new nation state. According to the historical records, written by non-Indigenous elites, the Apurinã were noble savages who could be civilized, Christianized, and turned into an able workforce (see Coutinho 1862; Chandelss 1866; Labre 1872). In the beginning of the twentieth century, the Brazilian state established so-called Indigenous posts (*posto indígena*) in the Amazon region, state official's houses and buildings for productive activities, with the aim of turning Indigenous people into "proper citizens," but also to act as places of intermediation between Indigenous and non-Indigenous populations. The state's aim was to educate the Indigenous population in order to carry out agricultural and other types of economic production, and these plans worked in tandem with the schools that were to be opened in the area (De Oliveira and Gomes do Nascimento 2012).

On the other hand, Indigenous people were also protected by the state from the violent attacks of settlers and explorers who were exploiting the region's natural resources. The agency responsible for this function was called the Service for Protection of Indians and Local Workers (SPILTN), but later it needed only to "protect" Indigenous People and in 1918 its name was changed to the Protection Service of Indians (*Serviço de Proteção aos Índios*—SPI) (Lima 1992). It was also put in charge of establishing and maintaining Indigenous posts. The Posto Marienê was situated in the Apurinã area of the Purus River, and it was influential for many Apurinãs (Schiel 1999).

14 School Histories in Amazonia: Education and Schooling ...   253

By that time, numerous Indigenous persons were employed by the Purus River region's rubber patrons, and they lived in poor conditions, as they could rarely cultivate their own lands. Instead, they had to buy products at high prices and pay with their labor, meaning that they were perpetually in debt to their employers. Those who were unable to pay back their debts, were obliged to continue to work for their bosses. The SPI wanted to turn Indigenous people into "proper" Brazilian citizens, but at the same time their number was declining. Diseases, hunger, and violence were common problems (Ramos 1998).

In the schools established in the area, Indigenous languages and Indigeneity were consequently forbidden, as the aim was to transcend cultural differences and unify the nation state. The state encouraged Indigenous people to learn practices that would help Indigenous communities enter the market economy, such as agricultural skills, learning to use sewing machines, and acquiring other mechanical skills that were beneficial to the national economy, but also encouraged hygiene (Henriques et al. 2007). The school buildings were equipped by the state with sewing machines, carpentry and other work objects (see De Oliveira and Gomes do Nascimento 2012). Indigenous Peoples were persuaded to dress up in the style of the period and were materially "made" into being members of the dominant society.

Numerous non-Indigenous settlers brought with them more Christian missions, which became places to educate Indians, as well as convert them to Christianity. Missions in the area had been established especially by the Jesuists, and later by other groups. On one hand, in the missions, Indigenous people received some protection from those interested only in exploiting the natural resources and riches of the region, but on the other, the missions forced Indigenous groups to adopt the rules of the dominant society and were forced into hard physical labor (Lima 1992). Missionaries coming from different backgrounds also offered schooling, putting Indigenous people even more under the influence of Western thinking. Most missionaries started to use Indigenous languages in their Christian teaching and missions and made efforts to transform them into a written form. In the missions, Christian sacred texts and chants were translated into Indigenous languages, including the Apurinã language. This process happened without collaboration and negotiation on orthography or standardization. Moreover, most missionaries prohibited the practices of traditional rituals and many other ways of life, such as the use of traditional medicine and shamanism, considering them demonic (see also Schiel 1999).

Due to criticism toward the SPI, its mandate was taken over in 1967 by the National Indigenous Foundation—FUNAI, and now Indigenous people were not only officially protected in paternalistic relations but given more agency (see Ramos 1998). In their schooling, Indigenous languages were slowly recognized, and with that aim, the teaching responsibility was also given to institutions working on Indigenous languages, such as the SIL—Summer Institute of Linguistics, a North American missionary institution specialized in translating Christian texts. In the same period, some nongovernmental institutions started pioneer activities in Indigenous teacher training and education. Such an attempt was made by the CPI—Pro-Indian Commission (*Commissão Pro-Índio*) in the Acre state at the end of the 1970s. At the same time, the Funai continued developing economic activities in Indigenous areas, such as cattle ranching and the cultivation of coffee, corn, beans, cotton, and so forth. These activities reorganized and broke family relations and kin ties, as well as social hierarchies related to knowledge in Indigenous communities.

In the 1970s, through the resistance of the civil society to the military government, Indigenous organizations were founded in Brazil. They were supported by various nongovernmental organizations, such as rubber tappers and pro-Indigenous organizations. The Indigenous movement and its supportive actors backed Indigenous peoples' rights (Ramos 1998). From the late 1970s, Indigenous leaders collaborated with pro-Indian nongovernmental organizations, such as CIMI—the Indianist Missionary Council (*Conselho Indigenista Missionário*) and CPI. Consequently, in the 1980s, Indigenous leaders demanded their rights and the demarcation of their lands. At the same time, the UNI—Union of Indigenous Nations of Acre and Southern Amazonas (*União das Nações Indígenas do Acre e sul-do-Amazonas*) was founded (see also Ramos 1998, 19). Apurinã leaders were among the most forceful actors in Indigenous politics. The Indigenous movement fought first for land rights, but soon after the battle for education and health rights began. This social movement also succeeded in designing and founding conservation units, environmental protection and social development projects, and a range of cooperative economic, educational, and health care projects in Indigenous territories.

Developing Indigenous Education: The First Decades After the Military Regime

In one of the first books in which Indigenous education in Brazil is mentioned, Fernandes (1975) noted that, since Tupinambá society was "traditional, sacred and closed," their traditional education had not prepared them to face new social situations in which Indigenous peoples had to defend themselves. Instead, it trained them to follow a collective way of living and to achieve their social realization as persons and human beings by acting in accordance with specific traditional criteria. However, Indigenous societies have never lived in isolation, and even in precolonial times there were long-distant exchanges.

In the Brazilian constitution of 1988, the Indigenous population was guaranteed for the first time the right to speak their language and carry out their traditional practices. Up until the 1990s, the state agency, FUNAI officially took responsibility for the education of the Indigenous population. Indigenous leaders and educators have worked hard to make schooling an instrument that would reproduce Indigenous knowledge and dignity, while at the same time receiving the same opportunities to study as others (Luciano 2013, see also da Silva and Ferreira 2001).

In 1991, differentiated education services for the Indigenous population were defined by law (Decree no. 26, 4th February, 1991— *Lei de Diretrizes e Bases da Educação Nacional*), and the responsibility for this was passed over to the Ministry of Education (see MEC 2017). In the same year, the Indigenous Education Committee in the Ministry of Education was established, which also became responsible for Indigenous education. Later in 2001, it was substituted by the Committee of Indigenous Teachers (see also other legal agreements in Luciano 2013). In its policies on Indigenous Education, the state focuses on the training of Indigenous teachers and offers school materials in both Indigenous languages and in Portuguese, and these efforts are financially supported.

From the 1990s onwards, Indigenous teachers' training became the official responsibility of the State Secretaries for Education, although the local actors, such as the CPI-Acre, or federal universities continued to be involved in their practical implementation. In the state of Acre, for instance, it was as late as 1999 that these developments had a real impact on the public articulation of Indigenous education in this state. The CPI-Acre, for instance, took into account the different needs and cultural differences of Indigenous peoples, and still today the state's Indigenous schools are showcases of successful and constructive Indigenous schooling.

With the help of state and nongovernmental sponsors, several Indigenous teachers have produced the first reader books in indigenous languages. However, the first Apurinã teachers who participated in the teacher training course did not have a very strong command of Apurinã, as they came from areas which were strongly influenced by the dominant society. Later on, when linguistic research was carried out in villages where the first language is Apurinã, new schooling materials were produced. The research has been done by Brazilian linguist Sidney Facundes and his students. Later, the first author of this chapter joined the team, while Apurinã teachers and elders were also involved through workshops which took place on Apurinã land and in the nearby cities. This collaborative work has produced first reader book, conversation manuals, dictionaries, and other teaching materials for Apurinã schools (see Facundes et al. 2019). However, their use is limited since there are not enough copies for all the schools on the reserves. Textbooks are mostly provided by the Secretary of Education, and are used more frequently. However, teachers say that only part of the state school material can be used, since its content is not applicable to their everyday lives. The literature can be very distant from the social, cultural and economic realities of the Indigenous reserves, such as the geography textbooks in Portuguese on Brazil's metropolitan cities.

Several dissertations have been written on the schooling of particular Indigenous groups in Brazil (see, e.g., Weber 2006; Collet 2006; Luciano 2013). According to our experience in the Purus River, the educational

14 School Histories in Amazonia: Education and Schooling ... 257

system still fails in terms of educating qualified Indian teachers and in employing state officials familiar with Indigenous realities. In general, the most common problems faced by Indigenous education at the state level are still the lack of funding and the inadequate organization and communication between Indigenous peoples and State Secretaries of Education. Studying school history at local levels, especially through the implementation of schooling policies, is a complex issue, as the local politics is related to power relations which constantly take new turns, and practical implementations of policies are short termed. The success of Indigenous education has largely depended on the realization of state funding arriving in distant Amazonian localities as well as collaborations with different NGOs (national and international), researchers, and other civil society actors. Today, in Brazil there are several Indigenous people who have completed their master and doctoral degrees.

The First Formal School in the Camicuã Reserve

The Camicuã reserve, one of the few dozen Apurinã reserves, is situated in the Southern Amazonas state, close to the city of Boca do Acre. According to Francisco, their first contact with the world of letters occurred in the 1980s with the arrival of the National Foundation of the Indian—FUNAI, which was responsible for the establishment of the first basic schooling unit in the so-called "White man's education." The school's floor and walls were made of logs, and *ubim* palm leaves provided its covering. In this way, the Apurinã of that territory took their first steps in learning to know, speak and write Portuguese.

Currently, the elementary school in this village is called the Municipal Indian Apurinã school and has over 200 students, who study until the fifth year. Besides them, more than 100 students study from the 6th grade up to the upper secondary school in the municipality of Boca do Acre. An increasing number of Indigenous youth study in urban areas. There they often face difficulties in entering schools and attending the classes, especially the many procedures involved in becoming officially registered at a state school. A registration fee has to be paid, and school shirts, books, and other school materials have to be acquired. FUNAI provides some Indigenous students with a small grant, but usually the aid is sufficient only for a few notebooks and pencils. The students face serious difficulties in continuing their respective courses, including problems concerning discrimination, prejudice, housing, transportation, and food—all factors that make it difficult to stay in school.

In the mid-2010s, still under the management of the former mayor of the municipality of Boca do Acre the Umanary Training Center was built in the Camicuã village. It was named after the current village leader, Umanary, who has been a leading figure in the Indigenous movement in the region.

In November 2016, the current mayor of Boca do Acre municipality received the strategic planning of OPIAJBAM—the Jamamadi and Apurinã Indigenous Peoples Organization of Boca do Acre, containing a set of actions, among them the proposal to set up an upper secondary school in the Aldeia Camicuã. At that time many things were verbally agreed upon between the mayor and Apurinã leaders, including the construction of the aforesaid school, but unfortunately these plans have not been realized. Traditional environmental and moral education is still provided to Apurinã youth in the community, as described in the earlier section of this chapter, but as many of them travel daily to schools outside the home village, their time is increasingly spent in the schools of the dominant society.

However, a very positive factor is that despite the difficulties faced by the Apurinã students outside their village, almost 30 persons from the reserve have been able to obtain new education from different university courses (health care, pedagogy, public management, and others), besides those who are currently attending these and other courses. Not to mention that in 2017, a group of 15 students graduated in a technical nursing course, and many of them are now practicing nurses.

School as Symbol of State Recognition

Previous studies have showed that for Amazonian Indigenous population, village schools have been important places to "become civilized" (e.g. Collet 2006). While investigating the meaning of schools for the

Piro (Yine in Peru), Gow (1991, 229–251) notes that schooling is a major symbol of state recognition and residential legitimacy, similar to land deeds. Furthermore, the school can act as a sign of acknowledging the dignity and well-being of the people in the village. These intellectual aspirations are one of the instruments for social reordering and state school education can be a source of power and a means of control during contemporary periods of change and uncertainty.

In general, for those attending classes, school is a place to acquire valuable knowledge. It is a custom that before the pupils attend classes, they always take a bath and change into fresh clean clothes, usually a T-shirt distributed by the local government. The school sets its own behavioral codes and references. Teachers call students by their Portuguese names rather than by the Indigenous names typically used in the community. Tassinari and Cohn (2009) have shown how schooling, in Karipuna and Xikrin perspectives and lands in Brazil, is valued as an "opening to the other", applying the term of Lévi-Strauss, especially gaining knowledge of mathematics, accounting, and Portuguese as well as other tools that could offer them means to reproduce their differences. During the course of our work, it was apparent that initially the students in the reserve studied for no more than a few years. Early marriages and pregnancies prevented young girls in particular from studying (Virtanen 2012, 73). Today, the students stay longer at school, but parents still demand and fight for better implementation of educational rights for their children.

When young Apurinãs are asked what for them is most important, the answer is often "to study." This dream is shared by families and by people in both villages and urban areas. Overall, the question of multicultural education is a complicated issue, since the overall priority seems to be the ability to read and write. Good quality and fully functioning Indigenous education is a dream for many Indigenous peoples.

Schooling became the main instrument for defining and contributing to their own well-being, through drawing on their social relations, knowledge, and language (see also Weber 2006). However, among Apurinã teachers, at local level, the state's support for the idea that Indigenous schools can apply different forms of learning, pedagogies, and values in Indigenous curricular and educational plans has been weak, as they have been harshly suppressed by attitudes of assimilation. In those villages that have managed to establish well-functioning multicultural Indigenous education there has been Indigenization of education and a clear valuation of Indigenous traditional knowledge. The students are then encouraged to learn about their environment, Indigenous language, traditional medicine, art, and history—while inviting elders to the classes, visiting the plantations and forests. But school structure by itself cannot rescue Indigenous knowledge and languages as they should also be integrated into the new areas and fields where young Apurinãs are active.

Due to the rarity of training events, such as those of the *Pirayawara* project, organized in the central Purus region, there are also only a few trained Apurinã teachers. The first teachers often achieved literacy while living and working outside the reserve. Being away from the reserve for quite some time resulted in that they rarely speak their Indigenous language well. This has impeded the concrete development of bilingual and multicultural schooling. A comparison between the southern state of Amazonas and the neighboring state, Acre, shows that local politics have played a key role in acknowledging Indigenous education on its own terms. It shows how acknowledging the traditional ways of life of Indigenous peoples vary according to the different local politics. For instance, since the end of the 1990s in the state of Acre, the meetings of Indigenous teachers have been frequent and they have supported the use of Indigenous languages. This state also has set up training for Indigenous teachers that is led by Indigenous persons.

For the last few years, Indigenous education has been managed by so-called Ethnoeducational territories (*Territórios Etnoeducacionais*), an attempt to reach better functioning regional Educational policies. However, some territories have various Indigenous peoples from different language families, and this makes the specific needs of different nations less visible, and gives undue emphasis to more vocal groups. Overall, one problem that has surfaced in all villages has been the lack of information and explanations, as well as the absence of trained Indigenous teachers.

Over recent years, indigeneity has facilitated access to schooling and job markets following the introduction of quotas for Indigenous students in higher education. In some Brazilian universities, specific actions are implemented to include Indigenous people in higher education, such as the Affirmative Action Policy, which allows Indigenous people to debate this policy and introduce their own opinions, perspectives and history in academia (Apuriná 2018, see also Mihesuah and Wilson 2004). However, most universities in Brazil do not currently have the basic and necessary conditions to sufficiently support Indigenous students in academia and in higher studies. Since 2005, Indigenous students have started studying at universities with the help of scholarships, offered, for example, by the FUNAI. However, this option is extremely difficult since many Indigenous students lack the necessary level of basic education to apply for such scholarships. Moreover, they also lack the necessary contacts with the Indigenous organizations capable of passing on information about these possibilities.

Many Indigenous youths feel that there is still a strong prejudice against the Indigenous population, and a way forward is improving education of Indigenous population. Their desire is to work in such areas as journalism, agronomy, medicine, law, business administration, and civil engineering, in order to become subjects in diverse areas of the society. On the other hand, many who live in areas where the environment no longer can provide game and other resources are acquiring education with paid work in mind. To date, a growing number of Indigenous persons have effectively invested in their education and learning experiences in urban offices, and actively take part in Indigenous politics (see discussion in Virtanen 2017). Overall, Indigenous political and cultural meetings have increased over the past years, and have allowed Indigenous peoples to become more conscious of other Indigenous groups and helped build collective resistance. Consequently, the current generations have gained more social power and space than the previous generations, who had to largely conceal their Indian roots, especially in the urban areas.

Indigenous Governance of Education

Indigenous traditional knowledge, values, histories, and languages cannot be separated from ways of receiving schooling, and their importance have been behind the claims for Indigenizing education. Our Apuriná case shows that even if Indigenous education and schooling are guaranteed by the Constitution and Education laws in Brazil, on local level, the practical implementation of Indigenous educational rights varies greatly. Thus, there are different school realities rather than just one Apurinã school history. Those Apurinã reserves that have succeeded well in designing their schools and their curriculums, have often benefited from constructive collaborations with governmental and nongovernmental agencies and far-reaching leadership. In this way, they integrate Apurinã ways of knowing and learning—just as they have been taught since the time of Tsura to the state schooling programs.

Amazonian Indigenous leaders and spokespersons have actively argued for Indigenous engagement and participation in governance of Indigenous education and educational policies regionally but also at state level. These leadership roles and positions have usually been the privilege of the well-networked higher classes of Brazil. It is also a loss for universities and fields of science if the Indigenous presence is not allowed agency in research. In the meantime, the dominant society still lacks adequate information about Indigenous people in general as well as their educational necessities. Solving these issues is crucial for better future-making, as Wilson (2013) has noted. This chapter has contributed to making one of the Amazonian Indigenous school histories more visible.

References

Apurinã, F. M. C. (2017). *O mundo xamânico dos Apurinã: Um desafio de interpretações*. Série Antropologia 458, Universidade de Brasília.

Apurinã, F. M. C. (2018). Um olhar reverso: da aldeia para a universidade. *Amazônica: Revista de Antropologia, 9*(1), 482–503.

Cabral, A. S., Monte, N. L., & Montserrat, R. M. F. (Eds.). (1987). *Por uma educação indígena diferenciada*. Brasília: Fundação Pró-Memória.

Chandelss, W. (1866). Ascent of the River Purus. *The Journal of the Royal Geographical Society, 36*, 86–118.

Collet, C. L. G. (2006). *Ritos de civilização e cultura: A escola bakairi* (PhD dissertation). Universidade Federal do Rio de Janeiro.

Coutinho, J. M. D. S. (1862). *Relatório da Exploração do Alto Purus*. Tipografia João Inácio da Silva.

14 School Histories in Amazonia: Education and Schooling ... 263

da Silva, A. L., & Ferreira, M. K. L. (Eds.). (2001). *Antropologia, história e educação: a questão indígena e a escola*. São Paulo: Global.

De Oliveira, L. A., & Gomes do Nascimento, R. (2012). Roteiro para uma história da educação escolar indígena: notas sobre a relação entre política indigenista e educacional. *Educação & Sociedade, 33*(120), 765–761.

Facundes, S. S. (2000). *The Language of the Apurinã People of Brazil (Maipure/Arawak)*. Ph.D. dissertation, University of New York at Buffalo.

Facundes, S., Virtanen, P. K., Freitas, M., Lima-Padovani, B., & Costa, P. (2019). Language Revitalization and Engagements in the Amazon—The Case of Apurinã. In S. D. Brunn (Ed.), *The Changing World Language Map*. Berlin: Springer.

Fernandes, F. (1975). *Investigação etnológica no Brasil e outros ensaios*. Petrópolis: Editora Vozes.

Funai. (2019). *Índios no Brasil. Quem são*. http://www.funai.gov.br/index.php/indios-no-brasil/quem-sao?limitstart=0#. Accessed 10 January 2019.

Gow, P. (1991). *Of Mixed Blood: Kinship and History in Peruvian Amazonia*. Oxford: Clarendon Press.

Henriques, R., Gesteira, K., Grillo, S., & Chamusca, A. (2007). *Educação Escolar Indígena: diversidade sociocultural indígena ressignificando a escola*. Brasília: Ministério da Educação.

Labre, A. R. P. (1872). *Rio Purus: notícia*. Maranhão: Tipografia do País.

Labre, A. R. P. (1889). Colonel Labre's Explorations in the Region Between the Beni and Madre de Dios Rivers and the Purus. *Proceedings of the Royal Geographical Society and Monthly Recording of Geography, 11*(8), 496–502.

Lima, A. C. D. S. (1992). O governo dos Índios sob a gestão do SPI. In M. C. da Cunha (Ed.), *História dos Índios no Brasil* (pp. 155–172). São Paulo: Companhia da Letras/Secretaria municipal de Cultura/FAPESP.

Lindenberg Monte, N. (1996). *Escolas da floresta: Entre o passado oral e o presente letrado*. Rio de Janeiro: Multiletra.

Luciano, G. J. D. S. (2013). *Educação para manejo do mundo. Entre escolar ideal e escola real no Altro Rio Negro*. Rio de Janeiro: Contra Capa/Laced.

MEC—Ministério da Educação. (2017). *Educação Indígena*. http://portal.mec.gov.br/educacao-indigena. Accessed 12 January 2017.

Mihesuah, D., & Wilson, A. (2004). *Indigenizing the Academy: Transforming Scholarship and Empowering Communities*. Lincoln: University of Nebraska Press.

Ramos, A. (1998). *Indigenism: Ethnic Politics in Brazil*. Milwaukee: University of Wisconsin Press.

Schiel, J. (1999). *Entre Patrões e Civilizadores. Os Apurinã e a política indigenista no médio rio Purus na primeira metade do século XX.* Campinas: Universidade Estadual de Campinas.

Tassinari, A. I., & Cohn, C. (2009). "Opening to the Other": Schooling Among the Karipuna and Mebengokré-Xikrin of Brazil. *Anthropology and Education Quarterly, 40*(2), 150–169.

Virtanen, P. K. (2012). *Indigenous Youth in Brazilian Amazonia: Changing Lived Worlds.* New York: Palgrave Macmillan.

Virtanen, P. K. (2015). Fatal Substances: Apurinã's Dangers, Movement, and Kinship. *Indiana, 32,* 85–103.

Virtanen, P. K. (2017). "All This Is Part of My Movement": Amazonian Indigenous Ways of Incorporating Urban Knowledge in State Politics. In H. Veber & P. K. Virtanen (Eds.), *Creating Dialogues: Indigenous Perceptions and Forms of Leadership in Amazonia* (pp. 259–284). Boulder: University Press of Colorado.

Weber, I. (2006). *Um copo de cultura: Os Huni Kuin (Kaxinawá) do rio Humaitá e a escola.* Rio Branco: Edufac.

Wilson, S. (2013). Using Indigenist Research to Shape Our Future. In M. Grey, J. Coates, M. Yellowbird, & T. Heatherington (Eds.), *Decolonizing Social Work* (pp. 311–322). Farnham: Ashgate.

15

Revitalization of Oral History in Wixárika Community-Based Schools and Museums: Working Towards Decolonisation of Art Education Among the Indigenous Peoples of Mexico

Lea Kantonen

Introduction

In this article I shall discuss the revitalization of Wixárika (pl. Wixaritari) oral history in community-based schools and museums in the context of formal and non-formal education and epistemic decolonization process among the indigenous peoples of México. In colonial and post-colonial America knowledge written with European alphabet has been privileged over other ways of knowing and learning. American pioneer of Performance Studies Dwight Conquergood reminds us that colonizing power relationships are still transferred to new generations of researchers and teachers as conventions of written forms and styles (Conquergood 1991, 101). Contemporary indigenous communities in México are, however, now encouraging themselves to found their own institutions in order to strengthen and develop non-literary ways of learning and their own forms of writing.

L. Kantonen (✉)
University of the Arts Helsinki, Helsinki, Finland
e-mail: lea.kantonen@uniarts.fi

© The Author(s) 2019
O. Kortekangas et al. (eds.), *Sámi Educational History in a Comparative International Perspective*,
https://doi.org/10.1007/978-3-030-24112-4_15

Wixárika history teacher Manuel de la Cruz Muñoz explains how oral history is understood in his community:

In our culture we consider as oral history everything that is learned at home, everything that our ancestors have transmitted to us generation by generation, voice by voice. Today oral history is still predominant [...] in the ceremonies, in the rituals, in the cultural activities, and all this is transmitted by oral history.

Cruz Muñoz with his colleagues at the secondary school Tatuutsi Maxakwaxi in the Wixárika community Tsikwaita see themselves as the guardians of ancestral oral knowledge. Oral history for them is practically the same as oral knowledge, and it includes for example practical knowledge of everyday tasks, knowledge of sacred places and routes between them, work instructions, collective problem-solving methods at community gatherings, habits, myths, stories of dreams, and memories of past events.

The Wixaritari (sing. Wixárika) live on the Sierra Madre mountains in Western Mexico on the area called The Gran Nayar inhabited by Wixaritari, Na'ayeri, Tepehuan and Nahua peoples. Wixárika language belongs to the Uto-Aztec language group and there are about 50,000 people speaking it. The mastery of oral language skills, the capacity of speaking beautifully, is highly appreciated (Hakkarainen et al. 1999, 52), for example in the selection of administrative and religious authorities.

According to Wixárika tradition the sacred ancestors of the Wixaritari rose up from the Pacific Ocean and started their journey towards the rising sun and the sacred land Wirikuta. They created the lands and waters and left part of their being as landmarks—hills, rocks and fountains—on their path. They established the sacred practice of annual pilgrimage to the Wirikuta desert, 500 kilometers northeast from the Wixarika area. The oral history of the first journey contains accurate knowledge for example of geography, agriculture, land ownership, nutrition and habits (Medina Miranda 2012; Liffman 2011). Wixárika oral tradition is not stable—it changes when the landscape changes, for example when dams and artificial lakes are built (Medina Miranda 2012).

15 Revitalization of Oral History in Wixárika Community-Based ... 267

The ritual specialists *mara'akate* (sing. *mara'akame*, 'the one who can dream' [Neurath 2013, 16, 133]) need a 10–12 years education at the *tuki* temple to learn to sing oral myths. Singing an agricultural ceremony usually takes two nights and two days, and there are many annual ceremonies to be remembered. The traditional education of a *mara'akame* also contains healing techniques, knowledge of plants, animals and celestial bodies, fabrication of ritual objects, singing and/or playing musical instruments.

The Wixaritari were one of the first indigenous peoples in Mexico to start decolonizing their educative structures in the late twentieth century, and the development of autonomous formal education in Wixárika communities as an alternative to the formal education in public or religious schools. The first community-based Wixárika school, Tatuutsi Maxakwaxi secondary school, has been studied by Mexican media researcher Sarah Corona Berkin (2002, 2007, 2011), Mexican pedagogist Rocío de Aguinaga (2010, 2015), American anthropologist Paul Liffman (2011), and Mexican anthropologist Angélica Rojas Cortes (2012). These writers, however, have not written much about formal art education—except Corona who has written on Wixárika photography at Tatuutsi Maxakwaxi school (Corona 2002, 2011).

Tatuutsi Maxakwaxi was founded in 1995 in the community of Tsikwaita by the community self governance, and it was followed by intercultural high schools in the Wixárika communities Tateikie and Uweni Muyewe, the Na'ayeri community of Muxatej, and others. The CEIWYNA network of the intercultural schools was founded in 2014, and community museums started to be planned by the indigenous teachers participating in the network. The planning has been supported by ITESO University, Finnish NGO CRASH, The Finnish Ministry of Exterior Affairs, the ArtsEqual consortium of University of the Arts Helsinki, and the Sámi museum Siida among others. I have visited the area repeatedly since 1999 with Pekka Kantonen, and worked periodically at Tatuutsi Maxakwaxi secondary school as an artist, art teacher, researcher, and translator as a member of CRASH since 1999 and, since 2012, in collaboration with universities. I recognize myself as a careful partial participant (see Brattland et al. 2018).

When I facilitate and translate art and museology workshops and invite Sámi museum professionals to advice Wixárika and Na'ayeri community museum activists, I participate in the collaborative founding process of community museums while researching the very same process.[1] My participation and the provisional outcomes—artwork, teaching material and research articles—are constantly evaluated and re-assessed in the indigenous community as well as in the community of other artist-researchers.[2]

I have together with my partner Pekka Kantonen described the community museum planning as a dialogical artistic and educative process (Kantonen and Kantonen 2013, 2015, 2017a) and the new institutions of schools and museums as part of contemporary ritual landscape (Kantonen and Kantonen 2017b); however, in this article I discuss how the Wixaritari are seeking to revitalize oral traditions and history in these new institutions especially in the context of art education. My research questions are: How are the Wixárika teachers revitalizing and planning to revitalize oral history in their community-based museums, especially in the case of Tunuwame museum in the community of Tsikwaita? How are they planning to apply art education in the revitalization process? What possibilities for revitalization, different from those of a school, do they see in the community-based museum?

I shall first describe the context of traditional Wixárika art education, next I shall refer to the literature of art education in pre-colonial, colonial and independent Mexico and especially on the Gran Nayar area of Western Mexico. I shall finish by reflecting upon recent encounters between formal, non-formal and informal art education in the process of museum planning. The teachers of Tatuutsi Maxakwaxi school together with their families have been my main informants.

---

[1]My research methodology can also be defined as artistic action research, see Lehtonen and Pöyhönen (2018).

[2]For example, the interviews for this article were recorded during three video workshops, *Taller de museología* (2014), *Aquí estamos sudando* (2015), and *Grabando al caminar* (2017) at Tatuutsi Maxakwaxi school. While writing this article I also processed the performance *Translating Other Knowledge* together with the Sámi linguist Irja Seurujärvi-Kari and the Wixarika history teacher Manuel de la Cruz, whose statement is cited in the beginning of this article.

Informal and Non-formal Indigenous Art Education

In the Wixárika communities the teaching of children and young people is seen as a sacred task (Eger 1978). The children learn informally by observing adults and by participating in everyday household chores rather than by following verbal instructions. The young people are gradually given more responsibility for taking care of crops, animals, small children, and for giving offerings to the divine ancestors. Art education is appreciated as an important part of Wixárika cultural practice, or as the Wixaritari call it, *yeiyari*, 'walking on the footsteps of the ancestors' (Neurath 2013, 12).

The Wixaritari oral histories are closely connected to visual arts and crafts (Schaefer 1989). Artistic skills such as embroidering, with their corresponding stories, are passed on in extended families. The children first observe the adults practicing their arts, listen to their stories, and follow them for their pilgrimages when they leave their artworks as offering at sacred places. They are then allowed to try art techniques, and if they show interest in the arts, they are given more challenging tasks. In the story by Apolonia de la Cruz technical learning is closely connected to oral history:

> I started learning when I was only three years old, first the *caminito*-stiches, and when I was seven, I already knew the three easiest kinds of stiches. [...] I learned first by embroidering, then I started talking with the adults, with my mother and the elder ladies in my community. (Cruz et al. 2014, 17)[3]

If a child shows special skill or interest to arts and there is no one in the extended family to teach her, the parents can contract and older artist to take her as an apprentice. The non-formal education of an apprentice is a firm commitment between the artist and the family of the child. Many of the artists are also initiated ritual specialists (Eger 1978).

---

[3]Translated by the author.

270   L. Kantonen

The relationship ideally leads to the initiation of a child. Cruz goes on describing her apprenticeship with her grandmother and explains how she gained her initiation:

> My grandmother used to take me to the sacred place that was called Parikatsie. I remember that when we were walking back, I carried my embroidering with me, and [when we stopped to rest], I started embroidering in the shade of an oak tree. My grandmother reproached me and said that I should rest because we still had a long way to go; I then heard my mother and grandmother whispering, I only heard a few words. They wondered how it had happened so soon that I already was embroidering. Later I learned that without me knowing they had prayed me a special skill for embroidering and weaving. They said that we should keep the six year promise and go to the sacred place every year, bringing artwork made by me and finally dipping the work in the blood of a deer and a cow for a blessing. (Cruz et al. 2014, 17)[4]

An initiated artist has a special gift of inventing new patterns and combining colours (Eger 1978). Other people order her craft works, so she can contribute to the economy of the household. Non-formal art education takes place in above described relationships of apprentice, or in ritual offices at the family shrine *xiriki*, and in a ritual community called *rukuriikate* for men and women striving for initiation and congregating at the *tuki*-temple (Neurath 2013).[5] The *rukuriikate* members are chosen by the elders to serve at the *tuki* with their spouses for five years and take the responsibility of arranging annual ceremonies and pilgrimages.

The annual ceremony of harvesting, Tatei Neixa or the Drum Ceremony, functions as a special non-formal art education event. By his singing the *mara'akame* (pl. *mara'akate*) leads the children to a flying

---

[4]Ibid.
[5]Since the Wixárika institution of *rukuriikate* is very old and its education often taking place at the context of the *tuki* temple is quite formal and rigorous, the concept of non-formal education might be misleading. However, it would be equally misleading to speak for example about *rukuriikate*-based, *tuki*-based or sacred education, because traditional art education happens in many contexts and places and because the dichotomy between sacred and non-sacred is foreign for the Wixaritari (Salvador 2017, 26–27).

15 Revitalization of Oral History in Wixárika Community-Based ...

tour to the sacred places and introduces them to the deified ancestors. When the child is five years old he or she has participated five times at the ceremony and remembers the *mara'akame*'s story about the sacred places. After the child has been introduced to the deified ancestors he or she can start taking small tasks and duties in the family temple, *xiriki*.

In contemporary Wixárika communities children and young people are also informally educated by mass media. Television and social networks are suggesting more individualistic paths for young people for the realization of their ambitions.

Making History as a Collective

In 2006 the delegation from Tatuutsi Maxakwaxi school travelled to Sápmi (Samiland) and Finland and visited many schools, universities and museums. The delegates gave a Power Point presentation at the schools and universities. I paid attention to the fact that in every place they gave a precise history of their school and explained in detail who had first dreamed the school, who had dreamed the name of it, which institutions and authorities had been consulted, how the place of the school building had been selected, how the vision and mission of the new institution was invented and articulated, and how the teachers were then selected and educated. In this way the history was used to justify the present condition that the school was functioning in Tsikwaita and the storytellers themselves had the privilege of working there. Listening to the same story over and over again in different places made me think that the history of the foundation of the community museum Tunúwame and the community museums network will be equally important in the future, and I discussed with the delegation how the different phases of the museum planning should be documented and archived.

The Wixárika decisions are made collectively, and it is necessary to remind everybody of the decision making process and the responsibility it implies. When the museum building will be erected and the new museum will need volunteer guides, guards and pedagogues, they will have better motivation if they will remember who was the person who dreamed the museum and its name and who were the experts consulted. The museum guides, guards and pedagogues will be proud of participating in the continuum of the collective history making.

The institution of *tuki* temple and the education taking place there and leading to an initiation, dates back to pre-colonial times (Liffman 2011). Some teachers of Tatuutsi Maxakwaxi are educated both non-formally in *tuki* temples and formally in universities, some are active writers and they have published research on their school and community (Salvador and Corona Berkin 2002; Tatuutsi Maxakwaxi 2014; Cruz et al. 2014; Salvador 2017). Their pedagogy can be seen as representing what Portuguese sociologist Boaventura Souza Santos (2007), calls pluralist epistemology. According to him a person can participate in two or more different or even contradictory knowledge systems at the same time. When she learns a new way of organizing knowledge she does not forget her earlier knowledge but she can navigate between different registers of knowledge-making. In their community the Wixárika teachers have learned an oral knowledge system transmitted for example by artistic forms, in the academia they have learned to apply Western scientific knowledge into their teaching.

The Wixárika communities see themselves as guardians of traditional knowledge as a collective. When the Wixaritari write or speak about their traditional knowledge, they usually do not like to be named individually, because individuals can never own the tradition (see for example Corona Berkin 2007; Smith 2012, 145–146). The researcher who asks questions and writes down the answers is even less the owner of the written research. The communities decide collectively which researchers are permitted into the community[6] and they want to see the research results given back to them. In the books published in collaboration by Wixárika communities and universities (Salvador and Corona 2002; Corona Berkin et al. 2007; Cruz et al. 2014; Tatuutsi Maxakwaxi 2014; Kantonen et al. 2017) the interviewed are often mentioned as the writers of the articles, and the names of the interviewers are sometimes not mentioned at all. However, the

---

[6]For example, Aguinaga, Liffman and Rojas who have written research on Tatuutsi Maxakwaxi school have also worked for Wixarika rights for many years as activists.

15 Revitalization of Oral History in Wixárika Community-Based ... 273

teachers at least at the Tatuutsi Maxakwaxi school agree that in scientific articles the name of the researcher should be mentioned because she is responsible for the truthfulness and the possible errors in the writing.[7]

The teachers who are responsible for developing the pedagogy of Tatuutsi Maxakwaxi school and Tunuwame museum are sure that their institutions will be remembered as important pioneers. Apolonia de la Cruz Ramirez concludes her speech in the teachers' meeting:

> [M]y research on teaching crafts, the Wixarika grammar and other knowledge that is taught to kids in school. In 50 years this all will be history. (Kantonen and Kantonen 2017a, 255)

Art Education in Pre-colonial, Colonial and Independent México

In the pre-colonial Aztec empire as well as in other pre-colonial Mesoamerican societies history and arts belonged together and formed a holistic unity. The written history was supported and mediated by different art forms: oral recitations, visual arts, and ritual drama. Oral history was taught in the context of indigenous philosophies and rituals in formal schools and dramatized in public ceremonies (Horcasitas 1974; Aguirre Beltrán 1992, 38–42; Fernández 2015). Colonial education fused pre-colonial and Catholic narratives into a diversity of syncretistic art forms, such as codex literature and theatre of evangelization (Arróniz 1979). Oral histories of colonization survived in the form of mythical stories and dramas performed in Catholic feasts and rituals (Bricker 1981). In independent Mexico education was secularized, written knowledge was privileged, and not much space was left for oral knowledge (Aguirre Beltrán 1992, 54–57, 75; Corona 2015).

---

[7]The teachers' council has not agreed to write or sign me a research permission. Because of the teachers' previous experiences with the *teiwari* (non-wixarika) they are suspicious about written agreements in general. The teachers say that research collaboration should be based on mutual trust and that an oral permission should be as valid as a written one.

Mexican revolution since 1910 emphasized public education as a tool to create a hegemonic and revolutionary nation. Much effort and enthusiasm was spent in founding rural schools as "houses for the people". Young promoters of rural and indigenous education called "missionary teachers" toured the country attending 2001 communities and 108,449 pupils in 1925 only (Aguirre Beltrán 1992, 74). Indigenous students graduated from secondary school were recruited as teachers, sent to rural schools, and further educated on short courses during holidays and weekends. School buildings were built, modern agricultural methods taught, cultural clubs, rural theatres and even local museums founded (ibid., 1992, 74). Indigenous languages, oral history and arts were not seen as valuable knowledge in the school context (Corona 2015), at its best they have been tolerated and paraded in national feasts as an exotic and colourful flavour in the multicultural nation. Folk dance was celebrated as an expression of national diversity: dances from different states of Mexico were modified for the school context and taught in every part of the nation—the diversity of cultures and languages was aestheticized (Rufer 2017).

The first conquerors came to The Gran Nayar area of Western Mexico populated by Wixárika, Na'ayeri, Tepehuan and Nahua peoples in 1530, but they could not overthrow the Cora (Na'ayeri) chiefdoms ruling on the mountains until nearly 200 years later. During the first half of the nineteenth century the Fransiscans funded missions in the three main Wixárika communities, congregated the people in the ceremonial centres, re-arranged the political and religious governments, and destroyed the *tuki* temples. In the end of the nineteenth century the Franciscans were expelled from the sierra, ritual art and architecture flourished again, and the Catholic influence on Wixárika life diminished (Lumholtz 1986 [1900], 14, 29; Liffman 2011, 45; Rojas Cortés 2012, 66–67). Because the missionary schools entered relatively late to the area and their teaching never reached the smallest villages, pre-colonial oral knowledge did not vanish (Liffman 2011, 40–44). The Franciscan missionaries were re-activated in the 1950s. In 1965 the first public boarding schools were founded into the region, and many of them are still functioning. According to the elders the missionary and public schools succeeded in partly colonizing the minds of the children and their families (Liffman 2011, 149–161; Kantonen and Kantonen 2017b).

Towards the Decolonization of Formal Education

The Zapatista uprising that started in the Maya area in the Mexican state of Chiapas in 1994 has had a strong influence in the indigenous schools throughout the country. The Zapatistas demand the right of indigenous children and adults for equal education, not only in Spanish but in their own languages and based on their experiences, philosophies, and world views. Their decolonizing pedagogics has been an inspiration for many other independent community-based schools in Mexico and elsewhere (Bertely Busquets 2015).

On the Western Sierra Madre mountains, in the Wixárika community Tsikwaita, the secondary school Tatuutsi Maxakwaxi School was founded in 1995, one year after the Zapatista uprising. It was the first community-based intercultural school on the Wixárika area. The community authorities, disappointed of the negative effects that the missionary and public schools had on the community, were decided in founding a different kind of school based on Wixárika values. The elders chose the first teachers, with good reputation and teaching skills, to be educated officially by the ITESO University. They were expected to educate the pupils as mediators between the Wixárika and the state authorities (Aquinaga 2010), however, the task of mediating was seen differently than in the mid twentieth century when indigenous promoters were expected to integrate the indigenous communities to the state-defined values and practices. Instead, the future mediators were expected to defend indigenous right of self-determinacy and to explain Wixárika traditions to the state authorities. They had to learn and conceptualize in pedagogical terms traditional oral Wixárika knowledge, so far transferred only informally and non-formally, as well as modern knowledge. According to Liffman the chosen teachers were conscious about the need of negotiation between tradition and modernity and self-conscious about their own role in the process (Liffman 2011, 139). For Rojas the pedagogy of Tatuutsi Maxakwaxi has accelerated a change from teaching cultural and religious practices to teaching articulation and cultural significations of those practices (Rojas Cortés 2012, 159–163).

Community Museum as a Meeting Point Between Formal and Non-formal Art Education

Many of the teachers and other volunteers who participate in the planning of the Wixárika and Na'ayeri museums have visited very few museums in their life. It is interesting that they show so much interest in developing a new institution in their communities. Museum is, after all, a colonial innovation. Why are museums needed in indigenous communities?

Though the idea of Tatuutsi Maxakwaxi school, for example, is to introduce Wixárika values into formal education, the practices or art education are not easily adjusted to the rhythm of the indigenous semi-nomadic way of life. School as an institution—however community-based—is too stable for fully teaching oral knowledge and artistic practices for the young people. Art as part of the school curricula is too narrow as a concept to include the multiple forms of traditional ritual artistic practices and their connections to the *yeyiari*, the traditional way of life.

The structure of the Wixárika non-formal art education as an apprentice relationship with a cultural specialist, based on oral and embodied ways of learning, dates back to pre-colonial times, however, it is very demanding and time-consuming. It also demands a strong commitment of the parents and the extended family. On the other hand, not all Wixárika children have the possibility of participating in the non-formal education in annual ceremonies and taking ceremonial duties, because of urbanization and seasonal migration: their families work as migrant workers on plantations or sell handicraft in cities, and they go to school outside the Wixárika area. The community elders are worried that the children and young people are getting alienated from Wixárika oral knowledge and art. Other diversions and international culture industry compete of young peoples' time and energy (Kantonen and Kantonen 2015, 29).

The planners of the community museums are developing a new kind of non-formal indigenous art pedagogy that attracts young people with contemporary participatory methods and digital media. It complements the formal art pedagogy of the schools, non-formal art pedagogy given in the ceremonies, and fills in the gaps between the ritual practice

15 Revitalization of Oral History in Wixárika Community-Based ...

and the articulation of significations (Kantonen and Kantonen 2017b, 12–16).

The headmaster of Tatuutsi Maxakwaxi, Carlos Salvador, who is himself a devoted photographer, gives an example of joint projects that could be arranged as a collaboration between the school, the *tuki* temple and the museum: he imagines that photography workshops would be arranged at school, the pupils would document traditional ceremonies arranged at *tuki* temple by the traditional authorities, and the results would be guarded in the museum.

> I believe that we could make an experiment in our drum ceremony, Tatei Neixa, and all the pupils would participate. We would arrange it [the workshop] in order not to lose our traditions: first we would give them the theory [of photography and of the oral tradition], then they could learn [taking photographs] practically, and if the child has a possibility, he would then go and participate in the ceremony. He would go with the knowledge in his mind, he would not go empty. The museum would then show the complete process. (Kantonen 2017, 28)[8]

As I understand Salvador he figures that the research part of the project would be arranged by the school and the devotional part by the religious authorities of the *tuki*, and the museum would be responsible for the exhibition and archiving of the results. In this way the museum would work as an organizing and mediating institution between the formal and the non-formal art education.

Unlike in the community museums in the southern states of México the Wixárika museums do not concentrate on archaeological findings but rather on the revitalization and documentation of oral history and art. Workshops based on traditional as well as of digital technologies are arranged. The pupils of the community-based schools participate in the research and documentation of oral knowledge. Research methodology, photography and video documentation is taught in workshops so that the students can document their own life and indigenous heritage in their families and communities. The documents will then be archived in the museum (Hirvonen-Nurmi et al. 2018).

---

[8]Translated by the author.

Since 2006 Wixárika and Na'ayeri teachers have visited other indigenous museums in Mexico and elsewhere[9] and taken courses in order to educate themselves in contemporary museum issues. Especially the Sámi museum Siida is a model for a museum based on indigenous world view. In the process of museum building and globalization the teachers and other voluntary museum workers need material of documentation methodology, conservation and storage of museum objects and digital data. Guidebooks of research, museology and Wixárika arts and videography are produced and published by the museum network and it's collaborators (Aquinaga 2008; Cruz et al. 2014; Hirvonen-Nurmi 2017; Kantonen 2017).

The teachers and museum planners, however, need to be conscious of the homogenizing tendencies of national education discourse. The Mexican researcher Mario Rufer (2017) has warned of the national institutions supporting and appropriating the emerging movement of community museums, risen from the very need to document histories not recognized by the national state. Even if the community museums succeed in recovering and retelling oral histories in pluralist ways, the participation of public schools—and their ritualized performative celebrations—in the museum events can lead to the domestication of these histories as mere examples of the "beauty" of the national culture.

Conclusions

In the CEIWYNA network of community-based museums, art education is seen as continuous with oral knowledge and values transferred informally in families and non-formally in the context of community life, rituals, and political gatherings. The aim is that the children learn

---

[9]In 2017 three members of CEIWYNA network, facilitated by members of CRASH, visited four indigenous community museums in the state of Oaxaca, Manuel de la Cruz Muñoz, representing Tunuwame museum, visited Te Tuhi gallery and many museums in Auckland, New Zealand, and Carlos Salvador, the rector of Tatuutsi Maxakwaxi school, visited the Sámi museum Siida. In 2018 Eduardo Madera, representing Tunuwame museum, visited indigenous community museums in British Columbia, Canada.

art according to same values that they practice at home and in the traditional religious institutions. The concept of art is understood in the context of the holistic world view and not separated between different art disciplines as in formal art education. Oral knowledge is supported by indigenous arts and is practiced, learned, and articulated by the community. At the same time the museums will function informed by and in collaboration with global indigenous movements. However, there is always the danger of getting assimilated by the nationalist discourses.

Wixárika communities have up to these days been led by elderly community leaders. Dreaming and verbalizing dreams in songs has been an important method in the transmission of oral history. As digital photography, video and sound recordings are rapidly expanding as methods of transmitting oral history among the young members of Wixárika community, it is interesting to see how these technologies will influence Wixárika understanding of their cultural heritage and the relationships between generations. Will video files replace songs and woven patterns in the transmission of oral knowledge from the elders to the young people who are following the footsteps of the ancestors?

Acknowledgments This research has been undertaken as part of the ArtsEqual—project funded by the Academy of Finland's Strategic Research Council from its Equality in Society-programme, project no. 293199.

I would like to thank Otso Kortekangas, Jukka Nyyssönen, and Sarah Corona for reading the manuscript of this article and making insightful comments on it.

References

Aguinaga, R. D. (2010). *Tatuutsi Maxakwaxi, una experiencia indígena de educación autonómica* (Unpublished doctoral thesis). Tlaquepaque: ITESO.
Aguinaga, R. D. (2015). Bases para una educación apropiada y pertinente en un contexto comunitario. In S. C. Berkin & R. Le Mûr (Eds.), *La cultura wixárika ante los desafíos del mundo actual: La negociación para la comunicación intercultural* (pp. 52–93). México, D.F.: Conaculta.

Aguinaga, R. D. (coord.). (2008). *Kiekari 'Iyarieya Wawamete—Buscar con el corazón el conocimiento de la comunidad. Módulo de Investigación.* Bachillerato intercultural Wixarika. Tlaquepaque: ITESO.

Aguirre Beltrán, G. (1992). *Teoría y práctica de la educación indígena.* Poza Rica: Universidad veracruzana.

Arróniz, O. (1979). *Teatro de evangelización en Nueva España.* México: UNAM.

Bertely Busquets, M. (2015). De la antropología convencional a una praxis comprometida. Colaboración entre indígenas y no indígenas en un proyecto educativo para construir un mundo alterno desde Chiapas, México. In: X. Leyva, et al. (Eds.), *Prácticas otras de conocimiento(s): Entre crisis, entre guerras* (Vol. I, pp. 225–252). San Cristóbal de las Casas: Cooperativa Editorial Retos.

Brattland, C., Kramvig, B., & Verran, H. (2018). Doing Indigenous Methodologies: Toward a Practice of the Careful Partial Participant. *Ab-Original, 2*(1), 74–96.

Bricker, V. R. (1981). *The Indian Christ, the Indian King: The Historical Substrate of Maya Myth and Ritual.* Austin: University of Texas Press.

Conquergood, D. (1991). Rethinking Ethnography: Towards a Critical Cultural Policy. *Communication Monographs, 59*(2), 179–194.

Corona Berkin, S. (Ed.). (2002). *Miradas entrevistas: Aproximación a la cultura, comunicación y fotografía huichola.* Guadalajara: Universidad de Guadalajara.

Corona Berkin, S., & other voices. (Ed.). (2007). *Entre voces… Fragmentos de educación "entrecultural".* Guadalajara: Universidad de Guadalajara.

Corona Berkin, S. (2011). *Postales de diferencia: La ciudad vista por fotógrafos wixaritari.* México, D.F.: CONACULTA.

Corona Berkin, S. (2015). *La asignatura ciudadana en las cuatro grandes reformas del LTG en México (1959–2010).* México, D.F.: Siglo XXI editores.

Cruz, A. D. L., et al. (2014). *Wixárika xuiyaya—Bordado Huichol.* Tlaquepaque: ITESO.

Eger, S. (1978). Huichol Women's Art. In K. Berrin (Ed.), *Art of the Huichol Indians* (pp. 35–53). San Francisco: The Fine Arts Museums of San Francisco.

Fernández, D. L. (2015). Children's Everyday Learning by Assuming Responsibility for others: Indigenous Practices as a Cultural Heritage Across Generations. In M. Correa-Chávez, R. Mejía-Arauz, & B. Rogoff (Eds.), *Advances in Child Development and Behavior—Children Learn by Observing and Contributing to Family and Community Endeavors: A Cultural Paradigm.* Amsterdam: Elsevier.

Hakkarainen, O., Leskinen, A., & Seppo, S. (1999). *Jyrkänteen reunalla: matka meksikolaiseen arkeen.* Helsinki: Like.

Hirvonen-Nurmi, K. (2017). Consejos museísticos sobre manejo de objetos, exposiciones y documentación. In L. Kantonen (Ed.), *Ki ti 'utame yu' uximayati—Museos vivos: Experiencias wixárika, na'ayeri y Sami* (pp. 87–90). San Miguel Huaixtita, Jalisco: Centro Educativo Intercultural Tatuutsi Maxakwaxí; Bancos de San Hipólito, Durango: Bachillerato Intercultural Takutsi Niukieya, Durango; Presidio de los Reyes, Nayarit: Bachillerato Intercultural Muxatena.

Hirvonen-Nurmi, K., Kantonen, L., & Kantonen, P. (2018). Miten voimme antaa museoesineiden puhua?—osallistavan esityksen dramatisointi. Ruukku Studies on Artistic Research 8.

Horcasitas, F. (1974). *El teatro náhuatl: épocas novohispana y moderna* (Vol. I). México: UNAM.

Kantonen, L. (comp.), Alonso Orozco, S. E., & Juarez, J. B. (Eds.). (2017). *Ki ti 'utame yu' uximayati—Museos vivos: Experiencias wixárika, na'ayeri y Sami (2017).* Tsikwaita, Jalisco: Centro Educativo Intercultural Tatuutsi Maxakwaxi; Uweni muyewe, Durango: Bachillerato Intercultural Takutsi Niukieya; Muxatej, Nayrarit: Bachillerato Intercultural Muxatena.

Kantonen, L., & Kantonen, P. (2013). Wirarikojen ja saamelaisten keskusteluja taiteen ja käsityön opettamisesta. In P. K. Virtanen, L. Kantonen & I. Seurujärvi-Kari (Eds.), *Alkuperäiskansat tämän päivän maailmassa* (pp. 393–424). Helsinki: Finnish Literature Society.

Kantonen, L., & Kantonen, P. (2015). Enseñando y exhibiendo arte y artesanía en el contexto cultural indígena. In S. Corona Berkin & R. Le Mûr (Eds.), *La cultura wixárika ante los desafíos del mundo actual: La negociación para la comunicación intercultural* (pp. 94–137). México, D.F.: Dirección General de Culturas Populares.

Kantonen, L., & P. Kantonen. (2017a). Tunúwame: Generational Filming in Collaborative Museum Planning. *Generational Filming: A Video Diary as Experimental and Participatory Research* (pp. 229–269), doctoral dissertation. Helsinki: The Academy of Fine Arts at the University of the Arts Helsinki.

Kantonen, L. & Kantonen, P. (2017b). Living Camera in Ritual Landscape: Teachers of the Tatuutsi Maxakwaxi School, the Wixárika ancestors, and the *teiwari* Negotiate Videography. *Journal of Ethnology and Folkloristics, 11*(1), 39–64.

Lehtonen, J., & Pöyhönen, S. (2018). Documentary Theatre as a Platform for Hope and Social Justice. In E. Anttila & A. Suominen (Eds.), *Critical*

Articulations of Hope from the Margins of Art Education: International Perspectives and Practices (pp. 32–45). London and New York: Routledge.

Liffman, P. (2011). *Huichol Territory and the Mexican Nation: Indigenous Ritual, Land Conflict, and Sovereignty Claims.* Tucson: University of Arizona Press.

Lumholtz, C. (1986 [1900]). *El arte simbólico y decorativo de los huicholes.* México D. F.: Instituto Nacional Indigenista.

Medina Miranda, H. (2012). *Relatos de los caminos ancestrales: Mitología Wixarika del sur de Durango.* San Luis Potosí: Universidad Autónoma de San Luis Potosí.

Neurath, J. (2013). *La vida de las imágenes: Arte huichol.* México, D. F.: Artes de México y del mundo.

Rojas Cortés, A. (2012). *Escolaridad y política en interculturalidad: los jóvenes wixaritari en una secundaria de huicholes.* Guadalajara: Universidad de Guadalajara.

Rufer, M. (2017). La inocua belleza. Tensiones entre museo, escuela y nación. In S. Corona Berkin (coord.) (Ed.), *¿La imagen educa? El recurso visual de la secretaría de Educación Pública* (pp. 19–34). Guadalajara: Editorial Universitaria.

Salvador, C. (2017). Por qué un museo cultural en Tsikwaita? In *Ki ti 'utame yu' uximayati—Museos vivos: Experiencias wixárika, na'ayeri y Sami* (pp. 87–90). In L. Kantonen (Ed.), San Miguel Huaixtita, Jalisco: Centro Educativo Intercultural Tatuutsi Maxakwaxí; Bancos de San Hipólito, Durango: Bachillerato Intercultural Takutsi Niukieya, Durango; Presidio de los Reyes, Nayarit: Bachillerato Intercultural Muxatena.

Salvador, A., & Corona Berkin, S. (2002). *Xapa taniuki maye'uxa meripai timieme hiki timieme/Nuestro libro de la memoria e la escritura.* Guadalajara: Universidad de Guadalajara.

Santos, B. S. (2007). Beyond Abyssal Thinking: From Global Lines to Ecologies of Knowledge. *Revista crítica de Ciencias Sociais, 80.* http://www.eurozine.com/articles/2007-06-29-santos-en.html/. Accessed 6 February 2018.

Schaefer, S. (1989). The Loom as a Sacred Power Object in Huichol Culture. In R. C. Anderson & K. L. Field (Eds.), *Art in Small Scale Societies: Contemporary Readings* (pp. 118–128). Englewood Cliffs: Prentice Hall.

Smith, L. T. (2012). *Decolonizing Methodologies: Research and Indigenous Peoples.* London: Zed Books.

Tatuutsi Maxakwaxi: Proyecto educativo comunitario wixárika. (2014). *Written and Edited by the Teachers of the Tatuutsi Maxakwaxi Secondary School.* San Miguel Huaixtita, Jalisco, Tlaquepaque: ITESO.

16

A Community of Ako, 1987–1995: Teaching and Learning in the ELTU and Po Ako, Auckland, Aotearoa NZ

Mere Kepa

Introduction

From the middle of the nineteenth century, migrants who were not users of English language began arriving in Aotearoa in large numbers (Waite 1992). In the 1960s and the 1970s large migrations of people arrived from the Cook Islands, Niue, and Tokelau, later from Samoa, and later still from Tonga. A repercussion of the migrations is that the number of the people residing in Aotearoa outstrips those who remain in the homelands. The major issues, trends and conditions were the migration of people from countries where English is not an official language, or the major language of the majority of the citizens. Moreover, a disproportionate number of the migrants from the south-west Pacific settled permanently in the city of Auckland.

M. Kepa (✉)
James Henare Maori Research Centre,
The University of Auckland, Auckland, New Zealand

© The Author(s) 2019   **283**
O. Kortekangas et al. (eds.), *Sámi Educational History
in a Comparative International Perspective*,
https://doi.org/10.1007/978-3-030-24112-4_16

Ako in Theory

In Maori language and culture, the word Ako means to learn, to teach, to advise, to study and to instruct (Kepa 2016). Ako is a conception that Maori language and culture shares with the Cook Islands Maori, Niuean, Tokelauan, Tongan and Samoan languages and cultures of the South Pacific region. Philosophically, a pedagogy of Ako is a sagacious and prudent response to the problem faced by Indigenous migrants from the South Pacific in secondary schooling, and that is, passively receiving useless information to do things for the prevailing culture and society. In a pedagogical sense, Ako is teaching and learning as a whole and not as a list of fragmented components. The conception is concerned with Indigenous teachers and students' knowledge and feelings about life, of gaining diverse experiences and skills to take their place in their community as well as the dominant English-speaking, New Zealand European, Pakeha society. Ako is concerned, too, with a cooperation of understandings to make a practical philosophy of dialogue without end, mutual learning, and mutual enhancement. As a Maori, Tongan and Samoan pedagogy, Ako is concerned with teaching and learning, the inseparability of language and culture, the value of good spirits, and passionate commitment to make a better education for migrants learning in the secondary schooling system; rather than abstract certainties or universal rules of conduct (Manu'atu and Kepa 2016). Pedagogically, unlike the prevailing universal practice of separating teaching from learning, Ako makes no distinction between teaching and teaching. Ako is a pedagogy through which teaching, learning, and cultural diversity are inseparable aspects of schooling, education, and life.

Ako in Practice

A deeper philosophy and a broader, richer practice of schooling and education is presented, here, through the examples of the English Language Teaching Unit (ELTU) and Po Ako (Kepa 2008; Kepa and Manu'atu 1998a, b). The ELTU and Po Ako were located at the large, state, coeducational Mt Roskill Grammar School. The adolescents were

Indigenous peoples from the Realm of New Zealand who migrated from Niue, Tokelau, and the Cook Islands (MFAT 2008). They came, too, from Tonga, Samoa, Fiji, Tahiti, Tuvalu, Japan, Indonesia, Thailand, Vietnam, Laos, Cambodia, the Philippines, China, Taiwan, Korea, Hungary, Russia, Venezuela, Chile, Peru, Israel, and the Netherlands. Through the ELTU, I shall share particularly the experience and practices engaged with the students from the self-governing islands of Niue and the Cook Islands, and the non-self-governing island of Tokelau. The people of Niue, Tokelau, and the Cook Islands are entitled to New Zealand citizenship under the Citizenship Act 1977 (MFAT 2008).

Through the Po Ako, I share the insights and practices of the homework project organised for the Tongan students and their parents by the ELTU's Tongan teacher (Manu'atu 2000b; Kepa and Manu'atu 1998b). Alongside Po Ako, I organised the homework centre for the Maori students at Mt Roskill Grammar. Both projects were designed to prepare the students to contribute and participate successfully in the secondary schooling system; to promote parental interest in the daily life of the school and the effects of the diverse communities' cultural practices on the educational life of the school (Manu'atu and Kepa 2004).

The English Language Teaching Unit

In 1975, the Minister of Education, Phil Amos, opened the ELTU in response to the large migrations of unskilled men and women and their children from the tropical islands to the north of Aotearoa, New Zealand. In the established phase of the ELTU, two pre-fabricated classrooms, across the driveway from the 'host' school, were allocated 24 students and 2 teachers. The term host school refers to the Mt Roskill Grammar in which the ELTU was organised in a formal but distant relationship. The students were withdrawn from their school of origin. Initially, they studied English, social studies, art, and music in the ELTU, and the specialist subjects of woodwork, metalwork, art, physical education, science, and mathematics in Mt Roskill Grammar, for two semesters. Partly as a result of its interrelated education activities, the principal appointed a senior executive as the official liaison person between the Grammar and the ELTU. From the outset the physical, pedagogical, language and cultural distance between the ELTU and the host school was at the heart of re-prioritising the pedagogy and to drawing together the grammar's technocratic or skills-based curriculum, the ELTU's teachers' experience and skills, and the students' languages and cultures.

The original teachers were seconded from Richmond Primary School in central Auckland city. One was a Maori Indigenous to the island of Rakahanga in the Cook Islands, and the other a New Zealander of Irish ancestry. I, an Indigenous Maori woman of Aotearoa, joined the staff as Head teacher in 1979. At this particular moment in the life of the ELTU, two of the teachers shared the cultural values and beliefs historically at odds with the prevailing English-speaking New Zealand European, Pakeha society. The third teacher was constituted in the assumptions of the dominant New Zealand English-speaking culture and society; simply put, he was a Pakeha (Kepa 2008).

In 1987, I proposed a new attentiveness to Ako. The central idea was that schooling and education is a harmonious unity (Kepa 2016; Manu'atu et al. 2016) in which both the school and Indigenous Maori, the school and Indigenous Tongan and Samoan migrants aware of our diverse languages and cultures represent the force for creating a richer pedagogical environment. The priorities included the clarification of the political capacity of teaching and learning in terms of the important concepts of language and cultural diversity, and ending marginalisation, or the domination of English language and Anglo-American-New Zealand European, Pakeha culture in the ELTU. The next priority points to the existence of people—parents, colleagues, community workers and so on—outside of the immediate environment of the classroom as important strengths in influencing both day-to-day experiences, and the outcomes of the teaching and learning partnership. And, that a critical Ako pedagogy can be practised apart or concurrently with the prevailing technocratic pedagogy as possibilities arise.

In setting up an innovative educational community for the migrant youth, the economic issue often plays the crucial role. Relatedly, for reasons situated in the government of day's process of allocating funding

16 A Community of Ako, 1987–1995: Teaching and Learning ... 287

to schools, the students' names remained on the register of the secondary school of origin as well as being recorded on the ELTU's document of application. The importance of the annual governmental allocation is that it enabled the teachers to select and purchase course materials independent of the host school's funds and prescriptions. The government allocation was supplemented by payment for the daily cleaning of the classrooms carried out by the students and the teachers. The money economised through this daily practice was allocated to meet the costs of numerous excursions engaged by the teachers to bolster the students' learning and education in and around the city; for example, visits to the Auckland museum, the art gallery, and the local aquarium to name a few places of interest. As well, the students' original school could benefit financially since each of the pupil's names remained on their school's register as well Mt Roskill Grammar's and the ELTU's.

Also worth noting is that the students who were withdrawn from the school of origin wore that school's uniform, paid no fees to Mt Roskill Grammar school, and brought with them stationary procured from their contributing school. The supplementary books and pens were purchased by the students from either the grammar school's stationery shop at a heavily discounted price or a store located in their own suburb. The teachers' and the students' travel expenses were reimbursed by the now defunct Department of Education. Upon the restructuring of New Zealand's education system in the 1980s, the teachers' expenses were recovered from the ELTU's bulk funding. In many instances, the students' school of origin generously purchased their bus tickets, or the students made private arrangements for their travel to and from the ELTU. These are no small matters since the issue of money was often the deciding factor in whether a student could attend the ELTU programme at all.

Likewise, human relationships are a prominent influence in whether a student will attend school or not. In the first place, the school of origin referred the candidates to the ELTU's staff members by official letter or a phone call; no electronic communication in the 1980s. Second, the students were interviewed and accepted by all of the ELTU's staff. Third, the students participated in the project with the consent of the custodial family. In terms of organising the contents of the education, the teachers in the ELTU worked collaboratively. The allocation of teaching time was organised by the Head of the project in cooperation with her colleagues and the teachers responsible for the host school's timetable. From 1975 to the early 1980s, the project's school year followed the two-semester system. On this practice, the staff visited each contributing school in the first 3 weeks of term one to talk with a candidate likely to be included in the programme. The year 9 students who were selected were removed from the contributing school for the duration of terms one and two. All of the students returned to their school of origin at the end of semester two. In the first 3 weeks of term 3 the school visits by the 3 teachers recommenced to observe and discuss with the class teacher, guidance counsellor, head of department or liaison person the appropriateness of the placement of the students and their educational enrichment. Also, the teachers selected students from Year 10 whom a contributing school's staff perceived as possible candidates to participate in the national examination called School Certificate in Year 11.

The cultural and academic demands of the students meant that tertiary study by their teachers was an important part of an educational programme. The point of view of radical education is for the teachers to take their own education seriously. Accordingly, in 1977, the first of the teachers began the postgraduate Teaching English as a Second Language course at Victoria University, Wellington. The paid study-leave established the ELTU tradition of constant university scholarship engaged by all the staff members who worked there throughout the 70s, 80s, and 90s. The last point is an important one since it was crucial that the teachers remained at the forefront of the particular professional field.

In 1979, the project was extended to include refugees from war-torn Indo-China. The enduring global upheaval meant that the ELTU was extended over its life to include adolescents from a range of cultural communities. In 1984, as part of the project teachers' ongoing response to bolster the students' education, the two-semester system was replaced with a 36 week or 900 hours schooling event. The influential aspect of the flexible organisation is that it allowed the students to return to their school of origin throughout the duration of the programme, for new students to be included throughout the school year and for the

16 A Community of Ako, 1987–1995: Teaching and Learning ... 289

incumbent students to continue learning within the programme the following year should they or their parents so choose.

In April 1987, a mathematics and science graduate, and active knower of Tongan and New Zealand European, Pakeha cultures joined the staff; she brought a new spirit and commitment to the schooling and education of the project's migrant students. Her appointment made possible the specific recruitment of Tongan-speaking migrants, and, also, offered the possibilities for all of the pupils to learn about mathematics, science, information technology, and economics through the English language. What is being pointed out here is that the novice's early lived experiences in Tonga, and her academic education in Aotearoa provided the project with another distinct language and culture. Importantly, by 1987, the staff consisted in an Indigenous Maori woman, an Indigenous Tongan woman, and an Indigenous Samoan man.

In the ELTU, the relationship between language and culture was pivotal to erasing much of the damage done by teachers whose teaching practice reflected a minimal willingness to understand the adolescents' lived situations and capacity to learn a new culture. The new relationship had several merits: First, the teachers in the project were of the cultures of Samoa, Tonga, and Maori of Aotearoa, New Zealand. Second, the relationship meant the Tongan and Samoan students could be provided an opportunity to speak with their own voices, to authenticate their own experiences, become aware of the dignity of their own beliefs and histories, and to begin to comprehend the value of their meanings and perceptions, particularly as they related to the technocratic curriculum. In this pedagogical relationship, the students could learn to think and act in ways that connected with different societal possibilities, and ways of learning. Third, the transformative pedagogy allowed the Samoan and Tongan students to continue their conceptual education whilst they were acquiring the school discourse. Fourth, the educational situation allowed the teachers to transform the curriculum to share their intimate experiences with the students' objectives and educational realities as required. Fifth, the culturally diverse pedagogy accentuated the teachers' ability to relate to the parents and students from a cornerstone of shared experience and understanding. Importantly, the relationship notified the secondary school community of the extensive possibilities of a pedagogy of Ako and the insights provided ideas to establish a critical pedagogy. Overall, the communal relationship announced a genuine undertaking by the teachers to promote teaching and learning enlivening the students' language and culture, and the technocratic approaches of practice to school authorities, students and parents from across cultures.

From 1987, the student body was divided into 3 classes established on concrete experience. That is, a class of adolescents from a range of cultures, educational experience, proficiency in the home discourse and exposure to the prevailing curriculum was formed. The diversity of the students' culture and the teachers' incapacity to speak *all* the languages of the students meant the particular group learned through the appropriation of school English. Of course, the students were never discouraged by any of the teachers to think, speak and write in their Mother tongue. What is being pointed out here is that all of the teachers encouraged the students to use their specific language and to translate it so the student did not feel learning the school discourse would alienate them from the cultural orientation they knew so intimately. As well, a class specifically for Tongan students was established. This class was characterised largely by students with minimal exposure to formal institutionalised learning, in most instances, lower primary educational conditions, and acquiring literacy skills in the parental discourse. Likewise, a third class of 12 Samoan students was set up. For the latter two groups, the educational ideas embraced learning mathematics, economics, general science, geography and history in the language of the homeland as well as in English in the ELTU. At the same time, the Tongan and Samoan teachers respectively carried out learning in the specific home discourse with their students by way of clarifying personal and social problems, accentuating their philosophy, politics, poetry, literature and histories, and enriching content across the curriculum. Therefore, the contents to learn, to talk about, to clarify to the students was guided, not set in concrete, by the prevailing technocratic curriculum.

The ELTU teachers' personal capacity to create, combined with their web of interdependence enabled their inclusion of Indigenous and conventional contents. In teaching mathematics, science, economics, geography and history the teachers related the subject-disciplines and made them concept rather than sequentially related. All of the staff struggled to unravel ways to simultaneously direct the students towards their re-entry into the official programme, and what the teachers perceived as critical education. The significant point is that there was always a real expectation that the students would contribute and participate in their schooling and education. On a daily basis, the ELTU teachers reflected, conversed, formed, and reorganised the content and practice; always looking for ideas and ways through which the students might learn to make sense of the world, and then to change obstacles to their learning.

The project was a period of exciting relationships of harmony, vast responsibilities to establish a sense of balance and varied tasks of renewal. Ironically, the late 80s and early 90s ushered in a period of marked change and possibilities for making learning a good experience for the migrants from the south-west Pacific. By 2005, the project's team was involved in research in the University; two of them held doctoral degrees.

Po Ako: Teaching and Learning in the Night

The label 'study clinics' has been used by the Ministry of Pacific Island Affairs, New Zealand Council for Educational Research, and the Ministry of Education to refer to homework centres that operated after-school hours, typically by a community of parents and concerned teachers. The agencies' notion of a clinic is equated with a pathological view of people; that is, people upon recommendation from say a doctor go to the clinic for the treatment of sickness and injury. The clinic is an institution where patients receive remediation and treatment. It is associated with psychiatry as well as the idea of an individual with a problem that needs treatment. The patients' records are kept in the clinic and they receive treatment at a cost. Study clinics are not only treatment centres, but might also be seen as a tool in the free market where projects are framed for the consumption or sale of education. In this way of knowing, the educational situation for the migrant students from the Kingdom of Tonga, for instance, is understood in terms of their consumption of materials produced by the free market to be purchased in the clinic. The marginalised students from Tonga are the clients for whom the clinics are set up to treat. My view is that the agencies' concept of a study clinic is ethically and politically undesirable to use in educational projects for Tongan people because of the relationship with the notions of cultural deficiency and treatment.

Po Ako, a Tongan project for teaching and learning in the night, or more simply, after-school hours, was formed through the extensive relationships and activities made by the ELTU's Tongan teacher with the Tongan students, their parents, and the Tongan academics and students within the local tertiary institutions. In Mt Roskill Grammar, the principal and two counsellors accepted the role to encourage the students and parents' involvement, who like themselves all came from a Christian-religion experience. Supportive roles were taken on by some of the Indigenous staff members in the Grammar (Manu'atu and Kepa 2004; Manu'atu 2000a; Kepa and Manu'atu 1998a).

Po Ako signals that diverse cultural communities can name their own ideas and projects. Also, the Tongan word signals that different frames of reference, reflects different meanings, values and relationships whereby people can be understood. Further, the naming of Po Ako by the Tongan community living in Mt Roskill was pivotal to creating the identity, purposes and control of the centre. Since Po Ako is located at the Grammar, deep knowledge about the prevailing New Zealand European, Pakeha culture and Tongan culture is of paramount importance to make sense of the meanings of the project.

In 1992, the Tongan parents named their community *Takanga 'a Fohe Taha 'i Puke Tapapa Incorporated Society* (Manu'atu 2000a). In the parents' view, the name articulated the educational position of Kakai (commoners) of Tonga in the school. Their view was that their children's education was like a Tongan canoe that was sailing in a rough economic, political, educational and cultural sea and the strong wind had an adverse impact upon the direction of their education. Expressed differently, the Tongan students experienced impoverished educational outcomes. The parents and their children believed that the good life for them lay in a fair education, good health, a good job and income so that they would be able to contribute and participate in their community as well as New Zealand society.

Po Ako was set up during the *Auckland Secondary Schools Maori and Pacific Islands Performing Arts Festival* held each year. In 1991 and 1992, the success of Grammar's Tongan Performing Arts group overwhelmed the Tongan parents and the students with mafana (warmness and friendliness). The sense of passion called in Tongan, mafana had enheartened the students to perform excellently in the festival; the passion moved the parents to talanoa (dialogue) with each other and their children, not merely about their success in performing Tongan hiva (songs and dance) but about the dismal performance of their teenagers in the national examination called School Certificate.

In February 1992, the School Certificate (1991) results indicated that not a single Tongan student at the Grammar had passed the important examination. Po Ako was set up to break the cycle of cultural and educational exclusion and operated every Monday and Wednesday from 7.00 to 9.00 p.m. Furthermore, from 1 October to mid-November, during the build-up to the School Certificate examination, Po Ako took place every night including Saturday.

The creation of a disciplined, respectful and formal Tongan educational context, in a government school, was critical to the success of the project. Po Ako drew strongly on Tongan language to clarify academic concepts that were not understood in English by the students, and in this way Tongan culture was included in the academic domain. Above all, Tongan language and culture was enriched and maintained in a real-life context. The point is that a language diverse pedagogy in which Tongan culture was paramount was accentuated.

The parents' participation was an important consideration. Po Ako established an influential point of contact between the school and this Tongan community. The parents were in custody of a formal forum wherein they expressed their concerns about their children's education directly to the grammar school's management. The relationship between the school and the community meant that the Tongan concerns were positively responded to in the educational institution. The Tongan students and the community' profile was evident on campus. Although

Po Ako operated as an after-school programme, it is one initiative whereby the community collaborated meaningfully with the school to address and encounter the academic failure of the Tongan students and the notion of cultural diversity.

It should be emphasised that Po Ako depicts an approach to teaching and learning that is part of a dynamic education relationship. The initiative depicts a project where a Tongan community was drawn together not simply to 'do' homework tasks but to po talanoa (dialogue in the night) about the values of the official curriculum. They were drawn together to query the notion of deficiency and treatment in the mainstream education thinking and practice.

Po Ako was a project through which these Tongan people learned to critically dialogue and understand the Grammar's and their own cultural formations. In the Tongan teacher's view, Po Ako was the only viable process whereby the Tongan students' schooling could be enacted by Tongan tutors, community workers, and the parents. Two points were emphasised: The parents could not engage a deeper understanding of the educational situation if po talanoa (dialogue) could not take place in the Tongan language (Manu'atu 2004). Tongan culture was a necessary condition to improve the students' achievement and the parents' understanding of living in Aotearoa as Tongan people. That is, the people's education is inseparable from their cultural, economic and political situations and only through their Mother tongue could they begin to talk about how these social orders influence what and how they know about themselves and education. The wider issues cannot be confronted by taking the people out of their context by way of discussing them in English. After all, English is a language that many of the parents and the students could barely talk, let alone read and write.

The parents were of the strong view that while money was necessary to pay the expenses, the most important objective lay in sharing knowledge and skills to deepen all of the participants' understanding of how Tongan people in the educational canoe can paddle against the powerful economic, political and social 'waves' and arrive safely ashore. The Tongan community maintained that Po Ako represented a context of learning moving towards better relationships through sharing understandings, resources and relations of power among the Tongan people, the Board, the teachers, the Indigenous Māori supporters and the Indigenous migrant peoples from the south-west Pacific in the grammar school. The contribution of the Indigenous Māori people's Parents group was to cooperate in the fundraising activities, to attend meetings in the school in solidarity with the Tongan community, and for the Indigenous Māori colleague of the Tongan teacher and coordinator to tutor the students.

The parents highlighted two aspects of the project. They were hopeful that through the appointment of youthful Tongan tutors, their students would come to know the importance of striving towards the successful accomplishment of local and national examinations. As well, the parents hoped that by employing these Tongan men and women a signal would be sent to other Tongan graduates to come and share their skills and knowledge in the Po Ako. At the heart of the community of Ako were the Tongan people, Tongan language and culture all of which are inseparable.

What is significant about the Tongan students' participation in the project is that their low level of achievement historically experienced by them in the school could be transformed. What it takes to begin the transformation cannot be the work of an individual or one group such as the parents; rather the commitment belongs to all of the teachers, tutors, parents, students, and supporters. More to the point, commitment to educational change does not simply happen and happen simply. Transformative education is culturally, socially and politically created through coming to understand the many aspects that contribute to success in education. Knowledge about the politics of education, the economic and social positioning of Tongan people in Aotearoa, and the possibilities for social and educational change depict the belief. The first 3 years of Po Ako demonstrate that sheer hard work is not enough. It is through the interconnection of theory and practice that social and educational change take place.

Po Ako provides an example of how one Tongan community came to tackle the issue of recruiting Tongan teachers. The provision of an educational context places the tutors in a location to begin learning how to work with Tongan students in school. As a communal relationship, Po Ako contributed to the young people's consideration of teaching their own people as a career. In fact, from 1992 to 1995, 5 tutors from Po Ako entered the then College of Education to train as secondary school teachers. Two taught in Auckland, two taught in Tonga and 1 worked in a non-teaching job and continued to tutor in Po Ako. Also, 3 other tutors returned to Tonga and worked in various levels of that country's education system. One of the tutors established a Po Ako in her own village based on the community at Mt Roskill Grammar.

Historically and culturally, working together is not an unfamiliar relationship for Tongan people. In New Zealand, Tongan people act communally within the extended family, church and school. In this way, Tongan people begin not to feel exploited and are permitted to act according to their collective values. On this cultural value, the Po Ako was used by numbers of Tongan students in government schools, and similar projects operated within the wider Tongan community across Auckland city.

To close: the ELTU and Po Ako were not merely education contexts, these were spaces where the students' language, literature, theatre, art, philosophy and love thrived. Learning and teaching as well as drawing upon a body of diverse languages and cultures are vital aspects of Ako in a community of Indigenous and Migrant teachers and students. Through Ako a novel pedagogy was introduced to maintain and enrich the students' cultures as well as learning to use English language and Anglo-American-New Zealand European, Pakeha culture. What has been emphasised is that it is necessary to understand that educating Indigenous and migrant students in government schools should not, ought not to be a factory-like experience, and that diverse languages and cultures are integral and critical to pedagogical possibilities for them.

Addressing educational change is one of the issues that unites Maori, Tongan and Samoan teachers in a collective attempt to dialogue about how to teach and educate migrant students whose language and culture is marginalised in secondary schooling. Moreover, to create ways to recognise the students' discourse in the technocratic pedagogical context is no small order; it is a political relationship, responsibility and obligation to changing teachers' discriminatory beliefs and practices. For the teachers, educational change meant acting in solidarity with the students, parents, colleagues, friends and relations to apprehend the limits of technocratic pedagogy that can be changed, and relating in work with each other. A community of Ako means the people beginning to resist Indigenous and Migrant cultures being reproduced by the force of technocratic teaching practice, and then, taking on the struggle to recreate themselves and all their realities as vibrant people.

Acknowledgements The author acknowledges the contribution and involvement of Dr. Linita Man'atu to the field of Indigenous and Migrant Education, the ELTU and the Po Ako. I acknowledge the contribution and involvement of the late Kathy Yuen, and Vavao Fetui, Ross Currie, Beverly Voisin, and Janet Clarke in the education and research undertaken in the English Language Unit.

References

Kepa, M. (2008). *Language Matters: A Richer and Curious Approach to Teaching English*. Saarbrücken, Germany: VDM Verlag Dr. Müller Aktiengesellschaft. ISBN: 978-3-8364-9198-3.

Kepa, M. (2016). On Thinking Ako in the South Pacific: An Indigenous Māori Point of View. In M. A. Peters (Ed.), *Encyclopedia of Educational Philosophy and Theory* (pp. 1–5). Springer. http://link.springer.com/referencework/10.1007/978-981-287-532-7/page/1. ISBN: 978-981-287-532-7.

Kepa, M., & Manu'atu, L. (1998a). An Attached ESOL Unit in a Coeducational Urban New Zealand Secondary School. In J. C. Richards (Ed.), *Teaching in Action: Case Studies from Second Language Classrooms* (pp. 74–80). Alexandria, VA: Teachers of English to Speakers of Other Languages Inc. ISBN: 0-939-79173-0.

Kepa, M., & Manu'atu, L. (1998b). A Tongan-Based Community Initiative in a New Zealand Secondary School. In J. C. Richards (Ed.), *Teaching in Action: Case Studies from Second Language Classrooms* (pp. 62–67). Alexandria, VA: Teachers of English to Speakers of Other Language Inc.

Manu'atu, L. (2000a). *Tuli Ke Ma'u Hono Ngaahi Mālie* [Pedagogical Possibilities for Tongan Students in New Zealand Secondary Schooling] (Doctoral thesis). Faculty of Education, University of Auckland, New Zealand.

Manu'atu, L. (2000b). Katoanga Faiva: A Pedagogical Site for Tongan Students. *Educational Philosophy and Theory, 32*(1), 73–80.

Manu'atu, L. (2004). TalanoaMalie Innovative Reform Through Social Dialogue in New Zealand. *Cultural Survival Quarterly, 27*(4), 39–41.

Manu'atu, L., & Kepa, M. (2016). *'Ofa, alofa, aroha, aro'a, Love in Pasifika and Indigenous Education.* Edited Collection. Saarbrücken, Germany: Lambert Academic Publishing. ISBN: 978-3-659-80476-2.

Manu'atu, L., Kepa, M., Pepe, M., & Taione, M. I. (2016). Spirits, People and Lands. In M. de Souza, J. Bone, & J. Watson (Eds.), *Spirituality Across Disciplines: Research and Practice* (pp. 123–133). Basel, Switzerland: Springer. https://doi.org/10.1007/978-3-319-31380-1_10. ISBN: 978-3-319-31378-8. ISBN 978-3-319-31380-1 (ebook).

Manu'atu, L., & Kepa, T. M. A. (2004). A Critical Tongan Perspective on the Notion of 'Study Clinics'. In T. Baba, O. Māhina, N. Williams, & U. Nabobo-Baba (Eds.), *Researching the Pacific and Indigenous Peoples: Issues and Perspectives* (pp. 145–158). Auckland: Centre for Pacific Studies, University of Auckland. ISBN: 0-908959-07-9.

Ministry of Foreign Affairs and Trade, New Zealand Handbook on International Human Rights. (2008). *Role of the New Zealand Human Rights Commission in the Pacific Islands Including Tokelau, the Cook Islands and Niue.* Wellington, New Zealand: MFAT.

Waite, J. (1992). *Aoteareo: Speaking for Ourselves: A Discussion on the Development of a New Zealand Languages Policy a Report Commissioned by the Ministry of Education.* Wellington, New Zealand: Learning Media, The Ministry. http://trove.nla.gov.au/version/26938575.

17

Education for Assimilation: A Brief History of Aboriginal Education in Western Australia

Elizabeth Jackson-Barrett and Libby Lee-Hammond

Introduction

It has been two hundred and thirty years since invasion/colonisation occurred in the place the world knows as Australia. Over this time, there has been a common thread to the language of deficit discourse and government policies relating to the education Aboriginal and Torres Strait Islander peoples.[1] The introduction to both English literacies

[1] We use the plural term of "peoples" to demonstrate the diversity of Aboriginal peoples in Australia—Aboriginal and Torres Strait Islander peoples are two distinct groups of people. Aboriginal people and Torres Strait Islanders throughout Australia have different thoughts, ideas and beliefs. Today their cultures are a mix of contemporary and traditional ways and practices (Australian Museum 2018: https://australianmuseum.net.au/indigenous-australia). The terms "Aboriginal" and "Indigenous" are used interchangeably and refer to those people who identify as Aboriginal and/or Torres Strait Islander. We, the authors recognise that Aboriginal and Torres Strait Islander peoples are not a homogenous group. The Term "Indigenous" is used to reflect this diversity.

E. Jackson-Barrett (✉) · L. Lee-Hammond
Murdoch University, Perth, WA, Australia
e-mail: E.Jackson-Barrett@murdoch.edu.au

© The Author(s) 2019
O. Kortekangas et al. (eds.), *Sámi Educational History in a Comparative International Perspective*,
https://doi.org/10.1007/978-3-030-24112-4_17

and western educational institutions for Aboriginal and Torres Strait Islander peoples is comparatively new considering Aboriginal peoples have lived and survived in this land for approximately 40,000 years–70,000 years (McGregor 2018). Aboriginal peoples' education Before Colonisation (BC) was grounded in people's relationship to Country and intrinsically linked to the interrelatedness of Aboriginal ways of knowing, being and doing. The knowledge received was notionally related to the seasons, agricultural farming practices, ceremony and family. After Colonisation (AC) Aboriginal peoples were dispossessed of Country[2] and culturally decimated by the colonial practices implemented against them. This intervention caused discontinuity in the ways traditional knowledge was conveyed. Once bricks and mortar classrooms were established by the colonial government, education policies excluded and marginalised Aboriginal peoples. In the twenty-first century, while progress has been made, the educational narrative for Aboriginal education is still one of the deficit, focussing on the "lack" of attendance, transience and low outcomes (Hogarth 2018). We must recognise that intergenerational trauma instigated by past policies has severely hampered Aboriginal engagement with the institution of education with "Indigenous youth remaining the most educationally disadvantaged group in Australia" (Calma 2008, 2).

In this chapter we explore the question of how past government policies have impacted contemporary Australian schooling for Aboriginal students. Using historical documents and government policies, we outline the narrative of education for Aboriginal students in Australia through a discussion of the impacts of these policies that have shaped the educational experiences of Aboriginal students since colonisation. Our particular context is Western Australia and we use this to illustrate the national picture that mirrors our local experiences. The reader will note that we refer to Federal and State policies throughout.

---

[2]Country: in Aboriginal English, a person's land, sea, sky, rivers, sites, seasons, plants and animals; place of heritage, belonging and spirituality; is called "Country" (Australian Museum 2018: https://australianmuseum.net.au/glossary-indigenous-australia-terms).

Traditional Education

Before colonisation, education for Aboriginal peoples was in the form of intergenerational knowledge transfer which was based on peoples' connection to Country, their place in the kinship system, gender and age and was established through the sharing of cultural heritage knowledge passed on by Elders. A combination of the frontier wars and the forced removal of Aboriginal children from their families and their associated kinship Country resulted in a fracturing of culture and peoples. Country is, for Aboriginal peoples, their "first teacher, derived from a land centred culture and based on very old pedagogies […] these old pedagogies acknowledge and honour the art and science embedded in traditional teaching practices" (Styres 2011, 717). This way of transferring knowledge was through an oral tradition grounded in the land, sky and waterways and was an essential part of life for the preservation of culture, language and stories.

Administration of Aboriginal Peoples

The history of the administration of Aboriginal people in Western Australia can roughly be divided into three periods. From 1829 to 1886 Aboriginal affairs was under the jurisdiction of the Colonial Secretary's Office. The second period covering the years 1887–1897 Aboriginal affairs were administered by the Aborigines Protection Board who were responsible to the Governor of Western Australia. The third period commences from 1897 when the responsibilities of the Aborigines Protection Board were assigned to the Aborigines Department under a Minister responsible to Parliament (Milnes 2005).

Initially, control of Aboriginal matters was in the hands of the British Colonial Office in London, which appointed protectors of "Aborigines" to administer policy at the colony level. However, local state laws also frequently contained clauses relating to Aborigines. When the state achieved self-government in 1890, Aboriginal affairs remained the responsibility of the British Colonial Office until 1898 when the Aborigines Department was established (Milnes 2005).

The Establishment of Schools for Aborigines in Western Australia

In Western Australia, a Native Institution was established by the colonial government in 1834 with the purpose of teaching English to local Aboriginal people and instructing them in living in a settled colony (Macfaull 1847). In 1840 a updated school for Aboriginal children opened in Perth, with the intent of this school of "civilizing and Christianising" Aboriginal children so they could be turned into a subservient class albeit stripped of their "cultural connections to Country and family" (Macfaull 1847, n.p.; Western Australian Government 1840). The Perth Native School was established in 1840 and the ensuing thirteen decades, Aboriginal children had limited or no access to a "western" style of education rather, receiving an education that prepared them for domestic work and labour.

In the late nineteenth century two orphanages for Indigenous children were opened in the southwest of Western Australia. Many of the children sent there had living parents (Haebich 1988). The children were educated and trained for domestic and farm work. Under the Industrial Schools Act 1874 children who were voluntarily surrendered to such an institution by their parents would remain under its authority until the age of 21 regardless of their parents' wishes. The manager of the institution could apprentice children over the age of 12 for domestic or farm labour.

Responding to atrocities committed against Indigenous people in Western Australia the British Parliament passed *The Aborigines Protection Act 1886* establishing the Aborigines Protection Board. Among the Board's functions was "the care, custody and education of Aboriginal children" (Western Australian Government 1886, n.p.). Resident Magistrates were empowered to apprentice any Aboriginal or "half-caste" child of a "suitable age" under an apprenticeship model that enabled employment with "no education and no wages ..." (Roth 1905, Number 2—Section C). The British Government, responding to concern about the treatment of Indigenous people in WA, retained control of Aboriginal affairs until the Aborigines Act 1897 was passed. Henry Prinsep, who had experience in colonial administration in India, was appointed Chief Protector.

Prinsep believed that Aboriginal children of mixed descent who grew up with their Aboriginal families would become "vagrants and outcasts" and "were not only a disgrace, but a menace to society" (Haebich 1988, 57). Lacking any legislative power to forcibly remove these children to the existing institutions and missions (which were not under his control), he endeavoured to "persuade" the parents to part with their children. In a circular letter to all Protectors and Government Residents in WA in 1902, Prinsep requested information on any "half-caste" children in their districts who could be induced to enter one of the existing institutions for their care and education. Not surprisingly, most parents refused to part with their children. In 1902, dissatisfied at his limited success in removing children from their mothers, Prinsep put forward the idea of extending his powers to enable him to remove children forcibly and without parental consent (Haebich 1988; Hasluck 1988).

1901 White Australia Policy

In 1901, after the federation of the Australian States and Territories, the formalisation of a "White Australia Policy" became enshrined in the Immigration Restriction Act 1901 nationally. This law specifically targeted "the prohibition of all alien coloured immigration" (Deakin 1901, 4804) and specifically sought to exclude Islander and Asian migrants. The law permitted only migrants of European descent to take up residence in Australia and also allowed for the deportation of "undesirable" people who had migrated to Australia prior to federation. In the context of this political and social milieu the 1905 Aborigines Act was established in Western Australia.

1905 Act

The West Australian Government in 1904 initiated an Inquiry into Aboriginal Administration. The brief of the Inquiry was to determine "the treatment of the Aboriginal and half-caste inhabitants of the State as well as the general administration of Aboriginal affairs within the state" (Human Rights and Equal Opportunity Commission [HREOC] 1997a, 2). The Inquiry found that "Aboriginal people were exploited, brutally controlled and malnourished" particularly by the police (Roth in Haebich 1988, 77). It was recommended that proper administration and appropriate legislation be introduced. A new Bill of Parliament to approach the "Aboriginal problem" (HREOC 1997b, Appendix 5) was introduced in 1905, however it dismissed the many recommendations of the Inquiry and favoured the prevailing political ideology grounded in Social Darwinism and survival of the fittest. This reflected an attitude towards Aboriginal peoples that was later captured by Biskup (1967) "all we can do is to protect them as far as possible and leave nature to do the rest. It is a case of the survival of the fittest but let the fittest do their best" (p. 63).

The 1905 Act provided the legal basis for the development of repressive and coercive state control over the Aboriginal population. The Act set up the necessary bureaucratic and legal mechanisms to control all Aboriginal activity, including contact with the wider community, and enforced assimilation of children, it enabled the State to determine the most personal aspects of Aboriginal peoples' lives including their education (Haebich 1988).

Impacts of the 1905 Act: Institutional Education—Mission, Settlement and Reserve Days

Missions, Settlements and Reserves were encampments built all over Australia. In Western Australia, these places were set up in the guise of "protection" of Aboriginal peoples under the direction of an appointed Chief Protector of Aborigines. Similar roles existed around Australia. The aim of mission schools was evangelistic, literacy learning was intended to enable children to read the Bible and to serve the aim of "Christianising" Aboriginal peoples thus stemming the tide of social problems identified in the 1905 Inquiry (Haebich 1988, 57). Missionaries of the era regarded themselves as those sent by god to save the souls of Aboriginal peoples but did not offer a broad liberal education. Missions, settlement and reserve schools sought to control every aspect of Aboriginal peoples' lives. The policy era of protection was fundamentally about biological absorption of Aboriginal peoples into white society (HREOC 1997a). The experience of schooling for Aboriginal peoples since the establishment of these policies of protection emphasise the ways in which education has been used for political aims, rather than the successful development of Aboriginal peoples so they could benefit from modern society. Aboriginal peoples were segregated from the mainstream Australian population and given an education based on an alternative to the usual 3Rs of reading, writing and 'rithmetic to instead represent an education that is Racist, Remedial and Ruinous (Jackson-Barrett 2011).

Education Under Assimilation Policy 1951–1972

The assimilation era extended from the 1930s but was officially sanctioned by the Australian federal government from 1951 to 1975. After the Second World War, with the atrocities committed by Hitler, the world was not the same. For Australia, this meant that Post-war immigrants were arriving and the assimilation policy implemented to immigrants was also dually promoted as a way to "culturally assimilate Aboriginal peoples into white society" (Haebich 2002, 62). Assuming that post-war Australia could assimilate new arrivals to its shores as well as the "Aborigine" (Hall 1989, 191). The Assimilation Policy did not focus on "race" but on an international push for human rights and decolonisation (Haebich 2002). Assimilation became a key policy that saw Aboriginal peoples elevated from a "doomed race" (McGregor 1997, 2) to one where citizenship was possible, particularly if "Aborigines" had access to an education enabling them to gain skills to contribute to modern society.

Education was high on the agenda at a conference held in the national capital, Canberra, where the Aborigines Department and state representatives met in 1947. This Act differed in a significant way from the 1937 Education Act as it included all Aboriginal peoples rather than excluding some based on blood quantum. This was underpinned by the belief that education would absorb the "Aboriginal problem" and the problem would be fixed (Bamblett in Duggan 2018; Haebich 2002; Ellinghaus 2003, 1). The State Ministers resolution at the Canberra Conference agreed that "the long term objective is education for full citizenship as part of the Australian Community" (State Ministers in Hasluck 1988, 66–69). What ensued was a policy that was supposed to give Aboriginal peoples an education and employment but in reality was one that became an assimilationist exercise by the Federal government designed to keep Aboriginal peoples at the lower levels of the socio-economic order with little or no education or employment and remaining socially isolated.

It is this historical context that has laid the foundation for Aboriginal education in the twenty-first century. Two hundred years of discrimination, marginalisation and exclusion have, not surprisingly, resulted in a host of educational challenges for contemporary Aboriginal students and education policy makers. In the following section we discuss some of the more recent attempts by policymakers to address the wide disparity in educational outcomes between Aboriginal and non-Aboriginal students in Australian schools.

Contemporary Policies

Closing the Gap

In 2008 the Council of Australian Government (COAG) made a decision to "close the gap" in the areas of life expectancy, child mortality, education and employment of Aboriginal peoples. In the COAG (2009) National Indigenous Reform Agreement there were three target areas in education;

1. ensure access to early childhood education for all Indigenous four-year-olds in remote communities by 2013;
2. halve the gap in reading, writing and numeracy achievements for children by 2018; and

3. halve the gap for Indigenous students in Year 12 (or equivalent) attainment rates by 2020 (p. A-18).

As a result of these goals, the policy of the present Australian government is to close the gap in literacy and numeracy between Indigenous and non-Indigenous students. In the latest and seventh "Closing the Gap" report the Federal government readily admits that "despite its good intention and considerable investment, the disparity in outcomes remain" (Abbott 2015, 1). We ascertain that before the literacy and numeracy gap can begin to narrow we need to address the discourse of deficit within the education community concerning Aboriginal Australia. Many Australians have not learned of the nation's history in relation to policies affecting Aboriginal participation education and all they see is the deficit without critically examining the causes. Educating the broader education community can only occur through a "pedagogy of interruption" whereby the next generations of Australians can fully appreciate the impacts of colonisation on the present experiences and life outcomes of Aboriginal Australians. This is what Biesta (2013) describes as coming to understand the intrinsic connection between the past and the present and all of our collective stories. We need a new language that moves them beyond the "terra nullius"[3] and a deficit discourse. Education professionals and the institution of education must move beyond the tokenistic attempts to incorporate Aboriginal culture into school settings to address the "cultural knowledge" gap with which many pre-service teachers enter their teaching degrees. Buckskin (in Price 2015) highlights that "governments and educators must show leadership to the rest of the Australian community by displaying genuine respect for Indigenous cultures and by basing all actions to close the gap on that respect" (p. 177).

---

[3]Terra Nullius is a latin term that means "nobody's land" and is the principle upon which Australia was colonised.

Standardised Assessments and Performativity

In relation to measuring Aboriginal school achievement Hughes and Hughes (2012) point out the risks associated with the analysis of national standardised testing. In their review of Indigenous Education they focus on the role of the Closing the Gap Strategy and the National Assessment Program for Literacy And Numeracy (NAPLAN) in constructing a deficit and racialised view of Aboriginal student performance. Analyses of Indigenous student performance on national tests tend to emphasise Indigeneity as the major predictor of poor NAPLAN results. This type of analysis links "cognitive ability with ethnic origin [and] is repugnant is civilised society" (Hughes and Hughes 2012, 16). In reality, the most important determinants of Indigenous education failure are the "quality of instruction" and "school ethos" (ibid., 15), both of which are excluded from the NAPLAN data modelling. One outcome of analysis that identifies race as the determinant of failure is the over-representation of Aboriginal students in special needs classes nationally (De Plevitz 2006). This is primarily due to culturally biased testing regimes rather than innate deficits in the students themselves (De Plevitz 2006, 47).

Prominent Aboriginal scholar Marcia Langton AM describes the continuing failure of Aboriginal students in Australian schools as a "crisis in education for Indigenous people" (2015, 12) and argues that while "education is a key ideological battleground, there is alarming evidence within mainstream education that there is a lack of capacity to educate Indigenous children" and "as such for Indigenous children, families and communities, poverty will remain" (p. 1). The slow progress of "Closing the Gap" targets is an indication that what Australia is offering Aboriginal students in their education is clearly not working. The challenge for our education system is to break free of the legacy of colonial education and to recognise that the knowledge held by Indigenous peoples is as important as everyone else's (Langton 2015).

At the heart of this problem is a system-wide lack of understanding, knowledge and appreciation for Aboriginal ways of knowing being and doing in Australian education. Santoro et al. (2011) stress the importance of "schooling systems and teacher education to formalise opportunities for non-Indigenous teachers and pre-service teachers to listen to, and learn from their Indigenous colleagues" (p. 66). Despite teachers best intentions, most have "inadequate understandings of appropriate pedagogies and the complexities of Indigenous cultures, knowledge and identities" (ibid., 66) we have noted this in our own field work with teachers over many years, where misguided but good intentions can cause irrevocable damage to relationships.

The over-readiness of institutions to lay the "blame" for educational failure at the feet of the student and their Indigeneity feeds a cycle of deficit. It is these colonial discourses that continue to shape and inform initiatives for Indigenous education in Australia and are often constructed through principles of compensatory, remedial or deficit models of education (Whatman and Duncan in McLaughlin 2013). These are not new problems but outcomes of intentional policies and practices rooted in Australia's colonial history (Taylor 2009, 7). To transform the current achievement gaps and educational disadvantage often associated with Aboriginal education new ways of working are needed.

Ways Forward in Aboriginal Education in Australia

The Australian education system has largely developed with little reference to Aboriginal culture and history. Initially, curriculum development actively ignored Indigenous perspectives. More recently there have been concerted efforts to include these perspectives across the curriculum (ACARA 2018) and to ensure that all Australian teachers engage with Aboriginal perspectives (AITSL 2016). These policy attempts, to integrate Aboriginal perspectives, are frequently restricted to explorations of Aboriginal art and music which are considered "safe" for educators (Bamblett in Duggan 2018) in fact, these may become superficial and tokenistic in that they don't address the complex and rich culture that underpins Aboriginal and Torres Strait Islander Peoples nor do they address the big historical issues impacting on Aboriginal peoples marginalisation in Australian society. By dispersing these perspectives across the curriculum there is a risk of diluting culture and perpetuating the national ignorance around Aboriginal ways of knowing being and doing (Bamblett in Duggan 2018).

Some initiatives more recently undertaken in Australia point to some promising practices for creating learning environments that are supportive of Aboriginal students and build on their strengths, competencies and connection to Country.

At the policy level, some mandated changes have taken place that require teachers to include Aboriginal content in the curriculum. The Australian Curriculum produced by the Australian Curriculum Assessment and Reporting Authority (ACARA) includes an acknowledgement of the failure of Australian education to meet the needs and aspirations of Aboriginal students and the necessity of the following priorities:

- that Aboriginal and Torres Strait Islander students are able to see themselves, their identities and their cultures reflected in the curriculum of each of the learning areas, can fully participate in the curriculum and can build their self-esteem and
- that the Aboriginal and Torres Strait Islander Histories and Cultures cross-curriculum priority is designed for all students to engage in reconciliation, respect and recognition of the world's oldest continuous living cultures (ACARA 2018).

These policy imperatives are an important national step towards engaging educators at what Nakata (2007) describes as the cultural interface. This interface is a means of generating dialogue among educators about the place of Aboriginal cultures and histories in the curriculum. The theory of cultural interface in education recognises that there are different perspectives about what constitutes knowledge and that success for Aboriginal students in education depends on educators recognising that scientific western knowledge is but one way of understanding the world and that there are diverse and multiple standpoints in regard to teaching and learning.

Building on the notion of a cultural interface, Yunkaporta (2009) developed an "Eight Ways" approach to explore how teachers can effectively work with Aboriginal knowledges in schools. In developing this approach, Yunkaporta recognised that Aboriginal pedagogies and learning processes are a dynamic way to frame curriculum rather than a focus purely on content. The application of Aboriginal pedagogies in the formation of authentic classroom learning for Aboriginal and non-Aboriginal students is understood to result in engaging students at a level of deep learning. One important element of this approach is the involvement of communities in partnership with schools. As the reader will recall, Australia's history of education policy in relation to Aboriginal peoples has been characterised by top-down, paternalistic approaches. It is only recently that calls for collaborative partnerships between schools and Aboriginal communities have gained traction. Our own work in Aboriginal education begins with the premise of community consultation and the engagement of Elders as pedagogues (Jackson-Barrett and Lee-Hammond 2018).

In addition to the Australian Curriculum, the Australian Institute for Teaching and School Leadership (AITSL) published professional standards for Australian teachers (AITSL 2016). These standards require teachers to demonstrate proficiency in a range of areas. Two of these areas are relevant to our discussion, one relates to *processes* for teaching Aboriginal students (what Yunkaporta describes as Aboriginal Pedagogies, ibid., 2000) and is the requirement for teachers to show proficiency in Standard 1.4: "Strategies for teaching Aboriginal and Torres Strait Islander Students" (AITSL 2016, 9). The second relevant standard for Australian teachers is: "Understand and respect Aboriginal and Torres Strait Islander people to promote reconciliation between Indigenous and non-Indigenous Australians" (AITSL 2016, 11). This latter standard is one we interrogate by asking: How do educators demonstrate their capacity/proficiency or accomplishment in being able to "understand and respect" Aboriginal and Torres Strait Islander Peoples?

In relation to this latter concern, the implementation of these standards in practice became the focus of a national study undertaken to determine how educators were meeting standards 1.4 and 2.4 in practice (Ma Rhea et al. 2012). This study found that the majority of Australian teachers expressed "fear and resistance" (p. 7) in relation to meeting these standards.

For many new teachers as well as the general Australian population, contact with and knowledge about, Aboriginal and Torres Strait Islander Australians is limited. Indigenous peoples have diverse identities with multiple languages. This, coupled with the way that Aboriginal and Torres Strait Islander peoples have been represented by governments and media organisations since colonisation have built up and added to the "fear and resistance" in non-Aboriginal peoples. Stereotypes have been perpetuated by what we term "government default" which is the non-teaching of Aboriginal and Torres Strait Islander studies and/or perspectives in Australian schools and within the curriculum. This historical form of hidden curriculum coupled with the history of colonisation and the impact of past government policies has up until recently focused on the Stolen Generations. Aboriginal Australia through the work of Aboriginal scholars like Langton (2015), Pascoe (2007), Nakata (2007), and Yunkaporta (2009) are now storying a different representation of Aboriginal Torres Strait Islander peoples. A story that demonstrates that Aboriginal society was highly productive, knowledgeable and sophisticated which has ensured Aboriginal peoples survival in this country for well over 60,000 years.

Conclusion

In this chapter, we have explored the notion that past policies of the Australian government have delivered devastating impacts on Aboriginal peoples in every sphere of their lives. We have specifically discussed the policies that originally excluded Aboriginal participation in a liberal education and subsequently have constructed a deficit discourse in relation to student outcomes. To change the dialogue of the past two hundred years requires a change of national attitude recognising not only the ongoing impact of history but the many strengths and competencies that Aboriginal students bring with them to school. In addition, education needs to recognise and involve communities in genuine dialogue to address some of the broader social circumstances impacting on student participation, engagement and retention.

If Australia is serious about "Closing the Gap" we argue that ways forward in Aboriginal education in Australia require a rethinking of curriculum to include Aboriginal peoples and cultures in authentic ways, for example, the use of Aboriginal pedagogies of learning on Country with the land, sky and waterways. This is consistent with Article 14 of the (UN) *Declaration on the Rights of Indigenous Peoples*, which states that:

[…] children, including those living outside their communities […] have access, when possible, to an education in their own culture and provided in their own language. (UN 2007, 7)

This will not only change the dialogue for non-Aboriginal Australians but impact on the success of Aboriginal students in Australian schools.

References

Abbott, T. (2015). *Closing the Gap Report 2015*. Canberra: Commonwealth of Australia.

Australian Curriculum Assessment and Reporting Authority. (2018). *Aboriginal and Torres Strait Islander Histories and Cultures: Australian Curriculum*. Retrieved October 15, 2018, from https://www.australiancurriculum.edu.au/f-10-curriculum/cross-curriculum-priorities/aboriginal-and-torres-strait-islander-histories-and-cultures/.

Australian Institute for Teaching and School Leadership. (2016). *Professional Teacher Standards*. Retrieved February 9, 2017, from http://www.aitsl.edu.au/australianprofessional-standards-for-eachers/standards/list.

Australian Museum: Glossary of Indigenous Australia Terms. (2018). Retrieved October 30, 2018, from https://australianmuseum.net.au/indigenous-australia.

Biesta, G. (2013). Interrupting the Politics of Learning. *Power and Education, 5*(1), 4–15.

Biskup, P. (1967). The Royal Commission That Never Was: A Chapter in Government Missions in Western Australia. *University Studies in History, V*(1), 89–113.

Calma, T. (2008). *Launch of Our Children Our Future Report* [Speech]. Retrieved from http://www.hreoc.gov.au/about/media/speeches/social_justice/2008/20080528_our_children.html.

Council of Australian Governments (COAG). (2009). *National Indigenous Reform Agreement: Closing the Gap.* Retrieved from http://www.federalfinancialrelations.gov.au/content/npa/health/_archive/indigenous-reform/national-agreement_sept_12.pdf.

Deakin, A. (1901, September 12). *House of Representatives, Debates* (p. 4804). Canberra: Commonwealth of Australia.

De Plevitz, L. (2006). Special Schooling for Indigenous Students: A New Reform of Racial Discrimination. *The Australian Journal of Indigenous Studies, 28*(1), 34–47.

Duggan, S. (2018, October 30). *The Silent Racism in Australia's School System.* Brunswick West, VIC, Australia: EducationHQ.

Ellinghaus, K. (2003). *Absorbing the 'Aboriginal Problem': Controlling Interracial Marriage in Australia in the Late 19th and Early 20th Centuries.* Retrieved from http://pressfiles.anu.edu.au/downloads/press/p73641/pdf/ch1128.pdf.

Haebich, A. (1988). *For Their Own Good: Aborigines and Government in the Southwest of Western Australia 1900–1940.* Nedlands, WA: University of Western Australia Press.

Haebich, A. (2002). Imagining Assimilation. *Australian Historical Studies, 33*(118), 61–70. https://doi.org/10.1080/10314610208596180.

Hall, R. A. (1989). *The Black Diggers: Aborigines and Torres Strait Islander in the Second World War.* Sydney, NSW: Allen & Unwin.

Hasluck, P. (1988). *Shades of Darkness; Aboriginal Affairs 1925–1965.* Carlton, VIC: Melbourne University Press.

Hogarth, M. (2018). *Words Matter: How the Latest School Funding Report (Gonski 2.0) Gets It So Wrong.* Retrieved from http://www.aare.edu.au/blog/?p=3243.

Hughes, H., & Hughes, M. (2012). *Indigenous Education 2012* (CIS Policy Monographs; 129). St Leonards, NSW, Australia: Centre for Independent Studies.

Human Rights and Equal Opportunity Commission. (1997a). *Bringing Them Home Report: A Guide to the Findings of the National Inquiry into the Separation of Aboriginal Torres Strait Islander Children from Their Families.* Sydney, NSW: Human Rights and Equal Opportunity Commission.

Human Rights and Equal Opportunity Commission. (1997b). *Appendix 5: Laws Applying Specifically to Aboriginal Children.* Retrieved from https://www.humanrights.gov.au/pulications/bringing-them-home-appendix-5.

Jackson-Barrett, E. M. (2011). The Context for Change: Reconceptualising the 3Rs in Education for Indigenous Students. *Australian Journal of Teacher Education, 36*(12). http://dx.doi.org/10.14221/ajte.2011v36n12.1.

Jackson-Barrett, E., & Lee-Hammond, L. (2018). On Country Learning: Improving the Social and Emotional Wellbeing and Involvement of Aboriginal Children in Early Childhood. *Australian Journal of Teacher Education, 43*(6), 86–104.

Langton, M. (2015). *The Right to the Good Life: Improving Educational Outcomes for Aboriginal and Torres Strait Islander Children* (CIS Occasional Paper; 133). St Leonards, NSW, Australia: Centre of Independent Studies.

Macfaull, C. (1847). *The Perth Gazette and West Australian Journal (WA: 1833–1847)*. Perth, WA. Retrieved from http://nla.gov.au/nla.news-title6.

Ma Rhea, Z., Anderson, P. J., & Atkinson, B. (2012). *National Professional Standards for Teachers Standards 1.4 and 2.4: Improving Teaching in Aboriginal and Torres Strait Islander Education.* Melbourne, VIC, Australia: Monash University. Retrieved July 13, 2015, from http://www.aitsl.edu.au/docs/default-source/default-documentlibrary/monash_study_final_report_09092012.

McGregor, R. (1997). *Imagined Destinies: Aboriginal Australians and the Doomed Race Theory, 1880–1939.* Carlton, VIC: Melbourne University Press.

McGregor, L. (2018). *Mungo Man: What Do Next with Australia's Oldest Human Remains?* Retrieved from http://www.abc.net.au/news/2018-02-12/mungo-man-what-to-do-next-with-australias-oldest-remains/9371038.

McLaughlin, J. (2013). 'Crack in the Pavement': Pedagogy as Political and Moral Practice for Educating Culturally Competent Professionals. *The International Education Journal: Comparative Perspectives, 12*(1), 249–265.

Milnes, P. D. (2005). *From Myths to Policy: Aboriginal Legislation in Western Australia*. Perth, WA: Belco Consulting.

Nakata, M. (2007). The Cultural Interface. *The Australian Journal of Indigenous Education, 36*(Suppl.), 7–14. https://doi.org/10.1017/S1326011100004646.

National Archives of Australia. (2019). *Land of Opportunity: Australia's Post War Construction.* Retrieved from http://guides.naa.gov.au/land-of-opportunity/chapter17/index.aspx.

Pascoe, B. (2007). *Convincing Ground: Learning to Fall in Love with Your Country.* Canberra: Aborigina Studies Press.

Price, K. (2015). *Aboriginal and Torres Strait Islander Education: An Introduction for the Teaching Profession.* Port Melbourne, VIC: Cambridge University Press.

Roth, W. D. (1905). *Royal Commission 'The Condition of the Natives'.* Perth, WA. Retrieved from http://nationalunitygovernment.org/node/1448.

Santoro, N., Reid, J., Crawford, L., & Simpson, L. (2011). Teaching Indigenous Children: Listening to and Learning from Indigenous Teachers. *Australian Journal of Teacher Education, 36*(10). http://dx.doi.org/10.14221/ajte.2011v36n10.2.

Styres, S. (2011). Land as First Teacher: A Philosophical Journeying. *Reflective Practice, 12*(6), 717–731.

Taylor, E. (2009). Foundations of Critical Race Theory in Education: An Introduction. In E. Taylor, D. Gillborn, & G. Ladson-Billings (Eds.), *Foundations of Critical Race Theory in Education* (pp. 1–13). New York: Routledge.

United Nations. (2007). *Declaration on the Rights of Indigenous Peoples.* Retrieved from https://documents-ddsny.un.org/doc/UNDOC/GEN/N06/512/07/PDF/N0651207.pdf?OpenElement.

Western Australian Government. (1840). *Colonial Secretary's Records* (Vol. 78/139). State Records of Western Australia Education Act (1893). Retrieved from https://www.legislation.wa.gov.au/legislation/prod/filestore.nsf/FileURL/mrdoc_14614.pdf/$FILE/Elementary%20Education%20Act%201871%20Amendment%20Act%201893%20-%20%5B00-00-00%5D.pdf?OpenElement.

Western Australian Government. (1886). *The Aborigines Protection Act 1886.* Retrieved from https://aiatsis.gov.au/sites/default/files/catalogue_resources/52769.pdf.

Yunkaporta, T. (2009). *Aboriginal Pedagogies at the Cultural Interface* (Professional Doctorate [Research] thesis). James Cook University. Retrieved from http://eprints.jcu.edu.au/10974/2/01thesis.pdf.

18

Conclusion: Promising Prospects—Reflections on Research on Sámi Education Yesterday, Today and Tomorrow

Otso Kortekangas

This chapter discusses two separate yet interrelated points. These points conclude the two thematic sections of this book: (1) articles on histories of indigenous education, with a special focus on Sámi education; and (2) articles on current and future trajectories of indigenous education. These two themes, in very general terms, are written by historians and educational scientists, respectively. These two different fields have their own specific theoretical and methodological traditions, as is reflected in the various articles of this book.

Jukka Nyyssönen shows in his chapter that the different perspectives of historians and educationalists can be systematized thus: historians take the results of education, such as assimilation, as the *end product* of their research, while educationalists use the results of education as a *starting off point* for their studies. In other, somewhat polemic words, historians are

---

O. Kortekangas (✉)
Division of History of Science, Technology and Environment,
KTH Royal Institute of Technology, Stockholm, Sweden
e-mail: otso.kortekangas@historia.su.se

Department of History, Stockholm University, Stockholm, Sweden

© The Author(s) 2019
O. Kortekangas et al. (eds.), *Sámi Educational History
in a Comparative International Perspective,*
https://doi.org/10.1007/978-3-030-24112-4_18

317

content to conclude what "actually happened" and close the case, whereas educational scientists take "what actually happened" as their action point, discussing also what is happening, and in many cases, what should happen in the future. Natan Elgabsi has discussed the difference between these two views in a philosophy of history setting (Elgabsi 2016). Elgabsi shows the ways in which the two perspectives can also imply two different approaches to the ethics of research. Given that research ethics is a recurring topic in indigenous studies, it may be helpful to remember that the discussions of ethics in these two traditions (history and more social science-oriented research, including education) use different concepts: whereas many historians tend to think that the most ethical research practice is to try to be as true to the sources as possible, the methodology used by educational scientists often suggests that the most ethical research practice is to utilize the space given in a certain publishing channel to advocate an active stance towards how the research results can be disseminated and used to promote social and political change.

These two different perspectives of research as a scholarly and ethical practice need not imply a schism or even a discrepancy between educational historians and educational scientists. This is well exemplified by the different chapters of this book. Together, they show that the two perspectives enrich and complement each other. In the following summary and comparison of the findings and results of the different chapters, the two types of chapters are discussed together, rather than separately. As explicated in the introduction, the chapters of this book compose a collection with an international, rather than transnational or cross-national perspective. This means that the chapters themselves focus in most cases on the educational history of indigenous peoples in a certain country. However, the results and conclusions of these chapters constitute formidable material for comparative conclusions, something this final chapter will try to carry out, if only in brief.

The diversity of chapters in this book poses an obvious challenge to anyone attempting to compare and offer conclusions about the findings of the chapters. In the following, I will, however, do just that, in comparing the chapters in a number of thematic parcels. My text follows the structure of the book. Sámi history is the main focus, whereas the other cases of indigenous education worldwide serve as points of comparison for many of the processes treated in the chapters on Sámi

18 Conclusion: Promising Prospects—Reflections ...

educational history. The discussion serves as a summary and conclusion of this book. At the same time, my text discusses the direction Sámi educational history is taking and should take, based on the chapters. I hope that this examination is read less as a critique of existing research and more as ideas for future research.

As a historian, it is easy to begin chronologically in the earliest years of Lutheran mission among the Sámi. The chapters of Ritva Kylli and Daniel Lindmark discuss early modern Sámi education organized by the Church of Sweden (the Swedish Lutheran state church established in the sixteenth century), with a special focus on gender. Lindmark shows that the employment of Sámi women in teaching varied over time and depended on the form and concept of education. In the case of stationary schools, Sámi women were not a prioritised group among teachers. In the case of the itinerant catechist school, however, they were. Lindmark explains this difference with the strong role that women had in domestic education (i.e., in teaching their children at home) within the Lutheran tradition. The itinerant catechist teacher travelled from village to village and taught children in their home environments. In this setting, it was natural for the church to hire women as teachers.

Kylli shows that in the catechist schools, both boys and girls were included in the sphere of elementary education already in the eighteenth century. This was rather remarkable compared to other school forms that had mainly male pupils. The gender balance reflects the home-like character of catechist tuition. Also, the schools were known to take heed of the Sámi culture as many catechists were of Sámi origin and used the local Sámi language varieties in teaching. As Kylli shows, Sámi catechists could also use their know-how of the traditional Sámi way of life and traditional religion to explain the core concepts of Christianity and thus aid and accelerate the learning of Christianity among Sámi children. From the perspective of the church, then, the policies are to a lesser degree to be interpreted as positive towards Sámi language and culture, and to a greater degree as positive towards efficient conversion and mission. Sámi language was an auxiliary of this process of Lutheranisation of Sámi children.

Yoko Tanabe's chapter on the Ainu schools in Hokkaido offers an excellent international case of comparison to Lindmark's and Kylli's chapters. Tanabe compares Japanese governmental schools and schools run by The Church Missionary Society (an Anglican mission society established in London in 1799) on the Island of Hokkaido, where the indigenous Ainu population resided. Tanabe shows that in the case of the Ainu, the school policies based on mission were more positive to local language and customs than the governmental schools were. The main explanation is the same as in the Sámi case: efficient mission was often carried through in the language the children understood best.

Pirjo Kristiina Virtanen and Francisco Apurinã examine the education of the Apurinã people in Brazil. Elizabeth Jackson-Barrett and Libby Lee-Hammond offer an overview of Australian governmental educational policies and their impact on Aboriginal peoples. Both chapters lay bare some of the negative effects of earlier educational policies and point out that in the future, more indigenous elements should be included in the curriculum. This inclusion is crucial not only in recognition and respect of indigenous cultures. It is also a prerequisite for political representation on equal terms that indigenous populations, such as the Apurinã in Brazil and Australia's Aboriginal peoples, have access to a qualitative education that includes indigenous elements without the threat of segregation. Virtanen and Apurinã also show that this kind of education has yielded good results in widening political and social representation and also participation among the Apurinã, especially in urban areas.

Lea Kantonen discusses the issue of indigenous elements in education in her chapter on the indigenous Wixárika community in Mexico. She shows that the role of indigenous teachers and pupils in the area has shifted from the twentieth century to today. Previously, pupils were educated to mediate governmentally set values and norms to their own peoples. Today, the perspective is the opposite, where pupils are expected to learn to navigate between their own culture and the government, between tradition and modernity. They learn to safeguard Wixárika autonomy and to explain their values to state authorities. Madoka Hammine shows in the case of Japan that there has been a lot of general rejection of the idea of indigenousness of the Ainu and Ryūkyūan peoples. Educational systems have played a substantial role in ignoring indigenous culture. Hammine shows that education could now be used as a force to disseminate knowledge about these peoples. This is a general wish and action point of many of the more future-oriented chapters of this book: to invert the earlier exclusive forces of education to be more inclusive and to disseminate indigenous culture rather than eradicating it.

What the examples of the early modern mission teaching and the modern examples of education as inclusive show is that the *function* of language in education has fluctuated over time. By *function* I refer to the purpose each indigenous language was to have in the context of education (see also Kortekangas 2017). The function of Sámi in Nordic Lutheran missions was the efficient dissemination of the Gospel. It is a delicate issue to draw parallels from seventeenth- and eighteenth-century ecclesial education to today's educational challenges in schools with indigenous pupils. Yet it is striking how culturally sensitive, to put it in radically anachronistic terms, the policies and practices of mission tuition were, even if the motives behind the policies and practices were based on notions of an efficient mission. The idea of taking the pupil and her or his culture as the focus of education is reminiscent of much later pedagogical developments. Within contemporary educational systems based on indigenous curricula, the function of indigenous language is ideally the dissemination of indigenous cultural values. In both cases, a function of intelligibility is also obvious—tuition in the language the children know best is a pragmatic argument difficult to refute.

Andrej Kotljarchuk's and Lukas Allemann's chapters illuminate the variety of functions that Sámi has had in the Soviet/Russian context. Kotljarchuk shows that in the early years of the Soviet Union, minority school policies included teaching material printed in Sámi, which differed from the policies in the Nordic countries at this time. The background to this policy was a general internationalist openness to the different nationalities and their languages in the Soviet Union. Times would turn grimmer with Stalin at the helm of the Soviet Union. Sámi teaching disappeared from schools and Sámi intellectuals were discriminated against and even eliminated. Lukas Allemann compares the processes of segregation and assimilation in Sámi education in the Soviet Union. According to Allemann, segregation has in many cases led to the stigmatization of the minority that assimilative tuition, for obvious reasons, has managed to avoid. Allemann shows in his study that the experiences of pupils in the segregated schools were worse than in the schools with no segregated education. These lessons are important when education based on indigenous curricula is discussed: how much can the indigenous schools deviate from the general educational systems in each country without being a disadvantage to the indigenous pupils in terms of access to the labour market but also in terms of cultural belonging and stigmatization?

Ekaterina Zmyvalova and Hanna Outakoski show that today, the legal framework in Russia supports Sámi-language teaching. However, in practice, the Russian educational authorities are passive in implementing Sámi-language tuition, and the pupils attend the existing (non-obligatory) classes sporadically due to the rather weak state of Sámi culture in Russia. The importance of individual actors is clear. This is also apparent in Marikaisa Laiti's chapter on Sámi-language early education in Finland. Individual teachers keep working for more Sámi-language tuition and more pedagogical content related to Sámi culture. This is hard work, however, since the curriculum of early education is based on Finnish norms and takes no special consideration to Sámi culture. In many ways, this resembles the case of the Riutula children's home that is the theme of Pigga Keskitalo's and Merja Paksuniemi's chapter: during the research period 1907–1950, Sámi cultural elements were included in the tuition and life at the residential school. However, as the teaching was in Finnish and based on Finnish values, a gradual de facto assimilation took place.

One of the obvious challenges, and also one interesting research topic for future research on Sámi educational history, is the possible conflict in ideology between the increasingly multicultural Nordic societies and the notion of indigenous education. The Sámi community is multilingual to begin with, not only in terms of majority language-Sámi bilingualism but also in terms of the different Sámi language varieties spoken today. As Inker-Anni Linkola-Aikio shows in her chapter, the integration of Sámi language education as a compulsory element in the tuition of the Sámi upper secondary school in Norway risks a de facto exclusion

18 Conclusion: Promising Prospects—Reflections ... 323

of pupils with other mother tongues than one of the dominant Sámi language varieties. The future of Sámi schooling should and will be multilingual. The same is true of most other indigenous groups in the world. Mere Kepa treats in her chapter the immigrants from the South Pacific to New Zealand, and the prospects of integration through Ako, a specific indigenous educational philosophy that takes into account the culture of newcomers. Even if the Ako can be seen as a possible way forward for integrating immigrant pupils, it is still local in the sense that South Pacific newcomers share a certain amount of cultural values with the New Zealand Maori. The case is thus rather similar to Linkola-Aikio's and highlights the commonalities and differences between indigenous peoples in a certain area (the different Sámi groups and the South Pacific-New Zealand indigenous peoples).

In both Linkola-Aikio's and Kepa's case, it is, however, crucial to understand that this kind of multicultural education is essentially different from the kind where pupils from several substantially different backgrounds come together. The latter is also the situation in an increasing number of Nordic schools. Torjer A. Olsen's chapter shows in what ways Norwegian curricula of different time periods have treated the Sámi. Olsen shows that the Sámi have been seen as a special case within Norwegian multicultural school policies, as the "most original" of the various "non-Norwegian" groups. The current national curriculum highlights the integrative forces of education in a multicultural society. It also makes claims that all Norwegian pupils should learn about the Sámi and about indigenous perspectives. It is worth asking to what degree integrating multicultural school policy is just another form of conformist school policy from the Nordic governments. Is school the place where the degree of cultural difference tolerated by each society is regulated in the future? The Sámi case, and other contexts of indigenous education, can serve as important lessons for educational policies, not only in the indigenous context, but also in the wider context where relations between culturally dominant societies and pupils from minority backgrounds are envisioned and negotiated.

Related to this question is the important discussion of indigenous and "non-indigenous" minorities. In recent years, Sámi educational history has benefited greatly from a strong international comparative practice with other indigenous groups. This frame of comparison is limited by at least two factors: the indigenous status, and the cultural dominance of the English-speaking world. This book itself is a case in point of the former. In the latter case, our collection proudly presents a variety of international cases of comparison: Mexico, Japan, Brazil, etc. The contributions from New Zealand and Australia are obviously equally important. But due to pragmatic issues related to the language skills of Nordic peoples, comparisons with indigenous cases in New Zealand, Australia and the US have had a disproportionate role in Sámi educational history. This is in a way ironic since many indigenous scholars from these regions criticize the overly dominant role of English language in their own societies.

To avoid repetitive research in the future, Sámi school history should try to liberate itself from these two limiting foci. We should ask whether we should take the indigenous status as an a priori research program, or rather be open to other kinds of comparisons, with minority populations not labelled as indigenous. An excellent empirical example is the Sámi intellectual, teacher and writer Per Fokstad, active in the first half of the twentieth century. Fokstad's period of literary activity preceded the period where *indigenous* was a self-evident, and, in many cases, the primary status of the Sámi. Of course, this does not mean that the same questions would not have been topical to Fokstad. Quite the contrary, he strongly felt that Sámi culture was under pressure from an occupying government, Norway. At the same time, he considered that the key to a strong and vivid Sámi culture in the future was an active cultural movement across the Sámi area, independent of the national boundaries criss-crossing Sápmi (Fokstad 1940). In Fokstad's reasoning, comparisons include such cases as the Welsh in the UK and the Jews of France (Bråstad Jensen 2004). Following Fokstad's lead, I think the time is ripe to break out of the current frames of research and boldly conduct comparisons across the Sámi area and with a myriad of international cases of comparisons, not limited to the English-speaking world, and not limited to the indigenous status.

References

Bråstad Jensen, E. (2004). Per Pavelsen Fokstad. En stridsmann for samisk utdanning, språk og kultur. In H. Thuen & S. Vaage (Eds.), *Pedagogiske profiler. Norsk utdanningstenkning fra Holberg til Hernes* (pp. 199–224). Oslo: Abstrakt Forlag.

Elgabsi, Natan. (2016). Var ligger historikerns ansvar? Benny Morris och Ilan Pappé om forskningspraxis, ångerpolitik och frågan om en ansvarsfull relation till det israeliska samhället. *Historisk tidskrift, 136*(3), 412–440.

Fokstad, Per. (1940). Veähaš jurdagak samii čeärdalaš tilii pirra. *Sabmelaš, 25*(1), 2–3.

Kortekangas, Otso. (2017). *Tools of Teaching and Means of Managing: Educational and Sociopolitical Functions of Languages of Instruction in Elementary Schools with Sámi Pupils in Sweden, Finland and Norway 1900–1940 in a Cross-National Perspective.* Turku: Iloinen Tiede.

Index

A

Ainu 9, 207–221, 226, 227, 229–231, 233–240, 319, 320
Ainu historiography 208
Ako 284, 286, 290, 295–297, 323
Alymov, Vasiliy 67, 68, 72, 73
Amazonia 247, 248, 252, 257, 258, 262
Apurinã 247–254, 256–260, 262, 320
Arctic 30, 92
Arctic region 27, 33
Assimilation 4, 5, 7, 8, 30, 48, 50–56, 58, 75, 77, 85, 126, 129, 130, 209, 229, 230, 232, 233, 235, 238, 239, 249, 259, 304, 305, 317, 321, 322
Australia 10, 127, 128, 161, 162, 299–313, 320, 324
Australia's Aboriginal peoples 299, 320

B

Batchelor, John 214, 215, 218, 219
Boarding schools 30, 65, 75, 76, 83–92, 95–97, 100, 101, 111, 114, 115, 131, 163, 180, 209, 215, 218, 221, 274
Brazil 9, 247–249, 251, 254–256, 261, 262, 320, 324

C

Catechists 5, 13, 15, 20–24, 31–34, 37, 38, 40–42, 50–52, 219, 319
Catechist tuition 319

© The Editor(s) (if applicable) and The Author(s), under exclusive license
to Springer Nature Switzerland AG, part of Springer Nature 2019
O. Kortekangas et al. (eds.), *Sámi Educational History in a Comparative International Perspective*,
https://doi.org/10.1007/978-3-030-24112-4

328 Index

Cherniakov, Zakharii 8, 65, 69, 70, 73
Children's home 161–163, 168, 169, 171, 181
Christian education 30, 31, 33, 34, 38, 40, 42
Christianity 16, 29, 32, 33, 35, 38–40, 42, 51, 170, 180, 213, 220, 253, 319
Church Missionary Society (CMS) 208, 209, 213–215, 217–221, 320
Citizenship education 3
Civilising dimension of education 4
Clerical recruitment 13, 20, 22
Colonisation 52, 54, 55, 149, 233, 240, 299–301, 307, 312
Committee of the North 68, 69
Cultural interface 310
Culturally dominant societies 323
Curriculum 19, 73, 92, 100, 115, 117, 125–127, 130–139, 150, 179, 189, 191, 198–200, 211, 215, 220, 233–237, 262, 286, 289, 290, 294, 309–313, 323

D

Decolonising education 3, 4, 48, 129
Decolonising methodologies 2, 3

E

Early childhood education (ECE) 126, 127, 134, 136–139, 187, 188, 190, 194, 306
Early modern Sámi schools 9, 319
Education 3–7, 13, 20, 22, 27–30, 32, 33, 35, 37–41, 50, 51, 55–59, 64, 67, 75, 77, 86, 93, 94, 106, 109–112, 118, 119, 125, 126, 129, 143–146, 148, 149, 151–157, 164, 165, 168, 169, 178–180, 188, 192, 193, 195, 197, 199, 200, 208, 210, 214, 221, 230–234, 237–241, 248, 254–256, 258–262, 267, 272, 275, 284–296, 300–310, 312, 319–323
Education as a resource 48, 51, 66, 191, 261
Education policy 30, 155–157, 211, 221, 306, 311
English Language Teaching Unit (ELTU) 284–292, 296, 297
Ethical practice 318
Ethics of research 318
Eurocentric way of doing research 2
Ezochi (Hokkaido) 319, 320

F

Female students 14, 17, 19, 22–24
Finland 4–7, 21, 27, 28, 30, 34, 35, 37, 38, 40, 50, 52, 55, 73, 162–167, 169, 172, 174, 188, 190, 192, 194, 195, 197, 198, 200
Finnish Lapland 21, 27, 28, 32–34, 38, 41
Fokstad, Per 324
Function of language in education 321

G

Gender 14, 17, 24, 301, 319
Governance 146, 228, 262
The Great Terror 8, 64, 73, 77, 78

Index **329**

Gremikha 99, 101
Guovdageaidnu 146–148, 150

H

Hakodate Ainu School 215, 217
History of childhood 165
History of ECE 126
History of education 1, 3, 4, 6, 47,
    164, 187, 311
Hokkaido Former Aborigines
    Protection Act 208, 209

I

ILO 169 120, 125, 126, 132, 134,
    136, 137, 139, 145, 227
Indigenous children 67, 84–86, 92,
    99–101, 106, 110, 112, 119,
    161–165, 179, 180, 247, 275,
    302, 308
Indigenous children's right to learn
    their native language 106, 109,
    110
Indigenous cultures 2, 307, 309,
    320
Indigenous curriculum 100, 126,
    132, 134, 136–139, 233, 237,
    309, 323
Indigenous education 1, 3, 9, 10,
    78, 143–145, 156, 157, 248,
    255–257, 259–262, 274, 308,
    309, 317, 318, 322, 323
Indigenous education policy 208,
    221
Indigenous languages 111, 112, 149,
    232, 237, 239, 253, 254, 256,
    260, 274

Indigenous perspectives in education
    248, 260, 309, 318, 323
Indigenous rights 227–229, 240,
    249, 275
Integration 7, 58, 66, 132, 139, 151,
    220, 323
International law 106, 109, 110, 113

J

Japan 9, 207, 208, 213, 219–221,
    225–233, 237–241, 285, 320,
    324
Japanization 210, 221, 230
Jews 136, 324
Johansson, Gustaf (bishop) 41
Jooseppi Guttorm, primary school
    teacher 41

K

Kola Peninsula 8, 9, 66, 67, 69,
    72–74, 78, 85, 107
Komi 8, 68, 73, 76, 86, 94, 96

L

Language and cultural enrichment
    50, 52, 54, 57, 86, 118, 148,
    179, 188, 195, 229, 236, 249,
    294
Language policy 143, 144, 146, 149,
    153, 155, 156
Lovozero 68, 76, 77, 83–89, 92,
    93, 99–102, 105, 107, 108,
    113–115
Lovozero school 106, 113, 114, 116,
    117, 119

330 Index

Lutheran education 28, 41, 321
Lutheranisation 319
Lutheranism 13, 42, 50, 319
Lutheran mission among the Sámi 319

M

Maori 196, 284, 286, 289, 296, 323
Maori education 286, 289, 296
Maori students and teachers 285
Meiji Restoration of 1868 207, 221
Mexico 9, 266–268, 273–275, 278, 320, 324
Migrant Education in Aotearoa 283
Modernity 58, 59, 275, 320
Multicultural education 237, 259, 323
Murmansk region 8, 68, 69, 73, 86, 87, 92

N

Narratives 3, 7, 47–56, 58, 59, 131, 273, 300
Nation-building 3
Native Institution 302
New Zealand 10, 127, 128, 278, 284–287, 289, 291–293, 296, 323, 324
Nomad school system of Sweden 6
Norway 2, 5, 9, 29, 42, 52, 54, 58, 63, 76, 107, 125–137, 139, 144–148, 152, 154, 156, 157, 194, 221, 322, 324
Norwegianization 129, 131

P

Perestroika 77
Philosophy of history 318

PISA studies 7
Po Ako 284, 285, 292–297

R

Remedial schools 85, 92–95, 101
Riutula children's home 162–165, 170–175, 177–181, 322
Russia 2, 8, 28, 29, 37, 63–67, 69, 73, 77, 78, 85, 86, 92, 95, 106, 107, 118, 119, 128, 227, 229, 285, 322
Russian Lapland 76
Russian legislation 110
Russian Orthodox Church 8, 213
Russian Sápmi 105, 109, 117, 119
Ryūkyū 9, 227–233, 235, 237–239

S

Sámi 2, 4–9, 13, 15, 19, 20, 22–24, 27–35, 37–42, 48–59, 83, 84, 86, 92, 99, 101, 106, 107, 111, 113–119, 127–132, 134–139, 143–148, 150–157, 169, 170, 172–174, 176, 178–181, 187–201, 220, 221, 319–324
Sámi children 6, 15, 30, 32–34, 42, 86, 94, 105, 111–113, 119, 130, 131, 134–137, 144, 162, 163, 169, 173, 178, 180, 181, 188–190, 192–195, 198–200, 319
Sámi culture 13, 20, 33, 53, 57, 130, 132, 134, 137, 176, 188, 194, 198, 200, 319, 322, 324
Sámi curriculum 135

Sámi education 1, 4–9, 14, 53, 106, 113, 115, 117, 143–145, 156, 317–319, 321–324
Sámi empowerment 48, 55
Sámi identity 8, 33, 148, 151, 154, 156, 189
Sámi intelligentsia 8
Sámi language 8, 9, 15, 19, 20, 30, 31, 33, 34, 40, 42, 50, 51, 55, 102, 105–107, 109, 111, 113, 115, 116, 118, 119, 128, 132, 135, 137, 139, 143–149, 150–156, 179, 187–200, 319, 322, 323
Sámi language teaching 115, 155, 157
Sámi school history 47–50, 53, 58, 147, 318, 324
Sámi schools 7–9, 13–24, 49, 50, 55, 58, 107, 116, 135, 144, 154, 323
Sámi secondary education 143, 146–148, 156
Sámi students 131, 132, 135, 139, 146, 147
Sámi upper secondary school in Guovdageaidnu 143, 146, 148
Samoa 283, 285, 286, 289, 290, 296
Sápmi 1, 5, 13, 14, 20, 83, 151, 271, 324
School experiences of the Sámi 4
Security dilemma 64, 75, 77

Security policies 4
Shūshin 212
Social Darwinism 220, 304
South Pacific 284, 323
Soviet terror 64
Soviet Union 7, 8, 64–66, 73, 74, 77, 85, 87, 321
Stalin, Joseph 8, 72, 75, 77, 78, 86, 321
Student recruitment 14
Sweden 2, 4–6, 9, 13, 14, 20, 21, 27–29, 38, 42, 52, 65, 107, 128, 164, 194

T

Third sector 162, 168
Tonga 283–286, 289, 290, 292–296
Tongan Homework Centre 285, 294
Tuhiwai Smith, Linda 2

V

Vulnerability of indigenous peoples 64, 72

W

Welsh 324
Wilson, Shawn 2, 3
Wixárika 265–272, 274–279, 320
Women teachers 22, 24, 41, 319